Indian Women in the House of Fiction

Indian Women in the House of Fiction

Geetanjali Singh Chanda

zubaan

ZUBAAN
an imprint of Kali for Women
128 B Shahpur Jat, 1st floor
NEW DELHI 110 049
Email: contact@zubaanbooks.com
Website: www.zubaanbooks.com

First published by Zubaan 2008
Second impression in 2009
First paperback edition 2014
Copyright © Geetanjali Singh Chanda 2008

10 9 8 7 6 5 4 3

ISBN 978 93 83074 73 0

Zubaan is an independent feminist publishing house based in New Delhi with a strong
academic and general list. It was set up as an imprint of India's first feminist publishing
house, Kali for Women, and carries forward Kali's tradition of publishing world
quality books to high editorial and production standards. *Zubaan* means tongue, voice,
language, speech in Hindustani. Zubaan is a non-profit publisher, working in the areas
of the humanities, social sciences, as well as in fiction, general non-fiction, and books for
children and young adults under its Young Zubaan imprint.

Typeset at FACET Design, D-9, Defence Colony, New Delhi 110 024
Printed at Raj Press, R-3 Inderpuri, New Delhi 110 012

For my parents Amarjit and Bhagwant Singh
and
for Nayan, Amit and Ateesh

ACKNOWLEDGEMENTS

It was a restless, April-hot Delhi day and I was almost 19. I read Anita Desai's *Cry, the Peacock*. The shock of recognition made me realise what I had missed in my study of canonical English Literature. It was not just the presentation of an Indian context or names and people who looked and spoke like me, but the texture of the emotionally nuanced mindscapes of Desai's women characters that resonated and called me to myself. That led me on a journey of discovery of other Indian women writers like Shashi Deshpande whose complex and layered novels have sustained, nourished and enriched life and literature. My heartfelt thanks are first to Indian women writers in English who have courageously continued to write even when women's writing and especially Indian women's writing in English was often viewed as mimicry. In creating this wonderful body of literature, they have also created a community of readers and writers. Feminist publishers like Urvashi Butalia at Kali for Women and now Zubaan are pioneers in making sure that women claimed their place in the writing world. I am honoured to be counted as a Zubaan author. Urvashi has managed to negotiate the thorny path between friend and publisher with unfailing good humour and charm. Her encouragement kept the project alive. Preeti Gill insisted that I should add the chapter on apartments to my narrative of women's space in havelis and bungalows. That forced me to rethink what I had written so far. It is a pleasure to thank Urvashi and Preeti for making this book happen. Inni Dhingra kindly put me in touch with Amrita and Rabindra Kaur Singh who enthusiastically responded to an email from an unknown person and generously allowed me to use one of their paintings as the cover for this book. My title *Indian Women in the House of Fiction* builds upon the thought provoking works of Henry James and Lorna Sage.

Traveling, living and teaching in India, France, Hong Kong, Australia and the United States has afforded me a very personal and constantly evolving insight into the minutiae of identity negotiations, geography and ethnicity as they are explored and articulated in daily life. My friends and colleagues have been a lifeline – as both guides and sounding boards in these ruminations. Foremost among these are Rajeshwari and Tushar Ghose, Staci Ford, Gordon Slethaug and Mani and Gita Subramanian, who not only shared my angst while I was plunged in the depths of my doctoral dissertation in Hong Kong, but whose constant friendship and support have followed me around the world. I sadly miss my friend Monique Mayer who is no more, but with whom I shared conversations, cooking, French and a love for travel. I have often had cause to recall the sage advice of my teachers and colleagues in Hong Kong, Elaine Ho and Douglas Kerr. Meenakshi Mukherjee was there at the beginning of my thinking about Indian writers in English and has been generous with her advice and encouragement at key phases of this process. Pogie Menon's warm reception and astute insights into the idea of looking at space and housing as a way into women's writing was crucial to get this project off the ground. Conversations with Ritu Menon have also kept me in touch with women's writing in India.

Teaching at Yale University these past six years has been an exhilarating experience, thanks in large measure to my students, who forced me to think about diaspora writers in different ways. More importantly though, they convinced me that these novels touched a chord for Indian and non-Indian readers living a world away. My colleagues Laura Wexler, Margaret Homans and Linda Anderson's enthusiasm for a new colleague and her work enabled an easy transition from Hong Kong University to Yale, and their supportive concern kept the book on the front burner during my first years at Yale. I am also grateful to Chip Long and Emily Bakemeier for their enthusiasm for my work, and to Peggy Liggett, Priya Natarajan Seema Khurana and Saveena Dhall for their friendship.

Writing is often a lonely process that would be infinitely poorer, if not impossible, without insightful critics. I feel blessed to have friends like Josie Woll (alas no more), Carol Honsa, and Phyllis Palmer in Washington, who prioritized my writing and made time to read and comment on drafts of various chapters. Michèle and Alain Archambault in New York were not only meticulous readers who helped me clarify my thoughts and the way I articulated them but their warm insistence also kept me on track for finishing the book. Ayesha Heble on a flying visit to Delhi made time to look over the proofs of the first couple of chapters and her suggestions were invaluable. Sujatha Rao has been a one-person band encouraging, badgering and bullying to make sure that the publishers and I were kept in line and focused on getting the book out. Conversations with Beatrice Wallerstein and Borje and Ulrika Ljunggren were necessary reminders that this work had a larger resonance.

Finally, how does one thank family? Without the boundless love and support of my parents, none of this would have been possible. My mother's indomitable spirit and joie de vivre has been inspirational. My parents-in-law would have been so proud to see this book and their absence is deeply felt. The quiet affection of my natal and marital families has been a source of encouragement and strength. Each member of the family provides a particular kind of nurturing and I can only thank all of them in Delhi, Calcutta, Bombay, Bangalore, Horsham and London for their (at times blind) faith and unstinting love and encouragement. I would particularly like to acknowledge my brother Pami, a renaissance man who dares to go where others fear to tread. In The Attic, he has created a space for real conversations with writers, artists and thinkers; and my brother-in-law Pulak who has always been interested in my writing. I am also indebted to cousin Mala and nieces Amba and Tuli whose unwavering interest and support has been a reassuring reminder that they think my work to be important; and Aishwarya and Kabir, whose inclusive and spontaneous generosity links the family generationally, braiding all of our life-stories together.

Amit and Ateesh are the kinds of sons one reads about – loyal, loving and sensitive – with a sense of humour to boot. However, this has not prevented them from being astute but supportive critics. Conversations with them have tempered and nuanced my thinking and their keen editorial skills have honed the written word. My husband, Nayan, a compassionate partner in this and all other journeys, has pushed me to fly higher, dig deeper and spread my wings wider. But for him this book and much else in my life may never have been, and certainly not seasoned with this rich sauce of celebrations, laughter and love.

CONTENTS

1

Introduction

The Indo-British encounter altered both the Indian landscape and its mindscape. The crucial site of this change was the domestic space. Both the actual homes and the relationships within the home were dramatically altered. The encounter forced a change in housing style, a reconsideration of notions of womanhood and of what exactly constituted Indianness in literature. Architecturally, as the joint-family haveli dwellings were replaced by the Western bungalow homes the haveli ethos seen as particularly Indian was carried over to the new homes. The transition from the indigenous patriarchal haveli to the Western bungalow dramatically affected women because of their centrality in the domestic and familial spheres. For them the transgression of traditional norms is further complicated by the identity politics of Indianness and womanhood. The nexus between modernity and nationalism led to the concept of a "new woman", one who was permitted to step out in ways that had not been possible before, but, equally one who was often contradictorily circumscribed by arbitrarily defined notions of Indianness. Traditionally perceived as guardians and transmitters of culture, women became active participants in this change. As they negotiated between a Westernisation, often seen as emblematic of modernity, and an Indianness read as tradition, that they documented in English. The English language, probably the most enduring legacy of the colonial encounter, was enthusiastically adopted by Indians but its 'foreign' status made Indian users question its validity as a means of communication. English as a vector of change affected women and men in very different ways. The gendered impact of English in India is further complicated by issues of nationalism and ethnicity that have dogged the process of assimilation of the English language and literature into India.

The Problem of English in India

From the inception of Indian English literature, it has been impossible to separate the issue of language and literature from that of nationality and ethnicity. The inability even to name the literature—as its various appellations from Anglo-Indian to Indian English to Indo-Anglian and Indo-English[1] —indicate the magnitude of the problem.[2] K.R. Srinivasa Iyengar and M.K. Naik's pioneering surveys of Indo-English literature highlight the dilemma that Raja Rau expressed best: "One has to convey in a language that is not one's own the spirit that is one's own."[3] The issue, however, has never been purely one of language or even aesthetics—politics needs to be taken into account. English has been the language of a colonising power and continues to be seen as the language of privilege. Svati Joshi notes that even today, although "various forms of indigenism" are on the rise, the status of English remains relatively unchanged:

> English still remains the language that regulates access to higher education, and is linked to class interest, economic benefits and with the production and reproduction of major forms of social power and cultural privilege.[4]

However, writers like Khushwant Singh and Keki Daruwala contend that "there is a strong bias against Indians writing in English" which Daruwala fears might even "drive the English language writer out of the country slowly."[5]

The shadow of Macaulay's "brown sahib"—Indian in colour but British in tastes and habits—continues to loom over the language issue. The unease with English can be traced back historically to the colonial project of winning the hearts and minds of the people through a cultural education. In *Masks of Conquest*, Gauri Viswanathan convincingly demonstrates how English Studies was used as a tool to create "consent" for political and cultural domination. Because literature in the colonizers language was divorced from its political function and defined as a vehicle of universal values it became, as Rajeswari Sunder Rajan says, easier to justify its continuance. She notes,

> It is this dissociation of English literature from its national origin that has made possible its unproblematic retention and continuance in the post-Independence education sylla-bus in India.[6]

English education which was linked to economic incentives thus subtly helped spread the message of British superiority.

In contrast, Modhumita Roy maintains that Indians were complicit and "volunteered" to assimilate because it afforded them better economic and social opportunities.[7] The hybrid class of educated and wealthy professionals who aspired to administrative jobs formed an English speaking elite. English was not only a passport to government jobs then, as it is to international jobs now, it was, and continues to be a link language among Indians from different regions. Nationalists, like Raja Ram Mohan Roy, though anti-colonial, also saw English education as a vehicle for social reform and modernisation. The status of women was a central issue in India's modernity. As Partha Chatterjee notes, the woman question had at the time become the measure of a superior civilisation. Katherine Mayo's controversial *Mother India*, for instance, highlights the plight of women to justify the "mission civilisatrice" of colonialism.[8]

Kumkum Sangari and Sudesh Vaid note that in their desire to help their women improve themselves and become "companionate wives," the Nationalists automatically turned to the "morally ennobling" texts of English culture.[9] But these texts proved to be a double edged sword. The English language with its very expressive ideologies gave women an unconventional set of tools with which to refashion themselves. Sangari and Vaid further observe:

> It is in this historical intersection that women begin to constitute themselves in journals, autobiographies, poems, narratives and diaries, and to which we owe the formation of an Anglo Indian literature.[10]

Women and men authors fashioned "modern" Indian women protagonists who strove to balance tradition and modernity, the home and the world. For the novel writer, as Meenakshi Mukherjee points out, this was a "two-fold adventure" since both the English language and the novel form were new on the Indian literary scene.[11] "The problem," she notes, however, was "to reconcile two sets of values—one obtained by reading an alien literature and the other available in life"(7). Laila, the young protagonist of Attia Hosain's Partition novel, *Sunlight on a Broken Column*, attributes her sense of rootlessness and painful disjunction to the chasm between her English education and an Indian lifestyle creating a distance that leads to the anxiety about belonging and community.

Linguistically, Indo-English novelists went through various experimental phases of mimicry and creativity to arrive finally at a confident and playful Indian English idiom. As Jon Mee notes, "Rushdie's great feat in *Midnight's Children* was to show that English could be productively unhoused for writing about India."(716)[12] Most recently Arundhati Roy's *The God of Small Things* is also testimony to an ease, playfulness and a casual Indianization of English. Author and critic Raji Narasimhan's bald statement, "[C]reative writing in English is not natural for an Indian,"[13] is not only unsustainable but has been proven invalid. The evolution of the literature, especially in the last ten years, bears testimony to a mature and confident style that has been internationally acclaimed (view for example, the various nominations and prizes). Raja Rao in the passage quoted earlier had gone on to lament that,

One has to convey the various shades and omissions of a certain thought movement that looks maltreated in an alien language. I use the word 'alien', yet English is not really an alien language to us. It is the language of our intellectual make-up, like Sanskrit or Persian was before—but not of our emotional make-up.[14]

Today these anxieties about original expression in a foreign language are less tenable because for those who write and read in English it is no longer a "foreign language." They have grown up with English as a first language and made it their own, even though many are bilingual.

The liberating aspect of English expression—both in the choice of subject matter and style—tends to be glossed over. Salman Rushdie attributes the omission to anxieties of political correctness.[15] However, I feel this aspect is deliberately minimized (often by the writers themselves) because their indeterminate status between Indian and English renders them particularly vulnerable to the fear of being labelled un-Indian; and un-Indian imperceptibly changes to inauthentic, and thereby undermines the very base of Indian English writing.

Professor B. Kachru's crucial question about the Indianizing of English shows the shift in the language debate by the 1980's:

What does it take to give a once imposed (foreign) language a national identity? What are the processes of acculturation and nativization a language must undergo before one can consider it one's own?[16]

Although ostensibly about language, the question opens up a Pandora's box about issues of the relationship between literature and national identity. Although two excellent studies, *The Lie of the Land: English Literary Studies in India* and *Woman Image Text: Feminist Readings of Literary Texts*,[17] clear the terrain for initiating such a discussion; I will for the present, take the question at face value. The concept of nation invoked is a loose one referring to an intangible sense of Indianness.[18] Linguistically, the Indianisation of English was achieved by devices like transliteration, translation of idioms or the unitalicized use of Indian words.[19] Mulk Raj Anand, one of the "big three" mentioned earlier, asserts that the "echoes of one's mother tongue" can be heard in Indian English. He, in fact, claimed that "the original vibrations alone can give authenticity to the contents of speech of the characters."[20] Thus authenticity begins to be conflated with the qualities of languages considered to be specifically Indian but gradually also includes contexts and characters deemed Indian over others that are inauthentic because they lack these characteristics of Indianness. Kachru's response to his own question is more extreme. He goes so far as to say that Indian English has no referent to its origins:

> The acculturation of English seems to be complete within the sociolinguistic context of India to which the "native" speaker of English has become marginal.[21]

It could be said that the continuity of English in India is, in fact, premised upon its de-territorialization and de-nationalisation. English has become a global language that does not carry the burden of colonialism or of a national location any longer. This of course is problematic and we will return to it later.

Women and Language

Some critics claim that for Indian English women writers, language offers a certain distance, acting as a kind of mask. This particular use of language has led to at least two very different interpretations of women's writing. Meenakshi Mukherjee criticises such authors as Kamala Markandaya and Nayantara Sahgal's writing style as flat and confining. She notes,

> Their prose style has the smooth uniform ease of English expensively acquired at public schools in India and private schools abroad. It is a highly readable English and it seems to control their choice of themes—instead of, what would be more desirable, the theme determining the language.[22]

Malashri Lal, on the other hand, reads the simple, if not simplistic, linear narrative patterns and the blandness of the language as a deliberate strategy for saying the unsayable. She argues:

> women's writing in English is *deliberately simple on the surface* because that is the only way the cries of agonized displacement can find space in writing. *(Emphasis in the original)*[23]

She sees the tension between a surface placidity and a "strenuous" subtext as almost formulaic in women's writing, its repetition in various texts convincing her that it is a deliberate ploy. In reading novelists like Shashi Deshpande or Anita Desai it behoves one to read against the grain and to look out for the quietitude that masks their often radical messages.

Language may open the space to address taboo subjects by creating a space or a distance from the regional-language home communities. The lack of a regional base freed Indo-English literature from the norms of particular literary traditions thus making experimentation easier. Many writers have also noted that they "choose a language other than their mother-tongue for writing they wish to keep from the readership within their own languages."[24]

At least two writers—Mrinal Pande and Kamala Das— have chosen to write their autobiographies in English.[25] The assertion of an individual self in English by writers who are generally known for their work in Hindi and Malayalam respectively is significant. The subject matter of their autobiographies as well as of others like Nayantara Sahgal's *Relationship* also defies conventions.[26] They tread on dangerous ground exposing themselves as desiring and suffering subjects when they write about sexuality, wife abuse and familial relationships.

Women's internalization of "male-stream" values continues to circumscribe and shape their choices of language and genre. The fear of homelessness in both a literal and a metaphoric sense seems to be an inherent condition of being women but most specifically of writing women. Two collections of conversations among English and bhasha women writers *Storylines: Conversations with Women Writers* and *Just Between Us*, confirm that women writers across a broad spectrum of

age, community, regions, caste and class are acutely aware
that writing is a subversive activity especially in patriarchal
societies and this "ultimate transgression" can render them
homeless. Social, religious and political censorship constrains
all writers, but women particularly suffer from what the poet
Imtiaz Dharker calls "the good girl syndrome".[27] In the 1930's,
some seventy years earlier, Virginia Woolf had already
exhorted women writers to "kill the angel in the house" but
evidently the shadow of her wings still continues to affect, if
not silence, women.

Categories of Indianness

Colonial rule having created a class of cultural and linguistic
"interpreters" or "translators", the question of Indianness was
inflected with notions of nationalist loyalty and identity.
Would what the African-American writer DuBois called "two-
ness" or double consciousness erase or limit one's Indianness
because of the addition of an English or Western
consciousness? Who could be classified as an "Indian" author?
What criteria should be used for ascertaining that an author
could be classified as Indian? Ethnicity, origins, citizenship,
location or language were arbitrarily deployed as some of the
criteria of inclusion especially among Indian authors writing
in English. This discussion already circulating in the 1960s and
before is exacerbated today. In the early anthologies, for
example, Ruth Prawar Jhabvala, born of Polish parents,
educated in England, married to an Indian, living in and
writing about India is included among Indian writers by some
critics like Naik but excluded by others like Meenakshi
Mukherjee.[28] The justification for including Jhabvala would
be that her subject is India and she then lived in India. But
equally she could be excluded on the grounds that she is not
ethnically Indian nor is she an Indian national. Similarly then,
how does one classify Attia Hossain or Kamala Markandaya?
Both lived abroad but were ethnically Indian and the question
of their being counted as Indian writers has never been raised.
Currently the increased mobility of a large number of the new
cosmopolitan group of writers who may be of Indian origin

but who write from abroad, often spending half their time in India and half abroad in various metropolitan locations makes these categorisations of who is Indian even more problematic. Salman Rushdie's polemical and controversial comment that, "Indo-Anglian" literature represents perhaps the most valuable contribution India has yet made to the world of books[29] was probably the last straw in a debate that had been simmering at home and abroad about who has the right to speak, for whom, and from where. Issues of privilege and Western academic hegemony are only one part of the debate. A politics of location has also become a critical factor in other, often more dangerous realms of existence, like the communalisation of India.[30] Sunder Rajan's apt definition of the implications of such a location is worth noting:

> Location, however, is not simply an address. One's affiliations are multiple, contingent and frequently contradictory . .
> . . location is fixed not (only) in the relative terms of centre and periphery, but in the positive (positivist?) terms of an actual historical and geographical contingency.[31]

The questions posed within this debate need serious consideration which, however, is beyond the scope of this work.[32]

To return, however, to the politics of location specifically in relation to literature, Rushdie's argument may not be very different from Sujit Mukherjee's mentioned earlier. The difference is that whereas Mukherjee and others would locate Indo-English literature in an Indian context, Rushdie, unsurprisingly, places it in a placeless diaspora. But the diaspora has its own context, as the global address for Indian authors living and writing from abroad, which Rushdie proposes as the site for reading Indo-English literature.[33]

Rushdie further accuses "vernacular literatures" of being "parochial" in their criticism of Indo-English authors' success in "breaking out."[34]

The debate has often been acrimonious and authors like Bharati Mukherjee stridently reject the labels and insist that they do not want to be categorised as either "Indian" or "women" authors because that diminishes their status as writers. The sub-text of the labelling game raises Spivak's questions raised earlier about who has the right to speak and for whom? These insistent questions hark back to issues of authenticity and authority that so haunt Indian writing in English. Does a west-based author's exploitation, of what Meenakshi Mukherjee calls, Indian raw material, entitle them to speak for and about India from privileged centers? Their location authorises their voices as often the only ones heard. The anxiety about India based English authors, novelist Deshpande notes, does not stem merely out of jealousy but out of a larger concern about the globalized market shaping and magnifying certain voices and concern over others. Critics like Aijaz Ahmad, among others, offer a three-fold critique contending that English writing is still unable to reflect the complexity of Indian life; post-colonial literature is primarily focused on the anxiety of foreign returned Indians and the framing trope is that of the Western-educated figure naval gazing at their elite marginal positions as both insiders and outsiders to India. For these characters and writers India is a metaphor not a lived reality.

The critique is harsh and a more relevant question may be what does being "Indian" mean at any specific time and place. The initial measure of "Indianness" was a result of, and in opposition to, a notion of "Englishness." Tharu notes that "a principal burden of this [Indo-English] literature can be regarded as a working out of the urgencies that arise from the Indo-British encounter."[35] The most dramatic terrain of change wrought by this encounter is visible through Indian novels in English in the reconfiguration of the notions of woman, home and Indianness.

Indeed, Rushdie's claim that "Literature has little or nothing to do with a writer's home address," is deeply problematic.[36] This body of literature as well as individual authors are profoundly aware of and shaped by "the home address". Literature's search for a "cultural self-identity," echoed in the texts, has everything to do with a home address whether real or imagined. Individual authors, write with an awareness of the boundaries of that home address.[37] Even in the literary space of the imagination, restraint and a keen sense of social, gender and class-bound realities set the limits. Transgressions, as noted above are camouflaged or, when openly violated, the consequences of no-return or eviction from the home are clearly understood. Indian women in the house of fiction reiterate the significance of a cultural Indianness. Lorna Sage justifies her title, *Women in the House of Fiction*, by suggesting that "'the house of fiction isn't, for my purposes, only a metaphor for containment. It's a reminder that fiction isn't placeless."[38] Extending Sage's premise, I want to suggest that both the Indianness and the womanhood constructed in and by this fiction are informed by place. The place here is the geographic, the national, and the metaphoric India which are the cultural parameters of "the home address" within which critics, authors and their protagonists frame their perceptions of an Indian reality.

Indian English Literature

Apart from issues about language and its place in India, at a literary level too, Indianness has been central in the development of Indo-English literature. K.R. Srinivasa Iyengar, a pioneer of critical work on Indo-English literature who popularised the term "Indo-Anglian" literature, asserts:

> what makes Indo-Anglian literature an *Indian* literature, and not just a ramshackle outhouse of English literature, is the quality of its "Indianness." (Emphasis in the original)[39]

Critics like Iyengar, Mukherjee and Golak among others have carefully delineated myths and legends, social contexts, choice of subjects, historic and regional particularities and textures of thought as some of the markers of this Indianness. Githa Hariharan and Shashi Deshpande's creative use and reinterpretation of myths can be read as markers, not only of Indianness, but also of a new feminist literary strategy of change.

Iyengar has always insisted on the status and centrality of English as a "link-language." He argues that, "Indo-Anglian literature, besides being a distinctive literature in its own right, is also a link-literature in the context of India's pluralistic literary landscape."[40] Meenakshi Mukherjee, however, notes that "instead of being a source of wealth, our plurality of languages becomes a pretext for preventing or silencing analytical discourse."[41] The competition among Indo-English and regional language literatures has reduced the possibility of communication or creative dialogue between them. In *Towards a Literary History of India*, Sujit Mukherjee bemoans the absence of a comparative framework for analysing Indian literatures or for formulating a literary history of India. The rhetoric of the oft-claimed unity of Indian Literature, though it is written in many languages, therefore remains merely a theoretical proposition.

The lack of dialogue between various Indian languages, even in terms of the translation of major works, continues to point to English as a link language. Aijaz Ahmad notes the irony that,

a Third World Literature would arise on the basis of Western *languages*, while Third Worldist ideology is manifestly opposed to the cultural dominance of Western *countries*. *(Emphasis in the original)*[42]

In specific and utilitarian situations, Ahmad and others are forced to concede the centrality of English, however problematic, on the Indian landscape. For example, Susie Tharu and K. Lalita's two-volume *Women Writing in India: 600 B.C. to the Early 20th Century* and Meenakshi Mukherjee's *Realism and Reality: The Novel and Society in India* can be seen as steps in the direction of opening the space for an intra-regional dialogue through English.

Despite Iyengar's plea that English should not be made into an "ideological issue," that is exactly what it continues to be. The "burden of Indianness" carried by authors and critics alike is especially onerous when Indian and English become conflictual binaries. In the early post-independence years Svati Joshi notes that the urban, English-speaking elite and their literature had to position themselves "both against colonialism and within the indigenous society."[43] Fifty years after independence, although English continues to carry some of the old scars, it is more firmly entrenched and accepted than ever before. Joshi attributes the allure and continuity of English in India to a new kind of community formation which negotiates heterogeneous culture and society, and which offers the perspective of both insider and outsider. If this is a difficult position to maintain within the Indian literary context, the issue becomes even more fraught and contentious in its relationship with the West.

Even though the first book by an Indian author in English, *The Travels of Dean Mahomet* was published in 1794, the debate over colonial English education continued to rage till much later.[44] In fact the place of English in India is still contested. In 1823 the nationalist reformer Raja Ram Mohan Roy's "Letter on English Education" argued in favour of establishing English rather than a Sanskrit school. The former, he believed, would "promote a more liberal and enlightened system of instruction."[45] Enlightenment and modernity was English's passport into India and even nationalists like Roy argued for the adoption of English on the strength of this argument. On the other hand Thomas Babington Macaulay's oft quoted 1835 Minute on Education argued for English education on the pragmatic and colonial grounds of creating a class of interpreters between the rulers and the ruled; "a class of persons, Indian in blood and colour, but English in taste, in opinions, in morals, and in intellect."[46]

Indian English Literature's Search for Home

Having adopted English, Indians not only made it their own by Indianising it, they also used it across a variety of genres from government tracts and legal drafts to essays, pamphlets, newspaper articles and letters; from autobiographies, poetry, fiction, history and biographies to limericks and doggerels. Broadly though, the history of Indian writing in English is traced back to the early nineteenth century. In *A History of Indian English Literature*, M.K. Naik chronologically demarcates four broad phases of Indian writing in English. Both poetry and prose were produced in the first phase from 1800 to 1857. In the second phase, between 1857 to 1920, poetry continued to be a significant genre, and names like Toru Dutt, who died at the young age of twenty-one, marks this period.[47] Susie Tharu and K. Lalita's meticulous research has revealed other writers like Pandita Ramabai Saraswati, Cornelia Sorabji and Rokeya Sakhawat Hossain in this early period. Tharu and Lalitha note, for example, that Hossain's "utopian fantasy," *Sultana's Dream* (1905), "was probably the first such work in Indian literature".[48] It predates Charlotte Perkins Gillman's better known *Herland* (1915) by a decade.

The novel genre was the latest to arrive in this period and was new to Indian literature. Even so, Meenakshi Mukherjee notes that "the Indo-Anglian novel came into existence long after the novel had become an established genre in other Indian languages."[49] Bankimchandra Chatterjee's *Rajmohan's Wife*, which first appeared in serialised form in 1864 and was posthumously published in book form in 1935, is considered to be the first Indian novel in English.[50] It was also this famous Bangla novelist's first and only novel in English. Krupa Satthianandhan (1862-94) is deemed to be among the earliest women novelists in English.[51] These were, however, stray examples and did not yet signal a body of Indo-English literature. Mukherjee remarks, "[T]he Indo-Anglian novel made a diffident appearance in the nineteen twenties" noting, however, that a few novels had appeared even before this period.[52] M.K. Naik recognizes with some surprise the discrepancy between lagging female education and the "early appearance of women novelists."[53] He names Raj Lakshmi Debi, Toru Dutt, Krupabai Satthianandhan and Shevantibai M. Nikambe as the four prominent women novelists before the turn of the century.[54]

The absence of women novelists in Naik's third phase, between 1920 and 1947, is therefore all the more striking by contrast. This phase is dominated by the "big three" male novelists—Raja Rao, R.K. Narayan and Mulk Raj Anand. In the fourth period from 1947 and beyond, Naik notes that women novelists "form a sizeable and significant school."[55] The four main novelists he names are Anita Desai, Nayantara Sahgal, Kamala Markandaya and Ruth Prawer Jhabvala. By this time there was a substantial body of novels by women and men in both regional literatures and Indo-English writing. Since Naik's writing, the field has grown considerably. As writer Champa Bilwakesh notes, "South Asian women have arrived like storm troopers into the diasporic English literary scene. Titles by South Asian women dominate shelf space at bookstores in a way South Asian men's never did."[56] Women novelists like Anita Rau Badami, Kiran Desai, Shashi Deshpande, Chitra Bannerjee Divakaruni, Jhumpa Lahiri, Bharati Mukherjee, Arundhati Roy, and many others who dominate the literary landscape today, are both from India and from the Indian diaspora abroad.

A search for community, central in Indian women's novels in English, has also been crucial to the body of Indo-English literature since its beginning in the early nineteenth century. While the dual heritage—Indian and English—has enabled a new community formation within India, it has also created in the literature a sense of un-belonging. In a multi-lingual society like India, Indo-English literature has had to negotiate a place both within a rich and vibrant circle of Indian literatures as well as internationally among other literatures in English. Unanchored from regional moorings, Indo-English literature's pan-Indian reach tends to be class-based. Ease with English signals a more Westernised, affluent class that has access to an English education. The terms "Indian" and "English" in this literature are not mere linguistic signifiers but are politically weighted by the history of colonialism in India. A brief exploration of the dilemma of Indo-English literature's search for an identity provides the background for a similar quest by women protagonists in this literature by women authors. Indian women's novels reveal that gender is a critical category in the notion of an "Indianness" which they embody and of which they, as women, are the principal caretakers.

The Indian Woman

The "home address" or the notion of Indianness is crucial in shaping identities and the construction of the Indian woman in post colonial Indo-English women's novels. Simone de Beauvoir stated, "one is not born a woman, but rather becomes one".[57] Tracing the path to becoming the gendered subject for the Indian woman, can however be problematic. In his seminal work *Orientalism* Said confesses to obeying Gramsci's injunction to compile a critical inventory of the traces of historical processes that have formed individual consciousness as a way of knowing oneself.[58] It is impossible to delineate exactly a cultural ethos or value system, but a consideration of ancient literature may provide some broad thematic links between the past and the present in the construction of women's identities within a larger cultural context. The specific time period is less important to my argument than the general ideologies that continue to shape specific aspects of both Indianness and womanhood. My concern with the "past" is only as it is perceived, interpreted and incorporated into the "present". The focus is on those aspects of the past that contemporary society has chosen to reject or retain, especially as indicators of Indian Womanhood.

Contemporary Indo-English literature reflects the continuing and inherent tension between the reinforcing of traditions and the resistance to recurrent cultural patterns. Spivak suggests that just as the narratives of Oedipus and Adam are cultural signifiers for Western tradition, indigenous legal tradition, scriptures and myths might be considered as "regulative narratives" for non-western traditions.[59] It is in their role as gender and cultural demarcators that classics, myths and legends serve as distinctive markers and reminders of Indianness and womanhood. Some critics of Indo-English literature like Shantha Krishnaswamy, have sought to trace and affirm the Indianness of women protagonists and to see them largely in the context of their relationship to men.[60] Her work *The Woman in Indian Fiction in English* (1950-80), like Meena Shirwadkar's earlier *Image of Woman in the Indo-Anglian Novel*,[61] considers women as a separate category but sees them strictly in relationship to men. Neither author analyses the differences, if any, between male and female authors. They map women's roles as mothers, wives and daughters, in Indo-English writing by women and men. Shirwadkar's largely descriptive work reveals the importance of certain gender stereotypes that persist in this literature, while Krishnaswamy emphasises women's roles as "the sisterhood of man."[62] Krishnaswamy concludes that, despite change, women protagonists emerge intact as "essentially Indian," but she does not question the construction of that Indianness.[63] Contemporary novelists, I suggest, are less sanguine. They explore archetypes and question both women's resistance and their complicity as they negotiate the wide divide between the idea of Woman and women as individuals or even a class in "civil society."[64] Women have been participants in the construction and transmission of these ideologies as they have also been shaped by them.[65]

Hinduism, as the dominant religion, provides the grid upon which the broad cultural framework of India is knitted into place. The cult of goddess worship, iconically represented in "mother goddess figures" that date back to the Indus Valley period, are vaunted as proof of Woman's high status in society.[66] Altekar's statement, "The apotheosis of the mother has reached a greater height in India than anywhere else," reflects a commonly held view.[67] Kamala Ganesh observes that the sacralisation of Woman as mother is indicative of female creative power, "She conveys not so much the ideas of physical motherhood but a world-view in which the creative power of femininity is central.[68] Bhattacharji, however, reads the deification of motherhood as "compensatory, seeking to recompense society's indifference to the mother."[69] Radha Kumar's excellent study of the women's movement in India notes how the mother-ideology continued to be deployed in the nationalist period, often equating mother-goddess with mother-India.

The first half of the twentieth century saw a symbolic use of the mother as a rallying device, from feminist to terrorist assertions of women's power as mothers of the nation, to terrorist invocations of the protective and ravening mother goddess, to the Gandhian lauding of the spirit of endurance and suffering embodied in the mother.[70]

The sacralisation of motherhood is inherently problematic. Mahasweta Devi's short story "Stanadayini" is a brilliant indictment of the glorification of the abstract idea of motherhood while ignoring the position of real mothers.[71] Githa Hariharan's *The Thousand Faces of Night* and Shashi Deshpande's *The Binding Vine* both indicate that for an older generation of women, often the only legitimate way out of imprisoning gender roles, be they of sacred motherhood or dutiful wives, was to follow in the itinerant footsteps of Mira Bai, the Bhakti poet who renounced the world for her god.[72] Change, in novels like Anita Rau Badami's *Tamrind Woman*, for example is often marked by showing different possibilities of renegotiation to mother and mother-country for both mothers and daughters.

The idea of mother goddesses is deeply connected with the idea of sexuality. The sacralised attitudes towards mothers and the unwritten taboo on mentioning sex have almost silenced contemporary women's writing on sexuality in general, and of mother's sexuality in particular. This is why Kamala Das's autobiography *My Story* was considered controversial, and, more recently, Roy's *The God of Small Things*, faced legal action on charges of pornography. Roy's case shows how the appeal to tradition justifies attempts to proscribe women's writing in the public sphere. That the appeal is being made reveals, in turn, how traditional perceptions of Woman's "proper" place endure in legal discourses, and continue to draw populist support.[73]

The good-mother/bad-mother binary in Indo-English fiction can be traced back to popular perceptions of the goddesses Parvati and Kali.[74] Although mentioned in the Epics and the Puranas, they come into prominence later. In the popular imagination they complement each other as archetypal images. Kali is in every way a contrast to the fair Parvati. Her independence (of any male god), her physical position above him, her dark and dishevelled appearance and association with cremation grounds are deliberate markers of otherness that locate her on the margins of society.[75] She is dangerous because she "threatens stability and order."[76] [Even the traits that Kali embodies are recognised as being tameable and trainable to preserve patriarchal domesticity, in legends as well as in contemporary literature.]

Parvati, on the other hand, is the upholder of societal norms. She embodies very specific cultural values of female strength as moral superiority, which we shall see again in Sita and Kannaki. Parvati as the "insider" goddess is part of the patriarchal structure of society while Kali the "outsider" goddess threatens that structure – and in doing so, the whole moral code. In both cases, however, the power of the goddesses is validated through their male consorts. David Kinsley's interpretation, which mirrors a more general point of view, cautions against women shaking the status quo because of the dangerous consequences that would follow. Woman's sexuality is the core issue in maintaining the balance of kinship relations in a society. The "experimental" or at least more flexible ways of thinking about female sexuality afforded by unconventional goddesses became codified by Manu in the second century.

Manusmriti, regarded as the most authoritative and earliest law book in India, helped to codify and systematize the subordinate status of women and enshrine it as documented rules.[77] I do not want to rehearse yet again Manu's aphorisms that have become not only a part of everyday language but also part of contemporary attitudes to women.[78] The text enshrines women's lack of access to learning into a religio-moral precept. Kumkum Roy notes the careful situating of a woman's place firmly within the home, as the initiation, student, householder periods of a man's life were paralleled stage by stage by analogous domestic duties for women. Marriage was the equivalent of religious initiation for a girl, serving the husband was the student stage for the wife, and household duties were the symbolic parallels of worshipping the sacred fire. Every stage of a woman's life was marked by extolling and valorising the men in her life and confining her strictly within the domestic sphere. What in earlier times had been merely custom, Manu inscribed, with all the force of written law. "The acceptance of such prescriptions," Roy notes, "would have meant that any non-domestic activity was viewed as unworthy or unwifely."[79] Nayantara Sahgal's *Rich Like Us* describes how in marriage, procreation, property, inheritance and other rights, Manu's shadow looms large over the Indian psyche. It was not only that women had no place outside the home, but even within, subservience and abject dependence were her lot. In his psychoanalytical study, Sudhir Kakar reiterates the same idea, noting that traditionally "an Indian woman does not stand alone; her identity is wholly defined by her relationship to others,"[80] as he defines the three stages of a woman's life by her gender roles of daughter, wife/ daughter-in-law, and mother.

Sita, the ideal wife and heroine of the epic *Ramayana*,[81] embodies Manu's attributes of the wife and domestic heroine. She dominates the popular imagination and "is revered as the model Hindu wife, who although the victim of injustices, always remains loyal and steadfast to her husband."[82] Although Valmiki's version does not emphasise her divinity, other versions grant her goddess status.[83] Ramanad Sagar's 1980's tele-serial of the *Ramayana* captured the popular imagination, revived the epic and fixed this particular version above others as the authoritative narrative and Sita as the exemplar of Indian wifehood.

The basic story remains unchanged in the many versions. At the moment of his son Rama's coronation as king, Dasratha, because of an earlier promise, is obliged to banish Rama from Ayodhya for fourteen years. Rama's wife, Sita, and brother, Lakshmana, insist on sharing his exile. In the forest Sita is abducted by Ravana. Rama ultimately vanquishes Ravana, destroys his kingdom and rescues Sita. However, he is loath to take her back because she has been with another man. At his bidding, Sita undergoes the test of fire. She emerges unscathed because of her moral strength.[84] Many years later, rumours about her purity resurface. Rama exiles his pregnant wife to the forest. She gives birth to twin sons. Even more years later Rama is willing to accept Sita again provided she undergoes another test of fire. She refuses and begs the earth to open up and take her back.

Three viewpoints have dominated the Rama-Sita mythology: their idealisation as an exemplary couple, Sita as the paragon of wifehood, and Rama as the ideal King. Sita continues to be the model for Indian wifehood, in life as well as in literature. Madhu Kishwar, founder editor of the feminist journal *Manushi*, testifies to her own and her readers' "obsessive involvement with Sita."[85] Before I take up Kishwar's argument, the three aspects of the *Ramayana* story that I wish to examine are Sita's "self effacing devotion and loyalty" which as Kishwar notes "have become the hallmark of the modern day stereotype of Sita"; her *agniparikhsa* or fire-ordeal; and the *rekha* (boundary line) that Lakshmana draws for Sita's protection as he leaves her to answer his brother's supposed cry for help.

The "Lakshmana rekha" has become the archetypal boundary line dividing an inside, safe space for women from a dangerous and threatening outside. The narrative unambiguously shows that even the most virtuous of women, Sita, is vulnerable outside the protection of domestic patriarchy. Ravana, disguised as a mendicant, lures her to step outside the protecive parameter and metaphorical limit drawn by her brother-in-law, before he can abduct her. The responsibility and blame for stepping out are hers. In Indo-English literature, the same metaphoric line operates to create psychological and spatial restrictions for women. In novels like Rama Mehta's *Inside the Haveli*, the physical demarcation between haveli and non-haveli dwellers encompasses a more abstract notion of "them" and "us" along class and gender lines. In Indrani Aikath Gyaltsen's *Daughters of the House*, the house as a patriarchal space is more ambiguous, but the distance between male and female spaces is equally rigid, as they are in Shama's Futehally's *Tara Lane's* clear differentiation between the corrupt, noisy, male world of the factory and the quiet, insulated world of women's domesticity. It cannot be surprising then that transgression is at the core of Indo-English women's novels, be it between notions of Indianness and Westernisation, inside and outside or male and female spaces. But the perils of stepping out can have disastrous consequences, as often there is no place for these "border-crossing" women to go. Malashri Lal labels this phenomenon "The Law of the Threshold." She explains:

> The threshold is a real as well as a symbolic bar marking a critical transition. Men have, traditionally, passed over the threshold unchallenged and partaken of worlds, the one within and the other "without".[86]

The home is a clearly gendered space that affects women and men differently. Lakshmana draws the line for Sita's protection, but by this act, security is transformed into incarceration thus reiterating the nest/prison duality of home. Women's association with domesticity and tradition has made their stepping out hazardous. The literature reveals that for women a sense of being Indian has meant conforming to gender roles of mother, wife and daughter. The parallel stories of women servants and upper class women in the novels show how both are marginalised because of their gender, and circumscribed by a feudal patriarchal ethos which offers protection in return for conformity.

Kishwar justifies Sita's unwavering loyalty as a sign of emotional strength and not slavery:

> She is seen as a person whose sense of dharma is superior to and more awe inspiring than that of Ram—someone who puts even maryada purshottam Ram—the most perfect of men—to shame.[87]

She is strong because her faith, her dharma makes her morally sure and hence fearless. Similarly, Kishwar suggests that Sita's acceptance of the first fire-ordeal was an act of defiance. Her refusal to submit to the second ordeal, choosing instead to return to her mother Earth, Kishwar asserts, "is interpreted not as an act of self-annihilation but as a momentous but dignified rejection of Ram as a husband."[88] In a letter to *Manushi*, a reader's absolute rejection of the Sita model and indeed other scriptural models pins the blame for women's erasure on the more culturally popular interpretations. She says:

> Now we must refuse to be Sitas. By becoming a Sita and sub-mitting to the fire ordeal, woman loses her identity . . . .. Our exclusion from the scriptures, from temples, from smritis, is also our strength. We can be fearless since we have no mod-els.[89]

Both Kishwar and the letter-writer look at the Sita figure not merely as a theoretical and textual paradigm but one that shapes their present everyday lives. In this context, the intersection between literature and society cannot be taken lightly.

In her later writing though, Kishwar does a volte face. Her justification is worth quoting in full because it indicates the pulls that push women, especially wives, to conform. It also highlights the ambiguity of an interpretation that seduces by promising community and by appealing to Woman's higher morality. Kishwar explains:

> There are several practical reasons why Sita-like behaviour makes sense to Indian women. The outcome of marriage in India depends not just on the attitude of a husband but as much on the kind of relationship a woman has with her mari-tal family and extended kinship group. If, like Sita, she com-mands respect and affection from the latter, she can frequently count on them to intervene on her behalf and keep her hus-band from straying, from behaving unreasonably. Similarly, once her children grow up, they can often play an effective role in protecting her from being needlessly bullied by her husband, and bring about a real change in the power equa-tion in the family, because in India, children especially sons, frequently continue living with their parents even after they are grown up.[90]

The premise of Kishwar's argument is based on her perception of an Indian "reality" which unquestioningly, and in spite of experiential knowledge to the contrary, offers conformity as a strategy for survival. Like Manu's strictures, this tactic endorses dependent, patriarchal power relations, just as the explanation reinforces divisive binaries of male and female roles. Surprisingly, given Kishwar's own activist background, the question of woman's agency does not even arise. She emphasises Woman's "being" rather than "doing" as a solution to social ills. But her complete reliance on societal "disapproval" as a regulating measure is not endorsed in reality, as seen by the various letters to *Manushi*, nor do women novelists present compliance in such a positivist mode.

The conflation of positive female power with moral rectitude and obedience to society's rules is also epitomised in the sixth century Tamil classic *Shilappadikaram*. Kannaki, the heroine, is able "by the power of her virtue" to burn down the city of Madurai and destroy the Pandya king.[91] As a chaste, dutiful and righteous wife, she is more powerful than even the mightiest ascetic or king. Sita and Kannaki are genuine daughters of Parvati in the traditional mould, and, as such, the exemplars of Indian wifehood. A psychoanalytically interpretive construct of the individual and society like Sudhir Kakar's is enabled by this continuity between past and present, tradition and modernity. Kakar points to this connection between suffering and righteousness as a "major fantasy" that protects Indian women from rage against their lot.[92] The fantasy of the suffering but righteous woman winning a real or moral victory in the end is also a staple of the Bollywood film industry.

The supposedly impenetrable armour of righteousness is an important detail in the idea that "good" women are divinely protected. This ideology perpetuates the myth that women have only themselves to blame for overstepping the line of good conduct and thereby inviting punishment. Desai and Krishnaraj point out that even someone of Gandhi's stature endorsed such a viewpoint: "Mahatma Gandhi too believed that a chaste woman should be able to ward off rape and if she could not she should give up her life."[93] These attitudes are not merely a case of blaming the victim. More dangerously, the conviction of moral or "divine protection" denies agency to individual women to protest or take charge of their lives. The subliminal links between passivity and goodness for women are deeply rooted in Indian culture, equating independence and action with a moral or spiritual lack. In fact, Kishwar acclaims that Sita, unlike Draupadi, did not even need to pray for help; divine help came to her unsolicited.[94]

The figure of Draupadi, the heroine of the *Mahabharata*, has not achieved a Sita-like popularity maybe because she questions male power and authority. In B.R Chopra's 94-episode television serialization of the *Mahabharata*, the moment of Draupadi's public disrobing is portrayed with melodramatic bathos.[95] In this story, Yudhishtar stakes and loses everything in a dice-game, including his four brothers and their common wife Draupadi. She is dragged by her hair into an open assembly for a public disrobing. Her husbands cannot protect her and the community of men who are her kinfolk, do not say a word in her defence. The God Krishna, however, responds to the prayers of this good and devout wife, and does not allow her to be dishonoured. While other myths use a similar theodicy to explain and justify the protection of "good" men who surrender themselves to a greater will,[96] women have internalised this message in a very particular way.[97] Current research on the Partition shows that in the conflation of Woman and nation, women became the assertive site of a national identity.[98] Jasodhara Bagchi comments, "[D]efilement of communal honour through the violation of female sexuality is a thesis that resonates through the entire process of our nation building."[99] The issue of rape in novels like Deshpande's *The Binding Vine* and Desai's *Fire on the Mountain* is a version of Draupadi's story—a misogynistic public humiliation for female transgression. Purshottam Agarwal's point bears reiteration here that "[V]iolence in general and sexual violence in particular, has always been an integral part of any authoritarian world view."[100] He argues that rape, at an individual or a collective level, "is not just a matter of sexual lust", but an unambiguous assertion of power. The underlying conundrum is that if divine help is not forthcoming, can that be taken as proof of a woman's immorality? The novels rage against such a prescriptive reading. Women novelists neither promote passivity against injustice nor blame the victim and hold them responsible for their victimisation, but these perspectives are recognised and addressed.

The *Vedas, Manusmriti, Shilappadikaram* and the two epics, the *Ramayana* and the *Mahabharata* have been major influences in shaping attitudes to women and of women themselves.[101] It is not surprising, therefore, that Indians extol the Vedic age as the golden age of Hindu womanhood.[102] Because the sacred texts proclaim that no religious ritual could be completed by a man without a *Saha Dharma Carini* (loosely translated as a co-religious traveller),[103] a woman's place by the side of the man became essential. However, she could not perform a rite independently. A man on the other hand could, for example, substitute an image, as Rama substituted a golden image of Sita, and still perform the ceremony. Furthermore, as Sukumari Bhattachrji points out, while each ritual benefited fathers, husbands or sons, it was the role of women as upholders of the patriarchal family that was especially crucial.[104] In the work of both Attia Hosain and Rama Mehta the young daughter and daughter-in-law are constantly aware of this burden of tradition. Women seers and savantes like Gargi may be mentioned in Vedic texts, but as Kumkum Roy reminds us, they stand out because they are interlopers, defying the norm.[105] Women during this period were defined in and by a patriarchal context. Their value lay in being obedient daughters, good wives and mothers of sons. To a greater or lesser degree the same ideologies are perpetuated in contemporary culture. The novels, however, question these constructs of womanhood. While signalling the importance of the past and especially a mythic past, they do not necessarily endorse or subscribe to traditional readings of these myths. For example, Githa Hariharan's Sita, in *Thousand Faces of Might* unlike her epic namesake, defies social strictures, and risking the consequences, grabs at a second chance of life on her terms.

If the fiction written by Indian English women novelists reconfigure the mindscape of the Indian past as it is represented in the popular ancient texts, then the concrete spatial landscape of havelis and bungalows reveals the physical dimensions of Indianness. I not only want to explore the ways in which gender and identity have been embedded in the very ground-plan of the havelis, but I also wish to interrogate aspects of that more traditional domestic pattern as it has been carried over into the more modern bungalow and apartment dwellings.

The Indian Home

Architecture shaped the visual Indian landscape just as literature had shaped a normative mindscape. In many Indo-English novels, gender relations are the site of contact and conflict between tradition and modernity or Indian and Western values. Kumkum Sangari and Sudesh Vaid warn that,"[B]oth tradition and modernity have been, in India, carriers of patriarchal ideologies" and that both are "eminently colonial constructs."[106] In order to circumvent what the Rudolphs call an "analytical gap,"[107] created by positioning tradition and modernity in a dichotomous relationship, I have tried to use the terms in a neutral way positioning tradition and modernity in a dialectical relationship.

The house, a multi-layered space is the site of renegotiations between women and men as well as between different generations of women. As a site of nostalgia, some homes allow a return to an eternal childhood that left indelible impressions of security even as it defined limits. More importantly, however, women in these texts return to childhood homes to reclaim and come to terms with their past. Natal and marital homes, though often confining, are also accepted as training grounds for cultural continuity. In most novels, the domestic space becomes the site of female friendships and of changed man-woman relationships. Gender and identity seem embedded in the ground-plan of the havelis and some aspects of that lifestyle are carried over to the more modern bungalow dwellings. Contemporary Indian English novels explore women's re-creation of both the home and of her place in it.

Havelis

Architecturally, the "haveli" style has been the prototype urban Indian home. Its origins are obscure, but Sunand Prasad points out that similar forms can be traced back to the Indus Valley period about 3000 BC.[108] The original haveli design was a series of rooms constructed around an interior, open courtyard which was the focal point or the centre. A 17th century Parisian bourgeois home, as described by Witold Rybczynski, bears a striking resemblance to the Indian haveli.[109] The open courtyard at the heart of the inward-looking haveli dwelling provided light and air, and was the site of women's household chores.

The architect A.G. Krishna Menon suggests that the haveli's inward, centripetal movement, from public to private, which is also replicated in town-planning and temple architecture, is indicative of a shared, pervasive, specifically Indian world view.[110] He notes:

> There is a progressive movement towards increasing privacy from the city to the *mohalla* to the katra and then the *haveli*, and within the *haveli* from the public to the private *zenana* domains. It is like the unfolding of the temple plan from the *nat mandir* to the *garbhgriha*.[111]

Wacziarg and Nath note that "just as the joint family system was the smallest economic unit in the social structure of medieval India, a haveli was the smallest survival unit in the civic structure".[112] The haveli can be seen as a pan-India idea of home, a common "icon of house desire" which largely subsumed all other significant differences of religion, climate and region.[113] Attitudinally, it reproduces in microcosm the Indian social structure of kinship pattern, where the family is privileged over the individual unit.[114] Ideologically, havelis projected the concept of a unified world view that elided differences of class and gender. V.S. Pramar's architectural description minimises even obvious class difference by insisting that "in architectural terms the haveli was merely a very grand version of the common urban house."[115] Mehta and Hosain's novels, however, suggest that class and gender differences are structurally and ideologically embedded in the haveli.

Etymologically, Sunand Prasad points out, "the word haveli may derive from "haowla," the old Arabic for partition."[116] At one level, the closely clustered havelis seemed to celebrate the concept of unified communities. At another level, each haveli was a self-contained world, enclosed by a high, windowless wall isolating it from other havelis. Within the haveli, too, the gendered division of space reinforced women's "conventional subordination."[117] The organisation of the haveli space would support Shirley Ardener's contention that the inter-linking of physical boundaries and social rules results in women being structurally "muted."

Women especially were bound to obey the complicated rules of inner/outer, male/female, family/non-family spaces. Thus Geeta (*Inside the Haveli*) is immediately reprimanded when she strays into the male domain. These strict internal boundaries were constant reminders that hierarchy and gender determined one's place within the home. Women's mobility was restricted to the women's quarters or the zenanas. The segregated spheres also emphasised the separate worlds of men and women who lived together and yet apart in the same house. Wacziarg and Nath confirm that the haveli

represented the rigid lifestyle of a society that segregated its men from its women. The architecture of the haveli was conceived around this social norm.[118]

Laila (*Sunlight on a Broken Column*) sees how the segregation can be positive in terms of the security it offers but the negative aspects of confinement are not lost on her either. *Daughters of the House* takes the question of isolation to its logical end and provides a most ambiguous portrayal of a house inhabited only by women as both a womenspace and a prison. This nest/prison duality is present in the haveli and in the very idea of home, but it is possible to see, as we will see later, how this patriarchal space can be transformed into a womenspace.

Doreen Massey is particularly critical of "the associations of `a sense of place' with memory, stasis and nostalgia," which she sees as "reactionary," "escapist" and "essentializing."[119] In her view, although rootedness or attachment to a particular place is often seen as confining, exclusionary and static, it does not necessarily have to be so. Mehta and Hosain present quite different versions of the haveli. Jeevan Niwas *(Inside the Haveli)* is time-bound, embodying elements of both staticity and exclusion. It could be read as a nostalgic and romanticised evocation of a lifestyle threatened by change, as it measures the distance between the new township and the older haveli community. Ashiana *(Sunlight on a Broken Column)* is associated with memory but it does not romanticise haveli existence. It recognises the necessity of change. The transformation of the haveli ethos here is seen almost in organic terms.

In the novels, including *Inside the Haveli,* natal and marital homes, though, are seldom the lieu of what Massey calls an "unproblematical identity."[120] The authors do sometimes evoke "home" in Bachelardian terms as first models -- the embodiments of hopes and of dreams.[121] The return to these homes is thus often nostalgic but it is not romanticised. For instance, when Laila *(Sunlight on a Broken Column)* returns to her natal home, she remembers the pain of growing up in that home as much as she remembers the innocent joys. The authors, especially Hosain, are not in any way suggesting a return to "a golden past." In fact, the complex and problematic nature of that past is never glossed over. Nor do the novels condone the hierarchy and gender bias of the haveli, but there is an attempt to reclaim what are seen as the haveli's positive aspects, just as there is an attempt to reclaim certain aspects of the mythic models. The haveli's assimilation into modernity suggests that the sense of community that it encouraged is one of those necessary requirements of the condition of womanhood mentioned earlier.

To return to the haveli courtyard, it can, at moments, be envisaged as a womenspace—a lieu where women come together. The courtyard is designed to be the kind of private space that Millett justifiably rails against, as one that becomes an "ideological prison."[122] Wacziarg and Nath confirm that this was in fact one of the intents of the haveli design:

The original function of a haveli, apart from providing residence, was to wall in the domestic life of a family. Secluded from the outside world, a haveli set its own pace of life.[123]

The novels, however, often question and undermine this prohibitive intention inherited from tradition. In Mehta and Hosain, although the haveli is a place where the womanly rituals of domesticity are undertaken to propitiate patriarchal deities of father, brother and son, the work itself unites the women. Class boundaries of who works and who supervises the work are temporarily blurred. It is a lieu where, to use contemporary corporate-culture terms, women network and gather and exchange information. An emotional support system among the haveli women is prominent in both Hosain and Mehta. The novels show how in the small, restricted circle of the havelis, place and community are deeply intertwined. As an "imagined community," the haveli is conceptualised more in terms of a commune than the politico-nationalist ones articulated by Benedict Anderson.[124]

In both real and fictional havelis, the open and yet enclosed space of the courtyard remains ambiguous. It is a general area and yet restricted by a careful cordoning off from the view of strangers particulaly non-family males. The duality recalls that the haveli structure is premised upon the distinction between public and private space. Carole Pateman notes:

The dichotomy between the private and the public is central to almost two centuries of feminist writing and political struggle; it is, ultimately, what the feminist movement is about.[125]

It may not be "what the feminist movement is about" but it is a crucial issue in all the novels under study, particularly in Mehta and Hosain where the haveli and its life-style are at stake; *Tara Lane* and *The Binding Vine* also focus on this issue in a more contemporary setting.

Alan Roland notes that Indians view space in terms of the "sacred" and the "profane."[126] Women's place in the courtyard at the centre of the house would be comparable to the *garbhgriha* or sanctum sanctorum in temple architecture noted earlier by Menon. The sacralisation of Woman, noted earlier in this Chapter, is spatially repeated here. Prasad links the courtyard to a "metaphysical" space. He compares it

> to the cosmos within the dwelling. In ancient "mandalas" the central square that of the courtyard belongs to Brahma who is the Creator; only bare earth and plants were traditionally allowed here. There is a parallel idea in Islam of the garden as representation of paradise.[127]

This comparison reiterates the paradisiacal resonances of the garden common to Hindu, Islamic and Christian mythologies. The invocation of Brahma recalls woman's biological role as creator. The location of women in this kind of a womenspace would emphasise and privilege their biological destiny. The idea of women who fulfil their role as protectors of the hearth and providers of sons to continue the family name is deeply embedded in the haveli ethos as almost a spiritual duty. The courtyard's associations with the inner sanctum-sanctorum and with nature shape a dual notion of femininity. It can be a place of retreat and community or it could be a patriarchally designated space for women symbolising specific constructs of gender which women themselves have internalised. A critical aspect of the courtyard space is that it is envisioned as "natural" as opposed to "built". If the link to Brahma raises issues of reproduction, its location as an interior space, where only "bare earth and plants" are allowed, re-poses questions of the links between nature, nurture and feminine roles as well as the issues of privacy. Menon and Pramar both note that havelis were built on the principle of "infill" -- filling in a plot according to need. Pramar elaborates that the ad hoc and rather random construction process of the haveli made no allowances for outward additions:

> Curiously, although the joint family knew that it was bound to expand, no architectural provision was generally made for this. As the family grew, members simply huddled closer together without feeling any sense of deprivation. This was

because the concept of an individualized space, or even of personal possessions, never arose.[128]

However, the romantic generalisation of this communal sense of space is unsubstantiated. There was no "individualised space" but that there was a gendered space remains unacknowledged. The novels reiterate gender divisions and notions of privacy, providing a very different perspective. They suggest that within the group-ethos of the haveli, notions of individuality and privacy are suspect, synonymous with selfishness and a betrayal of the social group code. Identity is conceived of as a fixed category derived from broad notions of race, ethnicity, religion, language and geography. Gender as a category of a different sensibility is not even considered.

Similarly, Pramar notes that "the attitude to architectural space was polyvalent -- space was multi-purpose and its functions could change without changing the enveloping form."[129] He elaborates:

> with the exception of the hearth, no part of the dwelling has any permanent function. There are no clearly defined places for sleeping, working or sitting about and no family member is assigned a private space . . . . Once the men have selected their sleeping places, the women will adjust theirs accordingly.[130]

Unlike Menon, Pramar ignores the obvious hierarchy. The spaces of the haveli may appear transparent and fluid but the users of the space were circumscribed by their positions within the family structure. For women in the haveli, the very patterns of existence are ones that require them to make the adjustments around the needs of male members of the family. This collective perception of "home," with its very definite ideology of women's place within, was what made the haveli the exemplar dwelling.

Womenspace

The terms "home" and "womenspace" as used here, need some explanation. Home is meant to evoke both its physical and emotional connotations. Witold Rybczynski elaborates the many-layered and positive meanings of home as:

Home brought together the meanings of house and of household, of dwelling and of refuge, of ownership and of affection. "Home" meant the house, but also everything that was
in it and around it, as well as the people, and the sense of
satisfaction and contentment that all these conveyed. You
could walk out of the house, but you always returned home.[131]

However, my use of the word also includes the more
negative, looming shadow of the home as an imprisoning space
that threatens reprisals if its strict rules and regulations are
disobeyed. Home is a gendered space with very different rules
for women and for men. The contradictory ideas of a safe haven
and a prison are structurally embedded in this space. In the
novels women's friendships with other women make the home
a haven and even when one leaves the original home of female
friendship a community of women is sought in the larger society.
The physically separate mandated women's spaces that were
the hallmark of the haveli look forward to a metaphoric
community of women even beyond the family circle.

The idea of "womenspace" is a development of, amongst
others, Elaine Showalter's mapping of women's writing.[132]
Showalter notes that feminist criticism developed as a part of
the international women's movements. The connection
between women's lives and women's work led to a sense of
belonging or community. As such Indo-English women writers
belong to a literary and linguistic community; second, these
novels point to a female community formation that transcends
class and age; and third, writing and reaching out to other
women often becomes for the authors and their protagonists, a
way of creating a sustaining community.[133] The concept of
"sisterhood" has in recent times been severely and justly
criticised in feminist communities as homogenising women and
erasing crucial differences of caste, class, race, and ethnicity.[134]
However, sisterhood, female solidarity and communitas are
crucial to an understanding of womenspace. Victor Turner
describes communitas as "a modality of social inter-relatedness"
which emerges from liminality or a shared outsider status and
is an "indispensable human social requirement."[135] In these novels

we see that the social segregation of women (especially, but not only, in the havelis) and their lower status often marginalises and silences them. Their work and their seclusion create moments that allow them to transcend barriers of class and age, and enables communication "as women". I am not suggesting that this womenspace is in any way structured, conscious or permanent; on the contrary, it is fluid, sporadic and unconscious. These are momentary alliances that can reverse themselves as easily as they were formed. This understanding between women is how I understand womenspace. Researchers and activists Gomathy and Fernandez in writing about their reaction to the film "Fire" testify that

> Almost all women in our society have experienced women-only spaces—for confidence sharing, healing, mutual comfort and support—at some point in their lives. Often deep bonds, intimacies and sensuousness—sometimes extending to the sexual—have characterised these spaces. At the interstices of a patriarchal society with the potential to maintain the structures that control women, or transform them, these spaces act as essential 'breathing spaces' and sources of energy for women to share and recuperate from the misogynist society that we live in. However, 'women-only' spaces are 'allowed' only if women in it are seen as sexually inactive within them".[136]

The womenspaces constructed within these novels are spaces of friendship and empathy where sexual relationships among women have not been explored. In keeping with a close reading of the novels I have not dwelt on this aspect either. I have tried to provide a nuanced construction of womenspace inspired by Kumari Jayawardena's articulation of a methodological "universality in diversity."[137] She exhorts feminists not to let difference divide them just as they should not let universality homogenise.

The adage "a woman's place is in the home" is given new meaning by Indo-English women novelists. Their creation of a womenspace from within a dominant, patriarchal space is similar to, and as deliberate as, their reinterpretation of traditional myths to make them resonate in a changed world. Their inclusive, palimpsest technique reinserts in the present what Rudolph and Rudolph call, "certain persistent requirements of the human condition that tradition, as it is expressed in the past of particular nations, can and does satisfy.[138] I see womenspace as framed by the "persistent requirements" of the condition of being Woman. The yearning for a women's community can be traced back to a segregated lifestyle concretised in the haveli. Different women authors have conceived of this space in a variety of ways but the common element seems to be the sense of community, or "communitas", amongst women. The inner courtyard, the distinctive feature of the haveli dwelling, could be read both as a traditional, segregated place for women and as a transformed womenspace.

This construction of womenspace may appear to under-privilege, if not erase, class, amongst other differences. Massey and Mohanty warn against feminist attempts that either institute boundaries and close spaces or open them to such an extent that all differences are erased.[139] I am not suggesting an erasure of difference. However, the novels' conscious attempts to highlight moments of female alliances across class and generation cannot be ignored either. At these moments, gender is the unifying factor that temporarily subsumes class, generation, region and other differences. This "coalition-politics," to borrow Johnson-Reagon's term, is not necessarily a political strategy but stems rather from a personal, subjective empathy that links women to other women and through that to a larger sense of community.[140] We see this reaching out among women on the basis of being women in a large majority of novels. In the havelis the parallel stories of servants and family women serve as a foil and a mirror to each other. In other novels like Alexander's *Nampally Road*, an emphatic and non verbal connection and communication is established between the protagonist and Rameeza Be who lies raped and broken in police custody. Again and again we see women transcending barriers of culture, race, class and age to forge bonds of solidarity. These alliances are not in any way fixed or permanent or even consciously sought tactics. However, the acknowledgement and celebration of female friendship, or a fleeting "communitas," in Turner's sense of the word, is a characteristic feature of Indo-English women's novels and one that, in large part, reflects the influence of women's' movements in India and abroad.

The change in dwellings in India from the indigenous haveli to the Western bungalow marks a significant moment of transition in values and relationships. But the strong bonds among women are sought even where the physical space does not any more enable women's togetherness. Home, both as a notional concept and as a physical reality, became the site of a new quest for identity. In novels like *Sunlight on a Broken Column* and *Inside the Haveli,* women's centrality in the domestic and familial spheres and their role as "cultural transmitters" lead to a questioning and re-evaluation of their traditional roles as mothers, wives and daughters. The haveli ethos of feudal patriarchy, conformity to rigid gender roles, and hierarchy that is sometimes carried over to the bungalow, as in *Tara Lane,* is further complicated for women by the identity politics of Indianness and Womanhood. As the bungalow replaced the haveli, westernisation, modernity, privacy, and belonging and homelessness became urgent issues. Women protagonists seek out other women as guides in this transitional moment. Even today, the haveli's construction of gender and gender relations continues to subtly shape various other homes like bungalows or modern apartments and the relationships within and without. The gendered spaces of haveli and bungalow homes provide blueprints of what Shirley Ardener has aptly termed "ground rules and social maps."[141]

Bungalows

In Indo-English women's novels, the shift from haveli to bungalow is marked by what Roland in a different context describes as a change from the "we-self" which "contrasts with the self of Westerners, which is implicitly always an I-self."[142] The haveli, as a dwelling for the extended family, was a concrete symbol of a group ethos seen as typically Indian. The bungalow, which is essentially a nuclear family dwelling, symbolises individuation and a narrowing of familial ties associated with a Western way of life. Geeta's search for quiet and privacy in *Inside the Haveli* are, in this context, seen as negative aspects of Westernisation. Until she unlearns the lessons of her cosmopolitan, Bombay life, she cannot adapt to the haveli existence which Mehta posits as authentically Indian. Women protagonists negotiate between the ideologies of a "we-self," socially approved if not enforced as a code of behaviour especially for women, and an "I-self," which while it may offer a greater degree of freedom, may not offer any substitute for the loss of community. Even in novels where bungalow-living is the norm, the search for "communitas" is a reminder of the haveli pattern. For instance, in *Ladies Coupe*, and *The Binding Vine*, Akhila and Urmi reach out across class barriers to women in the larger community. Other novels too destabilise haveli notions of Indianness by offering other community formations blurring the lines between fixed and emotive ideas of Indian and Western, tradition and modernity.

The haveli typology which had been the norm across India -- a unifying projection of "an icon of house-desire" -- was gradually dislodged by the bungalow. Prasad notes that hardly any havelis have been built since Indian independence in 1947. The bungalow, described by architect and writer Gautam Bhatia as "India's legacy of British domestic architecture,"[143] was conceived of and constructed as a single, whole unit without the random "adding on" of rooms according to need that characterised the haveli. It was designed to house a nuclear family with a clear allocation and use of specific rooms. Rybczynski notes that in Europe "Privacy and domesticity, [were] the two great discoveries of the Bourgeois Age" (p77). The links between privacy and domesticity were reflected in domestic arrangements by initially marking a separation between masters and servants and then came the separation between work and residence, public and private. He notes the increasing privatization of the home associated with a growing sense of intimacy till finally the house was identified exclusively with family life.[144] However, the most dramatic change between the haveli and the bungalow was that the latter was outward looking. The inner courtyard was replaced by the garden around the house. Commenting on the difference, Anthony King notes:

> Activity in this courtyard house was centripetal: movement was inwards, towards the courtyard. In the bungalow, it was centrifugal, outward, on to the veranda, and further into the compound.[145]

In novels like *The Day in Shadow, Nampally Road,* and *The Thousand Faces of Night,* the centrifugal movement out of the house is literal. For Sahgal in *The Day in Shadow,* a woman's ability to leave home becomes a mark of courage. Architecturally though, this is a significant inversion of what used to be the private space into an outer, almost public space. But as Bhatia notes, "the garden can also be seen as a distancing device like the walls of the haveli. It separates a house from its neighbouring house."[146]

There are two distinct moments in the evolution of the bungalow: the first signalled adaptation and the second, distance. Around the seventeenth century, with the advent of the Europeans (mainly the Portuguese and the British) in India, the traditional Bengali peasant-hut or "*bangla*" was modified to provide temporary shelter to these foreign travellers. It is important to remember that these first Europeans were travellers and traders, not settlers. This difference was marked in both the form and the materials used for the kind of houses they built. As King has pointed out, settlers and emigrants tend to make very different statements by their dwellings. They underline their origins and diifference by building houses that are modelled on cultural models that they may have left behind. But in India as Anthony King notes, initially around the seventeenth century, "the bungalow was a product of cultures in contact, an indigenous mode of shelter adopted and adapted for Europeans living in India."[147] The two major characteristics of the *bangla,* that it was temporary and built indigenously fitted their needs perfectly. King notes that the main features of early bungalows -- shallow foundations, cheap materials and *kuccha* (temporary) buildings -- structurally underline the transience of their occupants. By the time of the battle of Plassey (1757), travel and trade had given way to a concrete intention of empire. Many bungalows were set up to accommodate British administrators and soldiers. The British were living in India but not necessarily with Indians. Their bungalows were no longer a symbol of "cultures in contact." They came to exemplify quite specifically "a house for Europeans in India; the criteria were explicitly racial and cultural, and implicitly political."[148] The ethnic and racial categories of who was housed within its walls became more important than what kind of a house it was even in architectural terms.

By the mid-nineteenth century, the very word *"bangla"* had been transformed and appropriated. "Bungalow" was etymologically acknowledged as an Indian word, but for all practical purposes it had become a part of popular English language usage. If the mohallas, with their interconnected narrow streets, closely clustered havelis and market places, denoted a social involvement and interaction, then the bungalows were a clear and diametrically opposing statement about valuing isolation, the desire not to mingle, and the lack of ties with the dwellers of Indian towns and the social or religious life of the community. King astutely notes:

> The location of the bungalow-in-its-compound, away from places of Indian settlement, expressed the political and so-cial relationship between the occupants of both. Spatial dis-tance reflected social distance.[149]

The villa then became "the modern icon . . .—the detached house set in its grounds."[150]

Had this distance remained a Kiplingesque divide between East and West, the twain would not have met and each would have remained on their own clearly demarcated side. But already by 1824, with the consolidation of the empire, the *bangla*, or bungalow as it began to be called, became the urban dwelling space of the local elite. Many urbanised/westernised

Indians began to prefer living in bungalows as a sign of their status and modernity. The westernised dwelling, however, did not indicate an acceptance of Western ways or even closer relationships, as Santha Rama Rau's *Remember That House* indicates, the time was not yet ripe for the bridging of the socio-cultural divide or the coming together of an Indian woman and an English man.

If English was the linguistic marker of the Westernised Indian, then the bungalow became the iconic visual marker of India's Westernisation. Two significant factors that speeded up this process were mass urbanisation in the nineteenth and twentieth centuries and the entry of the Indian elite into colonial administrative service. Prasad notes, "A crucial factor here is that "Westernisation" was implicit from the start in the rise of Indian middle class."[151] Macaulay's Minute which articulated a deliberate policy of creating a class of English-Indians disturbed the roots of an identity that had thus far been taken for granted. Indian men realised that to advance it was in their interest to adopt not only the language but also the life style of the ruling class. But for women the same adaptation was often read as betrayal. The boundaries of Indianness had to be clearly demarcated and women's place was within these boundaries. Again, even for men, what may have been a purely pragmatic gesture of imitation for promotion did not remain just that. Macaulay's cultural hybridisation took root and flourished. At this historical moment, the crucial significance of the bungalow was that it became "an ideal house-form within the native culture."[152] The colonial administration's encouragement of Macaulay's hybrid Indian was a deliberate part of public policy. King notes a striking illustration of this even in the rules for "The Occupation of Public Works Inspection Bungalows" which in one province specified that "Asiatic officials are eligible to occupy these bungalows if they have adopted European customs."[153] When confronted by colonialism and this almost missionary zeal to convert Indians to semi-Britons, issues of class, religion and gender which could be internally divisive were largely ignored on the Indian side to provide a homogeneous and united front as Indians. The role of women as keepers of tradition took on a whole other inflection. Her domain of the home became seen as an almost sacred space that had to be protected and deliberately kept separate from the taint of Westernization. A nationalist monolith had to be created to combat the colonialist "other" which was deemed the "real" enemy.[154]

A broad and almost too easy continuum of tradition -- rural -- Indian was pitted against what was seen as its opposite, modernity -- urbanisation -- Westernisation, which in this instance had specifically colonial connotations. Nationalist discourse, as Partha Chatterjee eloquently argues, elaborated upon the binaries of tradition and modernity or spiritual East versus a materialist West, in spatial terms of inside and outside or the home (ghar) and the world (bahir).[155] The home was a protected inner space unsullied by contact with the outside. In this discourse Chatterjee notes:

> The home in its essence must remain unaffected by the profane activities of the material world - and woman is its representation. And so one gets an identification of social roles by gender to correspond with the separation of the social space into ghar and bahir.[156]

Women's association with domesticity cast them as the guardians of the home which was the nation -- India. More importantly, women were seen as the embodiment of an essentialised concept of Indianness associated with a sacred interiority and unchanging tradition. Men's adoption of Western norms was seen as a practical necessity, but Woman's westernisation was read as betrayal.[157]

The tensions between colonialism and indigenism foregrounded by the architectural change from haveli to bungalow gradually became conflated with issues of tradition and modernity which still reverberate in twentieth century novels as well as modern housing. Menon comments:

> A house is never merely a maximum utilisation of space but a projection of the self that often one would like to be. For the modern Indian, home is a palimpsest of haveli, colonial bun-

galow and post-modern structures that they have seen in their travels. And they want their homes to reflect all these tenden-cies and streams.[158]

The narration of home in Indo-English women's novels similarly reveals the extent to which the villa, bungalow, kothi and other models have been superimposed upon the haveli typology. The discernible tendency to map modernity onto tradition in these novels has led some critics like Jain and Mahan to lament the absence of "revolutionary change," especially in the status of women in Indo-English fiction.[159] However, I would suggest that there is an attempt to change the structures from within. The novels show an awareness that tradition should not be rejected, nor modernity accepted per se.

The logical continuation of a study of the domestic space from haveli to bungalow would have been to consider the apartment which is increasingly the dwelling of middle class Indians. But literature lags behind life and very few novels actually use the apartment as a site of domestic interactions. However, there are some creative alternate homes located in shops and ashrams which provide a very different way of looking at the idea of home and women's place in it.

References

1   Bhupal Singh's survey covers a century and a half of Anglo-Indian writing until 1930. His criteria include any novel in English about India, novels dealing with the life of Eurasians or Anglo-Indians, and he specifies that it does not include Indian novels by other nationalities than English. Indian writing in English is mentioned in an appendix at the end and dealt with summarily in the form of an annotated bibliography. See Bhupal Singh, *A Survey of Anglo-Indian Fiction*, (London: Oxford University Press, 1934).

2   Naik and Mukherjee have both documented in detail the various name changes and their implications. Naik notes that the Sahitya Akademi has "recently accepted `Indian English Literature' as the most suitable appellation for this body of writing." (p.5) However, I find the term Indo-English Literature the most appropriate and have used that to designate Indian writing in English.

3   Naik, *A History of Indian English Literature*, 1982. (p.3)

4   Svati Joshi, (ed.) *Rethinking English: Essays in Literature, Language, History*, New Delhi: Trianka, 1991. (p.3 & p.2)

5   Khushwant Singh and Keki N. Daruwala. Interview on Zee News. 31 December 1997. I am grateful to Gita and Mani Subramanian for bringing this to my attention.

6   Rajeswari Sunder Rajan, (ed.) *The Lie of the Land: English Literary Studies in India*, Delhi: Oxford University Press, 1993. (P.12)

7   Modhumita Roy, "`Englishing' India: Reinstituting Class and Social Privilege." *Social Text 39*, Summer 1994. (p.82-109)

8   American critics like Mary Daly have read Mayo's work as a feminist critique of Indian patriarchy. Mary Daly, *Gyn/Ecology*, Boston: Beacon Press, 1979.

In *The White Woman's Other Burden* Kumari Jayawardene notes how interventions like Mayo's led to a joining of ranks between Asian feminists and nationalists. Mrinalini Sinha's "Introduction" in Mayo's *Mother India* details its publishing history as well as the debates it has provoked at various stages.

9   Sangari & Vaid, eds. *Recasting Women*, 1989. New Delhi : Kali for Women.

Textual models were not the only ones that nationalists turned to. Jayawardene notes that the interaction between "new women" and Indian nationalists also showed the latter's admiration for particular women. Lajpat Rai, Aurobindo and Gandhi had for instance been deeply influenced by meetings with women who had been active abroad. In India, women like Madeleine Slade (renamed Mira Ben by Gandhi), Mirra Richard (called The Mother by Aurobindo), and Annie

Beasant (or Sister Nivedita as she was known) were revered. "These foreign women were not only spiritual figures, they also performed the role of organizer, manager, confidante, secretary and fund-raiser to the `great man'." See Kumari Jayawardena, *The White Woman's Other Burden Western Women and South Asia During British Rule*, New York: Routledge, 1995. (P.176)

10 Sangari & Vaid, (eds.) *Recasting Women*, 1989. (P.13)

11 Meenakshi Mukherjee, *Realism and Reality: The Novel and Society in India*,Delhi: Oxford University Press, 1994. (P.17)

12 Jon Mee "Not at Home in English?: India's Foreign-Returned Fictions" (2001)

13 Raji Narasimhan, *Sensibility Under Stress: Aspects of Indo-English Fiction*, New Delhi: Ashajanak Publications (no publication date given) (p.1)

14 Foreword to *Kanthapura* (1938) Bombay: Oxford University Press, 1947

15 Salman Rushdie, "Damme, This is the Oriental Scene For You!" *New Yorker*, (June 23 & 30, 1997) (P.50-61)

16 B. Kachru, "Indian English." *Seminar* 359 (July 1989) (P.30-35)

17 Sunder Rajan, ed. *The Lie of the Land*, 1993. Lola Chatterji, ed. *Woman Image Text: Feminist Readings of Literary Texts*, New Delhi: Trianka Publications, 1986.

18 I use the word "Indianness" as a predominantly cultural referent. The idea that this "Indianness" is constantly under construction and therefore fluid is central to my usage. From this point on, I omit the use of quotation marks to indicate its particular use.

19 See Mukherjee, *The Twice Born Fiction*, 1974, esp. (pp.165-197)

20 Mulk Raj Anand, "`The Changeling,'" Ramesh Mohan, ed. *Indian Writing in English*, Bombay: Orient Longman, 1978. (p.14-15)

21 Kachru, "Indian English," *Seminar*, 1989, p.35.

22 Meenakshi Mukherjee, "The Language of the Indo-Anglian Novelist," Ramesh Mohan, (ed.) *Indian Writing in English,* Bombay: Orient Longman, 1978. (p.153)

23 Malashri Lal, *The Law of the Threshold: Women Writers in Indian English*, Shimla: Indian Institute of Advanced Study, 1995. (p.9)

24 Joseph, Ammu; Kannabiran, Vasanth; Menon, Ritu; Salvi, Gouri; Volga. (Eds) *Just Between Us: Women Speak About Their Writing.* Women's WORLD (India), Asmita Resource Centre for Women: 2004.

25 Mrinal Pande, *Daughter's Daughter*, New Delhi: Penguin Books, 1993. Kamala Das, *My Story*, Delhi: Sterling Publishers, 1976.

26 I use the term autobiography in its broadest sense. Nayantara Sahgal

and E N Mangat Rai, *Relationship: Extracts from a Correspondence*, New Delhi: Kali for Women, 1994.

27 Joseph, Ammu; Kannabiran, Vasanth; Menon, Ritu; Salvi, Gouri; Volga. (Eds) *Just Between Us: Women Speak About Their Writing*. Women's WORLD (India), Asmita Resource Centre for Women: 2004. (p.132)

28 Mukherjee excludes both Jhabvala and V.S. Naipaul. She explains, "I have, however, restricted my use of the term *Indo-Anglian* to include only the writings of those who are Indian and who have written in English." See Mukherjee, *The Twice Born Fiction*, 1974 (p.14-15)

29 Rushdie, "Damme, This is the Oriental Scene For You!" *New Yorker*, 1997. (p.50)

30 Fundamentalist or right-wing groups and factions have gained monetary strength and a voice in the international media because of the support of overseas Indians.

31 Rajeswari Sunder Rajan, *Real and Imagined Women: Gender, Culture and Postcolonialism*, London: Routledge, 1993. (p.8)

32 Two volumes, *Interrogating Post-colonialism* and *Between The Lines*, and Indian feminists' interviews with Gayatri Chakravorty Spivak indicate the urgency, the breadth and the various levels of an often fractious debate. Harish Trivedi and Meenakshi Mukherjee, (eds.) *Interrogating Post-Colonialism: Theory, Text and Context*, Shimla: Indian Institute of Advanced Study, 1996. Deepika Bahri and Mary Vasudeva, (eds.) *Between The Lines: South Asians and Postcoloniality*, Philadelphia: Temple University Press, 1996. Gayatri Chakravorty Spivak interviewed by Rashmi Bhatnagar, Lola Chatterjee, and Rajeswari Sunder Rajan, "The Post Colonial Critic," Sarah Harasym, (ed.) *The Post-Colonial Critic: Interviews, Strategies, Dialogues*, New York: Routledge, 1990.

33 Salman Rushdie, *Imaginary Homelands: Essays and Criticism 1981-1991*, London: Granta, 1991. (p.17)

34 In a similar vein, Khushwant Singh attributes criticisms against Indo-English writers to "a strong element of envy" because those writing in English earn much more. (Singh's statement on <u>Zee News</u>. 31 December 1997).

35 Tharu, "Tracing Savitri's Pedigree," Sangari and Vaid, (eds.) *Recasting Women*,1989 (p.257). New Delhi : Kali for Women & Zubaan

36 Rushdie, "Damme, This is the Oriental Scene For You!" *New Yorker*, 1997. (P.56)

37 Dr Paul Smethurst (HKU), in a private discussion, suggested that writers like Rushdie and other expatriates may not be similarly constrained by boundaries. However, though the extent of the

influence of the home address varies amongst individual writers, its influence is felt even in what authors think they can write about.

38 Lorna Sage, *Women in the House of Fiction: Post-War Women Novelists*, New York: Routledge, 1992. (Preface ix)

39 K.R. Srinivasa Iyengar, "Indian Writing in English: Prospect and Retrospect," Ramesh Mohan, (ed.) *Indian Writing in English*, Bombay: Orient Longman, 1978. (p.8)

40 Iyengar, "Indians Writing in English," Mohan Rakesh, (ed.) *Indian Writing in English.* (p.6)

41 Meenakshi Mukherjee, "The Problem," *Seminar.* 359. July 1989. (p.12-14)

42 Aijaz Ahmad, *In Theory: Classes, Nations, Literatures*, Bombay: Oxford University Press, 1992. (p.80)

43 Joshi, ed. *Rethinking English*, 1991. (p.5)

44 Mehrotra, Arvind Krishna. *An Illustrated History of Indian Literature in English.* Delhi: Permanent Black, 2003. (p.2)

45 Roy saw English education as a gateway to learning "useful sciences." Excerpted in M.K. Naik, *A History of Indian English Literature*, Delhi: Sahitya Akademi, 1982. (p.11)

46 Mehrotra, Arvind Krishna. *An Illustrated History of Indian Literature in English.* Delhi: Permanent Black, 2003. (p.5)

47 For an incisive and contextual reading of Toru Dutt's "A Sheaf Gleaned in French Fields" see Susie Tharu, "Tracing Savitri's Pedigree: Victorian Racism and the Image of Women in Indo-Anglian Literature", Kumkum Sangari and Sudesh Vaid, eds. *Recasting Women: Essays in Colonial History*, New Delhi: Kali for Women, 1989. (p.254-268) Dutt's unfinished novel, *Bianca, or the Young Spanish Maiden*, was published posthumously in 1878.

48 Susie Tharu and K. Lalita, (eds.) *Women Writing In India: 600 B.C. To The Present*, Volume I. New York: The Feminist Press, 1991. (p.340)

49 Meenakshi Mukherjee, *The Twice Born Fiction Themes and Techniques of the Indian Novel in English*, New Delhi: Arnold-Heinemann, 1971/ 1974. (p.18)

50 Bankimchandra Chatterjee, *Rajmohan's Wife: A Novel*, (1835) with a foreword, notes and an afterword by Meenakshi Mukherjee, Delhi: Ravi Dayal Publisher, 1996.

51 She is variously spelt as Satthianandhan in Meenakshi Mukherjee's *The Perishable Empire* and as Sattianandan in Susie Tharu and K. Lalita's *Women Writing in India.*

52 Mukherjee, *The Twice Born Fiction*, 1974. (p.19)

53   Naik, *A History of Indian English Literature*, 1982. (p.107)

54   *The Hindoo Wife or The Enchanted Fruit*, (1876) by Raj Lakshmi Debi.
     The Young Spanish Maiden, a romantic love story set in England, (1878) by
     Toru Dutt. *Kamala, A Story of Hindu Life*, (1895) and *Saguna: A Story of
     Native Christian Life*, (1895) by Krupabai Satthianandhan.
     Ratanbai: A Sketch of a Bombay High Caste Hindu Young Wife, (1895) by
     Shevantibai M. Nikambe.

55   Naik, *A History of Indian English Literature*, 1982. (p.233)

56   Bilwakesh, Champa. "Today's South Asian women writers fill
     bookstore shelves" India New England News. Issue: 02/01/04.
     \http://www.geocities.com/champa_b/womenwriters.htm

57   Simone de Beauvoir, *The Second Sex*. Translated and edited by H.M.
     Parshley, New York: Alfred A. Knopf, 1952/1993.

58   Edward Said, *Orientalism*, (England: Penguin Books, 1978/1985) In
     the "Introduction" Said quotes Gramsci's *Prison Notebooks*: "The
     starting point of critical elaboration is the consciousness of what one
     really is, and is `knowing thyself' as a product of the historical process
     to date, which has deposited in you an infinity of traces, without
     leaving an inventory . . . . therefore it is imperative at the outset to
     compile such an inventory." (p.25)

59   Gayatri Chakravorty Spivak, "The Political Economy of Women as
     Seen by a Literary Critic," Elizabeth Weed, (ed.) *Coming to Terms
     Feminism, Theory, Politics*, New York: Routledge, 1989.

60   Shantha Krishnaswamy, *The Woman in Indian Fiction in English (1950-
     80)*, New Delhi: Ashish Publishing House, 1984.

61   Meena Shirwadkar, *Image of Woman in the Indo-Anglian Novel*, New
     Delhi: Sterling Publishers, 1979.

62   I borrow the phrase from Kathleen Newland's *The Sisterhood of Man*,
     New York: W.W. Norton & Co., 1979.

63   Krishnaswamy states in the "Abstract," "the Indian woman emerges, at
     the end of the study, as a human person, essentially Indian in sensibility
     and likely to remain so in the near future." Krishnaswamy, *The Woman
     in Indian Fiction in English*, 1984.

64   I use the word "Woman" in the singular, with a capital "W" to indicate
     an essentialised, almost monolithic idea of woman. This is to be
     differentiated from "women" in lower case and in the plural, which
     refers to the reality of individual or groups of women.

65   Peter Berger, *The Social Reality of Religion* (or *The Sacred Canopy*), London:
     Faber and Faber, 1969.

66   The Indus Valley Civilization circa 3500 BC. The two major cities
     excavated were Harappa and Mohenjodaro.

67 A.S. Altekar, *The Position of Women in Hindu Civilization*, 1938 Delhi: Motilal Banarsidass, 1978.

68 Kamala Ganesh, "Mother Who Is Not a Mother: In Search of the Great Indian Goddess," *Economic and Political Weekly*, 20-27 October 1990, p.58.

69 Sukumari Bhattacharji, "Motherhood in Ancient India," *Economic and Political Weekly*, 20-27 October 1990, p.50.

70 Radha Kumar, *The History of Doing: An Illustrated Account of Movements for Women's Rights and Feminism in India, 1800-1990*, New Delhi: Kali for Women, 1993 (p.2)

71 Mahasweta Devi, "Breast-Giver," translated by Gayatri Chakravorty Spivak, Ranajit Guha, ed. *Subaltern Studies V: Writings on South Asian History and Society*, (Delhi: Oxford University Press, 1987) Appendix A, pp.252-276. See also in the same volume Gayatri Chakravorty Spivak, "A Literary Representation of the Subaltern: Mahasweta Devi's *Stanadayini*," (pp.91-134)At a theoretical level, Nancy Chodorow, among other feminists, neatly points out the dichotomy between the abstract idea of mothering glorified by society and the chore-work of mothering that society does not even recognise, let alone compensate. See Nancy Chodorow, *The Reproduction of Mothering: Psychoanalysis and the Sociology of Gender*, (Berkeley: University of California Press, 1978).

72 The Bhakti movement is supposed to have originated in South India in circa 7th century AD with the Sangam poets. It then travelled to Maharashtra, Rajasthan, Bengal and Orissa. It spanned a period from the 7th century AD to the 16th century AD. For an overview of women Bhakta poets see Madhu Kishwar, "Introduction." (Women Bhakta Poets). Manushi 50,51,52 (Tenth Anniversary Issue) 1989, (p.3-8)

73 In a different context, Patricia Uberoi has described the dependence of legal discourse and indeed, decision making, on cultural assumptions regarding the nature of sexuality. She calls this "judicial *ethnosexology*." See Patricia Uberoi, "Hindu Marriage Law and the Judicial Construction of Sexuality," Ratna Kapur, ed. *Feminist Terrains in Legal Domains: Interdisciplinary Essays On Women And Law In India*, (New Delhi: Kali for Women, 1997)(p.185)

74 See David Kinsley, *Hindu Goddesses: Visions of the Divine Feminine in the Hindu Religious Tradition*, (Delhi: Motilal Banarsidass, 1986).

75 Kinsley notes that, "Iconographic representations of Kali and Siva nearly always show Kali as dominant . . . . and when the two are depicted in sexual intercourse, she is shown above him" See Kinsley, *Hindu Goddesses*, 1986, (p.120)

76 Kinsley, *Hindu Goddesses*, 1986, (P.120) I use Kali as an example because she is the most well known. But as Dr. Rajeshwari Ghose (Department

of Fine Arts, Hong Kong University), points out there is a whole genre of literature called *Parani (Pattani)* in Tamil which is devoted to this aspect of war and blood.

77   Prabhati Mukherjee, *Hindu Women: Normative Models*, Delhi: Orient Longman Limited, 1978. Mukherjee provides an interesting comparison between the *Arthashastra* and the *Manusmriti* with a view to investigating any differences that there might be between *artha* (material) and *dharma* (righteous) "points of view in regard to the `woman question'" (p.7). But what she does not seem to take into consideration is that the overriding imperative of both texts is patriarchal. The questioning of continuity in the material or religious life of the society glosses over the nature of society itself.

78   Sayings such as "Her father guards her in childhood, her husband guards her in youth, and her sons guard her in old age. A woman is not fit for independence." Manu, *The Laws of Manu*, translated by Wendy Doniger and Brian K. Smith. London: Penguin, 1991.

79   Kumkum Roy, "`Where Women are Worshipped, there the Gods Rejoice': The Mirage of the Ancestress of the Hindu Woman," Tanika Sarkar & Urvashi Butalia, (eds.) *Women and The Hindu Right: A Collection of Essays*, New Delhi: Kali for Women, 1995 (p.14-15).

80   Sudhir Kakar, *The Inner World: A Psycho-analytic Study of Childhood and Society in India*, Delhi: Oxford University Press, 1981/1978 (p.56)

81   The *Ramayana* is roughly dated between 200 BC and AD 200.

82   Kinsley, *Hindu Goddesses*, 1986, p.65.

83   The Sita of Kampan's *Ramayana* stands out as being very different. However, here I am referring to the popular image of Sita as in both Tulsi and Valmiki's versions. It is this version that has been further reinforced by Ramanand Sagar's T.V. film serial in the 1980s. The impact of the television version and its links to Hindu fundamentalism and communalism at a popular level cannot be under estimated.

84   The main story of the *Ramayana* ends here. The last part pertaining to Sita's second exile is found in the *Uttara-Kanda*, widely believed to be a later addition. However, this part is generally included in popular tellings of the *Ramayana*. See Maurice Winternitz, *History of Indian Literature*, Vol I, translated by V. Srinivasa Sarma, Delhi: Motilal Banarsidass, 1981/1987. See especially (p.473-475)

85   Madhu Kishwar, "Yes to Sita, No to Ram!: The Continuing Popularity of Sita in India," *Manushi* 98, January-February 1997. http://www.arbornet.org/~radhika/Manushi/issue98/sita.

86   Lal, *The Law of the Threshold*, 1995, (P.12)

87   Kishwar, 'Yes to Sita," *Manushi*, 1997. http://www.arbornet.org/~radhika/manushi/issue98/sita. (p.3)

88 Kishwar, "Yes to Sita" 1997, p.4. http://www.arbornet.org/ ~radhika/manushi/issue98/sita.

89 Madhu Kishwar & Ruth Vanita, (eds.) *In Search of Answers: Indian Women's Voices from Manushi*, (London: Zed Books, 1984) (p.299)

90 Kishwar, "Yes to Sita," 1997, pp.7-8. http://www.arbornet.org/ ~radhika/manushi/issue98/sita.

91 Ilango Adigal, *Shilappadikaram*, 1965, (p.208)

92 Kakar notes, "One major fantasy, protecting her [Indian woman] from feelings of depression and rage, is of the heroine, battered by fate and men, finally triumphing both through her suffering and her commitment to virtue." See Kakar, *Intimate Relations*, 1990, (p.68) This theme is also a staple of Bombay films.

93 Neera Desai and Maithreyi Krishnaraj, *Women and Society in India*, Delhi: Ajanta publications, 1987 (p.255)

94 Kishwar, "Yes to Sita", 1997 http://www.arbornet.org/~radhika/ manushi/issue98/sita.

95 Again the importance of the tele-film version watched by thousands cannot be ignored. In recent times, this popular "transmission" of ideology across generations, classes and religions is crucial to perpetuating a particular construct of womanhood.

96 I am using Berger's explanation of theodicy as a rationalization of anomic phenomena in terms of religious legitimation. See specifically Chapter Three in *The Social Reality of Religion* (or *The Sacred Canopy*), London: Faber and Faber, 1969.

97 Sunder Rajan draws a clear link between Draupadi's disrobing and the prevalent practice of eve-teasing in India, showing the connections between women's internalization and acceptance of their abuse at the hands of men. See Rajeswari Sunder Rajan "The Story of Draupadi's Disrobing: Meanings for Our Times" in *Signposts :Gender Issues in Post-Independence India*. Rajeswari Sunder Rajan (ed).

98 For some excellent studies of partition see Urvashi Butalia, "Blood," *Granta* India! the Golden Jubilee, March 1997, and *The Other Side of Silence: Stories from the Partition of India*. New Delhi: Penguin, Viking Books, 1998 Ritu Menon and Kamla Bhasin, *Borders and Boundaries: Women in India's Partition*, New Delhi: Kali for Women, 1998.

99 Jasodhara Bagchi, Introduction, Jyotirmoyee Devi, *The River Churning A Partition Novel (Epar Ganga Opar Ganga)* translated from Bengali by Enakshi Chatterjee, New Delhi: Kali for Women, 1995 (xviii- xxix).

100 Purshottam Agarwal, "Savarkar, Surat and Draupadi: Legitimising Rape as a Political Weapon," Tanika Sarkar & Urvashi Butalia, (eds.) *Women And The Hindu Right: A Collection of Essays*. New Delhi: Kali for Women, 1995 (p.30).

101 The different categories like metaphysical, ritual, and socio-legal, which these texts could fall into need to be considered separately, but that is beyond the scope of this thesis. I am aware of blurring chronologies and categories; however, the purpose of this section is simply to provide some understanding of the attitudes that recur in contemporary literature which is my main focus.

102 In *Hindu Women: Normative Models*, (1978) Prabhati Mukherjee has explored in detail the change in status of women in the *Arthashastra* and the *Manusmriti*.

103 This is not strictly Vedic, but evidenced much more so in the *Grhyasutras* Ritual Literature. My thanks to Dr Rajeshwari Ghose for pointing this out to me.

104 Sukumari Bhattacharji, "Motherhood in Ancient India," *Economic and Political Weekly*, 20-27 October 1990, (P.50-57). This is an excellent review of ancient texts and rituals which clearly demonstrates how motherhood is projected through rituals.

105 Kumkum Roy, in *Women and the Hindu Right*, 1995.

106 Sangari & Vaid, (eds.) *Recasting Women*, 1989, (p.17)

107 The Rudolphs explain that an "analytical gap" occurs "Because they [tradition and modernity] are seen as mutually exclusive, to depart from one is disorienting and traumatic, to enter the other alienating and superficial" Rudolph & Rudolph, *The Modernity of Tradition*, 1967/1984, (p.6)

108 Sunand Prasad, "The Havelis of North India The Urban Courtyard House," Vol.I. Dissertation, The Royal College of Art, London, Visual Islamic Arts Unit, Faculty of Fine Art, June 1988, (1.7).

109 Rybczynski, *Home*, 1987. Rybczynski's description of a typical seventeenth century Parisian bourgeois home bears a striking resemblance to the haveli. See especially (p.38)

110 A.G Krishna Menon is the Director of the Tulsi Vidya Bharati School of Habitat Studies, Delhi.

111 Personal conversation with Menon in New Delhi, July 15, 1994.

112 Francis Wacziarg & Aman Nath, *Rajasthan: The Painted Walls of Shekhavati*, London: Croom Helm Ltd, 1982 (p.21)

113 Prasad, 'The Havelis of North India,' Diss., 1988, 1.3.

114 Menon remarks, "Clusters of havelis were formed by affinity groups (kith, clan, guild) and were known as *Mohallas* or *Katras* in the North, *Pols* in Gujerat, *Wada* in Maharashtra and so on." Personal conversation with Menon in New Delhi, 1994.

115 V.S. Pramar, *Haveli Wooden Houses and Mansions of Gujarat*, Ahmedabad: Mapin Publishing Pvt. Ltd, 1989 (p.108) Pramar, however, admits

that the location, of each specific haveli was not random. Class hierarchies were clearly visible in that "the most substantial houses were generally located at the centre and the poorest at the periphery" (p.27)

116 Prasad, "The Havelis of North India." Diss., 1988, 3.1.

117 Doreen Massey, *Space, Place and Gender*, Cambridge: Polity Press, 1994. Doreen Massey describes feeling like a "space invader" as she consciously enters supposed male spaces. These spaces, she says, "were designed to, or had the effect of, firmly letting me know my conventional subordination." (p.185)

118 Wacziarg & Nath, *Rajasthan*, 1982. (p.22)

119 Massey, *Space, Place and Gender*, 1994, (p.119)

120 Massey, *Space, Place and Gender*, 1994, (p.146)

121 Gaston Bachelard, *The Poetics of Space*, (1958) translated by Maria Jolas, Boston: Beacon Press, 1964.

122 Kate Millett in *Sexual Politics*, quoted by Gillian Rose in *Feminism and Geography: The Limits of Geographical Knowledge*. Cambridge: Polity Press, 1993.

123 Wacziarg & Nath, *Rajasthan*, 1982, (pp.21-22).

124 Benedict Anderson, *Imagined Communities: Reflections on the Origin and Spread of Nationalism*, London: Verso, 1983.

125 Carole Pateman, *The Disorder of Women: Democracy, Feminism and Political Theory*, Cambridge: Polity Press, 1989.

126 Alan Roland, *In Search of Self in India and Japan: Towards a Cross-Cultural Psychology*, Princeton: Princeton University Press, 1988.

127 Prasad, "The Havelis of North India," diss., 1988, 3.3.

128 Pramar, *Haveli*, 1989, (p.80)

129 Pramar, *Haveli*, 1989, (p.115)

130 Pramar, *Haveli: Wooden Houses and Mansions of Gujarat*, 1989, (p.69-70)

131 Witold Rybczynski, *Home: A Short History of an Idea*, New York: Penguin Books, 1986/1987 (p.62)

132 Elaine Showalter, (ed.) *The New Feminist Criticism: Essays on Women, Literature and Theory*, New York: Pantheon Books, 1985.

133 This notion of writing as creating a specifically "womenspace" is much more evident in women's autobiographies.

134 See Maria C. Lugones in collaboration with Pat Alake Rosezelle, "Sisterhood and Friendship as Feminist Models," Penny A. Weiss & Marilyn Friedman, (eds.) *Feminism and Community*, Philadelphia: Temple University Press, 1995. Chandra Talpade Mohanty, Ann Russo

and Torres Lourdes, eds. *Third World Women and the Politics of Feminism*, Bloomington and Indianapolis: Indiana University Press, 1991. Barbara Smith, (ed.) *Home Girls: A Black Feminist Anthology*, New York: Kitchen Table: Women of Color Press, 1983.

135 Turner, *Dramas, Fields, and Metaphors*, 1974, (p.231 & 243)

136 Arvind Narrain and *Gautam Bhan* (eds). *Because I Have a Voice: Queer Politics in India*. New Delhi : Yoda Press, 2005, (p. 200)

137 Kumari Jayawardena, *The White Woman's Other Burden: Western Women and South Asia During British Colonial Rule*, New York & London: Routledge, 1995 (p.18)

138 Lloyd I. Rudolph & Susanne Hoeber Rudolph, *The Modernity of Tradition: Political Development in India*, Chicago & London: The University of Chicago Press, 1967/1984 Midway Reprint (p.4)

139 See Doreen Massey, *Space, Place and Gender*, Cambridge: Polity Press, 1994. Chandra Talpade Mohanty, "Cartographies of Struggle: Third World Women and the Politics of Feminism," & "Under Western Eyes: Feminist Scholarship and Colonial Discourses," Chandra Talpade Mohanty, Ann Russo & Torres Lourdes, (eds.) *Third World Women and the Politics of Feminism*. Bloomington & Indiana: Indiana University Press, 1991.

140 Bernice Johnson Reagon, "Coalition Politics: Turning the Century," Barbara Smith, (ed.) *Home Girls: A Black Feminist Anthology*, New York: Kitchen Table: Women of Color Press, 1983.

141 Shirley Ardener, (ed.) *Women and Space: Ground Rules and Social Maps*, London: Croom Helm Ltd, 1981.

142 Roland says the phrase "we-self" was coined by Drs Al Collins and Prakash Desai. He notes that for Indians "the experiential sense of self is of a "we-self" that is felt to be highly relational in different social contexts." Roland, *In Search of Self in India and Japan*, 1988, (p.8)

143 Gautam Bhatia, *Punjabi Baroque: And Other Memories of Architecture*, New Delhi: Penguin Books, 1994. Bhatia details how the original Bengali Bangla was transformed into a bungalow: "No other building could as easily sum up the spirit of the imperial enterprise. The bungalow was designed to make the best of things, the best of imperialism, and the best also of its hostile setting" (p.36)

144 Rybczynski, *Home*, 1987. (p.39)

145 Anthony D. King, *The Bungalow: The Production of a Global Culture*, London: Routledge & Kegan Paul, 1984 (p.34-35)

146 Personal conversation with Gautam Bhatia in Delhi, July 1994.

147 King, *The Bungalow*, 1984. (p.14)

148 King, *The Bungalow*, 1984, (p.1)

149 King, *The Bungalow*, 1984, (p.1)

150 Prasad, "The Havelis of North India" Diss., 1988. 1.7.

151 Prasad, "The Havelis of North India," Diss., 1988, 5:14.

152 Prasad, "The Havelis of North India," Diss., 1988, 5:13.

153 King, *The Bungalow*, 1984, (p.55-56)

154 A most thorough and convincing historical analysis of the hardening lines and creation of binaries is presented in Liddle and Joshi, *Daughters of Independence: Gender, Caste and Class in India*, New Delhi: Kali for Women, UK: Zed Books, 1986. On the complex relationship between coloniser and colonised see also Ashis Nandy's excellent study *The Intimate Enemy: Loss and Recovery of Self Under Colonialism*, (Delhi: Oxford University Press, 1983/1989).

155 Partha Chatterjee, *The Nation and its Fragments: Colonial and Postcolonial Histories*, (Delhi: Oxford University Press, 1994).

156 Chatterjee, *The Nation and Its Fragments*, 1994, (p.120)

157 As Chatterjee explains, "in the entire phase of the national struggle, the crucial need was to protect, preserve, and strengthen the inner core of the national culture, its spiritual essence. No encroachments by the colonizer must be allowed in that inner sanctum. In the world, imitation of and adaptation to Western norms was a necessity; at home they were tantamount to annihilation of one's very identity." Chatterjee, *The Nation and its Fragments*, 1994,(p.121)

158 Personal conversation with Menon in New Delhi, July 15, 1994.

159 Asha Kaushik, "From Indignity to Individuation: Women in the Indo-Anglian Novel." Pratibha Jain and Rajan Mahan, (eds.) *Women Images*, Jaipur & New Delhi: Rawat Publications, 1996.

2

Haveli

Attia Hosain recounts a visit to a doctor in England when she had begun to lose her hair. The doctor immediately diagnosed her problem as homesickness. She had left India in 1947 and except for a brief work visit in 1951 had not been back. The therapeutic visit home resulted in the writing of *Sunlight on a Broken Column*. It was a special kind of homesickness though, because neither the home nor the country she had left behind were the same anymore. Two hundred years of British colonialism ended in 1947, dividing India into two countries India and Pakistan. Families like Attia Hosain's had similarly separated and chosen different homes and different homelands.

Fourteen years after partition, Attia Hosain's *Sunlight on a Broken Column* (1961) is among the first novels by an Indian woman writer to narrate the trauma of that period. Mumtaz Shah Nawaz's earlier novel *The Heart Divided* (1957) also by a Muslim woman writer provides an interesting contrast. It tells of her gradual transformation from a Congress sympathiser to a Muslim League activist who finally opted for Pakistan. In this genre Anita Desai's *Clear Light of Day* (1980) also delicately evokes the emotional rift between a brother and sister caught up in these indelible choices. In an extensive interview in London in 1991 some seven years before her death, Hosain told Omar Khan,

I wanted to write about that agonizing heartbreak when we were all split up and a brother could not see a brother and a mother could not be with her dying son and families that had been proud to always collect together when there were weddings or deaths or births or anything, cannot be together.[1]

In this elegiac novel of memory and nostalgia, the pre-partition India that Hosain mourns is embodied in the haveli lifestyle. As the daughter of a prominent landowning or taluqdar family she knew feudal India from the inside. *Sunlight* is the story of an urban, elite India that still maintains its links with the land and the past.

The novel opens in India of the 1930s. The turbulence of the times is reflected inside the old house or the haveli where the patriarch Baba Jan lies dying. Laila, the young, parentless protagonist grows up in the haveli 'Ashiana' caught between the feudal ways of her grandfather's world and the looming historical changes that will tear apart her family, home and country. Laila's personal drama is part of the larger historical change as violent religious riots and communal strife call into question the very idea of home, family and identity. Each individual of the large joint family has to choose between staying on in India or moving to Pakistan to start a new life in a theocratic Muslim state. Even her family is divided as one brother privileges birth-place by staying on in India while another privileges the importance of a religious identity in moving to Pakistan. Laila is torn between the idea of duty and tradition that her surrogate mother, aunt Abida has inculcated, and, an independent, individualism learnt through the Western education her father had wanted for her. She steps out of the protective, purdahed haveli world of privilege and falls in love with Ameer, who is by her family's standards, a thoroughly unsuitable man. When Laila is expecting their first child, Ameer joins the army and dies in combat leaving her to bring up their daughter. Laila's story is paralleled by that of her maidservant Nandi, who transgresses the haveli's strict sexual code of conduct. To avoid scandal she is married off to a much older man, deliberately has a child by an itinerant hillsman, and then leaves her father and husband's home to join Laila in her house in the hills.

Western values, education and urban modernity are again seen as a threat to the indigenous existence of yet another haveli some sixteen years later in Rama Mehta's *Inside the Haveli* (1977). If partition and independence herald the moment of change in Hosain's *Sunlight*, Mehta's *Inside the Haveli* is set at a moment of heated national debates around the issue of the abolition of the princely privy purses. After Indian independence in 1947 the princely states were abolished, however, the controversial privy purses or the state stipend assured by the Constitution continued to be given to the princes till 1971. The legal abolition of princely privilege instigated by the then Prime Minister Indira Gandhi, resurrected debates around issues of existence in a feudal but protective tradition of *noblesse oblige* versus the faceless bureaucracy of post-independent India. Rama Mehta's novel *Inside the Haveli* seems to propose, for women especially, a holding on if not à return to tradition. The feudal haveli life-style ensures them a certain rootedness and protection that an urban, modern, post colonial life-style cannot seem to provide. The novel emerges as a fictional sequel to Mehta's 1970 sociological work *The Western Educated Hindu Woman*. Fifty western-educated, elite women, like Mehta herself, are the respondents in this study that examines the extent to which traditional customs and values survive the impact of modernity and westernization.

Inside the Haveli recounts the story of Geeta—a western-educated, urban dwelling newly married woman—and her acculturation into a traditional family from Mewar (Rajasthan). Marriage and joint-family living are a "re-education" as Malashree Lal terms it, for Geeta.[2] After her initial claustrophobia at the cloistered existence, she refocuses her priorities and finds her place in the familial continuum of haveli existence. The urban Bombay existence she was brought up in is gradually erased as she learns her duties and the rules of the marital home and vows to perpetuate its traditions. Geeta's story, like Laila's in *Sunlight*, is also paralleled by that of her maidservant Lakshmi. However, Geeta's acceptance of the haveli is matched by Lakshmi's rejection of it. Their first-borns are both daughters, born within hours of each other. Lakshmi enters the haveli when she is ten years old, is married to another servant of the haveli at fourteen, and becomes a mother at the age of fifteen. Soon after the birth of her daughter, she opts out of the haveli to live in the city, leaving her daughter behind. It is not coincidental that servants are central to both these narratives. Their connections with family women underline class differences, while suggesting the commonality of gender roles that bind both sets of women to gender codes of *izzat*, or honour. But I shall return to the issue of servants later.

At one level it is easy to read *Haveli* and *Sunlight* as thinly veiled autobiographies. Hosain was outraged at Cecil Day Lewis' comment. that *Sunlight* was very autobiographical. She recounts,

> I got very angry and I said, what does he mean by autobiographical? Every first novel or any novel will have to be part of oneself and people one knows, but it is not the people and it is not actually the events but it is at the same time yes.[3]

Almost two decades later in 1978, the prominent Indian socialist novelist Mulk Raj Anand wrote a profile of Hosain for another edition of the novel where he puts her in the same league as early Western suffragettes like Emmeline Pankhurst, Beatrice Webb and other upper-class women who had espoused the cause of women's freedom. He said, "There would have to be in India some women from the big houses, who would spill the beans about the taluqdars with their large estates."[4] Following Anand's lead a decade later, novelist Anita Desai specifically notes Hosain's sensitive treatment of servants in the novel, "perhaps the most attractive aspect of her [Hosain's] writing is the tenderness she shows for those who served her family, an empathy for a class not her own."[5] Unlike Lewis both later critics see Hosain's insiderism or insider status as an asset that gives her an added authority.

Autobiography aside, sociologist historian Antoinette Burton in her insightful study of three prominent 20th century women writers Janaki Majumdar (1886-1963), Cornelia Sorabji

(1886-1954), and Attia Hosain (1913-1997) suggests that women's fictional or autobiographical writings about home can and should be mined as valid historical archive or documentation about the colonial period. She notes that Majumdar, Sorabji and Hosain

> made use of memories of home in order to claim a place in history at the intersection of the private and the public, the personal and the political, the national and the postcolonial. All three were preoccupied with domestic architecture, its symbolic meanings and its material realities, because they were keenly aware that house and home were central to their social identities and the cultural forms through which they experienced both family life and national belonging.[6]

Hosain and Mehta were among the early generations of western educated, urban Indian women who struggled with issues of tradition and modernity raised in their novels. Their trajectories, like those of their protagonists, though were very different. Hosain continued to live and earn a living in England even after her husband got posted to Pakistan. Mehta, like her 'subjects' in *The Western Educated Indian Woman* and as her protagonist Geeta in *Haveli*, strove to juggle family and career roles and in the end gave up her career as a diplomat (though she continued to be a professional academic and writer) to follow her husband. I am not suggesting that the novels should be read as autobiographies but it is important to place the authors in their historical and social contexts. The concerns about modernity and the impact of westernisation on women and on the domestic sphere were lived issues for both authors. The nostalgia for past homes as well as the desire for a different concept of home, central to these novels, are shaped by real personal and historical anxieties about the changing nature of home and nation.

Haveli as an Indian Space

In Indian English literature the changes in dwellings from the indigenous haveli to the Western bungalow to the apartment are significant moments of transition. Attia Hosain's *Sunlight on a Broken Column* and Rama Mehta's *Inside the Haveli* capture the haveli, a pan-Indian dwelling, at a specific, historical moment of its disintegration if not demise.

Physically and architecturally the distinctive feature of a haveli dwelling is the central, interior, open courtyard. This is the focal point or the centre of the house, surrounded on all sides by rooms.[7] No outsiders or non-family members were permitted in this interior space. It is the heart of the house where women gather unveiled to do their house-hold work together.

Architecturally, the haveli was the prototype urban Indian home. Its origins are obscure, but Sunand Prasad points out that similar forms can be traced back to the Indus Valley period about 3000 BC.[8] Pramar notes that "the attitude to architectural space was polyvalent — space was multi-purpose and its functions could change without changing the enveloping form."[9] There were neither private spaces nor any utility-specific rooms like bed-rooms, sitting rooms, etc. The only permanent functional room was the hearth and for the rest, he elaborates, men would select their sleeping places and then the women would adjust theirs accordingly (69-70).

Attitudinally, the haveli reproduces, in microcosm, the Indian social structure of kinship patterns, where the clan or the family is privileged over the individual unit. Ideologically, havelis project the concept of a unified world view that elides differences of class and gender. The haveli with its divisions of sacred and profane, female and male, public and private spaces reinforces gender and hierarchy divisions that are seen as purely domestic. The haveli life-style in the novels however connotes a feudal, joint family existence where hierarchy and gender are the twin axes of a tradition that, like India itself, is threatened by westernization and modernity.

Hosain's description of the heavy gloom of ill health, "the sick air, seeping and spreading through the straggling house, weighed each day more oppressively on those who lived in it" (14), is indicative of the state of health of the country, the feudal system and Baba Jan himself. However, for the parentless Laila,

Ashiana is a home where the absolute authority of the feudal patriarch Baba Jan prevails. Its extinction is as unthinkable as Baba Jan's death. "Ashiana" literally means both nest and paradise. For the parentless Laila the safety of the nest is provided by the family. But as a nest, the necessary flight of fledglings is written into Ashiana. Time, as a process of inevitable almost organic change, is already signaled in the preface quotation from T.S. Eliot's "The Hollow Men". Furthermore the mood, and the four-part structure of the novel also vividly recall Eliot's "The Four Quartets". As paradise, Ashiana is a utopia coloured in the soft tones of childhood memories of a safer and a more innocent time. It may be worthwhile to note that Ashiana was in fact the name of Attia Hosain's own childhood home in Hyderabad.

History is a crucial element of Laila's identity, and as the narrator, she suggests that it is equally so for others. In this partition narrative, location or a sense of place is disturbed by a historical moment, posing stark and urgent choices. The common bedrock of shared culture that underlies this site splinters, leaving bereft both those who moved and those who did not. In the ensuing dislocation and relocation, identity alliances that anchored one to a birthplace are torn asunder. A home, a nation, is (re)created by privileging religious identity over other affiliations of birthplace, friendships, language and a name. Laila's cousin, Saleem, who had opted for Pakistan cannot repress the exultant feeling of a homecoming on his visit to India after many years of what, even to him, seems like an exile in his country of choice. People recognise him here. The address that he had taken for granted of family name, class, and kin, is recognised and acknowledged, giving him a sense of both belonging and a past. The new world utopia of an Islamic nation, where only a religious identity counted, has rendered him anonymous and, therefore, homeless. Can either India or Pakistan be home to Laila and her family? Hosain's own decision to stay on in England rather than choose between India and Pakistan may be indicative of how the very idea of home had become problematic for the generation that lived through the trauma of violence, betrayal and displacement.

In Rama Mehta's *Inside the Haveli* the haveli stands for a hierarchical feudal India which almost imperceptibly merges with natural phenomena. Despite the "objective" third-person narratorial voice this is essentially a "history from the top." The narrator's "naturalisation" of the haveli establishes an almost organic link between India, the palace of the king and the haveli of the feudal class. In the textual terrain of Udaipur, landscape and class merge to present the feudal haveli as symbolic of an eternal Indianness. The Rana or king's palace is ensconced amidst the natural background of the hills and lakes of Udaipur. It is the central point within the walled city, surrounded by the interconnected havelis. Socially too, a direct link is established between princely Mewar which includes the palace, the inner city, and the havelis. The elite of Udaipur are the focal point, and they become synonymous with Indianness in the course of the novel.

The locale of *Inside the Haveli* is Udaipur, which used to be the capital of the royal kingdom of Mewar. The invocation of the old name Mewar instead of Rajasthan, reiterates the feudal ethics of a not too distant historical past. It also links this novel to the genre of Raj novels. Although the Raj evoked here is not the British Raj, the emotional resonance of romance and nostalgia is similar. The haveli is featured as representative of a common popular ethos rather than a feudal one espoused mainly by the nobility. The end of Royal Mewar, when "the palace lights were dimmed and the flag of Mewar came down," (2) is nostalgically recalled as a common, shared experience, one when the people, and not just the Rana, lose their city: "No one can forget those days when Udaipur belonged to the people" (2). The city, the Rana and the people are not only interchangeable but are figured metonymically for a certain traditional ethos.

In *Inside the Haveli* three parallel movements, nature, tradition and feudal nobility, reinforce each other, leading inexorably to the haveli — a very Indian 'habitus' in Bourdieu's sense of the term.[13] Udaipur, as a microcosm of India is pictured almost as if it were a natural phenomenon. The hill and lake are not mere landmarks or locational grids but centres of everyday community life. There is a timeless quality to the human activities which link, for example, the lake and the people:

> Men bathe in it; washermen unload their donkeys and beat the clothes clean on slabs of granite on its shores. Women on the river banks go to ring the temple bells before they return to light the household fire (1).

The text privileges continuity and a specifically Hindu tradition with its particular inbuilt inscriptions of hierarchy and gender roles in this romanticised picture-post-card version of the daily, natural life cycle of a place. The conflation of the king and his public is repeated in this assimilative gesture that also subsumes the hill, the lake and the city in "nature." Any threat to the feudal status quo is perceived as a threat that will disrupt the basic harmony of life.

The first time a haveli is mentioned in the novel, it is likened to a banyan tree, a central symbol in Indian lore, conjuring visions of rootedness, belonging, and attachment to the land, and thereby marking this landscape as specifically Indian. The banyan tree like the haveli's deep rooted "naturalness", holds it firm against ill winds of change:

> But, like a banyan tree, once it had taken root it spread. Today the haveli has many courtyards with many rooms. Its roots have sunk deep into the soil and nothing shakes the foundations although the hot winds of summer dismantle the wooden shelters of the poor and the monsoon rains melt the mud walls of the poorer in the same gully (3).

The narrator's commentary on the houses of the poor being vulnerable in contrast to those of the rich is not ironic, merely an accepted fact. The haveli, as a physical and a social structure, is presented as durable and solid. Its very solidity and likeness to the banyan tree are essential to its projection as a protective agent. The king, the patriarch and the banyan tree, like the haveli, provide sanctuary and protection. The novel's particular perspective of the view from inside is also the view from the top, from the Rana's palace. In this particular perspective the benevolent patriarchy of the Rana and of the haveli collapse into each other jointly offering protection and security in return for an acceptance of gender roles and the rules of absolute loyalty and allegiance.

In Mehta the haveli is delineated spatially from the outset. The new township is a constant and visual threat at the doorstep of the old city. The narrator notes that a now-crumbling, four-hundred-year-old "bastioned wall" encloses and protects the city, although "in fact there are now big gaps, but the wall still divides Udaipur into two halves". The concepts of ancestry, belonging, and birthplace reinforce the haveli dwellers claims to the land — as a geographic possession, but also more importantly, as an emotional anchor. As outsiders, both literally and metaphorically, the new town people for instance are denied even visual access to life within the city: "There is no way they can look into the courtyards; the windows are so high that no one can look through them" (3). However, the new township offers an alternative life style and value system which a maidservant, like Lakshmi, can and does opt for. But it is seen essentially in terms of risk and loss —a cost that is too dear for the privileged Geeta to bear. The new town dwellers are rootless because they are unconnected to the soil and its history—they are transplants. The lure of money makes them uproot themselves, and so they are seen as not valuing tradition. One of the most obvious markers of otherness is their dwelling. "In the new town the rich and poor are separated by the rose gardens; they don't know each other; they live separate lives". The staccato prose description here suggests the isolation and disjointedness of the new town lifestyle, quite unlike the lyrical, long sentences describing the daily life by the river quoted earlier.

If the banyan-like haveli evokes rootedness and inter-connections which are seen as typically Indian then the rose, a flower specifically associated with England, sets up the binaries of English versus Indian. The rose gardens surrounding the bungalows of the new-town emphasise its Englishness and isolation, mimicry of westernised modernity. The rose gardens around the bungalows are inscribed as un-Indian because of the distance they create. The garden in the English bungalow (as we will see later) provided distance between neighbouring houses and between the inside and the outside. The havelis, by contrast, despite the dirt and congestion, are seen as connected to each other at both a physical and a psychological level. The rose and the banyan can be read as conflictual symbols of West and East trailing in their wake connotations of isolation and connection, ornamentation and utility.

The obvious tropes of the banyan and the rose aside the physical configurations of *Inside the Haveli* forces a binary reading of the novel. Within the haveli the values of a cosmopolitan Bombay embodied in Geeta are pitted against those of a traditional and feudal Mewar. It is always referred to by this name rather than Rajasthan. Outside, in the larger context of the city, the conflict between tradition and modernity is played out between the new town people and the haveli dwellers. Geeta, her Bombay home, and her co-educational, Western education are markers of a modernity that threatens the Rajasthani haveli from within, as much as the new township is a constant and visual threat at its doorstep. Geeta's story in fact reveals the cracks in the structure rather than its solidity. The inner-city dwellers are urgently aware of "the gaps in the wall." The threat from the outside is not from Mughal invaders, as in the past when the city was first built, nor from the new township, but from consciously risked change in the form of educated girls married into the haveli. Geeta poses a double threat because, "After all she is educated and on top of that she is not from Udaipur. What a risk to get an outsider, especially when there is only one son." (15) Geeta and Laila, the daughter-in-law and the daughter, the younger generation puts the continuity of the haveli ethos at risk and become willy nilly the harbingers of change.

The inevitable generational change as seen in both Laila and Geeta was complicated in India by western education. Education is the focal point and a divisive factor of conflict in both *Sunlight* and *Haveli*. Laila blames her Western education for her alienation within her own household and family; Geeta on the other hand threatens the hierarchical and gendered space of the haveli by wanting to start a school for servant's children which ultimately will enable them to seek a livelihood outside the haveli. *Haveli* registers this as not simply a question of modernity versus tradition but the choices of accepting or rejecting the haveli life-style are framed in terms of loyalty or, of patriotism almost, to a specific value system seen as Indian. Partha Chatterjee's seminal work on Indian nationalism maps how for women, particularly, the binary divisions between East and West or the home and the world become rigid inviolate zones.[14] Uma Chatterjee extends the premise to show that the construction of Indian womanhood was not classless. Both Laila and Geeta are elite, upper-class women even though one is Muslim and one is Hindu. They become emblematic of how the Indian woman, as Chatterjee and Chakravarti show,[15] came to be constructed as the guardians of an inviolable Indianness in a specific colonial context. The texts, especially Mehta's *Haveli*, present the choices for or against the haveli ethos as not merely individual options but imbued with a larger essential and national significance.

A moment at the heart of *Inside the Haveli* is when Geeta starts informal classes for the children and the maids of the haveli. She teaches a bit of reading and writing and some sewing and embroidery. Initially the women of her own and other havelis are outraged because it is seen as "undermining our authority and making rebels out of our servants" (134). But Geeta's school is a marker of how change is admitted and negotiated. Critics like Malashri Lal see the school as an instrument of "revolutionary" change.[16] I would suggest that such a reading fails to question the basis of the school's existence. It owes its survival to patriarchal permission. It could be seen almost as a bribe to appease the outsider daughter-in-law. If it is disallowed Geeta has the potential to disturb the haveli structure by not only leaving herself but also by taking away her husband and children. Their leaving would be a greater blow not only to the continuity of the haveli but also to patriarchal hierarchical order. Geeta is permitted to keep the school going because wealth, patriarchy, and hierarchy in the form of her father-in-law's approval has been granted. Geeta's mother-in-law reassures her, "Once your father-in-law gives his approval to something then I am not afraid of what the world says". Lal's approval of gradual change with patriarchal consent that Mehta seems to advocate may leave one feeling slightly uncomfortable. The viability of a change "with permission" remains dubitable.

Geeta, the symbol of modernity, must, according to Lal, "undergo her own `regressive' transformation from the `modern' to the 'ancient' before she can function effectively."[17] However, Lal fails to ask whether Geeta sees it as "regressive" and whether she "function effectively." Lal's view that the text "records a silent revolution as women pick up the tools of independent economic existence without displaying any aggressive rejection of tradition" (96) is based on her view of Geeta's school being a symbol of revolutionary change and empowerment. Geeta herself like other postcolonial women protagonists though exemplifies rather how liberal education and independence may not be useful for her development as a woman in a still patriarchal though independent India. The clear demarcation of the women's sphere as dependent upon the men's is re-encoded in the resolution of the plot. Geeta is softly seduced into being a prisoner albeit a "willing prisoner" by the status, ancestry, community and service offered to her as a mistress of the haveli. The reiteration of feudal values as specifically Indian values cannot be ignored in this narrative.

In *Sunlight* Laila and her cousin Zahra are apt examples of Paulo Friere's vision of how one learns the word and the world simultaneously through a particular language.[18] Laila apprehends the world through English and her sensibility is strongly shaped by the cultural burden of that language. Her cousin Zahra, on the other hand, can speak English but her primary learning is through Urdu and through Koranic religious instruction. Zahra's educational qualifications are lovingly recited by her mother, "she has read the Quran, she knows her religious duties; she can sew and cook, and at the Muslim School she learned a little English, which is what young men want now." Zahra's education has indeed equipped her for a specific role in a specific society where even education and language acquisition are based on what men want. Laila scoffs that Zahra "was now playing the part of the perfect modern wife as she had once played the part of a dutiful purdah girl". She has been groomed to adjust, at a superficial level, to the demands of a "changing world." She did not question her purdah state just as she does not question her 'freedom' after marriage. An unquestioning obedience is what society requires of her, and that is exactly what her mother has taught her. *Sunlight* unlike *Haveli* seems to condemn the emergent post-independence, post colonial society where patriarchal structures are still in place though camouflaged and women are required to have a veneer of modernity over a subservient core.

We are forced to ask what is the purpose of education? *Sunlight* suggests two objectives for female education. Conservative characters in the novel articulate marriage as the acme of a young girls upbringing. Education and upbringing are used interchangeably, where one often signifies the other especially when referring to a traditional education like Zahra's. But education is perceived negatively and in conflict with upbringing when referring to a Western education such as Laila's. Laila and Zahra's pragmatic aunt Saira sees education as necessary to women's roles as suitable marriage partners even in changing India. Echoing Zahra's mother, she crisply notes, "Young men want their wives to be educated enough to meet their friends and to entertain. Nowadays they lay down all sorts of conditions". Laila's socialist friend Nita also sees the desire for higher education amongst the elite as "typical of your class" which has marriage as its goal: "You think a degree is a piece of jewellery, an additional ornament to be listed in your dowry". And there is more than a grain of truth in her observation.

It is easy to dismiss Zahra and others who see education as a passport to a better marriage but Laila's surrogate mother

Aunt Abida's commitment to learning is very different. She exemplifies and articulates the central aim of education as a way to reinforce a sense of belonging. Her sense of entitlement and of who she is and of her place in the community and the world comes not only from her awareness of her social and class privilege but also from a rootedness and knowledge of what she sees as her culture expressed in her native language, Urdu. Her personal strength comes from her internalisation and total acceptance of a particular way of life. Her unshakeable faith in the notion of duty anchors her. She says, "we cannot control what happens to us, but we can control our behaviour. One must never blunt one's sense of duty." Abida sees her duty as unquestioningly upholding the tradition in which she has been brought up. Her ideas of gender specific duties have been internalised through her readings of religious and cultural texts in Urdu and Persian. She is centred because she does not admit any conflict even linguistically. This is the heritage that she wishes to bequeath to Laila.

In Abida's case, a traditional, religious education has shaped her and assured her a place in family and society. Her sense of self is deeply grounded in a cultural, and a linguistic and literary tradition. Her unhappiness with Laila's forsaking of her mother tongue is the belief that it leaves her incomplete: "One cannot live fully out of what is borrowed. You must love your own language and heritage" (139).[19] Abida's sense of duty to tradition is shaped by her reading – she is a scholar of Persian and Urdu literature. Her education is a commitment that bolsters an allegiance to class, deeply internalised gender roles, and a religious community that constitute her identity. This is not to imply a lack of new ideas or modes of behaviour in a vernacular education, but the aspect that the novel emphasises through Abida's strong and centered character is of a dedication to tradition through language, religion and culture.

Abida has internalised the rules of the haveli-tradition and of women's place within it. Her strength comes from a total commitment to this value system, which in turn rewards her by reinforcing her position in the family and society. Her steadfast belief in the essential value of this system is unshaken nearly to the end which makes her almost a tragic heroine. Ultimately, however, she is betrayed by the system. She bends but does not break the rules as she assumes the responsibilities of the household and the estates, albeit decorously from behind the veil. Her firm belief in hierarchy and separate spheres for women and men is unshaken. The sense of knowing her place, that is, being grounded in familial, class, literary and cultural traditions, and a proud acceptance, even a deliberate appropriation, of her role in social, gender and hierarchical relations are the basis of Abida's moral edge. Her Gandhian way of life interweaves the broad humanist concepts of duty, tradition and loyalty. Adhering to an unchanging past, Abida declares, "I am not of these times. But I am living in them. The walls of this house are high enough, but they do not enclose a cemetery" (21). Imprisoned by tradition while the world outside is changing, death becomes Abida's only alternative. The house, for her, literally becomes a cemetery. Ironically, her death, especially during child-birth, even denies her continuity in the form of children. Hosain unambiguously provides only two alternatives — either to change and move with the times or to die. There is no romanticisation of, or wish to return to, this past. The haveli in "time-present" becomes a monument if not a mausoleum to the traditional feudal lifestyle. Ultimately, death or dislocation is the only choices.

In sharp and ironic contrast, Abida as the surrogate mother-figure is entrusted to provide a Western education for her niece. She becomes the unwilling but duty-bound catalyst who will distance Laila from a sense of her historical legacy as well as from familial networks. In the Indian context, as writer and psychoanalyst Sudhir Kakar notes, the distancing from family would mean being un-moored in a very real sense, because women's identity stems from their "embeddedness in a multitude of familial relationships".[20] Her uncle Mohsin's damning accusation that Laila is unable to remember the correct forms of address for even close relatives underlines this point. He attributes this shortcoming directly to her Westernisation.

Mocking her he says, "I would surely achieve my nirvana and become so English that my aunts and cousins would be strangers to me". However, more importantly, Laila herself blames her sense of alienation on her education: "Why did you not bring me up like Zahra?" she cries when reprimanded for being disrespectful to her elders. Her orphan-status is only a part of the reason for her alienation from the family. Her English education makes her different from Zahra and the others in the haveli, and that is why she is most comfortable with her England-returned cousins Kemal and Salim.

Laila is set apart from the others from the beginning by the fact that she wears dresses, speaks English and is called Lilly. The name change, as we will see in Santha Rama Rau (Chapter 3) immediately sets up a dual personality and vision. The English governess hired to teach Laila Western manners begins the process of a more fundamental transformation. In their final rift Abida accuses Laila of having been "defiant and disobedient. You have put yourself above your duty to your family". Abida invokes acceptance of hierarchy, class privilege, and community ethos as aspects of a particularly Indian tradition — validated as much by its antiquity as by its rejection of "westernness." Given the historical context of Indian independence in which the book is set, this opposition is significant. Partha Chatterjee notes that in fact some of the early opposition to education for women was grounded in the idea that "bookish learning" would make women unfit for practical housework and waylay them to sit around reading romances all day. Opposition to Western education, in particular, stemmed from a fear of "both proselytization and the exposure of women to harmful Western influences." [21] Anjali Roy and Manasi Sinha attribute Laila's very defiance of authority to her specifically Western education:

> The reason why she even dares question the soundness of this system is the difference in her upbringing. The doubts and queries that occur in her are the result of her exposure to western notions of equality, liberty and individualism. For others like Zahra there has never been any question of choice. [22]

Certainly, one would have to concede that Laila's cousin Zahra does not "choose" to come out. However, one cannot deny that time, as Hosain clearly indicates, makes Laila's stepping out of the haveli inevitable. The small concessions to a "changing world," of the girls being present at the discussion about their marriage and Zahra's coming out of purdah after marriage, are indicative that a generational change, however superficial it may seem, is unavoidable, whatever the education.

Zahra too, blames Laila's education for her alienation and, more importantly, for the way it has altered Laila's perspective of the world. She admonishes Laila for being unable to differentiate between the real world and the world of make-believe perpetuated by her reading. She says, "do you know what is wrong with you, Laila? All those books you read. You just talk like a book now, with no sense of reality." (29) By "reality" Zahra means what is culturally acceptable. She attributes Laila's romantic notions to her specifically English reading. This, she warns, will lead her to imitate other English ways. Most importantly, on the question of marriage, she forecasts, "I suppose you're going to find a husband for yourself? Maybe you'll marry someone for love like Englishwomen do, who change their husbands like slippers." (30) Laila, of course, fulfils the prediction of choosing her own husband and marrying for love which in turn forces her to leave Ashiana.

Sunlight shows that education can be a way of anchoring one in one's cultural heritage like it does Abida or it can equip one to negotiate a modern marriage and play the game in a traditional patriarchal society as it does Zahra. That is on the marriage front but do women have other destinies either in addition to marriage or other than marriage? Uncle Hamid links marriage to responsibilities. He claims, "I have always believed in the education of girls; it is the duty of parents and guardians to give them the kind of education that will best fit them for their responsibilities in this changing world." The question then is what are women's responsibilities and what kind of an education will allow women to fulfil these "responsibilities" in a changing society? And what are the changes that he envisages? *Sunlight* if anything, seems to condemn the superficiality of the changes and of the roles post independence India continues to assign its women citizens. It questions if education will permit women to combat traditional societal mores and equip her to survive on her own if need be.

Antoinette Burton suggests that Hosain is quite "skeptical of the possibilities of a post partition, postcolonial modernity for herself and perhaps more generally for women like her."[23] Education for women is in itself problematic but an English education compounds the problem for women like Laila, muddying the waters with questions of ethnicity and nationality. These, though not clearly spelt out, are part of the text's exploration of tradition and modernity. Abida's burden in bringing up her niece has been the conflictual choice between a traditional and a liberal education. Can a father's theoretical framework practically equip a daughter for existence in a patriarchal society where the women at least are aware, whatever the rhetoric, that for a girl marriage is the ultimate calling? *Inside the Haveli* on the other hand, condemns an education that distances women from tradition. It postulates a negotiation and balance between change and modernity, but that option seems to be limited to women of a certain class. Geeta's "reeducation" in *Haveli* is a clear indication that marital success is predicated on the bride beginning as a tabula rasa and relearning the mores of the marital home.

In *Haveli* the choice of the cities of Bombay and Udaipur, are not coincidental.[24] They reflect two conflicting value systems. Bombay, with its high-rise buildings, is the most modern of Indian cities, often compared to New York. Aside from connoting urban modernity, its association with the film industry gives it a certain surreal quality: a celluloid world that offers possibilities — a city where dreams can be achieved or mercilessly destroyed. Can an urban Bombay apartment dweller of a nuclear family not only adjust but also assume the responsibility of the haveli's continuity as a lifestyle? Is "adjustment" for Geeta tantamount to what Lal un-ironically but aptly terms "re-education"?[25] For Geeta is re-education a process of unlearning and erasing the Bombay existence before she can fit in? As late 20th century readers should we read this move back in time from an apartment to a haveli as a regressive backward step, or shall we look at it with nostalgia as Mehta seems to. Can education and modernity become assets in showing a different path, or do they make her a perpetual outsider, caught between the old and the new?

It is essential to bear in mind though that the harbingers of change are themselves shaped by the dialectic relationship between modernity and tradition. Meenakshi Mukherjee reminds us that in the early post-Independence novels, "[t]he novelists who attempted to present this complex period in fiction were themselves products of this tension."[26] Although these authors continue to be framed by this dialectic, later novels indicate a new trend towards an alternate myth-making.

Haveli as a Classless Space

The haveli lifestyle, which segregated men and women, created by the same token a shared space among women that sporadically blurred class differences and enabled makeshift alliances between women servants and the women of the family. These novels insist upon the connections between rich and poor women both inside and outside homes be they havelis, single family dwellings or public spaces. I wish to clarify at the outset that I am not providing a Marxist reading. Nor do these novels mark a trend in a *Littérature engagée* they are not proposing an overthrow of the feudal or the bourgeois systems. But in some aspects they do enable a Marxist reading which as David Craig suggests provides insights into a class system that shows how power is held and who holds it.[27] Most significantly, the novels question the roles society imposes on rich and poor women alike.

The insistent pairing of servants and family women draws the readers' attention to different world views. The servant is often the Other, a lower class woman, who, by her presence, even if it is a silent one, destabilises the narrative. In fact the different rules and the very distance between rich and poor women affirms Chakravarti's thesis of the construction of Indian Woman as an upper class Aryan, Hindu woman.[28] By their conformity to rules and rituals elite women are presented in a way as more Indian than either poor women or Western educated women. The servants too may reveal their aspirations for higher status by mimicking haveli mores. Anita Desai tends to blur class and Indianness when she points to *izzat*; honour and *sharam*/dishonour as the "two ruling concepts of Indian behaviour" (IX). She sees this binary as "primal passions" that posess rich and poor alike.[29] In the example given "primal passion" may not be the motivating factor that leads Nandi's father to beat her up for a supposed sexual transgression. It could as much indicate his aspiration to higher class mores and value systems. Although Indianness is not stake Desai subsumes class motivations in her discussion.

Servants, however, are central in these novels for three reasons: First, they provide a parallel narrative to the narratives of the family women. The relationship between servants and family women show a community formation that bridges class and age differences. Second, the same strict conformity to gender roles of mother, daughter, and wife are required of servants as they are of family women. Class differences are of course central but the texts insist on the similarity in gender roles of both rich and poor women. Often the servants are the guides who initiate family women, especially daughters or daughters-in-law, into the rules of the house. As such, in this role, they are complicit with patriarchy in the same way that mothers or older women tend to be. Third, although their stories parallel the stories of the protagonists they provide a view from the other side. Their presence is a warning of the possible fate of family women if they were to step out or somehow lose their class privilege.

In *Sunlight* the younger servants like Saliman and Nandi are linked to Laila and Zahra generationally—they are the same age. Ashiana is Laila's natal home, and she knows its rules; the maids, however, provide her with a different class perspective. Their viewpoint constantly adjusts the focus of the narrative, never allowing Laila (or the reader) to forget that the rules for poor women are different and their choices are circumscribed by their poverty. Nandi's "Better to be my father's mule that sometimes digs in its heels and will not move even when it is beaten, than to be poor and a woman", (168) is a clear-sighted evaluation of their double marginalisation and a salutary lesson for Laila. As an upper-class girl, Laila is not even supposed to understand the reasons for the maid Saliman's quiet banishment when she becomes pregnant by the driver Ghulam Ali. Nandi "educates" her by reminding her that, as poor women, they cannot afford the luxury of innocence: "We are the prey of every man's desires" (168).

Through their access to power, Laila and Abida might gain a voice denied to Saliman, but we are forced to confront Spivak's question of not only "can the subaltern speak, but whether and to what effect can she be heard?"[30] Saliman, who is not even allowed to speak in her own defence, translates her voicelessness into physical effacement by committing suicide. But Nandi's is the subaltern voice that is increasingly able to assert itself in the context of political and social change. In the haveli, she is singled out from the beginning for her beauty and her outspokenness. She is sent back to the village for straying into the men's quarters. But it is a very different Nandi who returns to the haveli and deliberately plots her revenge by enslaving Ghulam Ali: "She tormented and tantalised him with the consciousness of her beauty, and the absolute rectitude of her conduct". Her final act bespeaks supreme confidence as she manoeuvres to have her friend's lover thrown out of the haveli. She seeks revenge as much in Saliman's name as in the name of all women.

Nandi and Laila both break the rules and end up together as single mothers. The class difference is not erased as Nandi works for Laila and their roles as mistress and servant are clear. But they indicate the possibility of creating alternative mutually supportive home spaces, maintaining the childhood links formed in the haveli. In *Inside the Haveli* we see the same paralleling between Geeta and Lakshmi. Both mistress and servant even give birth to daughters—Vijay and Sita—within hours of each other. But their stories take very different trajectories and Lakshmi, in this case is a reminder to Geeta of what she stands to lose by disobeying the rules of the haveli.

Geeta's assimilation into her marital haveli is poised between one servant's rebellion against it and another's total commitment to it. Sunanda P. Chavan reminds us that, "Its [the haveli's] world is characterised by concentric duality — the masters and servants contributing equally to the pattern."[31] Lakshmi and Geeta both pay a price for their different choices. Had she not opted out, Lakshmi would have taken over from Pari seamlessly as Geeta does from her mother-in-law. The timing of Lakshmi's self-exile from the haveli and Geeta's absorption into it is significantly between the hiatus signalled by Bhabasa's death, marking the end of an era, and Vijay's birth, signalling regeneration. Geeta, the educated outsider, symbolises modernity, and is poised as a harbinger of change in this in-between space of possibility; but it is Lakshmi, the maid servant, who steps out, separating herself from both Geeta and the haveli. Lakshmi's story interrupts the main narrative that seeks to subsume differences, and instead insists upon class as a shaping factor in the choices each of them make.

The central episode that dramatically changes Lakshmi's life is, again as in Nandi, Saliman and Laila's case, one that focuses on women's sexuality and its control by society. Heeralal, the driver, gives her gifts of a silk blouse, a sari, and some sweets. On each occasion, instead of returning the gifts or showing them to the mistress, as behoves a servant, Lakshmi hides them. When the gifts are discovered, her husband accuses her of being "worse than a street woman"(58). Enraged by the accusation, she walks out of the haveli. Lakshmi leaves the haveli but she remains a constant presence through her daughter Sita. She is a reminder and/or a warning, haunting Geeta with the possibility of life on the other side. She is Geeta's other who sometimes indicates parity and sometimes unbridgeable alterity.

Geeta's moment of epiphany occurs when she hears her son's gurgles as Dhapu the maid bathes him. In that moment, she realises that conformity and sacrifice of her individual fulfilment are a small price to pay for the privilege and cocooning that the haveli can provide for her children.

> Where else in the world could children be enveloped in such affection? This kind of devotion is almost superhuman. The servants go hungry if the children haven't eaten, they go without sleep if a child has a slight headache. And yet for all this they get so little in return. But they are always cheerful as if they have their own secret source of happiness that no one can touch (137).

The sentimental tone of the narrative highlights the selfless devotion of the servants while it effectively blurs the material reality of "how little they get." The final soft focus that illuminates an intangible "secret source of happiness" ensures that it remains untouched by material change. Geeta does not even consider material compensation; in fact, a suggestion like that would reduce the warm glow of happiness to crass monetary reality. Geeta, who has been made aware of her lack of roots by haveli standards, is determined that her children shall not be deprived of "a five-hundred-year-old ancestry" or the selfless love of servants that is an integral part of the haveli system.

Security, class privilege, and access to power facilitate Geeta's acceptance of the haveli. It is worth recalling that Geeta's first step towards a deeper identification with the haveli was through her understanding of male prerogative. Her voyeuristic peep into the male quarters allows her a perspective of the haveli which emphasises a male code of chivalry and honour. Hypnotised by this transformatory vision, "a glow of pride and affection filled Geeta" (34) and allows her to identify with the haveli. In this moment, she realises how her "little discomforts" have blinded her "to the great traditions of the family" (35). Her transition from rebel to supporter is enabled by the image of herself as the mistress of the haveli who will perpetuate its traditions.

Lakshmi, in contrast, opts out because of her opposition to the male establishment. At the same time Geeta is assimilated, Lakshmi is caught out in a moment couched in terms of sexual transgression. Her reaction to the driver's secret gifts exudes a childlike glee and a sensuous appreciation. Her body registers the implication of the gifts:

> She turned the pink blouse in her trembling hands and caressed it to feel better its soft, smooth texture. Her cheeks became purple with excitement. In spite of the shafts of fear that ran through her body, a soft glowing warmth filled her (41).

The act of accepting the gifts has tainted her and made her a marked woman. Every minor misdemeanour henceforth will be judged in the context of this transgression. Lakshmi is aware that the slightest hint of sexual infringement evokes the question of male honour. At an individual level, this implicates her husband who immediately accuses her of being a loose woman without even giving her a hearing; and at the community level, the honour of the haveli is implicated. As a woman and a servant, she is already marginalised in the patriarchal, male-centred space of the haveli. In these circumstances, the unknown outside seems less of a risk than life inside the haveli. However, the gift-giving driver begs forgiveness and stays on. His transformed presence as an emasculated shadow of his former self is a salutary reminder. If, as a man, he is reduced to this, then Lakshmi, as a woman and a servant, would have risked complete effacement by staying on.

Critics like Chavan argue that, unlike Lakshmi, Geeta's ambivalence towards the haveli is the result of the novelist's failure to develop her character consistently:

> Like Lakshmi, she faces the problem of choice—either to stay inside the haveli and lose freedom or to go outside and be free. Lakshmi's choice is clear and deliberate. She prefers to leave the haveli. Geeta, on the other hand, is strangely passive in spite of her desire to escape the haveli.[32]

I would suggest that Geeta's choosing to stay in the haveli

is as conscious and calculated a choice as Lakshmi's is to leave. Geeta becomes the obedient daughter-in-law, conforms and even justifies that which she has earlier found unacceptable because her stake in maintaining the status quo is greater than in breaking it. Neither Geeta nor Lakshmi's choice is as clear-cut as Chavan would suggest.

Critics entrapped in a tradition versus modernity reading of the novel regard Lakshmi as a symbol of individualism and modernity. The city-dwelling Geeta is assimilated into the cultural past of the haveli and becomes a representative of feudal India; Lakshmi is othered by her lower class status and rejection of haveli India. Her gesture of leaving the haveli has been contrasted with Geeta's firmer entrenchment in it. R.K. Asthana maintains that Lakshmi "stands in open revolt against it [tradition] in tune with modernity, no matter what hardship she has to face.[33] Others read it as a futile gesture that leads to greater suffering for Lakshmi.[34] However, the text remains non-judgmental about Lakshmi's crossing over. She is carefully presented in a sensitive and nuanced manner —neither the fallen woman nor the defiant heroine. Even her ability to leave, ironically, is enabled by the haveli. She leaves without a backward glance at her infant daughter, confident that the haveli as a collective will look after Sita as it has done for her and others before her.

The Haveli as a Gendered Space

The domestic space of the haveli in these novels is primarily a patriarchal space which women organise and manage for men. Since Habermas' study, the conceptual distinctions between the domestic and the public sphere have become less rigid.[35] However, in the havelis, they remain distinct and separate physical spaces. Etymologically, Sunand Prasad traces the word haveli back to "haowla," the old Arabic for partition. In havelis the clear boundaries between sacred and profane, or private and public spaces especially affected women's mobility as they were restricted to women's quarters or the zenanas. The segregated spheres emphasised the separate worlds of men and women who lived together and yet apart in the same house.

Wacziarg and Nath note that the haveli, not only "represented the rigid lifestyle of a society that segregated its men from its women, But add that the very "architecture of the *haveli* was conceived around this social norm."[36] This segregation placed women at the centre of the home in the most private and sacred of spaces. The two-fold outcome was that while the idea of Woman is elevated and sacralised, the actual position and treatment of women is ignored. Second, the demarcation between private and public, the outside and the inside or the home and the world became unfranchiseable barriers that could make home a prison for women.

Woman is positioned in these novels as subaltern and voiceless because of gender. Class difference though always present and important especially to re enforce tradition and Indianness is less emphasised in order to highlight the gender hierarchy which silences family women and women servants alike. In both novels, female sexual transgression signals an in-built male authority over Woman. The punishment or ostracization is levied specifically against Woman's sexuality, for stepping out of the bounds of patriarchal protection. Stepping out from the world of the zenana can be merely a physical act, as it is for Laila's cousin Zahra or even for aunt Abida who moves from the interior of the zenana towards the more public men's space to look after her dying father. Abida's "moving out," unlike Laila's, is a reaffirmation of patriarchal loyalty and a specific female gender role of nursing the sick and aged. Abida consciously appropriates and internalises the "inherited" or allocated space within the haveli. Although she is the harbinger of change, her own moving out is firmly anchored to the concept of filial duty. Laila, Nandi and Lakshmi's stepping out brook no return. Laila's questioning or defiance of the haveli ethos casts her out forever. Laila, like Sita in the *Ramayana* is a reminder that the price of transgression for women, regardless of particular religions, is often eviction and homelessness.

The question however is, whether the haveli is a redeemable space? The obvious way to read the zenana or the enclosed women's quarters is as a patriarchal prison. This is the kind of private space that Millett justifiably rails against, as one that becomes an "ideological prison."[37] Wacziarg and Nath confirm that this was, in fact, one of the intents of the haveli design. They note that, "the original function of a *haveli*, apart from providing residence, was to wall in the domestic life of a family. Secluded from the outside world, a *haveli* set its own pace of life."[38] The novels, however, often question and undermine this prohibitive intent of the haveli and of the zenana in particular inherited from tradition.

In both real and fictional havelis, the open and yet enclosed space of the courtyard remains ambiguous. It is a general area and yet restricted by a careful cordoning off from the view of strangers or non-family males. The duality recalls that the haveli structure is premised upon a notion of gendered space which seamless seems to map onto notions of public and private space. Feminist contentions that the 'personal is political' make this specially allocated women's space problematic.

The Haveli as a 'Womenspace'

The haveli with its segregated zenana spaces illustrate feminist contentions that physical rules and boundaries of a place imperceptibly shape social behaviours. The haveli ethos is an abstract concept rooted in a geographical pattern at a certain historical moment but this teleology of a gendered community continues in bungalow and apartment dwellings too. The patterns of female friendship established in the zenana enable Nandi, for instance, to almost feel entitled to a safe haven for her son and herself with Laila in her hill home.

The zenana is traditionally seen negatively as a confining and segregated space, but it also offers women a place and a sense of community with other women. Lila Abu-Lughad's study of Bedouin women suggests that it is possible to shift the gaze and assume

> the perspective of those for whom this community of women
> is the primary arena of social life, [so that] we get a more

accurate and nuanced view not only of its connection to the men's world, but of the nature of women's experiences and relationships within the community.[39]

I would suggest that the zenana within the haveli can and is reclaimed in Indian women's novels as a 'womenspace'.

A womenspace evolves from the physically segregated space of the zenana to an emotional bonding between women across class and generation. The "womanly" rituals of domesticity are undertaken to propitiate patriarchal deities of father, brother and son but the work itself unites the women. In the havelis, the bond between servants and family women are predicated upon gender — "women's work" — of ensuring the smooth running of the household.[43] Their joint participation in this work is posited more as a "common cause" of tending the home than mere work. American feminist historian, Phyllis Palmer, in her study of housewives and domestic servants in twentieth century America, notes, "housework has divided women along race and class lines, at the same time that they were joined in their commitment to tending for people and doing the job well."[44] The patterns of women's alliances and women's exploitation because of class and gender that Palmer maps in her sociological study find a literary resonance in several Indo-English women's novels. The segregated zenana in this context is a concrete demarcation between women's and men's spheres of work. In the hierarchical feudal structure of the havelis, family women and women servants are both second-class citizens. The nature of their work and the awareness of their place make them natural allies within the domestic sphere. The association of Woman and domesticity makes the home a safe habitat; the outside is, by contrast, constructed as unsafe and threatening. Woman's work and her supposedly natural nurturing tendency posit the home as the shelter and safe haven that all women aspire to.

The links between femininity and domesticity are reinforced by the ideologies of women as nurturers in both feminist and non-feminist literature. The coupling of home, women and work is not peculiar to Indian society. Witold

Rybczynski traces "the feminization of the home in seventeenth century Holland."[41] He observes, "the house had become the place for another kind of work — specialized domestic work — women's work." (70-71) Domestic work in a feudal household is not a simple cash transaction but is deeply tied into notions of belonging, service, and loyalty. Bruce Robbins, in his delineation of the role of servants in English fiction points out that, "according to common usage, servants did not look for work, like other members of their class, but for a "place."[42]

Sunlight on a Broken Column and *Inside the Haveli*, refocus on the zenana allowing it to emerge more positively as a womenspace. It can almost be seen as a relatively "free space" where women can be together and relax with each other as they carry out the daily chores. In this central open space, class barriers are less rigid as maids and the women of the house gather together. The women work together to keep the house running for the men, but their co-operation in sharing the space and the jobs, builds a sense of a community of women. In *Inside the Haveli* the women gather to do the chore work involved in the family rituals of births and deaths. And in *Sunlight on a Broken Column* we note that all the women respond to the changed atmosphere as Baba Jan's condition improves: "it seemed that cramping weights had been removed from the seconds of the day and each one of us felt the lightening of a burden" (44). They gather on the rooftop — some to dye chunnis, others to grind spices and still others to sit sunning cold and weary bones and idly chatting — and do so with a shared sense of relief.

These moments of easy friendship, however momentary, are also repeated generationally. At Muharram, the younger maids Nandi and Saliman watch the *tazzias* with Laila and Zahra. A sense of youthful fun and freedom unites the younger generation — maids and cousins — against the constant work discipline imposed by the older generation. These rare moments of communitas stand out as significant, especially as the world outside and around the haveli crumbles. I am not suggesting that the zenana is a totally "free space" where women meet as equals but as noted earlier, there is a definite trend in Indo-English women's novels to represent it as a possible lieu of women's friendships across class and generations. The valorisation of the concept of "sisterhood" of the feminist movements of the early 1970s echoes this gender alliance that continues to exist despite all odds. It is possible to read the zenana as a space that women take back and transform, at least textually, into a safe and mutually supportive space.

Without attempting to erase obvious differences, I feel we cannot ignore the novels' conscious attempts to highlight moments of female alliances across class and generation. At these moments, gender is the unifying factor that temporarily subsumes class, generation, region and other differences. This "coalition-politics," to borrow Johnson-Reagon's term, is not necessarily a political strategy but stems rather from a personal, subjective empathy that links women to other women and through that to a larger sense of community.[45] I also do not wish to suggest that these alliances are in any way fixed or permanent or even consciously sought tactics. However, the acknowledgement and celebration of female friendship, or a fleeting "communitas," in Turner's sense of the word, is a characteristic feature of Indo-English women's novels and one that in large part reflects the influence of women's' movements in India and abroad.

The fear of "essentialising" may have led feminist critics and readers alike to disregard simple woman-to-woman connections. In this context, Spivak's notion of solidarity between privileged women and ordinary women is particularly useful. She says, "our solidarity is not to speak for, not to speak about, but to speak tout contre."[46] She specifically uses the French because it implies both the notion of closeness and opposition. In talking about "ordinary people" and creating links, there is a danger of romanticisation, and certainly in some novels, the identification between women is described in very lyrical and romantic terms but as Spivak notes, the other face of romanticisation might be silencing, and that poses an even greater danger. We may do well to recall Jayawardene's concept of "universality in diversity" as a particularly apt formulation of a woman centered world view.

There is no romanticization of the haveli or zenana in Hosain. Laila leaves Ashiana without much regret, because she has outgrown it and broken the rules. Laila's natal home with the zenana at its centre is a primary affiliation that marks all her other homes. It was both a home and a refuge for this parentless child. Ashiana has "engraved" within her what Bachelard terms "the hierarchy of the various functions of inhabiting."[47] But Bachelard's house which "constitutes a body of images that gives mankind proofs or illusions of stability" is not entirely so for Laila.[48] Mankind in this context is aptly used, because for Laila and Nandi as women, that stability is laced with a tradition that they found suffocating. Even as Laila sits reminiscing in the dilapidated home, her journey from a past that, retrospectively and in contrast to a fragmented present, may seem whole and solid does not allow her the luxury of forgetting the pain which is also embedded in the house. Her new house in the hills allows a different paradigm where though *class* differences are not erased and Nandi will still be the servant and Laila the mistress, but they have moved to a different level of female friendship that enables and enriches each others lives. They are linked by a shared past and as single mothers who will provide for each others children in their various class capacities.

In *Inside the Haveli* the transitional moment of Geeta's ultimate acculturation into the haveli tradition is also portrayed as a woman to woman handing over of a sacred trust through ritual. The soft-focus is on the womanly continuity of domestic tradition as Geeta accepts the responsibility of perpetuating the patriarchal, feudal tradition of Jeevan Niwas. It is worth quoting this passage at some length to show the quiet dignity imbued in the moment when the outsider daughter-in-law becomes an insider and almost anonymously assumes the rituals of the household so that the pattern remains uninterrupted:

> For seventy years Sangram Singhji's wife had walked in the corridors of Jeewan Niwas as the trustee of the family traditions. She had lived always in the shadow of her husband's ancestors. While she carried out her duties, she had at the same time carefully instructed her daughter-in-law in the rituals and customs of the haveli. That was the only way to ensure the continuity of family traditions. Its tiny flame flickered as always in front of the family deity (50).

The Hindu religious symbolism of the tiny flame in the earthenware lamp is deeply evocative. The womanly passing on of family traditions is seen as a sacred trust. The passage foregrounds the continuity of the ritual in literal and symbolic terms rather than the individual women who perform the rituals.

References

1   Omar Khan, "Attia Hosain: Interview" (http://www.harappa.com/attia/attiahosain.html)

2   Malashri Lal, *The Law of The Threshold: Women Writers in English* Shimla: Indian Institute of Advanced Study, 1995 (p.91).

3   Omar Khan, "Attia Hosain: Interview" (http://www.harappa.com/attia/attiahosain.html)

4   Mulk Raj Anand, "Attia Hosain: A Profile" Attia Hosain, *Sunlight On a Broken Column* Delhi: Arnold-Heinemann, 1980 Preface.

5   Anita Desai,"Introduction," Attia Hosain, *Sunlight on a Broken Column* London: Virago Modern Classics, 1988.

6   Antoinette Burton, *Dwelling in the Archive: Women Writing House, Home and History in Late Colonial India"* Oxford: Oxford University Press, 2003

7   Rybczynski's description of a typical seventeenth century Parisian bourgeois home bears a striking resemblance to the haveli. See especially p.38. Witold Rybczynski, *Home,*(1987)

8   Sunand Prasad, "The Havelis of North India The Urban Courtyard House," Vol.I. Dissertation, The Royal College of Art, London, Visual Islamic Arts Unit, Faculty of Fine Art, June 1988, (1.7).

9   V.S. Pramar, *Haveli: Wooden Houses and Mansions of Gujarat* Ahmedabad: Mapin Publishing, 1989 (p.115).

10 Personal conversation with Menon in New Delhi, July 15, 1994.

11 Alan Roland, *In Search of Self in India and Japan: Towards a Cross-Cultural Psychology* Princeton: Princeton University Press, 1988.

12 Sunand Prasad, "The Havelis of North India The Urban Courtyard House," Vol.I. Dissertation, The Royal College of Art, London, Visual Islamic Arts Unit, Faculty of Fine Art, June 1988 (1.3).

13 Pierre Bourdieu, "Social Space and Symbolic Power," *Sociological Theory* 7 (Spring 1989):14-25. Bourdieu defines habitus as "a system of schemes of perception and appreciation of practices, cognitive and evaluative structures which are acquired through the lasting experience of a social position" (p. 19).

14 Partha Chatterjee, *The Nation and its Fragments* Delhi: Oxford University Press, 1994.

15 Uma Chakravarti, "Whatever Happened to the Vedic Dasi? Orientalism, Nationalism and a Script for the Past," Sangari and Vaid, (eds.) *Recasting Women: Essays in Colonial History* Delhi: Kali for Women, 1989.

16 Malashri Lal, *The Law of The Threshold: Women Writers in English* Shimla: Indian Institute of Advanced Study, 1995 (p.95).

17 Malashri Lal, *The Law of The Threshold: Women Writers in English,* Shimla: Indian Institute of Advanced Study, 1995 (p.64-85).

18 Paulo Freire, *Pedagogy of the Oppressed.*

19 This recalls the argument suggesting that Indo-English writers are similarly distanced from an Indian reality.

20 Sudhir Kakar, *The Inner World: A Psycho-analytic Study of Childhood and Society in India* Delhi: Oxford University Press, 1978/1981 (p.62).

21 Partha Chatterjee, *The Nation and its Fragments: Colonial and Postcolonial Histories* Delhi: Oxford University Press, 1994 (p.128).

22 Anjali Roy and Manasi Sinha, "Growing up In a Zenana: Sunlight on a Broken Column," Viney Kirpal, (ed.) *The Girl Child in 20th century Indian Literature* New Delhi: Sterling, 1992 (p.217).

23 Antoinette Burton, *Dwelling in the Archive: Women Writing House, Home and History in Late Colonial India* Oxford: Oxford University Press, 2003 (p.15-16).

24 For an interesting development of the idea of how the British-created Presidency cities of Bombay, Calcutta and Madras have figured in four Indo-English novels see, Janet P. Gemill, "The City in the Indo-

English Novel," Allen G. Noble and Ashok K. Dutt, (eds.) *India: Cultural Patterns and Processes* Boulder, Colorado: Westview Press, 1982.

25 Malashri Lal, *The Law of The Threshold: Women Writers in English* Shimla: Indian Institute of Advanced Study, 1995 (p.91).

26 Meenakshi Mukherjee, *Realism and Reality: The Novel and Society in India* Bombay: Oxford University Press, 1985/1994 (p.69).

27 David Craig, (ed.) *Marxists On Literature: An Anthology* Middlesex: Penguin Books, 1975/1977.

28 For a scholarly study of Nationalism's construction of Indian women, see Uma Chakravarti, "Whatever Happened to the Vedic Dasi? Orientalism, Nationalism and a Script for the Past," Sangari and Vaid, (eds.) *Recasting Women: Essays in Colonial History* Delhi: Kali for Women, 1989.

29 Anita Desai, "Introduction" *Sunlight on a Broken Column* By Attia Hosain. Penguin Boks/Virago Press.

30 Gayatri Chakravorty Spivak quoted in Arnold Krupat, *Ethnocriticism Ethnography History Literature* Berkeley: University of California Press, 1992.

31 Sunanda P. Chavan, "Inside the Haveli: Inadequate as a Work of Art," R.K. Dhawan, (ed.) *Indian Women Novelists*, Set I: Vol. IV New Delhi: Prestige Books, 1991 (p.239).

32 Sunanda P. Chavan, "Inside the Haveli: Inadequate as a Work of Art." R.K. Dhawan, (ed.) *Indian Women Novelists*, Set I: Vol. IV New Delhi: Prestige Books, 1991 (p.247-248).

33 R.K. Asthana, "Tradition and Modernity in Inside the Haveli," R.K. Dhawan, (ed.) *Indian Women Novelists*, Set I: Vol. IV New Delhi: Prestige Books, 1991 (p.196).

34 See Viney Kirpal, Santosh Gupta, Sunanda Chavan and others in R.K. Dhawan, (ed.) *Indian Women Novelists*, Set I: Vol. IV New Delhi: Prestige Books, 1991.

35 Jurgen Habermas, *The Structural Transformation of The Public Sphere: An Inquiry into a Category of Bourgeois Society*, translated by Thomas Burger, assisted by Frederick Lawrence UK: Polity Press, 1989.

36 Wacziarg and Nath, Rajasthan, 1982. (p.22).

37 Kate Millett in *Sexual Politics*, quoted by Gillian Rose in *Feminism and Geography: The Limits of Geographical Knowledge*. Cambridge: Polity Press, 1993.

38 Francis Wacziarg and Aman Nath, Rajasthan, *The Painted Walls of Shekhavati* London: Croom Helm Ltd, 1982 (p.21-22).

39 Lila Abu-Lughad, "A Community of Secrets: The Separate World of

Bedouin Women," Penny A. Weiss & Marilyn Friedman, (eds.) *Feminism and Community* Philadelphia: Temple University Press, 1995 (p.21).

40 Benedict Anderson, *Imagined Communities:Reflections on the Origin and Spread of Nationalism* London: Verso, 1983.

41 Witold Rybczynski, *Home: A Short History of an Idea* Harmondsworth: Penguin, 1986 (p.72).

42 Bruce Robbins, *English Fiction From Below* New York: Columbia University Press, 1986 (p.58).

43 For lack of a better term, I use "family women" to indicate the upper class women of the house. The novels do not reveal much about the family life of the servants; their role is to look after the family and the household of the employers. The term "employers" might be unsuitable because they are not necessarily direct employers nor are they responsible for cash negotiations. But they are the ones who supervise the domestic work of the servants, and the servants are directly answerable to them.

Bruce Robbins, *English Fiction From Below*, New York: Columbia University Press, 1986 (p.58).

44 Phyllis Palmer, *Domesticity and Dirt: Housewives and Domestic Servants In The United States, 1920–1945* Philadelphia: Temple University Press, 1989 Preface, ix.

45 Bernice Johnson Reagon, "Coalition Politics: Turning the Century," Barbara Smith, (ed.) *Home Girls: A Black Feminist Anthology* New York: Kitchen Table: Women of Color Press, 1983.

46 Gayatri Chakravorty Spivak, Interview, "Transnationality and Multiculturalist Ideology," Deepika Bahri and Mary Vasudeva (eds.) *Between The Lines: South Asians and Postcoloniality* Philadelphia: Temple University Press, 1996 (p.72).

47 Gaston Bachelard, *The Poetics of Space* (1958) translation by Maria Jolas, Boston: Beacon Press, 1964 (p.15).

48 Gaston Bachelard, *The Poetics of Space* (1958) translation by Maria Jolas, Boston: Beacon Press, 1964 (p.17).

3

Bungalow

The bungalow, unlike the haveli, is essentially a nuclear family dwelling. It symbolises individuation and a narrowing of familial ties associated with an individualistic way of life. The shift in location from haveli to bungalow in Indian-English women's novels, parallels what Alan Roland, a practicing psychoanalyst describes as a change from the "we-self" which 'contrasts with the self of Westerners, which is implicitly always an "I-self."'[1] The haveli, as a dwelling for the extended family, was a concrete symbol of a group ethos seen as typically Indian. The bungalow, on the other hand, is essentially a nuclear family dwelling largely associated with a Western way of life. The bungalow can be seen as a physical manifestation of a "contact zone" of east and west in India.[2] The conflict and negotiations between so called Indian and Western values is visible in not only the architectural transition from the indigenous haveli to the Westernized bungalow; the blurring of Indianness and Westernness and male/female spaces but also in the relationships within the bungalow.

Westernization through an English education system, travel and social contact gives these protagonists a Du Boisesque "double vision" or "two-ness" that puts them at odds with traditional family patterns.[3] Others have referred to this twoness in more derogatory terms such as 'Oreos' for

African Americans – brown outside and white inside, 'Banana' for the Chinese – yellow outside and white inside, 'ABCD's' – American Born Confused Desis and so on. But the issue for the so called 'Brown Sahibs' or memsahibs in this case is less about what others call them and more about the fact that they have so deeply internalized notions and attitudes of both east and west that it is impossible to disentangle the threads. It is perhaps not surprising that Madras born Santha Rama Rau, mainly a travel writer, who grew up at least bi-culturally explores the theme of duality. The daughter of a diplomat father and a mother who was a prominent advocate of health issues, she lived and travelled abroad extensively. Rama Rau was born and grew up in colonial India but was sent to England for further education. She graduated from St Paul's School (UK) in 1939 and from Wellesley College (USA) in 1944. She taught at Sarah Lawrence College and was a freelance writer.

Autobiographically too Rama Rau is keenly aware of her dual personality. In an essay entitled "By Any Other Name" she recounts the remarkable story of her first day of school where the headmistress, as was their wont in schools in India, Hong Kong and other colonies, changed her and her sister's names. She comments, "At that age, if one's name is changed, one develops a curious form of dual personality".[4] Rama Rau also did a dramatic adaptation of E.M. Forster's *A Passage to India* and the Forsterian legacy is visible in her third novel *Remember the House* (1956) where she explores the theme of East West dialogue. Contrary to Forster's novel though, her protagonist is a young Indian girl Indira or Baba as she is called. The pet name, Baba meaning child, is not random as this is the story of Baba's coming of age. The novel opens on New Year's eve 1946-1947 in Bombay where Baba lives with her father. This is a moment of both Baba and India's 'tryst with destiny" on the eve of independence. As Baba notes, "Indian independence, only months away, was felt by most of us first as a sort of wariness about our pleasure, later as a political achievement"(1). Baba befriends an American couple Alix and Nicky Nichols. The gap between East and West and the old and new India is explored as Baba views Bombay and Indians through the eyes of the Nichols and she questions attitudes hithertofore taken for granted. The house in Jalanabad, Baba's childhood home, a joint family dwelling, is the house of the title and the touchstone against which all other homes—her politician father's in Bombay and her mother's religious recluse in the South—are measured.

English education posed as great a threat to Indianness as political imperialism. Beginning with Edward Said, other postcolonial writers like Gauri Viswanathan and Bill Ashcroft among others have pointed to the power nexus of language, education and culture that destabilized existing hierarchies. In both Attia Hosain's *Sunlight on a Broken Column* and Rama Rau's *Remember the House* English education is held directly responsible for distancing children, especially girl children from their traditional familial roles and roots. In both novels Abida and Nani, the much loved mother-figures speak in the voice of an immutable and reassuring tradition. Baba's grand-mother recalls that in the post-mutiny (1857) period mothers used to frighten their children into good behaviour by the threat of the wicked white man. And now she notes, "... just look at your old Nani, she hears foreign ideas from her own granddaughter. The people that she most dreaded speak to her through her child's child. ... The West has come to us now in a new way, a much more insidious way. Will this, too, be a conquest?"(182-183) This internalization of a foreign and colonizing value system could of course be read as "a con-quest" but the idea of duality or two-ness proposed by Du Bois shows how what may have begun as "conquest" has been so assimilated and integrated that later Indian-English writ-ers feel that the colonizing baggage has been discarded and English can and should be seen as just another Indian lan-guage. Time, it is felt, would have wrought change, moder-nity and westernization with or without colonialism.

Change in the domestic sphere of the novels revolves around the marital relationship that is central to the nuclear or bungalow home. The conjugal home is often the contested site where wifely conformity and obedience are exchanged for status and security. And, Baba's grandmother argues, even love. As she tells her own story, she admits that initially just the idea of being married was enough and the love for her husband came later.

> At first I was simply obedient. It was years before I experienced also the glory of loving. It came to me gradually through many days and nights when at last I knew him as I know myself, when there were no more discoveries, when there was no longer need for forgiveness or understanding or expression, then I loved him as I have loved nothing else on this earth – more, even, than my children (183).

The idea of conformity and innovation or change from within as suggested by Nani is akin to the idea of Indian music where the strict discipline of the raga forms the structure and the basis. It is only when the musician has perfected that discipline that she can change it from within. Some of the novels quite clearly suggest that this mode of change, rather than an overthrowing of old norms, is the way for a smoother transition. Nani dismisses Baba's objections, "Just think—what is it, this 'love' of yours? A little excitement, a little impatience, much imagination—is that enough to found your life on? Can you base the structure of your feelings. Your fulfillment, your children, your whole being on so little?" (183)

Baba's own insecurities about love and marriage are exacerbated by the influence of the Nichols'. Her friend Pria who has a much more pragmatic, Kiplingesque view that "East is East and West is west and never the twain shall meet" approach reminds Baba, "... the Nichols , like us, can only function within their own limits. Ours are very different, though no less satisfactory"(122). When the issue is articulated in conflictual cultural terms of east versus west the protagonist is practically coerced into choosing sides almost as a way of asserting cultural allegiance. Pria's sureness and Nani's tough common sense approach undermines Baba's explorations. She goes back to the 'suitable boy' whose offer she had earlier rejected. Unfortunately, both her earlier rejection and her later acceptance seem reactive which diminishes her decision. That aside, though, the problem is what was acceptable for Nani,who was anchored in strict values and belief structures and could not contemplate other options easily, may not feel 'natural' or acceptable to Baba. She can contemplate rejecting the community or mainstream value system. The only problem is that the lack of a practical alternative is bound to limit her imagination to the available possibilities. In fact, Nani's absolute conviction of the rightness of her way, projected as the Indian way, is rejected if not subverted even by her own daughter, Baba's mother, who leaves her politician husband's urban home to live alone.

Protagonists negotiate between the ideologies of a "we-self," socially approved if not enforced as a behavioural code, especially for women, and an "I-self," which, seems to offer a greater degree of freedom. But does it? Some haveli ideas of patriarchal hierarchy and a separation of spheres are brought into the bungalow existence, creating tensions and an urgent need to re-examine issues of female sexuality, conformity to social and gender codes and the very basis of heterosexual marriages. Is the post-independence Indian woman equipped to either alter the power balance or step out of the domestic sphere and survive in a man's world? Women take on so-called male responsibilities of fending for the family but will they be allowed the same freedoms that men are allowed? Stripped of the community that was central to the haveli existence, women in bungalows return, often literally, to their natal homes to relearn or to reject the lessons of their mothers.

The zenana space of the haveli is evoked in women seeking out other women to learn from their stories. Even in novels where bungalow living is the norm, the search for "communitas," especially among women, is a reminder of the haveli pattern. Although some aspects of the haveli ethos like the joint-family existence were transposed into western-style bungalow or apartment homes, the change in dwellings among the urban Indian elite marks a significant moment of transition in values and relationships. The major change of course was the change is dwelling and perspective from the extended family grouping to a nuclear and individual focus. For women, the change raised new questions about sexuality, female individuality and egalitarian relationships between women and men but also among women. Questions about speaking and listening and silencing came to the fore as the marital pact had to be renegotiated in bungalow dwellings.

The narration of home in Indian English women's novels, particularly Santha Rama Rau's, *Remember the House* (1956) Githa Hariharan's *Thousand Faces of Night* (1992), Shama Futehally's, *Tara Lane* (1993), Shashi Deshpande's, *A Matter of Time* (1996) and, Anita Nair's, *Ladies Coupe* (2001), reveal the extent to which the villa, bungalow, kothi and other housing models have been superimposed upon the haveli typology, not so much architecturally but as a continuity of social patterns. The tendency to map modernity onto tradition in these novels has led some critics to lament the absence of "revolutionary change," especially in the status of women in Indo-English fiction.[5] However, the novels could be read, as mentioned earlier, as an attempt to question and change the structures from within. They show an awareness of the centrality of past patterns even while creating new patterns of existence.

A moving train rather than a static, physical house is the centre of Anita Nair's *Ladies Coupe*. The train of course evokes ideas of journeys and movement that are relatively new in Indian English womens's novels. In this work the strict rules of confining ideologies that stifle women even as they have to adapt to changing times are questioned, appropriately perhaps, from within the moving location of a train compartment. Nair recounts that the idea of setting the scene in a train compartment came from her own travel in a compartment reserved for ladies. She vividly recalls the easy camaraderie, the sharing of food and personal anecdotes among the women: "When 15 years ago I was travelling in a ladies' coupe the women around me began talking—I was on the top berth — there is an atmosphere of intimacy that comes in. People talk more openly to strangers—there is no judgment."[6] These ladies only coupes or compartments used to exist as an integral part of the Indian Railways system till the early 1990s. The protagonist, Akhila, undertakes a journey in search of an answer to the question that all the women in the various novels seem to ask—can a woman live alone and be happy? As the eldest daughter, Akhilandeswari or Akhila as she is called, shoulders the responsibility of the family when her father suddenly dies of a heart attack. She steps into the male sphere of responsibility by taking on a job to support the family. But her mother, siblings and society at large still expect her to conform to selective female gender and caste roles of a Tamil Brahmin woman. The siblings marry and have children, yet Akhila, a 45-year-old spinster, remains the "cash cow" who subsidizes her sister and her family. Almost crushed under the weight of duty, Akhila sets off on a journey in the ladies-only train compartment of earlier years. Each of the five women passengers recounts her story in response to Akhila's question: Can a woman stay single and be happy, or does she need a man to feel complete?

Patriarchal Lineage

Akhila lives in a man's world where social structures and relationships are grounded in patriarchal ideologies. The bungalow as the bastion of the heterosexual home and the nuclear family is the space where Akhila's question resonates. It is repeatedly posed in all the novels albeit in different ways. The subtext of the question explores the power relations within a family and specifically between a couple. In the move from the haveli to the bungalow, women gave up a feudal structure where the patriarch, normally the eldest male, ruled. But patriarchy continued even in the bungalow and beyond, socially and in familial relationships. The house itself seems to demarcate the boundaries and spaces. In *Remember the House* eight pages are dedicated to a fond description of the routine and attitudes inculcated in the Jalnabad house.

> In Jalnabad, I thought, no one made much of a point about happiness. We were given, and we accepted, almost without

thinking, certain precepts. The importance of the family—the one we were born to or the one we married into. Our place in a certain structure, a pattern of life, of birth, marriage, children, peace and death. Our debt to a world could be defined, but the promises were all unstated. With our framework we would make our own happiness. It was never suggested that we pursue happiness. We were not encouraged to waste our time (90).

Although the house is physically absent and no action unfolds there it is a living frame of reference for Baba to even think of her marital home to be.

In four of these novels, women review and understand their marital homes from the double gaze of looking backward at their natal homes while looking forward at the marital homes. They marry but return to the natal home to see more clearly. An understanding and empathy with the natal home provides the first step in renegotiating their place to make marital homes more viable. In three of the novels — *Thousand Faces of Night*, *Tara Lane* and *A Matter of Time* — the natal houses are in fact the framing background and the location of the action. The centrality of the house in these novels cannot be overstated. In an interview with Lakshmi Holmström, Deshpande confirms:

> For me it's essential - almost as essential as it is for a movie director - to have the shape of the house clear. I know all the houses in my novels ... as an architect does, all the rooms, even if I may not use them. If I have that clear then the rest of it can happen, because it is there that it is going to happen.[7]

Feminist publisher and critic Ritu Menon in her insightful essay on Deshpande notes that the ancestral home is often the locale and organizing factor in not only *A Matter of Time* but in most of Bangalore-based writer Shashi Deshpande's work.[8]

In *A Matter of Time* (1996) the lineage of the house is carefully etched and established in the first paragraph. The first of the three sections of the novel is even entitled "The House". The whole first chapter focuses entirely on the house, foregrounding it as a central character. In this novel, as in

Sunlight on a Broken Column, the house itself is under threat. Earlier, in both *Sunlight on a Broken Column* and *Remember the House* illness and death of the patriarch signal the end of a particular era and lifestyle. Here, similarly, modernity or development threatens the house as it threatens a particular haveli life-style in Rama Mehta's *Inside the Haveli*. Architecturally, in *A Matter of Time* the era of big sprawling houses is over. It was unique for its size and for the period when it was built. Now, like other houses in the neighbourhood, it will be razed to make way for high rise apartments. But the real threat in the novel is not a dichotomous struggle of tradition versus modernity manifested in architectural style. The maleness of this house built by and for men is at risk: "It is obvious that it was built by a man not just for himself, but for his sons and his son's sons" (3). The daughters know that "the male child belongs" (71). Daughters are mere visitors passing through, almost "refugees" seeking shelter. Even if nothing is said, "the walls of this house that seems to cry out that the very reason for their existence was a son."(71)

The second section of the book begins with a quote from the *Brhad-aranyaka Upanishad* that reiterates the primacy of the male and particularly the father-son bond:

Whatever wrong has been done by him,
his son frees him from it all;
therefore he is called a son. By his
son a father stands firm in this world.

In this home though, there is no son to free the father or enable him to stand firm. In fact, there was only one son in three generations and he was lost at an early age. However, the premise of the family and home as a male space is reiterated in entitling the second section "The Family". But again it is craftily undermined by the fact that women provide the continuity in this house built by men for men. The three generations of women who live here make this house a home. Classical Indian texts prescribed four stages of man's existence—childhood, student, householder and renunciation. The transition from one stage to another is meant to be timely and appropriate. *A Matter of Time* opens with a quote from the *Brhad-aranyaka Upanishad* about leaving the householder stage. The irony of the particular renunciations in this novel is their untimeliness. Neither of the two men who renounce their home and family have in fact fulfilled their duties as householders.

The story is quite simple. Sumi's husband Gopal announces that he is leaving home. Sumi and her two daughters Aru and Charu return to live in her parental home in "the big house" next door. In many ways Sumi's return is a replay of her mother's untold story. Kalyani too had come back to this, her parental home, when her husband had abandoned her. And, although her husband returns, he lives apart in a room at the top of the house, never speaking to his wife although the charade of family life is carried on. His daughter, Sumi, comes to terms with her existence as a single mother and abandoned wife in her natal home, where she also finds her vocation as a writer and teacher. She takes up a job in a different city but just before her planned departure both she and her father are killed in an accident.

The location of the natal and marital homes in both *A Matter of Time* and Shama Futehally's *Tara Lane* is interesting in that the marital homes exist almost in the shadow of the natal homes. The lessons of one house are carried to the other, even if marriage may have been a way to escape those patterns. In fact, when Sumi tries to conceptualise her ideal house she finds that she unconsciously but repeatedly sketches her natal home:

> It is as if there is a tracing of this house already on the paper, on any paper that she begins to draw on and the lines she draws have no choice but to follow that unseen tracing. (78)

The watermark of this particular natal home is exactly what we see in the larger context of the haveli typology that seems to shape bungalows and apartments too. In Sumi's case this curious return to the Bachelardian idea of childhood homes of happiness is odd because she, in fact, marries to escape the pattern of domesticity of her parental home. Sumi returns to the natal home because she has nowhere else to go. In confronting her mother's story and her childhood, she finds herself and is able to leave her natal home. This text, like the others, does not allow an escape from the past: the past has to be confronted and transcended. But her death at the moment of acceptance and self realization is puzzling as is the fact that she and her father die at the same time.[9]

In Shama Futehally's *Tara Lane* too, the natal home is the blueprint for the marital home. But Tara's move from her natal family to establish her own nuclear family is an extension rather than a rupture. *Tara Lane* is a sort of coming of age story of Tahera or Tara, as she is called, the elder daughter of a rich Muslim family. She is torn between loyalty to her parents and their privileged position and a new world order. Her marriage to a very 'suitable boy,' Rizwan, and the birth of her son promise a continuity with her feudal lifestyle. But corruption and chicanery are the hallmark of independent India. The family-owned factory is a reminder that her privilege is enabled by the work of others. The men in the family—father, uncle, brother and then husband—have to deal with officials who have to be bribed and with labourers who strike to demand better working conditions. Tara and the older generation face the stark choice of moving with the times and compromising their idealistic standards or going under. Home, as the woman's sphere, is Tara's only refuge where the confusion of changing times can be kept at bay. But this comes at a price. As a married woman Tara discovers that marriage requires complete obedience to the husband. Her cocooned lifestyle is possible only if she learns to willingly close her eyes and accept a narrower horizon.

Githa Hariharan's *The Thousand Faces of Night* (1992), which won the Commonwealth Prize for the best first novel, presents and rejects three different kinds of houses. In the first, the protagonist Devi leaves the house of anonymity in the United States to return to the cultural conformity of the Indian house of her mother aptly named after the mythological

Sita of the *Ramayana*. Her reintegration to the community is completed by the arranged marriage that moves her from her mother's house to her husband's home. Her mother-in-law Parvati had abandoned the care of this home to the servant Mayamma. The penniless and abandoned Mayamma who had fulfilled her duties to an abusive husband, mother-in-law and a wastrel of a son lovingly tends this home that is her refuge. But a lonely Devi is torn between the traditional stories of submissive, dutiful wives in her marital home and the stories of women warriors that were a staple of her childhood. Her father-in-law's stories of womanly conformity of heroines like Sita and Savitri are balanced by the remembered stories told by her grandmother of heroines like Amba who tenaciously braved all odds and finally succeeded in exacting their revenge. Finally, Devi also flees the marital home as her husband's mother had done before her. Parvati had left her home for Kashi the place of pilgrimages, whereas Devi abandons both her husband and her lover to reclaim her mother's home. However, to accommodate Devi, both Sita and her home change radically.

In all five novels, the home, a microcosm of a society, is seen as a male space. The patterns of patriarchy and women's roles are learnt in natal homes and carried forward into marital homes. But whereas in natal homes innocence protected the young protagonists, in their marital homes they have to take a conscious stand to either continue or alter the inherited pattern. Anita Nair's, *Ladies Coupe* is different in that she does not set up her own marital home but her future home whether as a single or a married woman will be dramatically different from the patriarchal home she has headed. The future homes of each of the protagonists are predicated on their natal homes which subtly orient future directions.

Bungalow

Marriage is seen as a first step in the creation of a nuclear home. In the conjugal home wifely conformity and obedience are often the price of status and security. The marital home is often a contested site between the cultural group ethos of the haveli dwellings and the more modern, post-colonial, individualistic notions of bungalow homes. These novels, while confirming the centrality of the marital relationship and home, also insist upon a closer scrutiny of the power relations that underlie familial and conjugal relationships.

Peter Berger delineates the dialectic relationship between the individual and the world as a mutually shaping process that enables the individual to make sense of the world and his place in it.[10] Berger and Kellner focus on the family as a microcosm and suggest that within this larger socio-cultural ideology, an essential function of marriage is its "crucial nomic instrumentality." Marriage is a socially sanctioned cornerstone of adulthood that offers protection against an ever-threatening anomie, or chaos. Marriage, they suggest, brings together the sacred, ritual, social, sexual, spiritual and emotional aspects of human nature. In choosing each other as creators and protectors of their joint reality through marriage, the couple, according to Berger and Kellner, becomes "the social site for the processes of romantic love, sexual fulfilment, self-discovery and self-realisation through love and sexuality"[11] which, aside from procreation, is the dominant themes of the marriage ideology. They see the marital partnership as "an ongoing conversation" (21), which validates each individual and his perception of reality.[12] The new conversation initiated by each couple is the "crystallisation of a so-called private sphere of existence" (22). They note that it is in this marital, domestic and private sphere "that the individual will seek power, intelligibility and, quite literally, a name, ... a world in which, consequently, he [sic] is somebody — perhaps even, within its charmed circle, a *lord and master*" (23) (emphasis mine).

Since Ernest Burgess' formulation of the family as "a unity of interacting personalities,"[13] most subsequent studies of the family have privileged the notion of family as a unit without considering either individual personalities or gender relationships. As the unit-identity is seen as more important than that of the individuals forming it, the assumption is that a family's identity is the result of an implicitly equal and mutual negotiation. In this context, Berger and Kellner's individual subject stands as a universal figure stripped of class, gender or hierarchy. They ignore that an individual's position within the family or even society is critically affected by age, class and gender. They allow for some variations but assume that the aberrations are individual idiosyncrasies. The systemic and inbuilt inequality of the family structure is not questioned by them or generally. In the Indian context the nostalgic remembering of the seeming solidity of the joint family, the "we-self" idea merges with gender specific notions of womanly sacrifice. The family becomes the raison d'etre of all existence, especially for women. Because Berger and Kellner, among many others, view the individual subject as genderless they do not see the gender inequality embedded in the institutions of marriage and family. However, in these novels the family is often portrayed as structurally imbalanced because of unequal gender relations.

Indo-English women's novels focus on the unequal partnership that slants the marital conversation. The family in these novels is seen as structurally imbalanced because of unequal gender relations. The authors insist on asking who has the right to speak and under what circumstances, and who listens?[14] The novels show that in the context of an unbalanced relationship, the only "conversation" permissible might be one that affirms the status quo. The idealised view of marriage as a safe haven neglects to question for whom it is a safe haven. The institution of marriage or the family as a unit may serve as a shield against anomie when pitted against a threatening "outside", but it does not consider the possibility of anomie within. The home is generally seen as a female space. Witold Rybczynski, Professor of Urbanism, links domesticity to the "feminization" of the home. He notes that in seventeenth century Europe, the idea of the home as an intimate space was also linked to "the growing awareness of individuality—of a growing personal inner life."[15] The woman or wife is generally placed at the center of the home and as a creator of the sanctuary, as Parvati is in *The Thousand Faces of Night*. But by the same token, it does not necessarily ensure her an un-qualified place in the sanctuary. Her individuality or inner life is, in fact, erased at the altar of family life just as it is for other wives in these novels. Within this enclosed domestic space, which in Indo-English literature is envisaged as both nest and prison, marriage becomes a socially sanctioned way of implicitly empowering a particular individual — the hus-band — to become "a lord and master." The home, be it a haveli or a bungalow, is indeed *his* castle that the lord and master both rules and protects at his whim.

Women in both *Tara Lane* and *Ladies Coupe* clearly recognise and even articulate the mantra of wifehood. Akhila's mother teaches her the rules:

> First of all, no good wife could serve two masters – the mas-ters being her father and her husband. A good wife learnt to put her husband's interests before anyone else's, even her father's. A good wife listened to her husband and did as he said. 'There is no such thing as an equal marriage' ... 'It is best to accepts that the wife is inferior to the husband. That way, there can be no strife, no disharmony. ... A woman is not meant to take on a man's role. (14)

And yet in Akhila's case specifically she is asked to or rather forced to take on a man's role in one sphere—provid-ing for the family. And yet she is denied male freedom in travel, sexuality or decision making. She is also completely denied the female gendered roles of wife and mother. Women or rather wives, in the other novels are financially, emotion-ally, or socially dependent and are the more vulnerable part-ner. But in Akhila's case, although she is the bread-winner and supports the family financially, she is rendered more vul-nerable by being excluded from both male and female spheres.

In a patriarchal society a successful marriage is predicated upon woman's vulnerability and upon her subordinate status vis-à-vis her husband. Amita Tyagi Singh and Patricia Uberoi's observation about short romance fiction applies equally to a novel like *Tara Lane*:

...reconciling love and marriage in this romance fiction is not a question of reconciling a woman to her mother-in-law, but rather of reconciling a woman to her loss of autonomy, individuality and selfhood in relation to her husband.[16]

The structural inequality of this kind of marriage relegates women to a separate sphere where she is enfeebled by the protective care bestowed upon her. Tara discovers that negotiating a balance, even in a nuclear home with two people, can be full of pitfalls. No border crossings are allowed and each demands uncompromising loyalty: "What I was not prepared for was finding that I had to be entirely with him or entirely apart" (86). Not only do institutions like marriage create binary male and female spheres, they also necessitate a choice between fathers' homes and husbands' homes.

Separate Spheres

Overstepping the mutually reinforcing boundaries of class and gender spells danger for Tara. Her existence is premised on a clear cut spatial demarcation between her home and the factory and the street that links them all together. She is particularly aware of the chasm of class and gender that isolates her from others, even in her own lane. The "main part" of Tara Lane was "crowded, squalid, and so shamingly the truth; here was no pleasant disguise of front lawns" (10). The bungalow lawns, the distancing device that separated the colonials from the locals in earlier times, here also mark the distance between the rich and the poor. Although the factory is the source of Tara's family's wealth, it is so "other" that it constantly threatens to engulf her own reality. The ugly main part of the street is more terrifyingly "the truth" and real to Tara than her own home; consequently her need to cling to home is greater. The separate spheres ideology of the public arena of work and politics being a male sphere and the domestic or the home being the private arena of the female are deeply ingrained in Tara. Maintaining the separation and distance between the home and the world are key to her sense of well being.

The separation between classes in *Tara Lane* is often translated as differences between male and female spheres. Edwin

Ardener draws male and female cultures as two overlapping circles where the common middle ground is shared territory.[17] For Tara, however, the overlap is a site of confusion; male and female spaces appear conflictual and she strives to keep them apart. As a child, the factory and her home formed the two ends of her world. She is precariously stretched between the two, afraid and vulnerable. Futehally, however, suggests that one cannot ignore the points of intersection. The factory, located at the end of Tara Lane, is by its very name, integral to and as inseparably a part of Tara as is the main, posh part of the lane. She tries to maintain the distinction between her home and the factory but the lane bearing her name connects her to both the squalor of the factory and the posh elegance of her home. Not surprisingly, the only haven in the factory is her father's air-conditioned, wall-to-wall-carpeted office right at the top. Placing the office at the top marks its dominant status just as much as its separation and isolation from the actual working area does. The same spatial and class distance was evident in *Inside the Haveli* where the Rana's palace on the hilltop dominates the landscape.

Feudal harmony in *Tara Lane* rests on the same foundations as marital harmony, and both stem from the consent to an unequal relationship. Futehally seems to suggest that an acceptance of one's place is essential for ensuring the status quo: "it was silently clear again that all the cares of the world rested on the men's shoulders and we had no business to ask or look askance or criticize." (150) Unless Tara is prepared to face the chaos of overlapping spheres and risk striking out without the cushioning of wealth and status, she has to accept the strict separation and the resultant silencing. After Tara marries, the spaces of the home and the factory resolve themselves as men's and women's separate worlds. Just as the plush office was indisputably her father's and then her husband's sphere, the home is her mother's and her sphere. The male sphere is posited as the outside, or *bahir*, the world that men have to deal with. The factory, which in Tara's mind is associated with noise, dirt and commerce, is the embodiment of the male sphere. In contrast, Tara's mother's home, like her own, symbolises the female sphere of domesticity, interiority, quiet and beauty. The male world of strife, noise and commerce, albeit filtered through the air-conditioner, is not allowed to enter the home. The peace of this home, however, is dependent upon the noise of the factory, just as the welfare of the workers and their families is contingent upon Tara's family's feudal goodwill.

In *Culture and Imperialism*, Edward Said reveals how imperialism has to be read between the lines, especially in colonial texts.[18] Said notes that Jane Austen's *Mansfield Park*, for instance, has to be read not purely as a domestic novel but "contrapuntally." Mansfield Park owes its existence to lands held in the colonies. These other lands, though never directly mentioned, enable a genteel English lifestyle. Futehally, on the other hand, overtly insists on underlining the interdependence between the feudally run factory and the home. The end of feudalism, however, is not marked by an exhilarating moment of a throwing off of shackles.[19] Futehally's novel, written well after Indian independence (1947), the Emergency (1975-77), the anti-Sikh riots (1984) and the destruction of the Babri Masjid (1992), presents the post-independence phase as a creeping malady of petty corruption of labour leaders and the new generation of owners. Tara's uncle, brother, and husband are all implicated in the prevailing corruption but despite her ostrich like stance Tara recognises her own complicity.

Women often collude in both the acceptance of inequality and in the creation of a particular version of home as the male lair. The subordinate position of both women and servants makes them the silent mainstay of these homes. In *The Thousand Faces of Night* the moment of this almost seamless change of places is marked when Parvati hands the keys of the house to the servant Mayamma. She says, "You know how to look after him [her husband], and keep him comfortable" (63). The transition points to the primacy of the gendered role of the wife over the individual wife—Parvati—in the home. It is reminiscent of the continuity insisted upon in Kunwarani Sa's automatically lighting the puja lamp after Bhaba Sa's death (*Inside the Haveli*). The narrator does not imply that Mayamma will take Parvati's place as a wife. But the wife's role is so diminished of emotional content that it is implied that a housekeeper can fulfil it adequately. By installing the destitute Mayamma in her place, Parvati clearly suggests that security is the main reason for a woman to accept this kind of a relationship. For Mayamma, fleeing from her own marital home, the house on Jacaranda Road provides a refuge. Ironically, as a servant in the house, Mayamma finds it a safe haven and an emotional anchor, whereas as the wives, both Parvati and Devi need to flee.

Arlie Hochschild convincingly argues that women, even in the commercial world, are socialised to nurture in order to compensate for their subordinate position. She links subordination and nurture rather than the commonly accepted essentialist link between femaleness and nurture. Hochschild suggests that women tend to offer "emotional labour," which in the context of novels can be read as maintaining a specific idea of home, as a "trade for economic support."[20] The links between women and domesticity also underscores the idea that nurture is not only woman's nature but also her job. A woman's "job," as Hariharan and Futehally illustrate, is making the home a retreat from the commerce and strife of the outside world for the husband or for the "family." We would do well to remember, however, that no union laws or minimum wages are guaranteed in this particular "job." Women's interrogation of their specific role and stake in these structures tends to upset the status quo. As long as the familial unit affirms and sustains a basically patriarchal ideology, the traditional family is seen to be strong: indeed, it may even hold anomie at bay. The price of self-effacement paid by women, particularly, regardless of class or race, has been internalised by women themselves as duty, tradition, and nature.

Marital Homes

Tara (*Tara Lane*) clearly views marriage as "nomos building" or as a bridge that brings two families of similar social status and backgrounds together. The new unit extends and replicates the familial unit. In the Bergerian vision the marital

unit is a process in the mutual construction of social norms —
between individuals and society. It is a way to order the world
in a meaningful way so as to shield oneself from anomie.[21]
Even as a child Tara avers, "Life, I knew, was like a piece of
cloth which was stretched too thin, so that at any moment
you could discover a large hole underneath you" (12). She's
haunted by the fear of either falling off the edge or tearing
the thin fabric of the sheet anchored by family and class that
will cast her out to the chaos that lurks everywhere. The fabric image, interestingly, is repeated in *A Matter of Time* and
the social approbation of facing the crisis as part of a nuclear
family as opposed to a joint family is felt intensely:

> There was a time when a man could have walked out of his
> home and the seamless whole of the joint family would have
> enclosed his wife and children, covered his absence. Now
> the rent in the fabric, gaping wide, is there for all to see.
> (*A Matter of Time*, 13-14)

Sumi does not leave the marriage of her own will but she
does have to deal with the emotional, social and financial consequences of creating a new home on her own without a husband. In the bungalow existence women are more vulnerable
and alone than in the haveli existence. Men's leaving is more
disruptive in the bungalow and women, distanced from family
and focused primarily on the nuclear family, may have less of a
support system. In the nuclear family bungalow women like
Sumi, Tara, Devi or Akhila have to figure out a different support network and have to learn to be much more self-reliant.

In *Tara Lane*, marriage, both as a social institution and as a
personal relationship, is invested with the power to patch,
reinforce and enlarge this precious fabric. But the fabric itself
is anchored by adherence to social rules. Conformity to a strict
demarcation of gender and class spheres will, Tara feels, protect her from the chaos that lurks around the corner. Conformity, "the propriety of it all" (66), thrills Tara. Her engagement ceremony is the acme of familial solidarity and a testimony to unquestioning acceptance and integration. "Wasn't

it all, after all, for this, for this closeness, for this rightness, for this intimate delight?" (68) The "it" referred to is not just her particular marriage but also the way in which a respectful acceptance of conventions can lead to a spirit of community where one can be sure of one's place. In this context, the ease with which her comradeship shifts almost imperceptibly from her sister Munni to her husband Rizwan is unsurprising: "In this new situation where there was no Munni, there was he instead; effortlessly, unasked. He had smiled with understanding and there I was, safe" (71). Safety is a recurring motif and concern for all the women protagonists but for Tara it borders on the obsessive. Marriage and conformity to rules will be her talisman against the fall into chaos and lower class status. She seeks protection in the clear demarcation of boundaries between male and female, rich and poor, the comfort of the known and the fear of the unknown. In her parental home her innocence as a child protects her from the knowledge of patriarchy and class privilege but in the marital home she, like the mythological Gandhari, has to willingly blindfold herself to the reality of her existence or to rock the boat and in some way opt out. The easy passage from Munni to Rizwan is replicated concretely by the positioning of Tara's natal and marital homes. A short walk through the garden links her marital home to her mother's home like an elongated umbilical cord. Tara, unlike Sumi or Akhila' cannot or is unwilling to give up familial and class privilege and so settles for the much narrower existence required of her.

Tara's world insists on a conflation of class and gender as the women's sphere. *Khandani* women or women with a lineage inhabit and shape this precious domestic front with its attention to details of flower arrangements and comfortable living. Tara's joyful acceptance of the marriage proposal from Rizwan's family is an affirmation of social and familial continuity. Marriage integrates her and assures her a place in the social system in her own right. Tara feels an instant affinity with Rizwan and his family:

And if we had all been photographed just then, at exactly the
second when the young man [Rizwan] laughed and
disclaimed, the photograph would have shown a oneness, a
feeling of belonging together, a oneness as delicate and excit-
ing as the arrangement of lady's-lace on my mother's dining-
table. (61)

She feels this sense of connection even before she realises
that Rizwan's family had come on an inspection visit to look
her over as a prospective bride for their son. The simile of the
"lady's-lace" arrangement is, of course, indicative of wealth
and a certain culture, but it also signals careful cultivation, fore-
thought, and fragility. A flower arrangement, consciously as-
sembled to decorate, is hardly a serendipitous meeting of souls.
It is meant to suggest the artificiality of the meeting. It is difficult to tell if Tara's excitement stems from the sheer craft of
such seemingly effortless harmony. But the perfect flower arrangement evoked suggests a perfect (arranged) marriage. The
arrangement itself seems to have become invested with the
aura of the togetherness of the living room. However one
chooses to read the simile, it is clear that Tara lays great store by
both familial solidarity and wealth, and the arrangement
symbolises both. An embarrassed Tara acknowledges that "some-
where in the background the thought that Rizwan's family had a
car and house and servants just like ours" (66) is reassuring. This
similarity of background helps conquer the niggling doubt —
the ever present "worm" of her conscience – "that I was taking
an easy way out of something or other" (66). The "something or
other" that she is opting out of is an assumption of responsibility, individual independence and a poorer everyday material
existence. She is honest enough to admit that the dusty bus ride
in search of a job had so exhausted her that she had to return in
a taxi. Similarity of class, religious and cultural backgrounds is a
recurrent theme in Futehally. Her short story, "Portrait of a Childhood," which in many ways resembles *Tara Lane*, clearly delineates the "uncomprehended gap" between the narrator's family
and others in terms of class and culture. This gap recalls the tear
in the fabric that so haunts an anxious Tara.[22]

But it is the niggling worm of doubt that also forces Tara to repeatedly equate marriage with some kind of an enfeebling illness. Tara sees the adult world as a sharing in misery; for her, marriage is not necessarily associated with adulthood. Marriage, like childhood, is another kind of retreat and dependency: "I could step quickly back into the warm, muffling quilt which was my marriage" (130). Marriage provides Tara a certain protection from the pain of adulthood, which she describes as "steadily acquiring a cold in the head" (49). The metaphor of illness notwithstanding, marriage is still figured as a buffer against the feared outside. Although it may be confined, dependent, and muffled, like the feeling of having a head cold, this is the world that promises Tara security. She does not question the dependence too closely. After their first and only altercation regarding the running of the factory, Tara assures herself and Rizwan, "Never would I forget my place again" (86). Her acculturation into adulthood and marriage has been the gradual stilling of her conscience. She notes her subtle recasting: "I was no longer the sort of wife who would ask questions which were not wanted" (92). In neither her paternal nor her marital homes has Tara been equipped to be her own person. She notes sadly, "The instinct that had made me think of marriage as a warm bath had been right — you were either inside it or freezing outside" (86). All Tara's analogies are domestic — the cocooning comforts of "muffling quilts" and "warm baths." The only two choices that she sees open to her are the dichotomous *ghar – bahir*, safe inside the home or vulnerable outside it. Education and class, which should have prepared her to step out confidently into a changing world, in fact seem to underline her dependence on the protection of men. Tara's story could be read as a process of deliberate moulding by individual mothers, like Sita in *The Thousand Faces of Night* who attempts to "train" her daughter as she does her bonsai plants; or by an acceptance and internalization of social norms as in the case of Baba, (*Remember the House*) Geeta (*Inside the Haveli*) and Tara who are eminently trainable and are gradually assimilated and acculturated into the prevailing ideology of womanhood. Akhila, Sumi, Parvati, Devi, and even Sita of an earlier generation,however, decide to finally opt out of the unequal relationships imposed by society.

As a protective gesture born of their own experiences some older women like the mothers in *Thousand Faces of Night*, *A Matter of Time* and *Tara Lane* try to teach their daughters the strict lessons of conformity. How does a woman who believes that marital harmony is based on a clear division of labour reconcile the irreconcilable? The reconciliation, if it has to happen, will necessarily reverberate in other spheres like the home. Having invested so deeply in a particular version of home, can Tara or her mother afford to rock the boat? In fact, neither Tara nor her mother is in the end, able to come to terms with the blurring of boundaries. If wealth and privilege in the commercial world are maintained by monetary bribes, then, Tara and her mother's compliance and submission to patriarchal domestic rules can also be read as the equivalent of accepting a different kind of a bribe. It could be argued that this silent acceptance may be their only survival tactic. But then that is exactly Rizwan's argument too, that in this new India it is impossible to run a business without bribery. In *Tara Lane*, as in the other novels, the home and the world are deeply intertwined.

Jacaranda and Gulmohar

But some women old and young do opt out or try and find an alternate version of home. Unlike Tara neither Sita nor her daughter Devi (*The Thousand Faces of Night*), accept the structural inequality of married life. To all outward appearances, Sita, like her namesake of the *Ramayana*, is the paragon of wifely duty, but it is not the *Ramayana* story of the dutiful wife who follows her husband into exile that is recounted here. This Sita is in fact linked to the fierce Gandhari of the *Mahabharata*. In the original version, Gandhari is portrayed as the perfect wife who, upon discovering that her husband is blind, blindfolds herself so she has no advantage over him. Similarly, Devi's mother metaphorically blindfolds herself by giving up her music. This gifted veena player tears out the strings of the veena, forsaking it for the pots and pans of domesticity. Sita's guiding motto of "Good housekeeping, good taste, hard work" (101) have been achieved with a determined penance like that of Amba in the epic *Mahabharata*, and "[o]nly Sita knew what relentless self-discipline had gone into the making of a perfect housekeeper, a blameless wife" (101). Sita's mother-in-law, Devi's grandmother accurately interprets these gestures not as signs of giving up or acquiescence but of changing the rules of the game. In her version, the motivating factor for both young wives — Gandhari and her own daughter-in-law — is not a passive acceptance of fate but a quiet, channelled, white-hot fury to perfect the assigned role.

Women's sexuality and its control though never overtly mentioned are at the core of familial relationships. In havelis and bungalows the patriarchal control of women's sexuality demarcates "good" women from "bad" women and in *Remember the House* a line is also drawn between Indian and Western attitudes towards love and marriage. In *Sunlight on a Broken Column* both Laila and Nandi's transgression revolves around the issue of sexuality. In *Ladies Coupe* Akhila's moment of "liberation" is the very male gesture of having casual sex with a stranger she has picked up. In contrast, her inheriting her father's mantle and having the male role of the family breadwinner thrust upon her, is seen in terms of the gendered stereotype of womanly self-sacrifice for the family. Her moment of sexual transgression is much more deliberate and self-aware. She also knows that this one act will place her on the other side of the *Lakshmana Rekha*. She franchises the boundary internalised by a majority of Indian women at least in the fiction of the eighties and nineties.

For Sita's daughter Devi in *The Thousand Faces of Night* the gulmohur and jacaranda trees become symbols of the choices she has to make in her marital home. The home itself is identified by its location on Jacaranda Road: the jacaranda's soft, hazy lavender blossoms surround the home, creating a peaceful haven for her gentle father-in-law who is steeped in ancient texts. This home is protected and cherished by the ser-

vant Mayamma. In the garden the gulmohur's deep, green
leaves and flaming orange blossoms offer a different promise
to the young, new bride. They recall the sensual youthfulness
of Devi's childhood companion the orphaned Annapurna. Devi
and Annapurna were joined at one level by their youth and at
another level—along with Devi's father—in their rejection of
Sita's strict discipline and effacement of self to duty.
Annapurna exemplifies an instinctive sexuality and passion
that Sita had sacrificed at the altar of wifehood. Sita, quick to
sense the potential threat in Annapurna's "unruly laughter"
(76) which fills her house, banishes her.

Devi's choices are stark. In choosing the jacaranda hues of
her marital home she accepts her mother's path of angry self-
sacrifice. In choosing the gulmohar however, Devi will redeem the pledge of nascent sexuality associated with
Annapurna. They had become blood sisters, as young girls do,
by pricking their fingers: "we stood on the *kolam* by the tulasi
plant and joined wounds together" (76). "The wound" that links
them across class backgrounds can be read both in terms of
their joint victim status as women, as well as unexpressed female sexuality. Although Devi's descriptions are couched in
the traditional metaphor of Indian love poetry and the boundaries of her feelings for this sister/ally are blurred, the sexuality is unmistakable. The discomfort with an acknowledgement
of sexuality is discussed in all the novels. Sumi (*A Matter of
Time*) re-writing a *Ramayana* story realises, "[F]emale sexuality.
We're ashamed of owning it, we can't speak of it, not even to
our own selves." (191) Men, and patriarchal society, threatened by overt female sexuality, have found ways of confining
it within the bounds of the jacaranda-like marital homes of duty
and reinforced by ancient myths and legends.

It is not coincidental that Devi recalls Annapurna at the
moment when the conscientious nest-building sparrows offer
a visual example of her future in the Jacaranda Road house.
She yearns for the passion of the gulmohur that she has been
denied — both as a child when her mother banished

Annapurna, and in her marriage, where her dull, corporate husband and the still security offered by the house suffocate her. The music of her lover-to-be, Gopal, wafting across the garden awakens her body. But her childhood friend Annapurna is recalled as the guide who will lead the way out of her jacaranda-curtained, gentle, "lush prison" into a world of risk and passion where "only the gulmohur blossoms fill the air with their noise of ripe colour" (78).

An unmarried Akhila (*Ladies Coupe*) has to sacrifice even the kind of sanctioned sexuality available to Tara (*Tara Lane*). The "heterosexual romance," Adrienne Rich notes, "has been represented as the great female adventure, duty, and fulfillment," and this is the promise fulfilled for Tara but is denied to Akhila. Certainly class and social status are key to the difference between Akhila and Tara.[23] Tara's sexual awakening is prefigured by her reading of D.H. Lawrence's *Sons and Lovers*. Lawrence's intensely male model of sexuality is part of Tara's "alternative world" (52) supplied by books. Lawrence's work, like the other texts she reads, adds another layer of romantic expectation to her already protected existence. Tara's description of the world of fiction – "like a film of gossamer, another world had descended from the air to cover the world I knew" (53) — hints at her awareness of its ephemerality. Economic necessity, on the other hand, forces Akhila into a more public, male world of earning a living. Her sexual awakening is a passive, secretive acceptance of furtive male groping in a crowded bus. The direct, public and tawdry experience leaves her feeling ashamed and unclean. Tara's appreciation of her sexuality, on the other hand, recalls the appropriate perfection of the flower arrangement and is well within the bounds of propriety that her background permits: "It was a miracle to me that so much joy could be without sin. But so it was; my married status proclaimed it, the family sanctioned it, the servants tiptoed away to allow it." (80) Akhila is barred from this world both because of class and because although she has crossed over to the male public sphere of existence she is still circumscribed by female norms of acceptable behaviour. As a woman in this male sphere Akhila denies her sexuality, her dreams of a higher education, marriage, colourful clothing and travel. Tara accepts the inequality of the marriage partnership because her one dusty, bus ride and search for a job have shown her that she is not equipped to survive independently. Sumi (*A Matter of Time*), who seems to have known sexual fulfillment, has to be jolted out of her quiet complacency to discover her place in the world as a woman alone. She seems to have indeed found a way of mapping her destiny and steps out confidently, only to be cruelly killed in an accident. Maybe Deshpande was unsure of a woman's ability to find her place without a man in an unequal society.

Jodi Ideology

It is possible to hold society at large – both women and men — responsible for women's suppression, as Anita Desai does. In an article entitled "A Secret Connivance," she asserts,

> There is a subtle, deep-rooted form of suppression, a secret connivance at the taking away of freedom for which I cannot blame the present or even the past regime, and for which a whole society, and its entire history with its burden of custom and tradition must be indicted.[24]

Desai claims that although there is no governmental suppression of freedom of speech in India, society, history and tradition can be held responsible for the silencing of women. She further surmises that men alone cannot be blamed for this oppression and explores some of the reasons why a woman "even when spirited and brave, adheres to the archetype."[25] Tracing the female lineage from Durga to Sita she concludes, "The myth keeps her [woman] bemused, bound hand and foot."[26] Questioning the myth, Desai avers, would be tantamount to "attacking the legend" that is the cornerstone of Indian family and society. Religion and gender scholar Julia Leslie, also claims that these myths are so much a part of an Indian woman's make-up that rejecting the myth becomes tantamount to rejecting herself. Those who resist the Sita model, she argues, "are resisting not only aspects of Indian culture but, in a very real sense, parts of themselves." [27]

Leslie concurs with activist Madhu Kishwar who notes that,

> the pervasive popular cultural ideal of womanhood has become a death trap for too many of us. It is woman as a selfless giver, someone who gives and gives endlessly, gracefully, smilingly, whatever the demand, however unreasonable and however harmful to herself. . . . Sita, Savitri, Anasuya and various other mythological heroines are used as the archetypes of such a woman and women themselves are deeply influenced by this cultural ideal. (46)[28]

However, Kishwar's current writing contradicts this earlier position. She now seems to suggest that myths and Sita-type role models are not "death traps" but rather, valid role models. The novels, for their part, indicate that Desai's view of women's "complicity" in their own subordination and silencing is more complicated than Desai would have us believe. All the stories in *Ladies Coupe* for instance are a testimony to the subtle ways in which women renegotiate the marital power balance. Desai concedes that women do not question the myth of womanhood because they may be fearful or emotionally and financially dependent, or because they have internalised patriarchal ideology. She accuses women writers, in particular, for failing to provide alternative myths. In a century where the "literature of self-analysis and psychology" has come into its own, she castigates Indian women writers for producing "a curious sameness of tone — melancholy, complaining, tearful."[29]

Sudhir Kakar, a well known writer and a practising clinical psychologist specialising in dysfunctional relations between men and women within and without the family, lays the blame on the Indian cultural ideology of the *jodi* or couple. He suggests that in fiction as in life, the all pervasive *jodi* ideology which even transcends class barriers, has been so internalised that it prevents women from leaving even unhappy or abusive marital homes. He notes that the yearning, particularly of the wife, for the "jodi" or couple is paramount:

"the intense wish to create a two-person universe with the husband where each finally 'recognizes' the other, is never far from her consciousness." (22) The cultural image of the couple, Kakar notes, is iconically represented by the *ardhanarishwara*, the half-man half-woman form of Lord Shiva; and in literature the stories of *pativrata* or devoted wives like Sita and Savitri have been held up as guides and models for the relationship between women and men. But the novels do not endorse the explanatory function of Kakar's work; while they are interested in the broader cultural inquiry inscribed in Kakar's discussion of individual psyches, they also question and critique his quasi-positivist positions. The five narratives in the *Ladies Coupe* work around this model to renegotiate the wife's place in the marital relationship. In Devi's jacaranda home too, the choices between a traditional home of wifely duty even in a bungalow setting are pitted against a new reconfiguration of a space that can be a home for women like Devi and her mother Sita.

The yearning for *jodi* notwithstanding, the Indian couple situates itself within and as an integral part of the extended family structure. Kakar notes,

> ...the fantasy of constituting a "couple," not in opposition to
> the rest of the extended family but within this wider network,
> is a dominant theme running through women's lives, actual
> and fictional. (22)

In fact, the *Stridharamapaddhati*, the oldest extant treatise on the duties of a wife, unambiguously asserts the importance of the joint family over the joys and sorrows of individual women or men.[30] The centrality of the couple as a part of family and society, Kakar proposes, gives woman her sense of identity as specifically Indian and as a woman. In this context the heavy cultural baggage of the *jodi* and of a joint family ideology would necessarily be carried even into bungalow dwellings as it is for Baba in *Remember the House*.

Kakar concludes that,

> gender relations seem impelled more by hostility than ten-

derness or love. The fantasies entertained by each sex in relation to the other are pervaded as much by hatred and fear as
by desire and longing. (114)

Kakar presents the gap between a cultural ideal and individual reality as a partial explanation of the tenuous relationship between women and men. He even attributes the crucial
importance of the notion of *jodi* to the fact that many women
choose suffering or even suicide over opting out of a bad
marriage. But he, like Berger and Kellner, does not question
the in-built inequality in the institution of marriage or the fact
that women may not have a place outside of marriage. Even
an educated and affluent woman like Tara is afraid of life
outside marriage. But again, despite all odds women like Devi
do leave marital homes and unhappy marriages.

Escape

The word escape is used four times in the first page of
Anita Nair's, *Ladies Coupe*. In earlier times women were able
to escape the confines of marriage by opting for the life of a
religieuse as Parvati (*A Thousand Faces of Night*) and Baba's
mother (*Remember the House*) do. That was one of the few ways
open to women. But Kashi or any other place of pilgrimage is
not Akhila's destination. Unlike Baba's mother or Parvati or
Devi she is not escaping the marital home, but she does pose
the question of women's survival in a patriarchal society. All
the stories recounted in the ladies train compartment deal
with how these particular women escape or renegotiate their
marital lives and homes.

In *The Thousand Faces of Night* both daughters in law, Parvati
and Devi, reject their marital homes. Parvati fulfils her duties
by providing a home for her husband, children and the
servant Mayamma. But once the children are away at boarding
school she finds the marital home inadequate. Like Gopal (*A
Matter of Time*), she too, repudiates the role of the householder.
But the option of *sanyas* was not open to women. Gopal is cas-
tigated and criticised by others for abandoning his wife and
daughters but his wife Sumi realises that emotionally he is ready

for *sanyas*. She sees his leaving as a renunciation—the final phase of the four stages prescribed in a man's life. She cannot blame him because she feels it has very little to do with her or the marriage as such. Gopal's leaving the home can be framed or at least understood within the larger cultural context of following the traditionally accepted path— even though the timing is unfortunate. But the stages in women's lives did not follow the same trajectory. A woman was not always allowed an education and was never released from the householder stage. The few historical examples of women who did renounce the world like the Bhakti poet Mira are seen as exceptional. When Parvati (*The Thousand Faces of Night*) leaves her husband's jacaranda house it is framed in terms of taking on a male perogative: "She had, like a man in a self-absorbed search for a god, stripped herself of the life allotted to her, the life of a householder."(64) Parvati's renunciation of the role of a Grihalakshmi, or household goddess, is a rejection of Manu's prescriptive role for womanhood. A role extolled in all her husband's stories later narrated to Devi. Rejecting the role of the housewife that erases her as a person, Parvati has only one option: the life of a religieuse in a holy place.

Generational difference could be one factor in whether or not, and, how women are able to leave home. Baba's mother and Parvati are of an older generation and their example in a way paves the way for the younger Devi to leave. Sumi and Akhila step out more cautiously having gathered themselves together from within the security of the natal home and the ladies compartment. But for Tara (*Tara Lane*), class rather than age seems to be the key factor that narrows her world to domesticity and leads her to accept an unequal partnership. Tara is the outsider par excellence: a woman in a patriarchal society and a member of a minority Muslim community in a largely Hindu country, to whom the outside world poses an inchoate threat. Her family's wealth and privilege equally isolate her from the majority, whose precarious existence in the urban slums around Tara Lane are guilty reminders of her complicity in their poverty. As a woman, her life on the fringes of the lives of her father, brother and husband distance her even within the home. Tara is an onlooker rather than an active participant on Tara Lane. The association of her name— Tara—links her irrevocably with the street, which makes her feel that "it was *my* lane"(9). The identification also legitimizes her right to narrate the story of the lane. Possession, however, is only one part of this equation; the other part hints that real possession would be in leaving the security of the cocoon to gather in the whole reality of the street. Squalor, poverty and ugliness are as much a part of the lane as the elegant homes and shaded gardens. Can Tara bridge the distance between home and the world, rich and poor, and assume responsibility for both as her namesake lane does?

The roads in both Meena Alexander's *Nampally Road* and Shama Futehally's *Tara Lane* serve as contact points that connect different spaces. The centrality of the road is underlined as each is specifically named in the title of each novel. Tara Lane, like Nampally Road, insists upon a two-way traffic rather than a delimitation of space. The lanes in both novels offer the women protagonists a way out of the house and the domestic world, but with the assurance of a way back in. In *Nampally Road*, Mira, a single woman, realizes the full potential of the two-way traffic offered by the road whereas Tara, as a married woman, seems to need various refuges rather than the adventure of the open road.

Malashri Lal terms this crossing of boundaries the "law of the threshold."[31] Lal notes, "the threshold is a real as well as a symbolic bar marking a critical transition".[32] This law, she argues, allows men "multiple existences" between the home and the world, but women's lives are circumscribed only within the home. Stepping out of allotted gender roles is tantamount to "an act of transgression" that will firmly shut one door. Girlhood, in these novels, is a preparation to enter into the culturally privileged world of the married woman. The texts question Indian society's belief that a woman's ultimate role is that of a householder — a wife and a mother. Sita (*The Thousand Faces of Night*), for instance, is propelled to meticulously mould every detail of her daughter's life to achieve the "one straight path to a single goal, wifehood" (103) for which she had sacrificed herself. Sita and Tara are both fully aware of the sacrifice – the giving up of self that allows them, like other women, to don the mantle of wifehood. The realist Sita is not motivated by a blind faith in tradition; she knows from experience that this is probably the only way to give her daughter "the best of possible lives" (108). Often in these novels, older women—grandmothers, mothers or surrogate mother figures—transmit a strictly gendered and hierarchical notion of Indianness and womanhood to their daughters often as a gesture of protection. An inherited legacy that they have earlier imbibed from their mothers, from popular myths or experientially from the constraints of their own everyday lives has already prepared the ground for an often resigned acceptance of these norms. But daughters hear, interpret and internalise stories in their own ways. Stories, and especially women's stories, often inspire women to action and understanding. Both Devi (*The Thousand Faces of Night*) and Akhila (*Ladies Coupe*) deliberately recall and seek out a specifically womanly wisdom. Neither seeks the subterfuge of escaping to Kashi or some other place of pilgrimage. In fact it is to confront the question of living within and as a part of society with and without men, that Akhila poses the question of womanly survival to the five — mostly married women — in the ladies coupe.

In a novel like *Ladies Coupe* the segregated woman's space of the zenana is replicated in the ladies coupe of a moving train. But in the other novels too even though the physical space is not demarcated the woman to woman connection is clearly maintained across class and generation. Older women do attempt to mould younger women into patterns of conformity but women's stories are also ways of transmitting alternative knowledge and living patterns.

Stories and Storytellers

Charles Merewether explains the pivotal role of the storyteller as part of an "interpretive community," who enables change by processing and coming to terms with the past: "The storyteller was an agent of change and a translator of experience, who worked with the material of an oppressive past."[33] In both *The Thousand Faces of Night* and *Ladies Coupe*, storytelling and especially women's stories are the agents of change that allow women to escape. The 'women only' space of the haveli's zenana is replicated literally in the physical space of the 'ladies compartment', as it is in the three generations of women who live in the big house in *A Matter of Time* and in Devi's final homecoming to her mother's house by the sea in *The Thousand Faces of Night*. In *Ladies Coupe* the five narratives could almost be read as separate short stories but each one is deliberately instructive and in response to the protagonist's question. Each offers a specific glimpse into the life of one woman, though each woman's story can become part of a larger canvas of how women negotiate issues of independence, sexuality, rape and ambition within their marriages. Their didactic intent links them to each other and to the protagonist Akhila's question of whether a woman can live alone, just as it links these stories intertextually to those in *The Thousand Faces of Night*.

Each house that Devi (*The Thousand Faces of Night*) inhabits comes replete with a storyteller as guide; the specific stories of and in that house form its grid. The "prelude" of the novel highlights the significance of the "story" as instructions on becoming "a woman warrior"(41). The invocation of Maxine Hong Kingston's novel *The Woman Warrior: Memoirs of a Girlhood Among Ghosts* recalls that these are instructions on the various ways of being a woman but each one is a fighting woman who does not passively accept her fate.[34] Kingston's stories are told in an immigrant context by a Chinese mother to her daughter in America as a means of providing a cultural framework. The purpose of both storytellers (Devi's grandmother and the mother in *The Woman Warrior*) is to provide a connection with the larger ethno-cultural and gender context to the next generation who might be distanced from it either geographically or temporally. The stories become one, among other models, of how they too can be integrated into the larger fabric of society without necessarily being suffocated by it. Both Kingston's and Hariharan's books are dedicated to their parents, reiterating that outside of the text too; legacy and continuity are crucial elements in these storytellings. Devi's prefers "the story that comes whole and well-rounded, complete with annotation" (vii). But the stories she has known have been the "sharp, jagged, tip-of-the iceberg variety" (vii). The stories of each of the houses she inhabits frame her at different periods of her life. Devi's grandmother's village house follows in the same continuum as Laila's village home in Hasanpur (*Sunlight on a Broken Column*) or Baba's childhood home in Jalnabad (*Remember the House*). These homes are reminders of connections with a "natural" world as well as a grounding with a specific notion of an Indian past. As places of escape or retreat, they provide an alternate model of existence away from the constraints of the everyday life in time present, and are largely associated with first homes or vacation homes. Devi's family, for instance, visits the family home only during the holidays. This is very firmly her grandmother's house and there is no suggestion that it would be a suitable lifestyle for the young Devi. Similarly, in *Sunlight on a Broken Column*, Abida and her sister retreat to the village home in Hasanpur. Zaira and Laila—the younger generation—are not allowed to sink back into the past; they have futures to negotiate.

Mayamma too reveals her own story on the eve of Devi's departure, as if to justify and enable her to leave. Her story gives the lie to the idea that conformity necessarily leads to the "happily ever after" scenario. Two interspersed voices tell her story: a third-person narrator and Mayamma herself. Mayamma directly addresses her story to "my daughters" (136). Her story is her "meagre wealth" (126) that she bequeaths to the daughters, emphasising a lineage of women. Despite her lower status as a servant, Mayamma's suffering and her age give her a certain moral authority to permit other women, especially the younger Devi, to step out. She recognises that age and circumstances make women's paths diverge, but validates their choice to escape just as she acknowledges hers to stay on in the Jacaranda Road house.

Devi's early and almost unconscious initiation into adulthood evolves amidst the contradictory forces of her grandmother's world of myths reinterpreted and linked to contemporary ways of women coping and to her mother's world of practicality. Their two houses—one of stories and the other of mottoes—also reflect this difference. Grandmother's storytelling, which sutures mythical characters like Gandhari and Amba to women like Devi's mother and her cousin Uma, creates continuity between a mythic past and the practical present. But to Devi, the stories open her mind to a world of "dangerous possibilities" (35). The instructive intent at the core of these mythical stories of idyllic marriages is women's power to channel their anger, transform them and change their fate. This, at least, is the lesson Devi learns. Akhila, too, learns the same lesson of transformation and assumption of control of one's life in the stories she hears in the train compartment. Both *Thousand Faces of Night* and *Ladies Coupe* subtly legitimise the defiance of mainstream norms of essential or "eternal" womanhood. Both texts present narrators who read epic stories against the grain and subtly subvert the conventional social expectations of wives. In her marital home on Jacaranda Road, Devi's father-in-law's stories "define the limits." Whereas her grandmother's are stories of resistance, "a prelude to my womanhood, an initiation into its subterranean possibilities", his stories insist on tradition as conformity. His stories "always have for their centre-point an exacting touchstone for a woman, a wife" (51). The siren song of conformity is one that seduces Tara (*Tara Lane*) and Baba (*Remember the House*) because as Desai, Leslie and Kishwar, note, certain myths have been so internalised that rejecting them would be a rejection of self. Then there is always the fear that that rejection will render one homeless.

Sumi and Devi find their vocation as story-tellers. Both are conscious of passing on these stories as alternative models to a younger generation. Sumi reinterprets traditional myths like the *Ramayana* from a womanly perspective, from the point of view of a Sita or a Sarupnakha (Ravana's sister), raising issues of sexuality and desire that were not often talked of in life or in these legends. In this the protagonist Sumi replicates author Shashi Deshpande's insightful short stories loosely based on myths. As a first-person narrator, Hariharan's Devi, is "greedy for a story of my own" (137). She sees her role as storyteller as both a link and a tribute to other women, "a mark of protest worthy of the heroines I grew up with" (95). Although her stories are linked to her "homecoming" and rebirth in India, she also sees them as the repayment of a debt. She remembers her grandmother's stories as filling a specific need:

> She chose each [story] for a particular occasion, a story in reply to each of my childish questions. She had an answer for every question. But her answers were not simple: they had to be decoded. A comparison had to be made, an illustration discovered, and a moral drawn out. (27)

These stories bridge the heroic tales "and the less self-contained, more sordid stories I saw unfolding around me" (31). As she matures, however, Devi sees the cracks in the bridge between past and present as "huge gaps," almost as if "the glue that held them together was counterfeit."(31) The mundane present lives, including her own, do not seem to fit into the framework of stories that her grandmother creates. Devi's grandmother is the decoder and interpreter who links the older stories to Devi's childhood. Devi, as the inheritor of a storytelling tradition, has to vindicate her grandmother and repair the gaps that are threatening to destroy the bridge of continuity. She does not adopt her grandmother's mythological framework but instead becomes the subject of her story. By inscribing herself into the story, Devi ensures that her voice is not silenced nor her selfhood erased as her mother-in-law's had been. The role of the storyteller is empowering and can itself be seen as a bulwark against the anomie that threatens. In these novels and especially in *The Thousand Faces of Night*, *A Matter of Time* and *Ladies Coupe* the storyteller is also someone who is equipped to decode, compare, illustrate and draw out the moral links of particular narrations to those of other women's stories. The storytellers and their listeners in both *Ladies Coupe* and *The Thousand Faces of Night* are aware that each story has a specific purpose—to fit an occasion. They are:

> Ideal moulds, impossibly ambitious, that challenged the puny listener to stretch her frame and fit into the vast spaces, live up to her illustrious ancestors. (27)

The panoply of stories includes and links women whose lives seem conformist and mundane to their more heroic ancestors. In fact none of the protagonists or even the secondary characters in these novels are presented as heroines. They are ordinary women who are compelled to carve their own niche, and their ability to do so and to survive, to cope, is heroic enough. In fact, Nair says of Akhila,

> She is typical of that generation. Not many have the courage to break away. You get sucked into the vortex. To me, Akhila in some sense enjoyed being a martyr. She's not an exceptionally strong woman. She is just somebody who has coped. All she wanted was to be a good wife and mother. It's a typical South Indian dream, especially for women of that generation.[35]

More importantly, though, the stories open a space for Sumi, Devi and Akhila to take their places among "her people" —both as a cultural community and within that, a specific community of women. Their particular stories become both a sign of individual protest and a beacon of encouragement to those who will follow. In fact, *Thousand Faces of Night* unambiguously states, "No heroine died without this powerful and destructive protest that left its mark, a memorial to a fighter, behind her." (40)

At a political and cultural level, the narratives in at least Rama Rau's *Remember the House* and Hariharan's *The Thousand Faces of Night* force a deterministic reading of the mother as mother-country because of the political and largely Hindu-Indian framework of stories. The mother's house by the sea in Hariharan also nicely pictorialises the map of India surrounded by the sea in the West, South and the East. Devi has known her grandmother's village home, the houses of strangers in America, her husband's home; the only unknown one is her mother's house. Both mother and daughter will discover this house as they create it together. The location of this house by the sea holds the promise that the wildness of the sea can yet enter the house.

Deshpande's *A Matter of Time,* Hariharan's *The Thousand Faces of Night* and Nair's *Ladies Coupe* extend the idea of a women's community as the basis from which to challenge culture from within. The houses and the train compartment in this novel suggest a more abstract social space. Sumi, the ladies and Devi weave their stories as part of a pattern of other women's stories. In Devi's case her grandmother, the housekeeper Mayamma, and the silent story of her mother-in-law all enrich her story at the same time as they contest and subvert her father-in-law's stories. Traditional stories and their reinterpretation are central to linking past and present and they in turn can provide the blueprint for an alternative domestic space in which mothers and daughters can co-exist. In returning to the big house with her daughters, Sumi recognises and comes to terms with her mother's pain. And her daughters in turn are direct participants and inheritors of the stories that they had been shielded against. In foregrounding Devi's return to the motherland and to her mother's house, Hariharan locates resistance within the parameters of the home community as both a metaphoric and an actual space.

The Thousand Faces of Night is unambiguous both about the transformative power of stories and storytellers and about the stories being specifically stories about women warriors that teach women to survive in a patriarchal society. The same seems to be true of Anita Nair's *Ladies Coupe* and yet the stated authorial intent in Nair's work is curious. In an interview she was asked if the book was about women. Her very defensive response not only equates women with feminists but also presents an extremely mainstream, if not malestream view of feminism. She responded:

I am not a feminist. I enjoy being in the house, I like to be
treated nicely and pampered. I don't think this book is about
feminism. It's about that inner strength which I see in so many
women that overwhelms me. It doesn't come naturally. It has
to be forced out due to unnatural circumstances — like in
Akhila's case.[36]

This may not be the place to digress and explore how
feminism is labelled as being antithetical to femininity or of
the hostility of some women writers to feminism, but it is a
question that needs further thought. The marital homes in
this novel do not provide a space for renegotiation. The texts
posit two possible models of survival for women warriors:
the Sita/Mayamma manner of perfecting and embodying
mythical models or the Parvati/Devi pattern of escape. *The
Thousand Faces of Night* makes clear, though, that young women
like Devi have to choose their heroines, and the stories with
which they identify, and that choice will shape the particular
women allies they find. At the end, poor and old Mayamma
is the only inhabitant in the abandoned house on Jacaranda
Road. Patriarchal tradition having betrayed the wives of the
house, she, the servant, remains as "the lone housekeeper of
the gods" (116).

The bungalow homes are a space where notions of In-
dian/Western and male/female are forced to confront each
other. Whether women choose to stay or to leave these homes
they do have to re-evaluate what Indianness and womanhood
means in this new, nuclear Indian dwelling. The haveli's zenana
or womanspace is being reshaped, at least in some of the novels, more firmly as the mutually supportive communitas of
women who depend on other women as their role models
and their guides. This women's community links back to its
more traditional past through grandmothers and mothers and
through mythological stories of Indian epics, although in many
cases the old stories are reinterpreted quite differently.

References

1   Roland says the phrase "we-self" was coined by Drs Al Collins and Prakash Desai. He notes that for Indians "the experiential sense of self is of a "we-self" that is felt to be highly relational in different social contexts." Roland, *In Search of Self in India and Japan*, 1988 (p.8)

2   Mary Louise Pratt's term.

3   These are the terms Du Bois used to describe the situation of African Americans or negroes as they were then called in the US.

4   Santha Rama Rau. "By Any Other Name" http://www.sad34.net/~globalclassroom/Library/Southasiaanyothername

5   Kaushik,"From Indignity to Individuation: Women in the Indo-Anglian Novel." Pratibha Jain and Rajan Mahan, (eds.) *Women Images*, New Delhi.1996.

6   http://www.hinduonnet.com/thehindu/lr/2001/12/02/stories/2001120200180300.htm. *The Hindu*, Sunday, Dec 02, 2001, Interview with Suchitra Behal.

7   Quoted in Menon's " No Longer Silent" http://ch.8m.com/cgi-bin/framed/1318/shashi.htm

8   Menon, Ritu. "No Longer Silent" http://ch.8m.com/cgi-bin/framed/1318/shashi.htm

9   In a personal conversation with Shashi Deshpande in Bangalore in 2004, I asked her why she had to kill off Sumi. She responded that she had struggled with it for a long time and then suddenly it came to her that this is how it had to be. This is what had felt right to her.

10 Peter L. Berger, *The Social Reality of Religion (or The Sacred Canopy)*, London: Faber and Faber, 1969.

11 Berger and Kellner, "Marriage and the Construction of Reality," Handel and Whitchurch, (eds.) *The Psychosocial Interior of the Family*, 1994. (p.22)

12 Critics like Norbert Wiley while agreeing with the main argument, have taken issue with Berger and Kellner's over-emphasis on speech as a pivotal aspect of conversation. See Norbert W. Wiley, "Marriage and the Construction of Reality: Then and Now," Handel and Whitchurch, *The Psychosocial Interior of the Family*, 1994.

13 E.W. Burgess, Handel and Whitchurch, *The Psychosocial Interior of the Family*, 1994 (p.3)

14 Here, I am deliberately invoking Gayatri C. Spivak's argument in "Can the Subaltern Speak" to suggest that the institution of marriage might be inherently marginalising for women as a whole.

15 Rybczynski, *Home*, 1986 (pp.110-111)

16 Singh and Uberoi, "Learning to 'Adjust,'" *Indian Journal of Gender Studies*, 1994 (p.102)

17 Shirley Ardener, (ed.) *Women and Space: Ground Rules and Social Maps.* London: Croom Helm Ltd, 1981.

18 Edward W. Said, *Culture and Imperialism.* London: Vintage, 1994.

19 This is reminiscent of Chinua Achebe's later novels. In his earlier (pre-Independence) work the nationalist euphoria dominates but in the later novels he is aware of the rot setting in and shows how corrupt politicians (like the labour leaders in Tara Lane) betray the earlier idealism.

20 Arlie Russell Hochschild, *The Managed Heart: Commercialization of Human Feeling,* Berkeley: University of California Press, 1983 (p.20)

21 Peter L. Berger, *The Social Reality of Religion (or The Sacred Canopy),* London: Faber and Faber, 1969.

22 Shama Futehally, "Portrait of a Childhood," Urvashi Butalia and Ritu Menon, (eds.) *In Other Words: New Writing by Indian Women,* Delhi: Kali for Women, 1992 (pp.49-57)

23 Adrienne Rich, "Compulsory Heterosexuality and Lesbian Existence," Snitow, Stansell and Thompson, (eds.) *Powers of Desire,* 1983 (p.197)

24 Anita Desai, "A Secret Connivance," *Times Literary Supplement,* 14-20 September 1990 (p.972)

25 Desai, "A Secret Connivance," *Times Literary Supplement,* 1990 (p.972)

26 Desai, "A Secret Connivance," *Times Literary Supplement,* 1990 (p.972)

27 Julia Leslie, Conclusion, *The Perfect Wife (Stridharmapaddhati)* by Tryambakayajvan, New Delhi: Penguin Books, 1989 (p.327)

28 Madhu Kishwar and Ruth Vanita, (eds.) *In Search of Answers: Indian Women's Voices from Manushi,* London: Zed Books, 1984 (p.46)

29 Desai, "A Secret Connivance," *Times Literary Supplement,* 1990 (p.976)

30 Tryambakayajvan, *The Perfect Wife (Stridharmapaddhati),* Selected from the Sanskrit with an introduction by Julia Leslie, New Delhi: Penguin India, 1989. Leslie notes, "Tryambaka is a collectivist. His concern is not with women as individuals but as parts that fit into and therefore strengthen the whole. While advocating conformity, however, the treatise is itself an admission of the power of nonconformist women to wreck the entire edifice of Hindu orthodoxy." (4)

31 Lal, *The Law of the Threshold,* 1995.

32 Lal, *The Law of the Threshold,* 1995, p.12

33 Charles Merewether, "Zones of Marked Instability: Woman and the Space of Emergence," John C. Welchman, (ed.) *Rethinking Borders,* Minneapolis: University of Minnesota Press, 1996 (p.108).

34 Maxine Hong Kingston, *The Woman Warrior: Memoirs of a Girlhood Among Ghosts,* 1976 Harmondsworth: Penguin, 1976/1977.

35 In conversation with Suchitra Behal, *The Hindu*. http://
www.hinduonnet.com/thehindu/lr/2001/12/02/stories/
2001120200180300.htm

36 In conversation with Suchitra Behal, *The Hindu*. http://
www.hinduonnet.com/thehindu/lr/2001/12/02/stories/
2001120200180300.htm

4

Apartments and Alternate Spaces

Partha Chatterjee notes that it would be pointless to look for traces of nineteenth and twentieth century women's struggles in public documents. In Europe and America the debates were often fought in the public arena but in India the struggle and change took place quietly in individual homes by individual women, "... the battle for the new idea of womanhood in the era of nationalism was waged in the home" (133).[1] Although contemporary women's struggles are now equally evident in the public arena the home remains a contested site of struggle. The apartment is a specifically urban dwelling space and one that is a relatively new, underutilized and unexplored domestic site in Indian English women's novels. Sharon Marcus notes that in nineteenth century London and Paris the apartment was a,

> uniquely urban form of housing that combined the relatively private spaces of individual apartment units with the common spaces of shared entrances, staircases, and partly walls, the apartment house embodied the continuity between domestic and urban, private and public spaces. (2)[2]

In the Indian context however, the apartment replicates some of the social patterns seen in earlier dwellings. The home space is different but the relationships within tend to yearn towards the same ideas of community formation and evocations of Indianness mentioned earlier. The newness of the dwelling notwithstanding, traces of previous home sites like the haveli and the bungalow come up imperceptibly like watermarks exerting conformity to older living-patterns even in this as yet uncharted space. Very few novels are set in apartments and its potential as a secular, intra-generational, community-forming enclave has not been adequately explored. Marcus' study notes that, "apartment buildings linked the city and its residences in real and imagined ways" (2) however, in these novels the apartment often remains the site of the isolation of nuclear or semi nuclear families, marooned among a sea of other such families similarly enclosed in their private little units. The awareness and real or imagined links to the city are not inherently closer in these apartments than they were in the havelis or bungalows of other novels. Diaspora writers use the apartment setting more frequently but even so, it remains a largely unmarked space. There is no geographical mapping of the apartment. Its interiority as a space, or even simply as a locale, remains untapped. It is curious that this particular urban dwelling—which has become fairly common in middle-class, urban, metropolitan India, and, especially among young, often single, working women—is absent from Indian English novels.

Class may be one explanation for this absence. Both English language women writers and their protagonists tend to belong to the upper middle class and are slightly older than the twenty something single, young, women white-collar workers who tend to live in apartments, especially in metropolitan cities like Bombay. Two of the novels by journalist and author Thrity Umrigar are set in Bombay. She herself moved to the United States from Bombay at the age of twenty-one. Explaining the Bombay apartment location and specifically the class divide in her novel *The Space Between Us* (2005) she says,

Growing up in Bombay, I was always aware of this strange, complicated, emotionally complex relationship between mistress and servant. With the dramatic class differences, with

the kind of apartheid that exists in middleclass homes—
where servants cannot sit on the furniture they clean, where
they have their own separate dishes and glasses etc.—it's a
relationship that would be easy to simplify and caricature.
But what I wanted to show in the novel was both, the connections and the separations, the intimacy and the distance between women of different classes.[3]

Neither the class divide nor the complexities of the relationships are specific to the apartment or indeed to Umrigar's
novels. The parallel lives of different classes of women have
been a recurrent pattern from havelis to bungalows and now
to apartments in Indo English novels.

Umrigar's *The Space Between Us* delineates the relationship
between Sera Dubash, a battered wife, now a relatively well
off widow who lives together with her son-in-law,Viraf and
pregnant daughter Dinaz in her (Sera's) apartment. Bhima has
worked for the family for twenty odd years and lives in a
nearby slum with her orphaned granddaughter Maya who is
also pregnant and refuses to reveal the name of the father.
The story revolves around the friendship and distance between Sera and Bhima. Despite their long association, the
master-servant hierarchy stands in the way of friendship. The
two women cannot, despite everything, transcend the class
barrier. Class distance in their case is measured by their starkly
different life-styles. One lives in an apartment while the other,
her domestic helper, lives in a nearby slum. The novel notes,
"Although her apartment building was located less than a fifteen minute walk away from the *basti*, Sera had felt as if she
had entered another universe" (113). The apartment, in both
of Umrigar's novels signals a particular class location. The
rather depressing conclusion is that despite the fact that Bhima,
the domestic servant, is Sera's only friend and nurse and
keeper of her secret of being a battered wife, Sera will choose
family and class over friendship. The choice is complicated as
it is rooted in a 'blood is thicker than water' ethos and simple
self-protection. Even within the isolation of the apartment Sera
and Bhima maintain the ingrained class distance as Bhima sits

on the floor sipping her tea from a stainless steel glass kept aside especially for her use while Sera sits on an upholstered sofa sipping her tea from a china cup.

Class, even between two apartment locations, signals a different social net-working in Shashi Deshpande's *That Long Silence* (1988). The protagonist Jaya is a lower middle class woman who grows up in a poor suburban apartment block on the edges of metropolitan Bombay. But as she and her marital family prosper they move into an apartment in the more posh Churchgate area in the heart of the city. The story of Jaya's self-discovery however, unfolds back in the suburban apartment. Under suspicion of malpractice, Mohan has to take leave from his job. He and his wife Jaya return to their flat in Dadar, a poorer Bombay suburb. An outwardly happily married couple with two teenage children and a beautiful home Jaya and Mohan are separated by a wide chasm of silence. The apartment, inherited from a relative and then bequeathed to Jaya by her brother becomes the locale for her re-evaluating herself as a wife, a writer and a person. The return to the apartment where she spent some of her childhood and which was also their first marital home is a hiatus from the posh Churchgate home with its rigid societal gender roles of wife, mother and woman. Here Jaya confronts the fears that have led to her self imprisonment if not erasure.

Jaya's marital home in Churchgate is not described so we don't know what kind of a dwelling it is. But author Suketu Mehta's experiential narrative about Bombay gives us some idea of a Churchgate home. Mehta notes,

> Coming from New York, I am a pauper in Bombay. The going rate for a nice apartment in the part of south Bombay where I grew up in is $3,000 a month, plus $200,000 as a deposit, interest-free and returnable in rupees. This is after the real estate prices have fallen by forty per cent.[4]

Jaya's personal drama takes place in the less affluent, suburban apartment in Dadar on the fringes of Bombay city. The contrast between the wealth of the central Bombay Churchgate home and the dirt and poverty of the Dardar apartment are noted at the very beginning and also mark the differences between what Mohan and Jaya are striving to escape.

As they walk up the stairs together Mohan seems to be almost absorbed by the squalor and poverty reminiscent of the childhood he had sought to escape. He climbs "gingerly, almost on tiptoe." Whereas Jaya walks "with the steadiness of familiarity, the dirt and ugliness obviously for her a normal part of the surroundings" (7). Her immediate ease and connection makes it apparent that for her the return is almost a comfortable kind of homecoming. Jaya acknowledges, "I only know that the bareness, the ugliness of this place pleased me more than our carefully furnished home in Churchgate... I had a queer sense of homecoming" (25). But she notes how different it is for Mohan who "prowled about uneasy and fearful, like a trapped, confined animal" (25-26). She feels as if "I had gone back to the days of my early childhood ..." (26) while Mohan on the other hand, sees it not as a homecoming but more an appalling return to an earlier time that he thought he had rejected and escaped.

Both Mohan and Jaya's childhoods had been problematic so this not quite the Bachelardian return to childhood the analogy therefore is curious. This insistent trope of staging a return to a known, earlier home, especially for women protagonists in many of the novels is not uncommon. The 'return home' seems essential for the protagonists to come to terms with their pasts so that they can reshape the future. The re-evaluation of their situation and their selfhood is possible only when they 'come home'. Laila (*Sunlight on a Broken Column*) like Jaya, has to return to the echoing, empty haveli of her youth to begin anew. The old home, regardless of whether it is a haveli, a bungalow or an apartment, seems to be the essential launching pad towards a future that will not repeat earlier patterns of confinement and silence often located in these very childhood homes. Early in the novel when she returns to the apartment, Jaya perceptively notes, "the ghost most fearful to confront is the ghost of one's old self" (13). Her acceptance of the apartment, dirt and all is an essential first step to an acceptance and confrontation with who she was. The "history of the flat" (41) is deliberately narrated as such to establish it as a concrete lieu with its own specific antecedents. In the intersecies of the intersections where the history of the apartment and Jaya's history meet lie revealed the kinds of ghosts that haunt her.

Jaya's ownership and place in the apartment are interestingly linked in that although the apartment was left to her brother he gifts it to her, his sister, rather than to his marital family. He does so partly because he feels it is their natal family inheritance. Jaya's childhood links to it give her a greater emotional right to it than simple patriarchal laws of inheritance that exclude her. As a woman, it is made clear to her that she is not entitled to even a place in her family genealogy let alone an inheritance of property. Class is also a factor and she notes cynically that her sister-in-law who lives abroad probably does not realize the real estate value of the place, and, like Mohan, she too "despised this part of Bombay, not just the filth and squalor, but the kind of people who lived here (42). Jaya's place in the family—natal and marital—and the kind of person she is and wants to be come together in this particular apartment space of childhood, relative poverty and couple existence.

Jaya accepts the squalor of this old home with as much ease as she does the poorer neighbours. The audible rhythms of their lives mark time and shape the patterns of her days in synchronic existence. As a child the constant noise had given her a sense of being "invaded, not just by sounds, but by a multitude of people and their emotions as well" (56), but now they form a familiar and comforting drone to the particular almost shared rhythm of life around her. She is equally aware of the cleaning women and their rough lives. She does not have to be told that the cleaning woman Nayana is pregnant yet again, and that the absence of her silver anklets indicates strained circumstances. Like Sera (*The Space Between Us*) she is aware of the class divide but her natural and instinctive sympathy allows her to form a bond with them without necessarily desiring intimacy or friendship. However, her husband Mohan's "indifference to things that did not concern him" (8) isolates him from his wife and also from the neighbours. It is the women who interact with each other across class lines, and, in fact they even wait till Mohan leaves to knock on Jaya's door. It is the easy and constant presence of neighbours even if at times irritating, that surrounds and sustains Jaya. It is the community of women, her neighbour Mukta and daughter Nilima as well as the domestic worker Jeeja and her grand-daughter Manda, who take care of Jaya when she is desperately ill and alone in the apartment. Gender deference and not wanting to intrude on the heterosexual couple-unit, along with Mohan's male-hostility, makes the women reticent. In fact, the absence of men—both physical and emotional—marks the lives of both the domestic workers and the apartment dwelling women and unites them in a common cause.

At one level the common cause is sheer survival. Mutual dependence enables and enriches womanly survival. Jaya honestly notes, "It was Jeeja and her like I needed; it was these women who saved me from the hell of drudgery. Any little freedom I had depended on them." (52) The housework done by other women frees Jaya to devote her time to writing. Jaya is aware of their different class and social positions and unlike Sera does not necessarily seek to bridge the class divide. However, Sera's relationship with Bhima is more intimate. Bhima does not merely ease Sera of the burden of housework but she also shares Sera's home space. Sera remembers:

> When the house felt tomblike, encased in silence, a silence that prevented her from reaching out to others, from sharing her darkest secret with even her closest friends. When Bhima was the only one who knew, the only one who felt the dampness of the pillowcase after long nights of shedding hot tears, the only one who heard the muffled sounds coming from her and Feroz's bedroom (18).

They have developed an intimacy and a language that does not need words. But their mutual dependence is similar to Jeeja and Jaya's.

The dependence is not a one way street either, whether it is a throwback to a feudal ethos or just mutual help Jeeja turns to Jaya when her drunken son is in hospital. She appeals to Jaya, not for financial help, she is fully aware that she can borrow money, but for contacts. She recognizes the doctor as someone who knew Jaya's brother. And she knows that Jaya's class privilege will open doors that are shut for the poor. Jaya uses her influence and class access to ensure that the son is well treated in the hospital. Similarly Bhima acknowledges that when her husband lay ill and abandoned in a government hospital, "Sera and Feroz Dubash had stridden in like movie stars and made sure that he got the best care. ... Rich, confident, and well-spoken, Serabai has a way of making doors open like a magician." (56) Where state institutions cannot be relied upon to provide services then class provides access and contacts to individuals within the system. Not only is Bhima's grand-daughter Maya's college education facilitated by Sera but equally Bhima anticipates,

...the good job that would inevitably await her [Maya], thanks to Dinaz's and Viraf's influence and business contacts, the escape from the menial, backbreaking labour that had marred the lives of her mother and her mother before her – that path would shrivel up, that much was certain. (21)

Domestic workers in both Deshpande's *That Long Silence* and Thrity Umrigar's *The Space Between Us* are aware of how the system works and parley the access their upper class employers enjoy to at least solve their immediate and specific problems.

Personal space and privacy are luxuries for Indian women of all classes. Women's lives generally, but in these apartments particularly, are open secrets and routinely passed on from one woman to another. The cleaning woman Nayana updates Jaya about her domestic helper Jeeja and how she had set up her daughter-in-law's small scale food-vending business. Similarly Jaya's neighbour divulges that she was aware of Jaya's secretive visits to the upstairs gentleman neighbour, Kamat. Sera's neighbour too knows exactly how often Sera goes to check in on her mother-in-law. The 'gossip' aspect of these interactions that were also evident in the haveli courtyard can be seen as an informal networking that creates a common pool of knowledge and concern. Women talking to other women are bound together in what Jaya terms a "conspiracy of women". (37) Men are not deliberately kept out, but, render themselves outsiders. Like Mohan, men are indifferent to things that don't necessarily concern them directly and they distance themselves from women's conversations. In fact the excerpt from Elizabeth Robins speech, "If I were a man and cared to know the world I lived in, I almost think it would make me a shade uneasy – the weight of that long silence of one-half of the world" that prefaces the book, explains the origin of the novel's title and sets its tone. [5]

Men's lack of caring is one aspect but, another related issue, is that not hearing women alters male perceptions of a situation. A case in point is Mohan and Jaya's interpretation of an incident from his poverty stricken childhood where he saw his mother as hroic and Jaya sees her as desperate. Mohan recounts how late one night, his father came home drunk. Having deprived the children and starved herself his mother had waited to cook afresh the little food there was for him. Enraged by the lack of chutney with the meal he flings it aside. Wordlessly and in the middle of the night, the wife borrows the necessary ingredients from a neighbour and with a child at her breast begins making the chutney. In Mohan's view this act bespeaks his mother's toughness and courage but Jaya sees it as pure despair:

> He saw strength in the woman sitting silently in front of the fire, but I saw despair. I saw despair so great that it would not voice itself. I saw a struggle so bitter that silence was the only weapon. Silence and surrender (36).

Silence is a persistent theme in Indian women's writing and is often encoded as punishment when men withdraw verbally; but it is also contrarily seen as both strength and/or weakness (depending on the situation) when women use it. Jaya notes how silence "links the destinies of women" even of mothers and daughters who may be very different from each other. Their suffering or their joys are often not told to the men even those closest to them—husbands, fathers or brothers—but they are not even told to other women as we see in Sera's case. The community of women is also bound together in a common silence that alienates them not only from the men but also from other women. In the return to the Dadar apartment Jaya has to also confront her many silences and silencings.

In Shashi Deshpande's novels womanly silence is often seen negatively as a silencing of women by patriarchy. In *That Long Silence*, particularly, Jaya's silence and her writing are linked. In the biography she has to submit to a newspaper she pares herself down to the barebones of "I was born. My father died when I was fifteen. I got married to Mohan. I have two children and I did not let a third live." In literary terms this would be the plot of her life. The sum total of the actions that happen. It does not at all reveal who she is. She notes that her diaries of the same period read like the neurotic ravings of a too sane housewife because they are so utterly dull and prosaic. But these diaries cleverly camouflage her real feelings.

> But of course, the truth was that there were only the bare skeletal outlines of that life in these diaries. Its essential core had been left out. The agonized cries—'I can't cope, I can't manage, I can't go on'—had been neatly smothered. As also the question that had confronted me every day—'Is this all?' (70)

The contents of the diary are heavily self-censored. Jaya does not, will not and cannot admit, even to herself, her real feelings. But the bland tone and style of her diary is a pertinent reminder of the critiques of Indian English writing mentioned earlier. Meenakshi Mukherjee puts this particular anodyne style down to class and a westernized education whereas Malashri Lal attributes the sameness of tone to being a deliberate strategy that masks subversive ideas. Jaya is self-reflexive enough to note with shock the narrowness of her vision. The diaries reveal a person who is so self obsessed by domesticity that she is oblivious of larger events in the country—famine, drought, scarcity of food (72). They parallel her Seeta newspaper column. The very pseudonym 'Seeta' is a subtle reminder of the Sita of the *Ramayana* but the different spelling also distances the two. The columns evoke the saccharine image of the dutiful Sita like the one popularized by Ramanand Sagar's television serial that was based on Tulsidas's version. The Sita of certain folk traditions, women's versions and regional retellings like the *Kamban Ramayana* is portrayed very differently and probably lies latent in the column and the different spelling. Unsurprisingly the people who love the Seeta column are stalwarts of conformity like Mohan, the newspaper editors and mainstream readers.

> But for Jaya the Seeta column had been the means through which I had shut the door, firmly, on all those other women who had invaded my being, screaming for attention; women I had known I could not write about, because they might—it was just possible—resemble Mohan's mother, or aunt, or my mother or aunt. Seeta was safer. I didn't have to come out of the safe hole I'd crawled into to write about Seeta. I could stay there, warm and snug. (149)

Coming back to the apartment though, Jaya sees that every decision comes with a price tag. She could stay in this hole of conformity "warm and snug" but it is not enough for her either as a writer or as a wife. When she writes what she feels is real, Mohan is devastated. He sees Jaya's writing as self-revelatory, "washing our dirty linen in public". Interestingly, as noted earlier, some critics also tend to see Indian English women's fiction as 'masked autobiographies'. In Mohan's case the problem with his wife's writing is two-fold, one is its revelatory nature which he feels exposes their family life and relationship and the other is that Jaya's taking her writing seriously is tantamount to her taking herself seriously. And the sub-text in that he is not the sole focus of her existence. He would prefer her writing to be a kind of hobby, in the way that education was seen to be in *Sunlight on a Broken Column*, that adds a bit of ornamentation to her and allows him to boast about 'his wife the columnist'. But anything more might displace him and diminish his centrality in her life. Jaya though is too honest to lay the blame for her being a failed writer entirely at Mohan's door.

She acknowledges her neighbour Kamat's assessment that she is "scared of writing. Scared of failing" (148). And the fear is that of exposing her real self. The self that dares to stand alone. She feels that in a way she had chosen to silence herself and crawled back into her comfort zone of the purely domestic space. From there it was easy for Mohan to propel her into another kind of writing – the Seeta kind. Just as Tara (*Tara Lane*) for instance, lets Rizvan guide her back to her comfortable home because one dusty bus ride proves to her that she is afraid and ill-equipped to cope with it on a daily basis. Or Geeta (*Inside the Haveli*) who chooses the haveli over an independent existence in the city. The non- conformity demanded of the protagonists may entail a price that, in the end, may not be worth it, at least not for them.

The seduction of conformity is often also portrayed as gender duty. Jaya is "scared of hurting Mohan, scared of jeopardizing the only career I had, my marriage." (144) Marriage is articulated not just a relationship but also a career. But it is more bonded labour than a simple job. The social stigma of opting out ensures that there are few second chances. Wives in these novels are aware that even though education and social status may give them more options than were available to their mother's generation they may not be equipped to survive as single women in a hostile social environment. Nonconformity which in the novels is often seen as 'being oneself' is like the ever threatening anomie that haunts Tara (*Tara Lane*). In *The Space Between Us*, at a critical point Sera is aware that the choice of speaking out or not will set her in a certain direction in her married life. Although she sees the moment she chooses to silence herself as a moment of self betrayal, she feels helpless as if she has no other choice.

> ...she was aware of a feeling of let down, of having betrayed herself. She knew that she had taken the easy way out that she had let the steam escape from the boiling pot of her emotions. ... What she had wanted to say was "I love life," a self-declaration as naked and real and authentic as an X-ray. And then, a door slammed shut somewhere in the inner recesses of Sera's mind.

But self-betrayal is tied into self preservation. Sera is convinced that she cannot talk to Feroz because he will not understand. And the lack of understanding can spell the end of the marriage. Her class, her education, her upbringing and culture have made all other choices impossible.

Jaya blames the institution of marriage rather than her individual husband, "it was not Mohan but marriage that had made me circumspect." (187) She feels that systems, structures and institutions tie women and men down. Fear had bound her, like it did Sera, and she understands, "I'm Mohan's wife, I had thought, and cut off the bits of me that had refused to be Mohan's wife." (191) The recognition that no one can do this to you but that you do it to yourself allow her to envisage change in a way that Sera cannot. Jaya feels that the system helps in wearing women down because injustice and inequality is systemic and encoded in the state of wifehood.

Jaya, learns the lessons of wifehood by example from the women in Mohan's family.

> Terrified of his disapproval, I had found out all the things I could and couldn't do, all the things that were womanly and unwomanly. It was when I first visited his home that I had discovered how sharply defined a woman's role was. They had been a revelation to me, the women in his family, so definite about their roles. So well trained in their duties, so skilful in the right areas, so indifferent to everything else. I had never seen so clear, so precise a pattern before, and I had been entranced by it. (83)

The reward of following in the footsteps of the women of Mohan's family is keeping at bay the threat of anomie. Doing her duty as a wife, the conformity to a prescribed gender role may not spell happiness and self-expression but she hopes it will be enough. "That way lay—well, if not happiness, at least the consciousness of doing right, freedom from guilt." (84) The choice for wives like Jaya, Sera and many others is a guilt-free conformity or a rejection of the socially confining roles of wifehood. For some, like Geeta (*Inside the Haveli*), an acceptance of the specific feudal gender role of a haveli dweller entails unlearning the cosmopolitan, more liberal upbringing of her urban, apartment dwelling childhood. The fear that haunts these wives is if they give up their wifedom then what is left? On her wedding day Jaya's aunt reminds her that "a husband is like a sheltering tree." (32) Later as she recalls her aunt's words Jaya thinks,

Without the tree, you're dangerously unprotected and vulnerable. This followed logically. And so you have to keep the tree alive and flourishing, even if you have to water it with deceit and lies. (32)

As single women, alone, can they afford to be left unsheltered? Sera betrays herself and Bhima by choosing her family and security over what is right. And in her case that could be attributed to age. She can only look to her children for support and in any case she had already erased herself in her relationship with her husband. But Jaya is at a cross roads where she feels that a renegotiation is still possible.

Jaya recalls that at the end of the *Bhagavad-Gita* sermon, after Krishna has explained the philosophy of life and given Arjuna knowledge, he also gives him the freedom to choose his path, "'Yathecchasi tatha kuru' Do as you desire." (192) In her return to the Dadar apartment and to her past Jaya (like Laila before her) feels equipped with a certain self-knowledge. At this moment of a second choice of who she wants to be she feels she can no longer provide the conformist, pleasing answers expected of her. She has to find her own voice. This is her moment of epiphany. In Sanskrit drama she had learnt that women were not allowed to speak the Sanskrit spoken by men. They had to speak Prakrit—which to her ears sounded like a baby lisping. A diminished, inferior tongue. And she realizes "I have been speaking Prakrit myself" (193). The mainstream voices had applauded her Seeta column because it too spoke Prakrit and reinforced a conformist and acceptable image of womanhood, whereas the kinds of real women she wants to write about resist gender conformity and are unafraid to show their emotions. Deshpande insists that only by breaking the silence of womanhood can women be freed. Bhima and Jaya are able to cut the strings that tie them down. But Sera is not given the same release or moment of epiphany. She is a hostage to class, age and family and retreats into silence and lies to protect all that she thinks she has left.

Thrity Umrigar's earlier novel *Bombay Time* (2001) is also set in an apartment in Bombay. If the haveli was the pan-Indian icon of house desire then "the apartment is much more the icon of cosmopolitan and urban Bombayite's desire".[6] Apartments are and have been the norm in urban Bombay unlike other metropolitan cities like Kolkata and Chennai or even Delhi which is essentially a government capital of bungalows, although all that too is fast changing. *Bombay Time* unlike *The Space Between Us* focuses more on community than on class. Much like Rohinton Mistry's *Stories from Firozsha Baag*[7] it focuses on the minority Parsi community.[8] Umrigar is as self conscious about her intention in exploring community in this novel as she was about exploring class in *The Space Between Us*. In an interview she notes,

> In *Bombay Time*, I was interested in exploring the bonds of community across time. My focus was this broad canvas where each member of this community is a single strand of thread that makes up this canvas. The focus of *Space* is different.[9]

The apartment block, Wadia Baug, in the novel works as a kind of uber haveli where all the residents are Parsis. The bonds of community within the larger living space unites them as familial bonds united the haveli dwellers.

The Prologue of the novel locates the city of Bombay as the larger canvas and then almost cinematically zooms in on Bomanji Road and speicifically on Wadia Baug on Bomanji Road as the central locus. The rhythm of the awakening of the city is localized and measured by how Wadia Baug as a collective awakens and faces the day. Each group begins the day in their specific ways from the butcher, milk and bread sellers who deliver their wares to the apartment block where wives bargain and awaken the children, to children getting ready for school, to working men readying themselves for office and the older generation gradually awakening later. Wadia Baug's awakening to a new morning is a microcosm of how Bombay heralds the new day.

The novel could be read as a multistory compilation rather than a straight novel. The story of the loving and successful family man Jimmy Kanga who returns from England to settle in Wadia Baug is contrasted with the sadly disintegrating family of Rusi and Coomi Billamoria and their daughter Binny who has already settled abroad. There are other stories, like Dosa's - married at age twelve because her father made a drunken promise to Sorab's father. After years of a hostile life together Dosa does finally fall in love with her husband only to lose him soon thereafter. The resident drunk Adi is haunted by the ghost of the girl he raped and who subsequently committed suicide. None of the neighbours know his secret and yet they all look out for him ensuring that he has food and is brought home at night. The cast of characters is large and varied as are their particular problems. However all the stories reveal how people of the building are linked to each other and how their lives are intertwined. They have known each other over the years, so their common past links them. But, a stronger link is belonging to the same small and diminishing minority Parsi community with its particular problems of where and how they fit into India. Their insiders-outsider status and the awareness of being a dwindling community almost necessitate their banding together.

The individual stories of the various residents of Wadia Baug are set against the backdrop of Jimmy Kanga's son's marriage. Mehernosh's wedding brings all the residents together in a celebration of union and new beginnings but it is also where the past is reevaluated. Jimmy has invited the residents of Wadia Baug to stay back after the other guests have left. He presents each with a photo album of their collective memories "Memories of Wadia Baug". As in Rushdie's "Imaginary Homelands" where a photograph of his house becomes the catalyst for a return to the past, here too they are the touchstone for nostalgia and reevaluations. Rushdie's reading of the past as a "foreign country" from which everyone is an immigrant to a present where everyone is necessarily partial or incomplete because they are displaced from their past is reclaimed in this album of memories that will complete them and propel them into the future. The fact that they are given their past, at the wedding, a moment of unions and new beginnings marks it as a legacy and inheritance. The photos are a link to the living examples or models for the younger generation. For the older generation though they are a poignant reminder. As Soli says "... what you have given us is more than a few pictures. You have reminded us of who we are and what we are to one another. You've given us ourselves back, our youth and our promise. Our real selves back..." (269). In this reclamation of their "real" selves as individuals and as a community they provide the way forward for the newly wed generation. They are singled out as a group to reaffirm their group identity as Wadia Baug residents. Their identity as Parsis does not need to be reiterated as only Parsis live in Wadia Baug. The photo album strengthens past links and binds them together firmly as a continuous community. It is a reminder to the new generation in the face of impending change and relocation to a richer milieu of South Bombay's Cuffe Parade area that they should not forget their roots, community and families.

Jimmy Kanga's own story nicely illustrates the insistence on these particular roots. He came as an orphan to his uncle in Wadia Baug. He studied law at Oxford but returned to India. He returns not so much for the idea of community but because he knows that whereas in England he would be one of many immigrants, "In Bombay, his uncle's contacts, his Parsi heritage, his light skin, his fluent English, his Oxford education— all these would make him a star. Unique. A big fish." (58) But it is his second return to Wadia Baug that is more complex if equally considered. Jimmy marries Zarin and, as a successful and rich lawyer, moves to a Cuffe Parade apartment. But all of them, he, Zarin and their son Mehernosh are unhappy there. They return to Wadia Baug, to be amongst their own people. The elevation in class and status in England or on Cuffe Parade Jimmy realises does not make up for being 'among their

own people". They find the more affluent Cuffe Parade people
to be snobs. Zarin complains that "the people here are so different" (72). And the difference is both in their cultural het-
erogeneity as well as the isolation of the rich. Zarin notes that
even children don't have free access to each others homes
"and everybody keeps their doors locked. ... Here, you could
go for days without anybody stopping by" (72). The isolation
of Cuffe Parade harks back to the isolation of Jimmy's life as a
foreigner in England, alienated from "one's own people". But
it is also the isolation of the bangalow dweller as compared to
the haveli dweller.

The isolation is especially hard for Zarin who is home alone
all day. She decides to move back to Wadia Baug with her son,
saying, "You don't know what its like during the day. The
quiet. When the wind blows from over the sea, it moans, like
an old woman crying. I just miss the hustle-bustle of our old
building. I miss our friends, all the joking around. I miss the
smell of Parsi food being cooked next door to us." (73) She
craves the feeling of community that is measured by familiar
food smells and the ease of being among known people and
cultural habits. Jimmy's epiphany triggered by Zarin's threat
to leave is not really about marriage but about community life.
He reiterates and enlarges on an old Indian adage that when
you marry you don't just marry an individual but the family.

> He had foolishly thought that Zarin and he were married
> only to each other. In reality they were married to an entire
> group of people, a neighbourhood, a way of life. Despite his
> love for her, he alone could not save Zarin. She needed all
> those others, their friends and relatives, in order to be whole
> and happy. ... he had been surrounded by a wealth of people,
> and he hadn't even known it. ... But they were his commu-
> nity. His people. They had befriended him when he hadn't
> had two nickels to rub together, cared for his only son, shel-
> tered his wife, held up his marriage. And he had left them
> behind like yesterday's newspaper (74).

He does not spell out what exactly constitutes community
and "his people" aside from the fact that they are a 'caring

community'. But he knows that whatever community means for him it is located in Wadia Baug. But he is almost shocked when a client whom he tells about his move back spells it out for him. The client says, "You are a Parsi, born and raised among Parsis. Here at Cuffe Parade, you are forced to live among Gujus, Punjabis, Sikhs. Very hard adjustment to make, I'm sure" (74). Brought up in the ideology and rhetoric of secular India, which he has vociferously espoused, he is shocked at the client's assumption that he is ill at ease in the mixed community setting of the Cuffe Parade apartment. He thinks that the boring sameness of Bombay's elite, secular class ambitions distance him from other Cuffe Parade residents. But is forced to rethink this when he catches himself automatically turning up his nose at the smell of different, non-Parsi cuisine wafting in his new apartment block. Ultimately the return to the old neighbourhood is for the homogeneity of community and a common past. Their move back to Wadia Baug replicates Jimmy's return from England (Oxford) and his son's from America.

The dislocation figured in the novel is not only of the younger generation moving away from Wadia Baug but also moving Westwards away from India.

> So many of them had lost their sons and daughters to America or England. They had worked hard all their lives, saved their pennies, complained about the rising prices of milk and chicken and sugar, postponed their own dreams—and still they couldn't hold on to their children or give them the lives they would have in the West. And so they performed the ultimate act of love—they unclasped their children from their bosoms and let their children go (27).

The moving away has specific implications for Parsis as the move not only distances parents and children but it will further loosen the bonds and opportunities of marriage within the community which in turn will impact the diminishing demographics. In the 1960s this westward migration of Indians was seen as a 'brain drain' and today in the 2000s it is seen as a move towards global opportunities. But the impact on families and communities is the same. For some of the Wadia Baug children, the move away is for better opportunities even though America is also figured as " that woman, kidnapping all our children"(251). But for others the move away can be read more as an escape than abduction. Rusi for instance, knows that his daughter Binny had to "escape"—the country, the city and the home. Although it is clear that she is primarily escaping their sad home, but, she is also escaping "this graveyard of a city, where women got struck with rocks and young men lay writhing in their own blood" (265). Wadia Baug may be a safe haven in the middle of a brutal Bombay but even in Wadia Baug the individual apartments enclose and hide their own share of unhappiness that the younger generation may seek to flee.

The geographic distance, however, also marks an emotional distance and a loosening of ties not merely between an individual and the community but also between an individual son or daughter and the parents. In providing what they consider to be better opportunities for their children the parents may unwittingly widen a mere generation gap into something more. The distance between non-returnees is marked by an ever increasing silence. The silence between Coomi and her daughter Binny for instance grows with each international phone call. Binny's notion of family has shrunk to encompass only her parents, the nuclear family whereas for her mother the whole neigbourhood, all of Wadia Baug, is family and Coomi wants to share their news with her daughter. Binny's shrunken notion of family however makes her impatient with news of the larger community. Coomi's world is closed to Binny and the mother-daughter relationship is in jeopardy.

Geographic distance marks an emotional distance that is also linguistically rendered in *Bombay Time*. Dosa's son Zubin marries and moves to Pune. Pune is only some 220 kilometers from Bombay. But even that short distance ruptures communication between mother and son. Dosa writes to her son in Gujerati which he cannot read or write. She takes this as being a sign of his not being interested in her life. But he justifiably responds that she sent him to an English medium school especially at the cost of the home language, so how can she now expect him to read Gujerati. Parents provide an English medium education to children to ensure their access to an international job market. But in so doing, the younger generation is linguistically distanced from their parents.

This is not to suggest that parents should hold onto the children in the face of inevitable change. But *Bombay Time* suggests that change can be renegotiated. Jimmy and Zarin's son, Mehernosh, becomes "the custodian of their future" (250), he is the beacon of this new renegotiation. Like his father, Mehernosh forsakes the lure of America to return home—to India and to Bombay, even if not specifically to Wadia Baug. This return is a renewal of hope. As Rusi says,

> it felt like a victory of sorts, a body snatched from the jaws of the monster that had swallowed up so many Parsi children. Mehernosh had been inside the belly of the beast but had remained unmoved by its glitter and promise.

His return and his marriage suggest community continuity. The heavy burden placed on the young couple demands:

> You have not only a right but a *responsibility* to be happy. ... All of us gathered here are like your own family.. Most of us saw you the day you were born. We need you to be happy, *beta*. For us. For all of us. It's the only way to make sense of all this—this city that's hell on earth, this life where we've all suffered. Our chance has come and gone. ... But young ones, ... you are our hope and promise. ... we need this for you and *from* you (249). [*emphasis in the original*]

The unspoken contract between the older and the younger generation is that the former's deferred pleasures will be realized by the latter. At the sunset of their lives the parental generation needs to know not only that their individual struggles were worth it but also that the community will survive in and through their children albeit in different locations.

The intention of the novel is spelt out and underlined. It closes with the omniscient narrator proclaiming much like a Greek chorus, "Yes, they will remember Wadia Baug and they will do their best to forget the city that it is housed in. They will choose memory over imagination. It is less dangerous that way" (271). The photograph album of past memories and the moment of the wedding and new community formation underlines the message of the importance of retaining the essence of Wadia Baug. Its crumbling edifice is built on a solid foundation capable, almost, of withstanding time and transcending relocation. However momentary and fleeting the feeling may be it is the heady mix of a shared past, sense of belonging and oneness that holds this group together. The everyday reality may be made of petty bickering but these are the mundane building blocks that cement relationships and create the bedrock of community.

Amulya Malladi's fourth novel *Song of the Cuckoo Bird* (2006) is located in an essentially women's community in a semi religious ashram setting that is very different from the Parsi community in *Bombay Time*. Malladi was born in India and studied engineering in Hyderabad and journalism in Tennessee. She now lives in Copenhagen. She says that she initially started writing the story of *Song of the Cuckoo Bird* when she was fifteen years old. It took many more years to find the appropriate vocabulary and for the ideas to mature. Interestingly the novel includes, at the end, a conversation with her mother. Malladi feels that the book is as much her mother's as it is hers in fact, many of the stories were recounted to her by her mother. Her mother's perspective may, in part have influenced the narratorial viewpoint and that may account for some of the tensions in the deeply problematic and disturbing ashram location.

The story is narrated from the viewpoint of Kokila who is often both narrator and protagonist. Kokila is the cuckoo bird of the title—Kokila also means cuckoo. As a betrothed child-bride who is then orphaned Kokila is brought to the ashram—Tella Meda, at the age of eleven. When Kokila reaches puberty, as was the custom, her husband's family come to reclaim her. She, however, refuses to go with them, choosing instead to stay on at the ashram. Charvi a young woman of twenty-one is the spiritual head of the ashram. Her father Ramanandam Sastri who first saw divinity in her at the age of fifteen had declared her a guru. Kokila's decision to stay on at the ashram is partly because she is in love with Charvi's brother Vidura. Vidura, however, runs away from the ashram and his father Ramanandam later becomes Kokila's lover.

The ashram is located in the small South Indian costal town of Bheemunipatnam. Set by the sea like Sita's house (*Thousand Faces of Night*) the romantic description evokes female sexuality and, in this case, erotic desire. Tella Meda is lyrically described thus, "on a full moon night the house glittered as if diamonds were studded all over it and its outer walls shimmered from the reflection of the waters of the Bay of Bengal" (4). We are also told that the foundation of house was first laid in 1947, which is the date of Indian independence, clearly aligning the ashram house to the house of India by the common date of Indian independence. But, the house like the postcolonial nation seems to have teething troubles as hurricanes destroyed each attempt to build it. Finally it is completed in 1955 but ill luck continues to dog it as at the moment of the *gruhapravesham* the owner's wife dies. No one actually ever lived in Tella Meda till it was handed over to Ramanandam who starts the ashram and installs his daughter as the guru. The parallels between house and nation seem to stop at this point except for the rather forced links of current event snippets preceding various sections that seem to want to continue the connection. The novel self-consciously spans forty years from 1961 to 2000 in the life of the ashram and of India. But, in fact, there is very little connection between the two except for an exterior, temporal contextualization between the current affairs of the nation and the events in the ashram. This may, in fact, be deliberate to indicate the isolation of the ashram existence. The narrator comments that,

> Kokila didn't care about any of that [politics, government and India's border problems]. She had lived in the closed world of Tella Meda for so long that the larger issues of the world weren't relevant to her (130).

But, in fact, this is said in the context of her increasing awareness of the emotional distance and age difference be-

tween her and Ramanandam. The gap between Tella Meda as
a microcosm or even an inset in India is unclear from the historical factoids. The two are tangentially linked only twice in
the novel and that too in a cursory manner. The lack of connection and purpose between the suggested outside and inside worlds in fact detracts from the narrative.

The ashram itself is a complex space:

> Tella Meda was an *ashram*, a religious dwelling where a *guru*
> led her folk to the right path through prayer and the reading
> of scripture. But it was not a conventional *ashram*. The *guru*,
> Charvi, refused to be called *"guru"* or *"amma,"* as the norm
> was for those as enlightened as she. Charvi went by just
> Charvi and would not call her home an *ashram* but just a
> home, hers, which she willingly and openly shared with those
> who were in need (4).

The reluctant guru however gradually accepts her status
and in fact the material survival of the ashram is dependent
on its being an ashram, a religious space, with a guru who
provides consolation and to whom people bring offerings.
Charvi's sister Lavanya, however, characterizes Tella Meda
as "a free inn for losers"(40). She and Vidura both insist that
it is not a home in any sense of the word. In fact Vidura warns
Kokila that not only is Tella Meda not her home, "It is no
one's home. ... This is an *ashram*, not a home...." (21). The
author, herself asserts in the mother-daughter conversation
at the end of the book that "Tella Meda is part *ashram*, part
women's shelter, part orphanage, and part home for the eld-
erly" (379). Ashrams in India as noted earlier are often the
only acceptable and available refuge, especially for women
without families and Tella Meds is portrayed as such.

The multi valent space is also contradictorily described as
both refuge and prison. The nest/prison dichotomy is not
particular to this ashram home. Other, more traditional, domestic spaces be they havelis, bungalows or apartments have
equally been both a refuge and a prison. Tella Meda is "a
home for the weary, a safe harbour for lost souls, the last
refuge for some and the only home for others" (4). Yet when

Subhadra, the cook who has been at the ashram since its beginning, anxiously contemplates leaving Tella Meda to live with her sister, Kokila compares her reluctance to that of long term prisoners who "when freed had trouble adjusting to the idea of the world outside. They preferred to stay in prison rather than go out and live with real people in the real world" (259). The ashram as prison resembles another women only home Gyaltsen's *Daughters of the House* which is also compared to a prison. Charvi is criticized for not encouraging the women to leave the ashram and the women are also compared to a tethered goat who does not explore the pasture. But the criticism seems harsh since, in the novel, the world outside the ashram is inhospitable to women. Aside from a strident insistence on marriage no options are offered. Even if they wanted to, where could these women go? They are barely safe when they are inside, how would they survive outside? This fear of the existence outside the relatively safe home spaces is constant in many novels such as *The Space Between Us, Tara Lane, Inside the Haveli, Thousand Faces of Night* among others. Kokila, for instance, feels homeless and orphaned because of the absence of gender roles that would attach her to people and give her a place in society. This is what Sudhir Kakar refers to as the strength and raison d'etre of Indian womanhood. Not only does Kokila have no where to go, she feels she does not even have an identity partly because "she was no one's daughter, no one's wife, no one's anything"(116). Outside these gender roles her life appears meaningless. The importance of family, even an ashram family of women, is better than being alone on the outside. Malladi's mother acknowledges that "they are a family at Tella Meda" ... And there is security with family" (380). Prison though it may appear to be, when biological families fail, and the state does not provide any kind of a security net then surrogate families like the one in the ashram become essential for survival.

The central contradiction of *Song of the Cuckoo Bird*, however, revolves around sexuality. Textually, at the core of the plot and of the ashram space, is the fact of a relationship be-

tween a much older man, Ramanandam, who sleeps with
Kokila, a woman younger than his own daughter. Everybody
knows of the relationship but let alone talking about it no
body even challenges or questions it. The open secret is covered in a "conspiracy of silence" and in subtle ways it even
increases Kokila's power in the affairs of the ashram. From
Ramanandam's openly articulated view-point the relationship
is not a problem because he has always espoused gender equality and ideas of free living and thinking. But it goes against
the grain of the conventional connotations of an ashram.

A "compulsive heterosexuality" to use Adrienne Rich's
phrase is central in this all women space.[10] Tella Meda evokes
the haveli with its ten rooms that surround the courtyard.
And the insistence on the courtyard being a female space written over by patriarchy is evident in the Tulsi plant at its centre.[11] The Tulsi is a symbol of matrimonial harmony and pros-
perity of the hearth. Married Hindu women often offer prayers
to the Tulsi plant. In the centre of the courtyard in Tella Meda
the tulsi pot stand sentinel. And as if the symbolism of the
tulsi were not enough we are told that the pot was "painted
red and yellow, auspicious colours that signified *kumkum* and
turmeric and were the colours of a married woman" (6). In
this ashram community that is largely inhabited by women—
unwed girls, single mothers or spinsters— all of whom have
been abandoned by men and a patriarchal society. And yet
the central symbol at the heart of their daily activity is the
tulsi. That this is not in any way meant to be ironic is clarified
by the dialogue at the end where the author's mother asserts,

"... all the others who lived at Tella Meda were people who
had lost something before they came there. Kokila came there
and lost her life. ... she lost the chance of having a life... you
know, to be a wife and mother" (376).

Kokila does in fact adopt a son the author reminds her
mother. But the latter avers, "it isn't the same thing. She had
no man, no husband" (376). And the text itself explicitly states,
"at Tella Meda she [Kokila] had a roof over her head but not

the respectability of a married and decent woman" (89). This clearly articulated alignment of decency and womanhood with the marital state is especially curious in an ashram location that is headed by a woman and where the women inhabitants are marginalized because of the men in their lives. The text simultaneously also reiterates that the women in Tella Meda are outcasts. The text suggests that the problem is both systemic and also in their individual men that these women are condemned to live on the fringes of society. Charvi herself is not exempt from this judgement. Malladi and her mother both feel that Charvi, despite her elevated position, is the saddest character in the novel because she is plagued by self-doubt. By way of explaining her possessiveness of her father the text also reiterates, "She had no other man in her life and never would. Ramanandam had named her a goddess and had therefore thrown her into the land of spinsters and loneliness"(35). The status of being a guru is seen as inferior to that of being a married woman. As a guru Charvi does not even have the option of exploring her feelings for the American photographer who stays in the ashram. The insistence on normative heterosexuality and prescriptive conformity to traditional gender roles is jarring especially in the ashram location.

Kokila's view of the ashram too, changes dramatically from when she first arrives as a child and is entranced by the beauty and comparative (to her thatched home) grandeur of the ashram. In her childish perception the ashram was "a place where there was always food, even if meagre amounts, and clean clothes, four walls, and a roof. As a child Kokila had thought that would be enough" (89). But for Kokila, the woman, the need for so-called decency and societal acceptance become crucial, "as a woman she had begun to realize that by choosing Tella Meda she had condemned herself to live on the sidelines of society"(89). The censorious, narratorial voice reiterates,

> after all, the women living at Tella Meda were not the most respectable. Women like Kokila couldn't expect marriage and family; no decent man would marry a woman who lived in

the *ashram,* an orphan, a discard of society who had spurned one marriage already (162).

The author, narrator and the text seem to insistently reinforce this viewpoint. For people within and without Tella Meda marriage and normative heterosexuality seems to be the only key to 'respectability', especially for women. This alignment of marriage and womanly decency not only colours society's perception of Tella Meda and its inhabitants, but more importantly it is a view-point that the women in the ashram seem to have internalized. *Song of the Cuckoo Bird* privileges retrogressive conservative, patriarchal traditions. In the link of ashram with nation this seems particularly jarring as nationalist reformers even in colonial times had fought vociferously to overthrow these misogynist traditions from their vision of modern India. Kokila, for instance, accords Renuka the right to criticize the ashram and its inmates because as a widow Renuka had followed the strict rules of widowhood by shaving her head and wearing white. The acceptance of traditional rituals elevates her status and confers upon her a sense of entitlement denied to others.

At the end, though, unconvincingly Kokila pays lip service, lists the house's lineage and acknowledges the privilege of having lived with "brave women". These ordinary women warriors are named and their sheer gutsy survival applauded. In this context the constant insistence on normative heterosexuality and conformity to tradition as superior and more valid lifestyles is odd and cannot but create a sense of readerly unease.

Chitra Bannerjee Divakaruni's *The Mistress of Spices* (1997) draws together the strands of self-discovery, Indianness and community in the most unusual of alternate domestic locations —a spice shop. A domestic, commercial space finally succeeds in presenting itself as part of the cityscape and the streetscape. This novel was short listed for the Orange Prize (England) and chosen by the *Los Angeles Times* as one of the best books of 1997. Starring Bollywood's lead actress Aishwarya Rai, *The Mistress of Spices* was made into a film in 2005, by Gurinder Chadha of

Bend it Like Beckham fame. Divakaruni was born in India and now lives in California. A multi-genre writer she has published poetry, essays, short stories and novels; her interests in community and women are evident in her fiction including *Vine of Desire*, as well as in her personal life as the President of MAITRI, a help line for South Asian women.

The Mistress of Spices begins in India with the birth of an unwanted girl child Nayan Tara. She acquires magical powers, is abducted by pirates and becomes their leader and then flees to a mysterious island of spices. In the Utopian island existence she, along with other women, learns the magic of spices and graduates to become a mistress of spices. In her role as mistress and healer she settles in an Indian spice shop in a poorer neighbourhood of Oakland California where she helps "all those who have suffered from America" (183)—these are the South Asian immigrants who have to negotiate their existence in a new country to make it home. Her instructions are to help her own kind and to never step out of the protective space of the shop which serves as a protective *Lakshman Rekha*. Rebellious and always a rule breaker, the now renamed Tilo, not only leaves the shop but also falls in love with an American. In the lyrical, magic realism mode of *Like Water for Chocolate*[12] her personal story is interspersed with the stories of others whom she helps with the aid of an exotic and esoteric knowledge of spices.

Tilo's arduous search for "the island of spice" recalls earlier adventurers, especially Columbus who set off looking for India and spices and found America instead. The connection may not be deliberate but the parallels lurk beneath the surface. Tilo's knowledge of Indian spices (the spices are always referred to by their Hindi or Bangla names) gives her an entry into America. She enters this new life and landscape not as an ordinary immigrant struggling for survival or even as a professional in search of better opportunities but as a wise woman in touch with her roots and able to help other Indian immigrants with their problems of acculturation. However, like other utopias in women's literature like *Herland* or *Sultana's Dream*[13], this too, is a women only island. On the island the mother is the supreme authority and "her power alone prevails" (24). The lessons of the island also foreground community and sister-hood—learning from each other and the ability to empathize without the necessity of words. Tilo recounts,

> We lived our days without hurry, and yet each moment was urgent, ... But much of our time was spent in common things, sweeping and stitching and rolling wicks for lamps, gathering wild spinach and roasting chapattis and braiding each other's hair. We learned to be neat and industrious and to work together, to protect one another when we could... (54).

The tasks on the magic island are surprisingly mundane and they are also extremely gendered. They are what could be seen as traditional 'women's work' the kind of work that women in the haveli did.

Female lineage and birthland (India) are evoked from the start in *The Mistress of Spices* where they are not merely identity referents but also markers that offer security, protection and sense of self to immigrants in their new countries of adoption. But the India evoked is an exotic India worthy of the Raj genre of novels: "But the spices of true power are from my birthland, land of ardent poetry, aquamarine feathers. Sunset skies brilliant as blood. ... there is no other place in the world quite like this"(3). And yet there is no irony indicated in the fact that the novel opens with the unwanted birth of a female child who, but for luck, would not even have survived in the same India merely because she was born female. A romanticized picture of India or Indian culture is often evoked especially in diaspora Indo-English women's novels without comment; while at the same time the stereotypical tropes of unwanted girl children, dowry deaths and arranged marriages —the cultural bias of an Indian patriarchal society that oppresses women—already common currency in the west is further foregrounded. On the utopian spice island the potential spice mistress's desire to link with and belong completely to the first mother could also be read as the yearning to belong to a romanticized birthland of beginnings. The pain of displacement as well as the longing of nostalgia intensifies the need to belong to the original home or motherland.

The grocery store 'Spice Bazaar' in America, like the Asian Cultural Centre in England (*A Wicked Old Woman*), are very particular spaces that locate food and culture as key ingredients to Indianness. But both are in their own ways problematic 'home' spaces for the community. The 'Spice Bazaar' is an Indian space of nostalgia and belonging if not a synecdoche for India. The store is described in loving detail from the outside in. The dried garland of mango leaves at the entrance leads onto a

> grease-smudged window. Looped letters that say SPICE BAZAAR faded into a dried-mud brown. Inside walls veined with cob webs where hang discolored pictures of sad eyed gods, their sad shadow eyes (4).

This is not a modern chrome and glass American grocery store that evokes modernity and efficiency. From the containers of rice and lentils, to rental video movies that go back to the black and white era, the text deliberately and specifically frames the space as an age-old and yet timeless past, an oasis of nostalgia. The listing of material products in the shop also takes on a sonorous almost incantory, chanting quality as if the mere naming of "atta and Basmati rice and masoor dal" (4) has the power to conjure up India. Colours and their referents similarly evoke a nostalgia tinged with exoticism. "Bolts of fabric dyed in age-old colours, New Year yellow, harvest green, bride's luck red" (4). The India recalled in and by the store is the 'eternal India' sentimentlly evoked in various genres of literature and painting among others. Tilo as the store-keeper, the mistress of spices, is the embodiment of an atavistic link to that palpable eternal past. She can empathise with the feeling of lost homes because she too has forsaken many homes including the perfect home of the utopian island. The grocery store is Tilo's home and for others a venue for meeting and connecting with India and their roots through Tilo. But in and of itself it is also a space of a specifically Indian sustenance through food and spices. Tilo's presence as the owner of the grocery store and a mistress of spices is necessary to ease their way in the new land. In the store she stocks all the necessary ingredients that will enable a smooth acculturation without losing ones roots, "... I have brought together everything you need in order to be happy" (7). These ingredients for happiness are rooted in India and available in this Indian space through the medium of a high priestess of spices who has herself successfully escaped the land of her birth and given up an utopian existence to arrive on these distant shores to re-make herself. The much valued mythos of reinvention is specifically American, but here it is enabled by recourse to and an acceptance of the past that is India. The immigrants view of India is filtered through what Rushdie terms "guilt coloured lens"—guilt at having forsaken the mother land. The particular idea of a timeless India, an island haven, which will sustain while allowing change is not merely seductive but essential for diaspora Indians who want to maintain links with their past and home country while reinventing themselves and living and acculturating to the mainstream culture of their adopted land.

The Spice Bazaar is a little patch of India that fits into an American street as if it has always been there. It is located on the "crooked corner of Esperanza"(4), an American street of immigrant hopes. The aspirations of the Indian Spice Bazaar lean towards the barred windows of Rosa's Weekly Hotel which is next to a Chinese sewing machine and vacuum repair store. All the immigrant cultures are lined up side by side in their struggle out of relative poverty towards the American Dream of the Gold Mountain and American entitlement. In *The Mistress of Spices* the immigrant nostalgia for a simpler past and their dreams of a successful future are, however, both coloured by betrayal, "their longing for the ways they chose to leave behind when they chose America. Their shame for that longing... (5). A visit to the spice store is seen as an "excursion into the land of might-have-been" (5-6) and is deemed especially dangerous for "brown people" because a foray into the past reveals all that has been left behind and also shows up the unfulfilled dreams of the move into this new future. The double betrayal of the "American dream" by America's rejection of the immigrant and the immigrant's resistance to new ways is unbearable, especially for the immigrant because these ways divorce them from their past and distance them from their children. The stories of Geeta the young business executive who wants to marry a Chicano man or of Jagjit the young sardar boy who, ostracized by his class mates, is adopted by homeboys. He cuts his hair and sheds his turban and becomes a drug peddler in a false move towards friendship, status and power. But the attempts at assimilation into mainstream culture by the younger generation often render their immigrant parents alone and homeless in both India and abroad. America for the older generation becomes a place to which they lose their children as in the Parsi community of Wadia Baug (*Bombay Time*). In *The Mistress of Spices* although parents share the same geographic space as their children they register similar feelings of loss and alienation from their children. (This will be discussed further in Chapter 7 "Diaspora Homes") The children too, speak a different emotional language so they are not unable to hear "the frightened love in your father's voice losing you to America" (82), nor do they understand parental fears.

For the younger generation the Immigrant Dream though is not only to be in America but to become American. Becoming American for some, like Gogol (*The Namesake*) is not merely acquiring citizenship or even material comforts but something less tangible and more crucial. In *The Mistress of Spices* the Barbie doll becomes the icon for a young immigrant girl's longings. For her, being American would necessitate a physical racial transformation to whiteness. She yearns for the fair skin, blond hair and blue eyes of Barbie and also for the emblematic sexualized female body replete with high heels, breasts and pin-thin waist. Torn by divided loyalties and conflicting cultural notions she laments, "and even though I know I shouldn't, I must be proud like Mother says to be Indian, I wish for that American skin, that American hair, those blue blue American eyes so that no one will stare at me except to say WOW." (66). The racialized and sexualized female body seen as American is the antithesis of parental notions or desires of Indianness especially in its women. Tilo's own transformation from a wrinkled, old woman to an attractive young one worthy of being desired by an American who can see through her disguise to the real person reiterates a similar transformation even though it is not a racial one. The film version, in casting Aishwarya Rai, Bollywood's leading lady and judged the world's most beautiful woman, alters this particular premise of being able to see the reality beneath the mask.

The Spice Bazaar however is not merely an Indian space restricted to Indians only. For the American who dares to cross the threshold and enter this foreign space it becomes the lieu of America's fantasies about India and the mysterious orient. The "exotic east" is located in the smells and materiality of the spices, but it is embodied in the Mistress of Spices herself. She is the ever old/young wise and caring mother/lover figure. Initially Tilo is a performer of ethnicity in this space. She is the witch/mother/sister/friend – and above all the healer. Tilo chides Raven for what he sees in her,

> You have loved me for the color of my skin, the accent of my speaking, the quaintness of my customs which promised you the magic you no longer found in the women of your own land. In your yearning you have made me into that which I am not (309).

But Raven because of his Native American heritage has the capacity to see beneath the surface and intuit. Their common borderless empathy and intuition links them and makes them equal. He did not take the path of magic once offered by his great grandfather because he was too young. And she, Tilo, having taken the path, is now ready to forsake it for the normalcy of everyday life that she had once spurned. The exotic and orientalized space of the Spice Bazaar is transformed into what Mary Louise Pratt terms a "contact zone". At the end although Tilo and Raven acknowledge that each may love the "exotic image" (331) rather than the reality of the other, Divakaruni insists on the upbeat American mantra of multicultural existence, "let's teach each other what we need to know" (331).

At a personal level, however, the Spice Bazar is Tilo's home.

She lives and sleeps there. It is also like her second body. She compares it to a snail's shell,

> ... the store was already around me, its hard, protective shell. The spices too surrounded me, a shell of smells and voices. And that other shell, my aged body pressing its wrinkles into me. Shell within shell within shell, and inmost of all my heart beating like a bird (133).

Thus, when she leaves the store for the first time, the layers that mask and protect her innermost self are peeled away and she is "struck by the sudden vertigo of homelessness" (137). In stepping out of the protective space she renders herself vulnerable like any ordinary woman. The momentous stepping out of women protagonists in Indian English novels is often a subconscious recalling of the mythological tradition of Sita crossing the protective boundary in the *Ramayana*. The protagonists are acutely aware of the price they will have to pay for stepping across the *Lakshmana Rekha* of patriarchal protection.

One has to wonder how location impacts the possibilities of change. Charvi (*Song of the Cuckoo Bird*) cannot even envisage giving up the ashram even though it becomes a home turned prison. Tilo on the other hand is able to think fearlessly of breaking the rules and walking out of the spice shop in America. Laila (*Sunlight on a Broken Column*), Urmila (*Vine of Desire*) and Jaya (*That Long Silence*) do step out of constraining homes be they havelis, bungalows or apartments in India but their stepping out seems to be weightier as if they are fully cognizant of the rough road ahead and the real fears of vulnerability and homelessness. These are the fears that prevent Tara (*Tara Lane*) and Geeta (*Inside the Haveli*) from walking out. A post colonial westernized and western educated woman living in India faces a very different reality from an Indian-American woman. In the Indian context even an alternate living space like the ashram suggests its own temporariness and unreality as a viable feminine community or domestic space.

The protagonist's ability to reshape or remake oneself anew

is a less loudly celebrated trope in India based women writers. Name changes as a signature of identity change for example in the Indian context is not viewed positively as this is often imposed by the marital family, as we see in Shashi Deshpande's *Binding Vine*. America based writers like Chitra Divakaruni and Bharati Mukherjee however view it more positively from the perspective of remaking oneself. But even there there is a difference between Tilo and the young protagonist of Bharati Mukherjee's *Jasmine*. Both use the idea of changing names to reinvent themselves and new personas indicate turning points in their lives. But unlike Jasmine, Tilo is not dependent on each new man in her life to bestow a new name and reshape her identity. Even in the loving space of the island she does not let the mother give her a new name—she chooses it herself. And when she chooses her last name, Maya, it is a very deliberate, thought through gesture of choosing a name that is not specifically Indian or American. She does not want a hyphenated existence as Asian-American or Indian-American but "one that spans my land and yours, India and America, for I belong to both now" (337). The over-articulated cheesy words and sentiments however don't diminish Tilo in the way that Jasmine's name changes seem to reduce her.

The search for new homes and communities whether in India or abroad are tinged with expectation and nostalgia. If, as Homi Bhaba says, memory is the essential link to cultural identity then the new homes envisaged in these novels will have to be literally 'remembered' or put together. The novels seem to insist that even new domestic spaces are anchored in the past and have to emerge into the present from that past however felicitous or traumatic the past may have been. Postcolonial critic Leela Gandhi notes that the process of "forging the reparative continuity between cultural identity and the historical past ..."[14] is essential for analysts and the novels indicate that this is a work that at least women authors take very seriously. Their evocation of Indianness, community and womenspace in the various domestic spaces of haveli, bungalow and apartment link past and the present and draw them into a slightly altered but essentially seamless future.

References

1 Partha Chatterjee. *The Partha Chatterjee Omnibus"* OUP. Delhi. 1999.

2 Marcus, Sharon. *Apartment Stories: City and Home in Nineteenth-Century Paris and London.* Berkley,London: University of California Press, 1999.

3 http://www.umrigar.com/interview/indian_express.html Indian Express interview By Sujeet Rajan

4 Mehta, Suketu. *Maximum City : Bombay lost and found.* London : Review, 2004.

5 Elizabeth Robins, in a speech to the WWSL, 1907. Quoted as prologue to Shashi Deshpande's *That Long Silence.*

6 http://www.umrigar.com/interview/

7 Mistry, Rohinton. *Swimming lessons, and other stories from Firozsha Baag.* Boston : Houghton Mifflin, 1989.

8 The Parsis were political refugees from Persia, members of the close-knit Zoroastrian community who came to India about a thousand years ago. They are largely concentrated in Bombay and are among the more affluent communities. They integrated linguistically and in terms of dress but kept their distinct customs and rituals like other minority communities. The strict rules against marriage outside the community has led to a demographic dwindling of population. For further information see http:// en.wikipedia.org/wiki/Parsi

9 http://www.umrigar.com/interview/india_currents.html India Currents Interview By Jeanne Fredriksen

10 Rich, Adrienne. "Compulsory Heterosexuality and Lesbian Existence" (1978) *Blood, Bread and Poetry: Selected Prose 1979-1985.* W.W. Norton & Company, New York, London, 1986.

11 Holy Basil or *Ocimum tenuiflorum* is an important herb in Ayurvedic medicine. The name tulsi or tulsai means "the incomparable one". Tulsai is the symbol of Vishnu and Lakshmi.

12 Esquivel, Laura. *Like Water for Chocolate.* New York : Doubleday, 1992.

13 Gilman, Charlotte Perkins. *Herland* (1915). New York : Pantheon Books, 1979.
   Rokeya, Sakhawat Hossain. *Sultana's dream and selections from The secluded ones.* New York : Feminist Press : 1988

14 Gandhi, Leela : *Postcolonial Theory: A Critical Introduction.* New York: Columbia University Press, 1998 [10].

5

Women-Only Homes

The physically segregated women's space that was the hallmark of the traditional haveli-style dwelling was absent in both the Westernized bungalow and in the urban apartment. The contradictory pulls of opening up and yet guarding the domestic space evident in colonial times were replicated in postcolonial India in extradomestic spaces. In *Same-Sex Love in India: Readings from Literature and History* Ruth Vanita notes that,

> if the court and the all-male communities around it disappeared in independent India, such communities reappeared in different guises elsewhere. And if the women's quarters began to meld into a shared family space (a process by no means complete today), women's schools, colleges, and hostels provided new all-women environments into which men were not allowed.[1]

But the physical absence of segregated women's spaces at home masks the emotional continuity of a 'womenspace'—where women seek out other women for emotional support. The pattern of womanly empathy and emotional support continued in both the bungalow and the apartment dwellings even though the physical space was no longer a part of these new domestic structures. A woman to woman connection was maintained in women's friendships even as the housing styles changed from haveli to bungalow to apartments. I am not suggesting, and, neither do the novels suggest, a homo-erotic community of women. There is an absence of sexual love among women and I agree with Vanita's contention that "Love need not take an explicitly sexual form, but it is nearly always expressed in language of poetic excess and metaphoric power."[2] In these Indian English novels however, even this language of excess is missing. It is possible to attribute this silencing to the "new homophobia" that was a result of colonial values. As Vanita explains it is not as if homophobia did not exist in precolonial India but this new virulent strain that continues in contemporary India is a colonial import. There are thus no sexual, lesbian overtones in these novels unless one wants to follow Adrienne Rich's mapping of female friendships as being on a "lesbian continuum." Rich defines the term "lesbian continuum to include a range—through each woman's life and throughout history—of woman-identified experience".[3] And the novels do point to "woman-identified" experience where women reach out to and link with other women across class, caste and age. Since the abstract idea of 'womenspace' originates from a concrete physical domestic space it seems logical to try and relocate it in a domestic setting. How does the zenana or womenspace of the earlier dwellings transform, if it does, when houses become women-only homes?

If traditional feudal homes or colonial patriarchal homes and even religious refuges are more prisons than havens for women, is it possible to conceive of distinctly separate domestic spheres or 'women-only' homes? Early feminist utopias like Rokeya Sakhawat Hossain's *Sultana's Dream* (1905) or Charlotte Perkins Gilman's *Herland* (1915) provide one kind of model for separate women's homes and communities. Anita Desai's, *Fire on the Mountain* (1977), Indrani Aikath-Gyaltsen's *Daughters of the House* (1991) and Shashi Deshpande's *The Binding Vine* (1993) explore the possibilities of different women-only homes. The homes in these novels are different from the

earlier utopian genres, and also from earlier haveli, bungalow and apartment homes, as well as from each other. However, all three pose the question of whether and how the absence of men affects domestic space and domestic ideologies
including women's community formations. Some Indian
women may have acquired, not only rooms of their own, but,
homes of their own, however the novels suggest that that is
not enough. Neither women nor their homes are an island
unto themselves. Women-only homes may provide a temporary refuge but in these novels they are not seen as permanent or viable dwellings. A sense of community and connection with the world around them including men and the male
community seems to be essential or these homes risk turning
into dystopias.

Shashi Deshpande's *The Binding Vine* (1993) stands apart
from the other two novels. Although specific homes are the
location of the action and the denouement of the plot, she
focuses on an abstract sense of women's community as home.
The Binding Vine constructs a virtual home through narration.
An exploration and concern with so-called women's issues
link women in domestic and extradomestic spaces. Their common trials and joys in patriarchal homes and societies lead
them to seek each other out as support systems. In the other
women-only homes in Gyaltsen and Desai the zenana or
women's space of the original haveli is enlarged or even physically transformed into becoming a house for women only.
However, like the zenana within the haveli, these homes are
not necessarily free or liberated spaces. Women, even in
women-only homes, can become authoritarian tyrants. And
the question of the viability of an isolated existence remains.
Although the sense of community among women is maintained
to a more or less degree in all three novels, the structures of
patriarchy and particular domestic ideologies have been so
internalized that they continue to impinge upon women's existence. In each of the novels we note the geographic isolation
of women-only houses, delimiting the boundaries and spaces
of male and female interactions, of what is kept in and what is

relegated to the outside. Second, we note the specifically female lineage and the legacy of the houses where class and
generational boundaries are blurred. The female inheritance
of houses is linked to a self-revelation whereby the house
itself is configured as a repository of the history of its earlier
women inhabitants. Third, we see that issues of power and
women's sexuality are central to the interaction between
women and men both inside and outside the house. Rape is
seen as the logical end or the culmination of a systemic power
imbalance between women and men. Each of the novels provides a very different answer to the possibility of living along-
side, if not with, men, even in women-only homes.

Location

In Indrani Aikath-Gyaltsen's *Daughters of the House* (1991)
and Anita Desai's *Fire on the Mountain* (1977), the houses under consideration are – 'Panditji's House' and 'Carignano'.
Panditji's house is located on a sort of island separated from
the mainland by a river and Carignano stands on a mountain
top in Kasauli in the Simla foot-hills. As in many utopian literary works, isolation and inaccessibility signal the liminality of
these houses. Their very existence is threatened by a looming
outside world that can, and ultimately does, disrupt their particular women's way of life.

Indrani Aikath-Gyaltsen's fledgling literary career ended
dramatically at the age of forty-one. She was said to have
committed suicide in the wake of the scandal over the discovery that her acclaimed novel *Crane's Morning* was allegedly a
plagiarization of Elizabeth Goudge's 1956 novel *The Rosemary
Tree*. Others, including her husband, suspect her family—
mainly her mother and sister— played a part in her death by
not getting her immediate medical attention for an asthma
attack. It is ironic that she died in her natal home, a disputed
property, in a women's house that she occupied with a mother
and sister with whom she was not on speaking terms.[4]

Panditji's house in Gyaltsen's *Daughters of the House* (1991)
stands in contrast to earlier patriarchal houses like Ashiana
(*Sunlight on a Broken Column*) and Jeewan Niwas (*Inside the*

Haveli). It is probably the most clearly articulated statement of the spatial division of women's houses from those of men. In fact, a river serves as an almost organic, natural, if fluid, boundary between male and female homes. Four women— Madhuchchanda, her sister Mala, their aunt Madhulika, and the servant Paro—live in a female household in "Panditji's house." The women live on the edge of poverty and the servant, Paro, makes subsistence possible by drawing from her savings. The genteel lifestyle of the women is disrupted by the unwelcome news that the aunt Madhulika has married their neighbour Pratap, who lives on the other side of the river. The house of women is thrown into turmoil by this male intrusion. Soon after the newlyweds return home, Madhulika falls ill and dies. In the meantime Madhuchchanda (called Chchanda for short) and her aunt's husband become lovers. At the end, although she is expecting Pratap's child, Chchanda refuses to marry him. The house remains a patrimony of daughters.

The women's house of quietude and role reversals where the servant is literally a part of the family and her savings and earnings keep the house going is contrasted by the maleness, loudness and plenty of the landowning lawyers of the Thakur's house named "Wagner's House" on the other side of the river. "Thakur Sahib's house, a replica of Panditji's but in reverse. It was a household of men and of plenty."(13) The narrator explains the deliberate evocation of Wagner, comparing him to the Thakur "because of his loud voice."(13) The Thakur's son, Pratap, is "the enemy" who crosses over from the male space of "Wagner's House". The rather obvious contrast between male exteriority and female interiority is reified in Pratap's potential to seduce the women by his access to the outside world. He is seen as not merely an innocent outsider, but as a coloniser who invades and occupies the territory of the home and the body. He disrupts the female patterns of life, but, more dangerously attempts to alter the structure to conform to the heterosexual and patriarchal norm. His maleness is an intrusion into women's lives and their bodies (at least Madhulika and Chchanda's) and into the house that Chchanda views as a temple. He does not and cannot understand the secrets and rituals of the house: "Then the stairs creaked under the footsteps of a man whom two infatuated women had not been able to teach in over ten months that the sixth step was broken." (111) This everyday unfamiliarity keeps him a perpetual outsider and a potentially dangerous one who is often described as a "prowling" beast.

Daughters of the House envisages a concrete and separate existence for women, notwithstanding the male ownership of the house, reiterated both by the consistent reference, "Panditji's House" and Pratap's threatening male presence that seeks to dominate, circumscribe and enforce a malestream model of conformity by integrating it into a mainstream patriarchal mould. However, the reality of female occupancy over the legality of male ownership establishes the house as a female space. The domination of ownership is subverted and undermined by the women's ease and easy occupancy of the house that renders it theirs—a distinctive female space. The second chapter of the novel does not carry the plot forward but digresses to narrate the house into being. In what Shirley Ardener refers to as a "genealogical space", the female identity and lineage of the house is foregrounded.[5] Chchanda traces its lineage matrilineally, recalling that this was her maternal grandfather's house that her grandmother and Paro had looked after. Furthermore, her mother, aunt, sister and she were all born in the house; whereas the forefather had only "set himself up there" (7). It is a patriarchal structure, occupied by three generations of women,—all only mothers, daughters and sisters—none of them wives.

The matrilineal genealogy in *Daughters of the House* is traced literally along bloodlines. But, in Anita Desai's *Fire on the Mountain* (1977), the genealogy transcends familial, ethnic and national boundaries. An anti-domestic, anti-wife genealogy of loneliness links the women—British and Indian—who have lived in Carignano, the isolated house in the hills. *Fire on the Mountain*, Desai's fifth novel, won both the 1978 National

Academy of Letters, or Sahitya Akademi, and the Royal Society Awards. The protagonist, Nanda Kaul, is an older woman. Now retired, she lives alone in Kasauli, a small hill resort on the Himalayan foothills which served as a poor second to the summer capital, Simla, in colonial times. Nanda presents the house, Carignano, as a safe haven, away from the demands of family and society, where she can finally be herself. But Nanda cannot escape familial ties when her great granddaughter Raka is sent to the hills to recuperate from an illness. In addition, her childhood friend Ila Das, now destitute, ekes out a living as a government-employed social worker in one of the villages in Kasauli. As a social worker, Ila works to stop child marriage which is illegal. In particular, she tries to prevent a local villager from marrying off his seven-year-old daughter. On her way back from visiting Nanda, Ila is raped and murdered by the irate father, Preet Singh.[6] The novel ends darkly with not only Ila's brutal rape and murder but also a forest fire, caused by Raka, and Nanda's ambiguous end.

Nanda although Indian, is a legitimate and natural successor to the English women who have lived at Carignano. If Chchanda's inheritance of Panditji's house seeks to pass on a womanly legacy of quiet role reversals and equality, Nanda's inheritance of alienation and pain is more problematic. Her isolation and cultivated quietude are deliberately interrupted by the bridging figure of the postman who connects her with the outside world. His womb-like, fecund canvas bag bulges with the social obligations of domesticity. Nanda reacts with distaste to "the sight of him, inexorably closing in with his swollen bag, rolled a fat ball of irritation into the cool cave of her day, blocking it stupidly." (3) The postman, like the telephone later, is a public conduit—like Pratap or the river in *Daughters of the House*, which links the womanly home to the world of gendered social expectations. In both novels outside communication, in the shape of letters, shatter the carefully created interior, private space of the house and its inhabitants. The letters are seen as clamouring demands of society. The history of Carignano though inhabited mainly by women is mediated through a male chronicler. The postman is the laconic record-keeper, the self-appointed historian who is able to trace back the house's inhabitants from 1843 to 1947 and then adds Nanda to the list of earlier inhabitants as their natural successor.

Carignano embodies the deep seated links between women and domesticity fundamentally unaltered by historical and political change. In 1947, at the moment of Indian independence, Nanda is able to buy a house in Kasauli—the ownership changes from British to Indian, she stands at an historical crossroad. In the transition from colonialism to post-coloniality, the ownership of the house is transferred but the gendered structural pattern of the house itself remains unchanged. The text strongly suggests a seamless continuity by placing Nanda at the centre. She is linked back to the previous English owners as her spiritual ancestors, and she looks forward to her great granddaughter as a possible inheritor of Carignano just as Chchanda looks forward to her daughter Madhumita inheriting Panditji's house. Desai's associative pairing of contrasting images of the eagle and the cuckoo, barrenness and fertility, freedom and imprisonment reiterate the stark dichotomous choices that the wives who inhabit Carignano, then and now, might have had to make. Nanda identifies completely with even the physical landscape of her chosen home. The text asserts that both have achieved a "state of elegant perfection" (31). Raka reaffirms the almost seamless melding of her great grandmother with the house, noting, "She saw the old lady who murmured at her as another pine tree, the grey sari a rock—all components of the bareness and stillness of the Carignano garden." (40)

A leading scholar and literary critic, Malashri Lal, endorses Nanda's Carignano existence as one of quietitude and acceptance however. She claims:

Nanda Kaul represents a fairly discernible stance in Indian feminism as documented in social histories and biographies pertaining to the early twentieth century, a feminism which supports the domestic role of women while recognising their secret longing for an opportunity to function individually in the world outside the home. The mood is not of rebellion but calm acceptance of a sequence in women's lives.[7]

But this is to take Nanda's defensive assertions at face value. Nanda's silence is indeed deafening, and I would suggest that "calm acceptance" is not even aspired to in this novel. The setting of the novel in Kasauli is deliberate and signals a flawed paradise. Kasauli is an army cantonment area, colonial Kasauli with its cobbled paths was a verdant hill station—a quick escape from the scorching plains of Delhi. But the smoking chimney of the Pasteur Institute stands as a lone, looming, phallic sentinel dominating the landscape. The institute set up by the British in the 1900s produces anti-rabies vaccines. A reminder of madness and disease even in the midst of this lush refuge. Cronin notes the associative disjunction of the setting:

> The Institute is a factory in Shangri-la, a reminder that the stillness that Nanda Kaul finds in Kasauli, the stillness that she weaves around her, is not a natural but a manufactured product, an antidote to the madness of involvement refined as painstakingly as the doctors of the Institute refine their rabies serum.[8]

The threat to the vision of Kasauli as a peaceful idyll is compounded by Raka's restless wanderings, the forest fire, Ila's cruel rape and Nanda's own end, all of which are an antithesis to what Lal reads as "calm acceptance." The links between woman and house are fairly clearly articulated in both *Fire on the Mountain* and *Daughters of the House* but at another level it is also possible to read both novels in the Jamesonian way as allegories of nation. Furthermore, in both novels the links between home and body cannot be ignored either.

Home as Nation and as Body

Educated, middle class women like Nanda, Ila and Chchanda, prepared to step boldly into a new India were stopped short. Indian modernity was still deeply linked to a patriarchal past that adhered to strict rules about women and their place both inside the home and outside. As women-only houses sometimes replicated the patterns of feudal ideologies of hierarchy and lineage of earlier homes the links between home as nation and home as body persisted. In *Daughters of the House* the connection between house and nation are established in the very naming of the house. Jawaharlal Nehru, independent India's first prime minister, was popularly referred to as "Panditji". This house then recalls the larger house of India led by Pandit Nehru. But the temptation to read Gyaltsen's novel as "a political allegory" in the Jamesonian way raises many troubling questions about women's place, and indeed men's place, in independent India.[9] This house is "a property, and therefore an address, of certain reputation" (129). It remains, however, a deeply troubled dwelling for women who are unable to live in it with or without men, and equally so for men who are completely marginalised if not rejected in this narration. In spite of the many connections suggested between home and nation, they remain an unarticulated, hinted at subtext of this novel.

If one were to continue to read the parallel of home and nation then the postcolonial home that Nanda is finally allowed to buy is not that much of a change from the colonial home. It is a barren, womanly inheritance that perpetuates and passes on a legacy of loneliness and arid isolation. Shyam Asnani reads hope in Desai's usage of incompatible couples like the sparrow and the eagle as a "metonym for a new morality". He feels that "her fictional milieu is the India in transition with its cultural and ethical values in the melting pot."[10] But the end of the novel belies that hope. The sombre mood of destruction and death in the flawed paradise of Kasauli and postcolonial India seems hardly more hospitable than that of pre-colonial or even colonial India. Ila's death finally forces Nanda to confront the lie that her life has been. The fantasies she spun about her exotic childhood to beguile Raka are as hollow as her projection of Carignano as a longed-for retreat. In the end she is forced to confess that, "She did not live here alone by choice—she lived here alone because that was what she was forced to do, reduced to doing." (145) It was not a choice or Woolf's longed for 'room of one's own'. Necessity and ultimately a lack of options force Nanda Kaul to retreat to the hills. Carignano and Panditji's house are both initially depicted as safe havens or utopias that turn out to be painful exiles if not dystopias. We are unsure whether Nanda or the Carignano house survives the forest fire but Raka the heir-designate certainly rejects the Carignano legacy. And if we continue to read the house as even in some way associated with nation then the younger generation like Raka not only reject the legacy of this home and nation, but, even deliberately destroy it. And although Chchanda's daughter is still a baby her future seems to be in a nation where men and women have to live apart for women to have even a modicum of independence.

At one level houses can be read as nation in these novels but at another level one is almost forced to draw the obvious connections between house and body. Men are physically kept out of the home/body. A young Chchanda clearly articulates her relief at the absence of men. For her, men are minimised to mere penises. "Mala and I had no reason to envy the normal family lives of the few children we knew, nagged by tyrants with penises" (11). Shirley Ardener notes that in heterosexual homes, "the peripheralisation of men in the home . . . . is also a form of exclusion by women."[11] In these women-only homes men are not merely marginalized but physically excluded. Women as individuals and as a community resist men whether those men force their way or are invited in. In these home/bodies/nation men are episodic, useful only in helping to— ironically in the patriarchal Indian context of male gender preference—produce girl children. Chchanda's mother married and produced two daughters. But Madhulika's marriage to Pratap at the age of forty-five precludes continuity in the form of children. Paro's fear of him is based on the knowledge that if he is not there to serve the purpose of producing daughters, his presence signifies a threat to their unique situation that exists on the margins of a male dominant, patriarchal status quo. Madhulika allows a man into a house that for the past fifty years has been the sole preserve of women. Although the house and the women of the house reject the male presence initially, he is later accepted and even loved, but ultimately cast out as his presence tends to overwhelm and upset the careful balance of women and domesticity.

Structural Boundaries: Sexuality

The river is one of three sites of action in the novel, and becomes the central symbol of sexuality, marginality and liminality. It is a boundary that separates but also allows for the possibilities of both coming and going. It has the potential to bridge the distance between the two opposing sides, reconciling Wagner's house with the house of women. The novel opens on the inside of this dividing line. Sexual awakening is foregrounded in the image of Chchanda standing shivering at the riverbank, ready to dive in. Her child's body is revealed in her spontaneous undressing and her awareness that her breasts don't quite fill her aunt's hand-me-down brassieres—a forewarning of things to come. The mix of innocence and sexual awakening is repeated in Chchanda's suggestive description of the fish at the bottom of the pond:

> A long tapering one lying perfectly still, its nose at the mouth of the trap and a round one swimming frantically against the sides of the net, its silver scales gleaming. Uncle Katla and Aunt Rui. (3)

Until the fish are identified as such, we do not know that Mala and Chchanda are observing two fish, designated as "uncle" and "aunt" that are swimming around the trap. The trap, though, is clearly identified as belonging to "Wagner." The salient elements of the plot are allegorically narrated in this moment as Chchanda stands poised to dive. Chchanda's intervention can be read as sexual awakening, survival, and protection. The sexuality has been hinted at in Chchanda's awareness of her own unformed body. The only way of survival and continuity for her and for the house is ensuring that there is a next generation of women to inhabit the house. Materially, Chchanda justifies her dive for the fish—even if it means stealing them from the trap—because it will supplement their normal, meagre diet. Later, they also justify their aunt's marriage to Pratap as a way of solving their financial problems.

In the opening chapter of the novel, we are carefully brought back from the periphery of the river boundary with Chchanda's nascent awakening to sexuality, to the outer court, then into the inner court, past the purdah-like wall, and into the kitchen. The path back is meticulously mapped. It is on this path, on the return from the watery boundary but not yet safe in the house, that Paro hands Chchanda and Mala the letter from the outside that will disrupt their isolated female existence. It announces their aunt's marriage and explodes their cloistered world. The narrator reminds us that the house is "an oasis", an isolated female space. Curiously, however, the house is contradictorily described as both a matriarchy and yet sexually pure: "the matriarchy of Panditji's House was a universe of nuns, young and old." (11) The home/nation/body that is constantly referred to by its patriarchal ownership—Panditji's house—enforces a specific nun-like abstinence. The trinity of house, body and nation closes its doors against any incursions or dominations. The house cannot accommodate wives with husbands or bodies that accept occupation.

Structural Boundaries: Domesticity

Sexuality is one kind of boundary that divides women-only houses from the heterosexual norm. But the gender specific ideology of domesticity that had been challenged by women protagonists in haveli, bungalow and apartment homes is rejected outright in both *Daughters of the House* and *Fire on the Mountain*. In Desai particularly, a virulent, anti-domestic ideology that transcends both nationality and chronological time, connects Nanda to the earlier British women dwellers of Carignano. The narrative blurs the lines between the house and its inhabitants. It is a sanctuary edged with sadness. Positioned as a tentative refuge from the world, but the threat of violence lurks both within and around every corner of Carignano. The history of the house itself is marked by random violence and madness. Initially Carignano was built for a Mrs. MacDougall and her "ominously pale children" (6) as a refuge from the heat of the plains. The house is permeated with her pathetic sorrow as she forlornly gazes "out across the valley to Sabathu where, amongst the white flecks of the gravestones in the military cemetery, their own seven children came to be buried, one by one."(6) The next inhabitant was the short-tempered Miss Appleby who chides the gardener, whipping him for planting marigolds in her garden. She is succeeded by the pastor's wife who not only refuses to make him his much-yearned-for apricot jam but plots incessantly to kill him. Ironically, it is she who meets a violent end by falling down the hill and splitting her head open on a rock. The house itself is implicated in the random violence by the roof flying off and decapitating a coolie, way down in the plains. (6) The house itself seems to warn against anyone perceiving it as a haven. Its apparent isolation and calm serenity mask a dystopic space.

Nanda clearly articulates her distaste for the hollowness of the domestic ideology that her predecessors' stories have hinted at and that have driven her to seek refuge in Carignano.

> The care of others was a habit Nanda Kaul had mislaid. It had been a religious calling she had believed in till she found it fake. It had been a vocation that one day went dull and drought-struck as though its life-spring had dried up. (30)

Her own sad tale becomes another weave in the tapestry of the earlier angry, betrayed women who dwelt in the house. Her husband's lifelong affair with a Christian teacher whom he could not marry because of her religion is a double betrayal of both women. Confronted with the duplicity of the situation she, like Sita (*The Thousand Faces of Night*), had resolved to perfect the role of wife even though her faith in the domestic ideology had been destroyed, "But the truth is that outside of this role Nanda has nothing else to turn to."[12]

The mother and wife roles that Nanda plays mask her thoughts. If, as Ila claims, their upbringing and education had rendered them helpless to face a changing world, Nanda's example also shows that the domestic ideology that she had been trained for and the need to adjust have quite erased her.

It is easy to see Nanda as a forewarning or an older version of what Tara (*Tara Lane*) is doomed to become. Continuity of the womanly, if not the matrilineal, inheritance is suggested by placing Nanda at the centre looking back to the emotional inheritance of the British women that permeates the very walls of Carignano and looking forward to her great grand-daughter Raka as a possible inheritor of Carignano.

Carignano extends the lineage and association of woman and home by implying that biology and even nationality can become secondary to a specifically female condition that is rooted in patriarchal domestic relations. Women's loneliness within these largely unsatisfactory relationships is an organising feature of their domestic existence. A Nanda Kaul, like others before her, may finally escape a heterosexual home of inequality but the new home is permeated with the sadness of the earlier failed homes. The biological inheritance of flawed mother-daughter relationships that is passed down from Nanda (through her daughter) and on to her great grand-daughter, Raka, is a part of the complexity of *Fire on the Mountain*. It is possible to read Nanda, Raka, and Ila on a continuum, though they are differently shaped by class, social status and generational differences. Premila Paul and Padmanabhan Nair claim that Carignano is "synonymous with loneliness".[13] They see different kinds of loneliness as the link that unites the three main characters — Nanda, Raka and Ila. Nanda seeks to bequeath this dubious estate that she has inherited to her great granddaughter. Raka's recognition of a pattern of victimisation through her "broken, twittering mother" (64) leads her to firmly reject, and to deliberately destroy both Nanda and the Carignano legacy. The devouring forest fire has the potential to burn down the forests around and also to destroy the house, thereby ending the complicity of women and domesticity.

Structural Boundaries: Religion

Sexuality and domesticity are reinforced in the way religion and more specifically Christianity is curiously placed in the intersections of nation, and a women-only-home-culture in both *Fire on the Mountain* and *Daughters of the House*. Christianity is positioned against a male-dominated Hindu India and it may also be possible to read the novels in terms of the role of minority communities in an all-absorbing majority Hindu ethos that infiltrates the psyche and social patterns of even the minorities. Ila, a Christian, once-upper-class-woman, sees her religion as enabling her to be open to change and survive even when she loses her class status. Her own example leads her to believe that women, even poor Hindu women, who are willing to be taught could transcend cultural barriers and accept change. But, in the end, the liberal laws that she, as a government worker, is enjoined to implement are no match against traditional practice. Legislation that may be beneficial to women, like the abolition of child marriage, is seen as threatening traditional male authority. Cultural Hindu traditions and religion are embodied in the "oily priest" who actively prevents women from improving their lot (129). In this context, the priest's opposition to Ila's efforts at reform have to be seen on the same continuum as Preet Singh's rape.[14] The priest's passive aggression makes him complicit in the rape even if he does not himself commit the act.

In *Daughters of the House*, Paro's Roman Catholicism is her first link to the house that was built on church ground. The specifically Christian imagery in this case overtly suggests religion as a form of imprisonment especially for women. The novel defies any simplistic reading, but the themes of temptation, the fall, betrayal, guilt, and finally the notion of the house as having been "saved" (124) set up certain cultural referents and a sense of community that interrogates and resists mainstream Hindu ideologies of India and of women's roles in it. Parvati, the Christian maidservant with the (unconverted) name of a Hindu goddess, is the guardian of the house and of the women within.[15] Her role as surrogate mother, guardian and jailer is just one of the ambiguities of the text.[16]

The Christian identity of the house is more or less lost or erased as it becomes "Panditji's house"—a marker that signals Hindu Indian ownership. But the moment of Chchanda's transition from sexual innocence to knowledge is again figured in Christian terms. A self-aware Chchanda describes the moment:

> I suddenly recalled the tales of Roman Catholic saints that Paro was so fond of telling us. I had the odd notion that, in my slip, with the light shining through my hair in a sort of aureole, I must look like a holy virgin about to be martyred for 'the faith'. (61)

But the faith for which she may be a martyr remains unclear. Is it the Christian faith of the house or the womanly faith of this particular home? For Paro, the house is the embodiment of both a female community and Christianity.

This is not a Christian female community but one where a cultural Christianity pervades. Religion per se does not seem to be particularly relevant, even to Parvati herself. Her vision of a womenspace is described within a framework of Christian imagery as a nunnery. In this context she views Madhulika's marriage almost in terms of original sin. Re-visioning the house as a nunnery links it back to its Christian origins but also alters the position of women within. Pratap's intrusion is thus framed in the context of a dual legacy of femininity and Christianity. Parvati is the moral and spiritual guardian of the house. Seen through her Christian lens, Pratap's entrance disrupts the matriarchal, female space and violates the nun-like state of its inhabitants: "The matriarchy of Panditji's House was a universe of nuns, young and old. It was an oasis" (11). Paro, as Mother Superior, has to keep the wolf at bay and protect the integrity of the house as a shelter from male presence.

Madhulika's marriage and Chchanda's seduction are both seen within the Christian framework of sin. Their "fall", is both betrayal and alienation. Eve is evoked in the secret sense of knowledge and pleasure that the body feels, but the loss is nonetheless poignant. The separation from the virginal body of innocent childhood brings pain, blood, and a renegotiation of the self's relation to the outside world. Chchanda recalls the moment of her "betrayal" in specifically Christian imagery. She notes the sense of a religious abandonment in her liaison with Pratap: "I was left as unprovided for as a nun who has lost even her faith" (113). The loss of faith is not only a Christian one but a female one too — that of a community of women. The name Pratap calls out, "Madhuchchanda," is to her "My name but not my name alone" (61). The multiple betrayals of the house as nunnery and a womenspace and of a woman by another woman, an aunt by her niece, are explicitly stated.

The rejection, however, is reciprocated by the house. The house, where until the moment of sexual transformation Chchanda "knew her way by instinct" becomes "a house that does not know me anymore." In a very Forsterian moment, everything seems to conspire to say no to their relationship:[17]

> And Panditji's House seemed to resent me, every tree twisted by the violent March winds protested at my treachery. They would bend to the right, straighten up, then bend to the left, saying, No . . . . no . . . . no . . . . It was the voice of the house itself I seemed to hear (58-59).

This is a pivotal moment when both the house and the women in it betray and reject each other. In different ways, both Chchanda and Madhulika are "punished" for their transgressions.

Madhulika steps across the Lakshmana rekha or what Malashri Lal calls the patriarchal "law of the threshold", of the house's matriarchal protectiveness and is both punished and rejected for doing so.[18] The house with the "yellow room" at its heart is the second site of action in the novel, and like the river earlier, it too emphasises a specifically female space, while additionally signalling an inter-textual reference to Charlotte Perkins Gilman's 1892 short story, "The Yellow Wallpaper". The parallels of the two similar yellow rooms are ironic and deliberate. Both texts view domesticity as the root of women's oppression. That was a yellow room where a wife was imprisoned (for her own good) by a husband. But here, in *Daughters of the House*, the punishment comes from within, or almost, from the maternal house. The text suggests that the lupus that ravages the beautiful Madhulika almost as soon as she returns home after her marriage should be read as a punishment.[19] Madhulika's confinement in the yellow room seems to be a punishment for breaking the strictly female and Christian code of the nunnery/house. Is she being punished for her "desertion" of the house?[20] The house here takes on enigmatic and almost sinister proportions. In Gilman, the house is a patriarchal structure where the doctor husband offers care and protection but his overwhelming care transforms the house into a prison. The patriarchal structure of Gilman's story is mirrored in Panditji's matriarchal house.

Stifled by love in this house of women, all Madhulika asks for are the same rights to marriage and children that other women have. But this house/nunnery is a house where only single women are permitted. Madhulika, despite her love for Paro, accuses:

It's your fault, you know it. You have confined the world. I want to be happy. You want to have me here for the rest of all our lives. That's the way you love me. But I'm tired of carrying the entire burden. I want to be happy. You are too demanding. (20)

Madhulika's simple desire for heterosexual conformity cannot be allowed in a nunnery or a house of women only. And like the husband in Gilman's "The Yellow Wallpaper", Paro, the servant and surrogate mother, becomes the jailer. Her outrage at the news of Madhulika's marriage is in sharp contrast to her very different reaction to Chchanda's liaison with Pratap. The permanency that marriage implies, rather than mere sex, is the issue. Paro reiterates the stereotypes of male behaviour that inevitably displace women and render them homeless as reasons for not accepting the marriage. The subtext is clear: if these daughters of the house could be treated so shabbily, then she, as a servant, would be doubly vulnerable. Sexuality or virginity can be overlooked especially if a temporary liaison can provide another daughter, as it has in the past, to carry on the legacy of the house. But permanent occupation is a threat that undermines the fundamental basis of the house.

Chchanda's being with a man, even her uncle, is seen as quite different from her aunt's choice. Pratap is not blamed for seducing her. He may be the outsider, but Chchanda willingly becomes his mistress. This sense of agency is also a strong component of Laila's character (*Sunlight on a Broken Column*). Laila knows that her love for Ameer changes her situation and not necessarily something that Ameer does. Chchanda, too, acknowledges her participation and the contradictory emotions the relationship elicits:

> But he had also succeeded in silencing what remained in me of yesterday's virgin, stifled now in her ecstatic shame, stupefied at recovering her former modesty together with the bitter recognition, the tenderness of her whole flesh, the very joy of drawing breath with another body which has just revealed to you the insistence of your own. (70)

The virgin Chchanda is silenced but sexual pleasure is seen as less of a threat to the house. The more problematic aspect is what Chchanda herself is the first to recognise. This liaison gives her "a taste for another kind of existence so that in the end it would be easier to wean me away from the soil of Panditji's House." (49) Uprooting and dislocation are uppermost in Chchanda's evocation of the idea of roots in her invocation of "the soil of Panditji's House." She sees Pratap's seduction as an effort to uproot her. And she is honest enough to acknowledge her own fleeting temptation and desire. The text posits an alliance with Pratap as an alienation from a natural female inheritance and genealogy embodied by and rooted in the house. Pratap threatens dislocation not only in terms of a womanly life-style of equality and harmony but an uprooting of that very feminine, anti-domestic ideology.

Gyaltsen seems to reinforce, disturbingly, not only the male-female opposition, but also links them in a continuum of male/city/confusion/wickedness/riches against female/country/interiority/genteel poverty. The equally rigid binaries on either side tend to make border crossings fatal. The deaths of both Chchanda's mother, Aparajita, and her aunt Madhulika bear testimony to that. Panditji's house is as much a cemetery for them as the marital zenana is for Abida (*Sunlight on a Broken Column*). Both sisters resist the "nun-like" single state of the house and assert their right to marriage and childbearing. They struggle to break free of the stranglehold of the possessive love of house, nieces, and Paro through marriage. Madhulika protests: "[a]fter all, I'm a woman and have the same right to marriage" (21) but the supposed permanency of marriage upsets the status quo of Panditji's house and cannot be permitted. Women's sexuality remains an organising principle of this house of women just as it is in other houses—havelis, bungalows and apartments—in the novels. The "virgin" Chchanda may indeed have been willingly silenced, but from the text it would appear that the "sexual woman" has not yet found a voice even in a house of women.

Silencing

Shashi Deshpande's *The Binding Vine* weaves an intricately complex narrative that incorporates the stories of three women of different ages and social backgrounds. Their stories though intensely individual and personal are inflected and highlighted by larger issues of women's solidarity especially around issues of public and private in women's lives. The narrator, Urmila, is a college teacher, coping with the grief of losing her infant daughter. Although her mother and childhood friend, Vaana, offer support, she finds escape, sanity and the will to cope in decoding and gradually understanding her long dead mother-in-law Mira's letters and poems; and in caring for Kalpana, a rape victim, who hangs between life and death. The story of Kalpana's rape is mediated through her distraught mother, Shakutai, who alternately blames her daughter and herself for the rape. At the same time Urmila uncovers Mira's story of marital rape through her writings.

The narrative juxtaposes issues of private and public in relation to issues of women's silence and sexuality. Deshpande links writing and rape as acts that women try to hide and label as private issues. Although them in the public sphere can render individual women vulnerable. The text suggests that women's conspiracy of silence regarding these issues could lead to a stronger community formation among women as the issues are specifically gendered. Although breaking the silence and foregrounding it in the public domain may endanger the tenuous ties of a familial community, it could also create a larger virtual community of women who could in fact be empowered by these revelations. The issues raise questions of women's silence, sexuality and of their interaction with men in the home and outside. Urmila's involvement with Shakutai draws her out of herself and her middle class milieu into the lower class, poorer world of a chawl-dwelling, working women. Transcending generational and class boundaries, Urmila rethinks her life through the connections she establishes with the deceased Mira's writings and Shakutai. The narratives link these women's lives and comment upon each other, imperceptibly transcending the boundaries of inside/outside spaces, time, and class.

The sense of community that Urmila creates with other women is based ultimately on empathy, individual friendships, honesty and respect rather than on abstract notions of sisterhood that often try to elide rather than face differences even between women. At one level it is possible to read the notion of women's community located only in the domestic space or in the specific links among women like Vaana, Urmila, Shakutai and Mira. However, a novel like *The Binding Vine* raises larger questions about what in fact, binds women to each other in strong sisterly bonds that sustain; and what they need to do as women to reshape relationships with the particular men in their lives and with patriarchal societal structures. Family loyalty, because it is often the only available support network, is highly valued. In novels like Umrigar's *The Space Between Us*, for instance, it can seem to be overvalued if not a concrete obstacle to women's friendships. In *The Binding Vine*, the question of a female, familial support network is posited against the larger issue of perpetuating womanly silence to protect the notion of family honour.

In a penetrating article on widows as a literary subject, Susie Tharu notes, "in modern Indian literature the choice of

the widow as protagonist should be read as an announce-
ment that the text is an intervention in feminist theory."[21]
Although the choice of a protagonist is not particularly note-
worthy in *The Binding Vine*, the issues it raises are an overt
intervention and an exploration of some key issues in feminist theory. Urmila—the mother, sister-in-law, friend and
daughter-in-law—at the centre of the narrative explores familial and gender roles that tie down and silence women. The
woman-to-woman bonds of birth, biology and nurture, unite
women but Deshpande also questions issues of women's silence as a consequence of their subaltern status that have been
the focus of feminist discussions. Silence, in this novel, as in
many of Deshpande's other works, is seen as an erasure of
woman. Although the recovery of women's writing has been
a significant feminist project in establishing a history and tradition of women's writing, this novel also reveals the very
real constraints on women writers and on the price that may
have to be paid in uncovering their writings. In the two volumes, *Storylines: Conversations with Women Writers* and *Just Between Us: Women Speak About their Writing*, Indian women writers of ten major languages conclude that "writing is a subversive activity in patriarchal societies. To take up the pen and
write one's destiny is the ultimate transgression …" They reveal the "gendered" nature of censorship whether it is imposed by family and society or whether it is self-imposed by
women.[22] Urmila is faced with exactly this dilemma of whether
she should publish her mother-in-law's work and thereby bring
"shame" by outing what is seen as an essentially "private" or
family matter. Psychologist Sudhir Kakar, among other anthro-
pologists, classifies India as a "shame culture" rather than a
"guilt culture" and in shame cultures family reputation and
notions of honour are of paramount importance.[23] In the same
vein, Shakutai and Urmila have to choose between keeping quiet
about Kalpana's rape to keep the respect or "*izzat*" of the family intact or to out it and place the blame where it truly belongs, on the perpetrator rather than on the victim. Deshpande
is balanced in her gradual working out of society's role in the

silencing of women and in women's own collusion in perpetuating the silence, and the price of breaking that silence.

Women's House of Words—Legacy

The deceased Mira's writing, as discovered and mediated
by Urmila, is an escape and a form of resistance from a domestic and marital confinement. In many ways Mira's secret diaries prove to be a virtual retreat in the way that the physical
house Carignano is a retreat for Nanda in *Fire on the Mountain*.
The focus on Mira foregrounds both her marital rape and her
writing, and the two are organically linked. As Mira emerges
through her writing, Urmila sees that her mother-in-law's writing is her real inheritance. She sees it as a gift of womanly
knowledge for all women, and not for her alone. Sharing the
secret of her marital rape, as revealed in the diaries, will show
other women that they are not alone. I will return to the issue
of rape later. But here I would like to note that Mira's writings
are seen as a women's inheritance just as the houses were an
inheritance that Madhuchchanda and Nanda wanted to bequeath to their daughter and great granddaughter respectively.
In *The Binding Vine* a woman-to-woman bond of genealogy
and legacy is established and transmitted through the writing
for all women. The house is recalled, but the writing and revelations are what link Urmila, Shakutai, Vaana, and Akka in bonds
of womanly solidarity and concern that transcend family ties.

For Urmila, the reality of Mira is established through her
writing. The jewellery that her step mother-in-law, Akka, cer-
emoniously hands over to her as the daughter-in-law underscores Urmila's traditional place in her husband Kishore's family. It establishes a link and continuity with his mother. But in
the handing over of the trunk full of Mira's writings, her books
and papers Kishore is bypassed and a direct woman to woman
connection is foregrounded. Urmila astutely notes the difference in the two presentations and remarks, "She [Akka] did
not mention Kishore at all, as if she was now directly linking
me with Mira"(48). She is Mira's inheritor as both a daughter-
in-law, thereby asserting the familial connection, and as a
woman, thereby emphasising female friendship and shared

experiences. The two objects of inheritance—jewellery and an old trunk—are themselves careful symbols: one of womanly ornamentation, and the other, possibly of female sexuality, as Freud might see it.[24] Through her writing, Mira bequeaths her the real wealth of self-revelation. And the self-revelation is that of a woman writer. Urmila knows that "the next time I open the trunk, it will be in search of Mira" (49). The writing — poems, diaries and random notes scribbled in books—reveal Mira's hidden life:

> As if in opening the book, we had released a genie; she came alive, she was suddenly all about us—in the books with her notes scribbled all over, in the scraps of paper on which she had written words, lines in Kannada (43).

Urmila wants to extend the bond to a larger community of women and men by publishing Mira's writing. Within Urmila's close circle, women's primary affiliations to each other are based on a shared past or the common experience of gendered roles of wives, mothers and daughters. Urmila is sharply aware of the sense of community with other women and realises that giving Mira a voice she may be empowering other women across generations who continue to be silenced by similar experiences. But initially Urmila is hesitant to even read Mira's personal thoughts, for fear of trespassing, "to violate her [Mira's] privacy, to lay bare her tragic story" (51). The move to publish would not only extend the hitherto private into the public sphere; it would jeopardise the intricate web of relationships since the poems implicate men who are husbands, fathers and sons. Especially the one man who was husband to Mira and Akka, and is Vaana's father and Urmila's father-in-law.

Two integrated aspects of Mira's writing are language and secrecy. The issue ties in with Mira's choice of writing her diaries in English whereas the poems are in Kannada. In uncovering Mira's journal and poems Urmila gradually sees the integral connection between public and private, and life and art. Mira's bilingualism, as Urmila herself notes, is not unusual. However, the clear choice and allocation of language to genre is significant. In Indian English writing it is worth noting that bilingual women writers like Kamala Das and Mrinal Pande, for instance, write prose and poems in one language but choose to write their autobiographies in English.[25] Das and Pande might have felt that writing their life stories in English allowed them a certain freedom and distance either in terms of the writing itself or in terms of the audience. These autobiographies, as well as memoirs like Meena Alexander's *Fault Lines*, articulate the anxiety of claiming individuality and separating from the group, which is seen as especially difficult for a woman and an Indian woman bound by the "we" ethos mentioned earlier. Traditionally in literature, diary writing is considered to be a preferred feminine genre.[26] But in the end Urmila realises that the poems and the diary inform each other despite the fact that Mira herself made a conscious linguistic distinction between the two. But to uncover Mira, the woman and the writer, both her diary in English and her poems in Kannada have to be considered.

Gender is an important consideration in Mira's awareness of herself as a writer. Through her writing we glimpse how tentative the deceased Mira was about her identity as a writer. She hones her craft in secret, afraid of being mocked for her effrontery, and full of self-doubt about her worth:

Huddled in my cocoon, a somnolent silkworm
will I emerge a beauteous being?
Or will I, suffocating, cease to exist? (65)

Mira's suffocation and diffidence stem from her choice of a male normative model. Her hero is a young male poet, Venu. Acceptance of this male model dooms Mira to silence. The real conflict is not so much between Kannada and English or even, as Urmila points out, between the difference in genres of the poetry and the diary form. It is not really a choice, as the women writers quoted earlier note, in male dominated societies, including Mira's conservative Indian society, the mainstream tends to be a normative "male stream."[27]

Mira writes in secret because she is afraid. The secrecy and anxiety in Mira's writings, both the diaries and the poems, stem from the fear of trespassing into non-womanly spheres. She is aware of being a transgressor. As a writer she is afraid of being mocked and as a woman she is fearful that an assertion of self will bring dishonour to her natal family and expel her from her marital home. Her account of her encounter with Venu and his crass rejection of her or any woman writer in a "biology is destiny argument" is revelatory. She carefully quotes his rebuttal in her diary. He asks, "Why do you need to write poetry? It is enough for a young woman like you to give birth to children. That is your poetry. Leave the other poetry to us men." (127) Mira was silenced and submitted to his verdict out of her own diffidence and fear. But Urmila wants to break this conspiracy of silence even though she knows that it will jeopardize her marriage and especially her relationships with her female familial community. She will have to risk breaking out of the prison of silence and try to navigate an uncertain future.

Mira's assertion of selfhood can be seen in her poetry, but both the poetry and the diaries remain secret and hidden away. Marriage is a turning point for women in terms of sexuality and in attenuating the links with their childhood and past. The old custom of even changing the first name of the bride is testimony to the erasure of an individual past. Mira describes this ceremony of acquiring a new name:

A glittering ring gliding on the rice
carefully traced a name 'Nirmala'.
Who is this? None but I,
my name hence, bestowed upon me.
Nirmala, they call, I stand statue-still.
Do you build the new without razing the old?
A tablet of rice, a pencil of gold
can they make me Nirmala? I am Mira. (101)

Pathetically, it is only within the safety of this secret writing that Mira can assert her individuality, defying the transformation that her marital state insists upon.

Mira's protest in *The Binding Vine* raises questions about the politics of naming (or renaming) but also queries the possibility of erasing an individual personality to "build the new," that is, mould a human being to fit into a particular family.

The name Mira is suggestive as it invokes and refers back to Mirabai, the renowned poet of the Bhakti period.[28] Legend has it that she gave up a palatial existence and rejected her husband, the Rana, proclaiming that she had already vowed herself to the Lord Krishna. Her defiant assertion, "I am Mira", is a statement of individual identity rather than a gender (or role) identity. Mira's ringing "no," parallels Mirabai's defiance,[29] and is a refusal to accept the erasure of Mira to accommodate "Nirmala," meaning the clean—a tabula rasa on whom the imprint of wife and mother in the husband's family can be engraved. This is quite unlike the name changing in Bharati Mukherjee's *Jasmine* or Jhumpa Lahiri's *Namesake* that see name changes as a step to acculturation in a far more positivist manner. Mira's poems, written secretly and tucked away, and her refusal to answer to Nirmala are her ways of resisting, albeit safely.[30]

Power, Sexuality and Rape

In these three novels as in others, women's sexuality is a constant theme. Meena Alexander (*Nampally Road*) and Nayantara Sahgal (*Rich Like Us*) among others consciously promote the idea of a women's community through shared concerns, rituals of birthing and motherhood. The "biology is destiny" argument is often presented positively as empowering rather than restrictive. Meena Alexander says:

> ...giving birth and taking care of young children, with all the difficulties and pleasures, has allowed me to think back through to my mother and her mother and allowed me to see the female condition more richly.[31]

One of many feminist projects of retrieving a matriarchal genealogy and, to use Alice Walker's phrase, the "search for our mother's gardens," is evident both in the invocation of an Indian cultural past and in the links women trace across generations with a Sybil-like ancestress.[32] This celebratory mode invokes mutually empowering female friendships across class.

The darker side of a woman-to-woman connection, however, is the link between women as victims. In these novels, rape is the most extreme manifestation of an in-built male authority over woman. It is a punishment specifically against woman's sexuality, for transgressing the bounds of patriarchal protection. Rape is seen as the pivotal moment where control over women is asserted through sexuality. In her *Against Our Will: Men, Women and Rape*, Susan Brownmiller convincingly argues that since man began to view his penis as a weapon he began to use it as such. She states,

> ...the basic truth [is] that rape is not a crime of irrational, impulsive, uncontrollable lust, but is a deliberate, hostile, violent act of degradation and possession on the part of a would-be conqueror, designed to intimidate and inspire fear...[33]

Rape is the physical and symbolic assertion of man's violent authority over woman. Passion and sexuality as such have little to do with rape. She concludes, "rape is nothing more or less than a conscious process of intimidation by which all men keep all women in a state of fear." (391)

The recurrence of rape in many of these novels, and in fact twice in *The Binding Vine*, is indicative of its centrality as an assertion of power. The male presence as an extension of the lurking violent world outside is explicit in Desai's chilling narrative. The house, Carignano, is the fixed locale of the three-part structure of *Fire on the Mountain*. The third part, although entitled "Ila Das leaves Carignano", is about Ila's first and last visit to the house. Ila is twice introduced into the text and Carignano as a disembodied voice before she appears physically. Both times, the telephone, normally a means of communication and connection with the world, signals a disruption of Nanda's carefully cultivated isolation. The first time, the ringing is described as "extraordinary, ominous." (20). The second time, violence and pain are signalled more clearly: "Then a scream rang through the house, tearing it from end to end. It was the telephone" (101). The third time, "the sharp, long sliver of the telephone's call cut through the dusk" (143), and the description replicates a chilling event outside. In the house, Ram Lal the male servant, has "silenced, decapitated the telephone" (143) just as Preet Singh has silenced Ila. The instrument itself "lay, in two divided halves, black, beside the open window from which the sky looked in" (144), mimicking Ila's position as she lies raped and murdered in the open field with the sky looking on.

In her reading of *Fire on the Mountain*, Florence Libert argues that "Preet Singh's act is one of revenge executed under passion".[34] But the text clearly suggests, as indeed Libert herself notes later, that it is a pre-meditated act. Preet Singh has hinted as much to the grain seller who warns Ila not to walk alone in the dark. The rape is retaliation against Ila, a woman, challenging Preet Singh's authority. Libert notes that Preet Singh "wants to assert his power and superiority over her. This he can do by raping her, thus violating her womanhood, something that murder alone would not have accomplished" (576). It is worth recalling Purshottam Agarwal's contention that "sexual violence in particular has always been an integral part of any authoritarian world view."[35] Since patriarchal houses are projected as basically authoritarian, it should come as no surprise that sexual violence or rape is embedded in their very structure.

Although fear of rape might affect all women, class obviously plays a key role in woman's capacity to defy mainstream structures. Deshpande and Desai are both acutely aware of class but they articulate it in very different ways. In *Fire on the Mountain*, Ila and Nanda belong to the same social class but Ila's poverty has reduced her to servant status and Nanda treats her as a poor relative who has to be endured. Nanda's wealth and status, on the other hand, offer her different choices. She secures her position by bowing her head and allowing what she perceives as the "noose" of duty—a loveless marriage and social decorum—to tighten around her neck. Nanda is the Other that Ila has always aspired to be: "all through her ragged life Nanda Kaul had been there, standing at a height, like a beacon, like an ideal" (112). The distance that separates them, "you [Nanda] in your manorial hall and I in my village hut down below" (113) is unbridgeable partly because Nanda knows, but does not quite acknowledge, the price she has paid to not be Ila.

On many levels, their lives have run along parallel lines. If Ila is alone physically, Nanda is so emotionally; Ila's rape at the end parallels Nanda's loveless coupling; and even Ila's lack of children conversely replicates Nanda's excess — too many children all unnamed and undifferentiated. Neither acknowledges the similarities. Ila has always been there on the fringes of Nanda's life, a constant reminder of the past she is trying to erase and of the price she has paid to not become Ila. Ila recalls Nanda as the elegant and efficient Mrs. Vice-Chancellor, the ideal wife and mother, but both know that image is superimposed upon that of Nanda the betrayed woman, unloved by a husband who "had only done enough to keep her quiet" (145). Nanda's silent acquiescence to that relationship and to bearing children who she says "were all alien to her nature" (145) pave her way to the manor.

From the security of the manor, Nanda recognises her responsibility to Ila: "She, well and strong and upright, she ought to protect her [Ila]. She ought to fight some of her battles" (133), and in a limited way she has done so. But Nanda's own hurt has created an impenetrable wall around her. She is unable to connect with Ila, which may be a question of class, but then neither is she able to reach out to her great granddaughter Raka. Nanda is unable to provide a sense of community because she is estranged from herself. Ila scares and horrifies her because her pathetic life is a fearful warning of the consequences of stepping out, and a reminder of the hypocrisy of her own life. Unlike Nanda, however, Urmila, (*The Binding Vine*) in her own clear statements as well as in the way she sees the links between Kalpana and Mira, privileges the gender bond between women. Structurally, each part of this novel begins with an excerpt from Mira's poems. Part two, for instance, conjures the image of Laxmi and her consort, the divine couple in Hindu mythology.[36] The prose narrative, however, recounts the story of Kalpana's rape.

In *The Binding Vine*, we see a deliberate erasure of class boundaries, a collapsing of gendered public and private spaces and, despite Deshpande's hesitation in labeling herself a feminist, an explicit and pointed illustration of the feminist slogan of the 1960s that the personal is political. In this novel, a supportive community of women is conceptualised both inside and outside the domestic space. But unlike Gyaltsen's *Daughters of the House*, the possibility of including men beckons in the recognition of consciously working towards systemic changes in society. Deshpande explores the intertwining of gender and class through two parallel narratives. The first story revolves around the discovery of Mira's writing and the gradual understanding of her marital rape. The second narrative is about Kalpana's rape by her uncle when she refuses to marry him.

The Binding Vine shows that the basic inequality and power imbalance between women and men colour all heterosexual relationships. Kalpana's mother, Shakutai, emphasises the class barrier as she distances herself from Urmila, explaining:

> Women like you will never understand what it is like for us. We have to keep to our places, we can never step out. There are always people waiting to throw stones at us, our own people first of all. (148)

Urmila's narration, however, refutes the two premises of class and place in Shakutai's outburst. Almost paraphrasing Brownmiller's contention that "all men keep all women in a state of fear" because of "Man's structural capacity to rape and woman's corresponding structural vulnerability"; the shadow of fear looms behind poor and rich women alike. In this novel none of the female characters—Urmila, Inni, Vanaa, Shakutai, Mira—are free from fear. It does not, in all cases, boil down to a fear of rape—but there is a fear that emanates from upsetting the gender balance that the men seem unaware of and that the women dare not articulate.

Economic independence does not necessarily translate into social change. Shakutai vainly warns both her daughter and, later, Urmila about transgressing gender boundaries but her caution falls on deaf ears. In response to Shakutai's assertion that Urmila cannot understand her because of class difference, Urmila protests:

You don't understand, Shakutai said to me. But how can I
not understand when the warning signposts are all about
me? It is different for you, Shakutai said, but it is not. (149)

Shakutai, schooled in the clear demarcation of male and
female spaces and roles, is haunted by the fear that her daughter may have called the rape upon herself.

Her lament underlines two unwritten rules that mould
women's behaviour and especially poor women's behaviour
—fear, and the untranslateable notion of '*aukaat*' (knowing
one's place). Kalpana broke both rules. She did not know her
place; as a woman and that too a lower class woman. And she
further compounds the first mistake by breaking the cardinal
rule—of womanly fear. Her mother complains, "I warned
Kalpana, but she would never listen to me. 'I'm not afraid of
anyone,' she used to say. That's why this happened to her . .
. . women must know fear." (148) Having acquired some education, vocational training and a degree of economic earning
power, Kalpana steps out fearlessly, unwilling to repeat her
mother's life of drudgery. But she is taught a brutal lesson
reminding her who she is and where she belongs—both in
terms of class and as a woman. The fear she must know is of
her own vulnerability as a woman vis-à-vis man.

Mira, on the other hand, knows the rules better even
though she is of an earlier generation and a higher class than
Shakutai and Kalpana. She writes in secret because she is
afraid. As a writer she is afraid of being mocked and as a
woman she is fearful that an assertion of self will expel her
from her marital home. As a wife she questions the sacrosanct
institution of marriage that permits a husband not only to
possess his wife but also to rape her. One simple problem is
the problem of language. It is not merely whether she writes
in Kannada or English, but in what language and with what
vocabulary can she express her fear of and her revulsion for
her husband? The subject itself is taboo.

Sexuality and eroticism remain rather hidden subjects in
Indo-English writing generally. In other novels we have seen
that the house itself seems to regulate female sexuality.

Feudal, patriarchal, haveli norms rendered both Laila and Nandi (*Sunlight on a Broken Column*), rich and poor women alike as outcasts when they transgressed the sexual codes of proper female behaviour. Similarly in bungalow dwellings marriage and obedience to the husband authorised women's sexuality within the heterosexual marriage. In the configuration of India as home, women as culture-bearers had to conform to nationalist notions of what it meant to be an Indian and a woman. In these women-only homes sexuality remains the cornerstone of male and female power and is explicitly stated as such. Girls become wives but it is as if the authors have not yet found the idiom in which to articulate the sexual experience. Bhakti poetry in Indian literature provides one model — the blurring of boundaries between the spiritual and the erotic. Despite their westernisation, Indo-English writers also tend to conflate the spiritual and sexual. It may be because of the privacy of the experience which links it to the inner or real world, or because Indian society over the last century has remained essentially puritanical, thus reinforcing the silence about sexuality. In *Sunlight on a Broken Column*, it is alluded to in platonic terms, and in *Daughters of the House*, the moment is passed over almost without the reader realising what has happened. In *The Binding Vine*, Mira alludes to a personal situation by enlarging it to a general, abstract plane. She astutely removes it to a higher level by invoking the socially accepted mythical paragons of divine sexuality, Laxmi and Shiva, to question the sanctity of the marital bond:

> But tell me, friend, did Laxmi too,
> twist brocade tassels round her fingers
> and tremble, fearing the coming
> of the dark-clouded, engulfing night? (56)

Mira's marital rape remains a private and secret agony that she cannot talk about. It is cloaked linguistically in spiritual metaphors and literally by the fact of it being both written in secret and then hidden in a trunk to be discovered long after her death. On the one hand, only religious terminology is deemed appropriate to describe the sexual moment. On the other hand, an overt indictment of male sexual violence within marriage would be unacceptable because it queries the presupposition of a husband's right to his wife, which is the cornerstone of the institution of marriage. Marriage, Kishwar and Vanita note, has very different implications for men and women: "for men, marriage means extended alliances, for women it means losing whatever little foothold they had in the natal family."[37] Mira's silence is as much about self-protection as it is about protecting her natal family and ultimately knowing that outside the marital home there is no place for her. In *The Binding Vine*, the narrator understands that art and life cannot be separated. Urmila acknowledges that in publishing Mira's writings both Mira the poet and Mira the sexual being will be exposed and her family—including Urmila and her nearest kin—will have to face the consequences of that revelation. It would be so much easier and hugely tempting to respect the status quo and keep the secret and the silence of Mira.

The story of Kalpana's rape is more complicated and sinister. It is embedded in the un-elaborated story of Shakutai and her sister, Sulu. The fear of homelessness is palpable in Sulu's anxiety at her childlessness, and the consequent anxiety that her husband "would throw her out and take another wife" (192). To complicate matters, she develops disfiguring skin patches which cause her husband to reject her physically. The physical disfigurement recalls Madhulika's lupus (*Daughters of the House*). Although the consequences are different the similarity of the two examples that open the way to an uncle-niece liaison are startling. Sulu's fears about her own marriage and Shakutai's anxiety about finding a suitable boy for Kalpana lead them to conceive of a plan whereby Kalpana would marry her aunt's husband. Sulu justifies the plan, "I have no children, she said. If Kalpu marries him, she can be mistress of the house, she doesn't have to do anything, and I'll do all the work, everything"(192).

Sulu's suggestion is not entirely selfish. No doubt it will ensure a roof over her head but in return for it, she is offering to do all the work, recalling how Shakutai in her early married days had felt like "a free servant" (110) for her husband. Shakutai, for her part, is not averse to the idea either. The marriage will help a sister whom she loves dearly, and ensure a safe home for her daughter. The fear of what marriage can hold for a daughter and a rejected wife makes the plan seem almost reasonable, and so little is expected from husbands anyway, that the sisters see this as an acceptable solution to both their problems.

But Kalpana has other plans for herself. When Sulu's husband learns of her forthcoming marriage, he rapes her. The publicity caused by the newspaper reports results in Kalpana's case being reopened, forcing Sulu's husband to come to her for an alibi. Sulu, shocked by the knowledge, tells Shakutai. For herself, however, Sulu sees no option but self-annihilation. The ever-dutiful wife: "She finished her cooking, gave him his breakfast and then . . . . The neighbours told me she was like a torch when she ran out, burning from head to toe" (189). Sulu's death evokes images of bride-burning or the so called dowry-deaths, and, of course, of the forest fire caused by Raka in *Fire on the Mountain*.

Fire can be read as a specifically feminine symbol. In the Indian context, particularly, fire evokes notions of purification, most literally recalled in Sita's test by fire in the *Ramayana*. But it is a richly layered image associated with women's suffering, especially in the context of Sati and bride burning.[38] In an interview with Desai, Lalita Pandit notes that the Indian word "*davanala*" literally means forest fire. She suggests that in Indian literature this metaphor was associated with "feminine sexuality," and writers "use it to suggest the socially/morally disruptive consequences of sexual transgression of women."[39] Pandit, however, commends Desai for being able to "reconstruct the metaphor," saying, "as if to retrieve it out of the accumulated conventional associations, you transform its meaning."[40] Despite Pandit's perceptive reading of the symbolic dimension of the fire metaphor, which Desai does not comment upon directly, its literal potential for destruction cannot be elided.[41] The text's refusal of life—at least two of the three women die—is in fact more than mere refusal. *Fire on the Mountain* insists on underscoring their sinister and violent end, and makes the question of a womanly legacy deeply problematic.

The difference, though, between the fires in *The Binding Vine* and *Fire on the Mountain* are that Sulu's is an individual gesture that ends her life, but in the other fire Raka is perceived to be destroying the structure or the surroundings that imprison women. By talking to the newspaper Shakutai breaks the silence that leads to Sulu's death but it may also somehow redeem the violence done to Kalpana. Shakutai's agonised struggle over whether or not she should talk about her daughter's rape and thereby expose her "shame" and her brother-in-law to the police is firmly contextualised by her individual place as a poor woman, alone in an uncaring society. But it also links Urmila's dilemma of whether or not to reveal Mira's story of marital rape thereby risking her own familial security.

Law and the police—the foundation and protector of civil society—reveal the patriarchal and class bias of the society. In *The Binding Vine* as in *The God of Small Things, Nampally Road* and many other novels these authority figures become emblems of an uncaring society. The policeman, for instance, refuses to change the initial incorrect hospital report from accident to rape and tries to justify it on various grounds of paternal caring. Reiterating the dichotomy of shame and honour he argues that it will bring dishonour to the family and ruin her and/or her sisters' prospects of marriage. His ultimate argument, however, reiterates the class and gender ideology that shapes mainstream attitudes. "Girls of that class always have boyfriends, the families know nothing about it," (88) he asserts dismissively.

The newspaper, another organ of the mainstream view, reports the case in a sensational and accusatory tone. The "blame the victim" viewpoint is widespread and internalised by women and men alike. It is Kalpana's mother who, in a pathetic mea culpa, cries, "she was stubborn, she was self-willed, she dressed up, she painted her lips and nails and so this happened to her" (148). All these transgressions mark

Kalpana as deviant. The sub-text of the posed photo published in the newspaper conveys the same message, that by being defiant and different, she "asked for it."[42] The photograph projects Kalpana not as a poor or shy victim but a pretty, young girl smiling confidently and directly at the camera. By dressing well, using make-up and her confident gaze Kalpana steps out of her *aukaat* (place). Her looking straight into the camera is read as her defiant and "forward" attitude. The mention of her job and independence is indicative of her assertion of her right to be on the street—a public and therefore a tacitly assumed male space. In a malestream patriarchal society the transgression justifies the punishment.

The juxtaposition of the two rapes, Kalpana's and Mira's, one outside and one inside the home, collapses the boundaries between the home and the world. Domestic boundaries that are meant to protect women are also envisioned as sites of inescapable suffering by these women authors. Deshpande shows how false the very notion of protection is, especially if the "enemy" is within. Marriage, in patriarchal societies, is seen as a marker that can safeguard women from the dangers of the public space, but it does not ensure safety within. Susan Brownmiller's comprehensive study on rape traces the idea of women needing protection historically as "the price of woman's protection by *some men* against an abuse *by others*.[43]" *(Emphasis in the original).* For poor women like Shakutai, Urmila explains, marriage is crucial because it is linked to the notion of protection and possession. Urmila could almost be quoting Nandi (*Sunlight on a Broken Column*) when she ventures that poor women, especially, need marriage for security: "You're safe from other men . . . . it usually gives them that guarantee of safety. It takes much greater courage to dispense with a man's protection." (88) By stepping out of the Laxmana rekha of male protection onto the streets, Kalpana calls the punishment of rape upon herself. The specifically sexual nature of the punishment is an assertion of male power. The formation of at least a virtual women's community where women help each other is one suggested way of combating unequal and cruel asymmetries of power.

Conclusion

Why are women particularly caught in this nexus of silence and fear? Individual men or patriarchy are not the only jailers that can silence women. In these novels women too can become veritable jailers and gender-code enforcers. But power is at the centre of any understanding of human relations most particularly in the microcosm of the home. Economic, social and sexual disenfranchisement has rendered women particularly vulnerable.[44] It is not merely that women are bound by the codes of a "normative heterosexuality", but that these codes have been internalised so deeply by both women and men that a life outside, for women especially, seems inconceivable. At one level it is easy to see how women-only homes can become confining for women because they exist within the ambit of male-dominated spaces and cultures. But Gyaltsen presents a very different understanding of what makes Panditji's house a prison. In this house it is the configuration of economics, religion and culture that are pitted against a women-only existence. The desperate struggle to maintain the sanctity of the women-only home ultimately transforms the servant and surrogate mother Parvati, or Paro, into a veritable jailer in *Daughters of the House*.

Recurrent themes of female friendships and finding their voice even in a male dominated society underlie these texts including *Daughters of the House*. I do not wish to suggest an unproblematic construction of Woman (as a monolith with a capital W) through these texts; nor do the texts themselves present women as an unmarked category.[45] Theoretically, it may be possible to link women in a global sisterhood as was done in the early stages of the Indian women's movements as well in the early phases of Western feminisms, but internationally and locally, this has proved to be an untenable position.[46] Woman as the subject of feminism continues to be debated, as does the question of her "complicity" as a perpetuator of patriarchal norms.

These novels create moments of "womenspace" or a female community that stem from a shared victimhood as well as a shared sisterhood.[47] The 1970s, an important moment in feminisms and women's movements were also formative years for some of the authors. As such, the writings are often marked by a valorisation of the idea of female friendships. The crucial role of servants and the connections between women despite class points to an awareness of the necessity of a coalitional politics on the part of the authors. The servants or lower class women are neither the subjects nor the protagonists in this literature; nor do they have any interiority, but their presence and parallel narratives interrupt and question the main stories. The recurrent themes of female friendships and recovery of voice that underlie these texts can be attributed to more recent feminist influences.

In all the novels there is a conscious attempt to transcend the barriers of class, generation and even nationhood. In the havelis, nurture and mutual caring between servant and mistress was imposed or facilitated by the feudal domestic context. Although *Daughters of the House* is similarly situated in a domestic sphere the roles of servant and master/mistress are reversed and the hierarchy is minimal if not entirely erased. In *Fire on the Mountain* and *The Binding Vine* female parallels, if not exactly friendships across class, are formed outside the home. A common link of caring and nurture and the inherent fear of female vulnerability is the basis of their relationships. A distinctive female legacy both positive and negative is articulated and examined. Anita Desai's *Fire on the Mountain* stands apart in observing the failure of female friendships and women's isolation from each other inside and outside the home. The chronology is deliberately disturbed to indicate that the continuity of a latent pattern of women's alliances— even when they fail—has been a part of Indo-English women's novels.

In the haveli and bungalow style dwellings, the feudal life-style and westernization were identified as the main threat. In the apartment dwellings, although the boundaries between home and the world were blurred, women were still circumscribed by conformity to notions of Indianness manifest mainly in the strict adherence to gender roles. But in

Daughters of the House and *Fire on the Mountain*, women-only homes are not seen as the solution either. Their very existence is premised upon a sheltered and isolated marginal space apart from mainstream society. The raison d'etre of women-only homes in these novels seems to be the asymmetrical power balance between women and men which are the foundations of mainstream heterosexual patriarchal families. The home as a homo-erotic womanly space is not even hinted at here. Although the link between fear and silence forces women to either re-evaluate their place in family and society or to try and opt out of these authoritarian structures that diminish and silence them. The novels posit both fear and love as the bedrock upon which these womanly alliances are formed, and both, it is suggested, are inherent in the condition of being woman. All three novels, but particularly *The Binding Vine* suggests that a women's community is an essential part of the condition of being a woman. But that does not necessarily lead to the viability of women-only homes. These homes are seen as temporary dwellings that often provide essential sustenance and community for women, but in the long run, the novels posit the home as a place for women, men and children but one where women are not silenced by the fear of sexual or emotional vulnerability or of being cast out and rendered homeless.

References

1 Ruth Vanita and Saleem Kidwai (eds.) *Same-Sex Love in India: Readings from Literature and History*. New York: St. Martins Press, 2000. (p.198)

2 Ruth Vanita and Saleem Kidwai (eds.) *Same-Sex Love in India: Readings from Literature and History*. New York: St. Martins Press, 2000. (p.200)

3 See Adrienne Rich, "Compulsory Heterosexuality and Lesbian Existence," Ann Snitow et al, (eds.) *Powers of Desire: The Politics of Sexuality*, New York: Monthly Review Press, 1983 (p.192)

4 For a detailed report see Moore, Molly. "Plagiarism and Mystery" *Washington Post* Foreign Service 04/27/94 http://www.sawnet.org/news/aikath_gyaltsen.html

5. Ardener, (ed.) *Women and Space*, 1981, (p.18)

6. Desai recalls that the character of Ila is based on an actual person with an awful voice: "This woman entered the book quite against my will, I hadn't planned it; she broke into it. And then I remembered that she did go and live in Kasauli and was murdered there, in exactly the way I described in the book. She seemed to enter the book like a ghost, as if she, too, belonged in it." "A Sense of Detail and a Sense of Order: Anita Desai Interviewed by Lalita Pandit," Hogan & Pandit, (eds.) *Literary India: Comparative Studies in Aesthetics, Colonialism and Culture*, Albany: State University of New York Press, 1995 (p.157)

7 Malashri Lal, "Anita Desai: Fire on the Mountain," N.S. Pradhan, (ed.) *Major Indian Novels, An Evaluation*, New Jersey: Humanities Press, 1986 (p.246)

8 Malashri Lal, "Anita Desai: Fire on the Mountain," N.S. Pradhan, (ed.) *Major Indian Novels, An Evaluation*, New Jersey: Humanities Press, 1986 (p.246)

9 Richard Cronin, *Imagining India*, London: Macmillan Press, 1989 (p.51)

10 Fredric Jameson, "Third World Literature in the Era of Multinational Capitalism," *Social Text* Volume 15, fall 1986, (pp.65-88)

11 Shyam Asnani, "New Morality in the Modern Indo-English Novel: A Study of Mulk Raj Anand, Anita Desai and Nayantara Sahgal," R.K. Dhawan, (ed.) *Indian Women Novelists* Set 1: Vol.I New Delhi: Prestige Books, 1991 (p.109)

12 Shirley Ardener, (ed.) *Women and Space, Ground Rules and Social Maps*, London: Croom Helm, 1981 (p.27)

13 Similarly *Sunlight on a Broken Column* suggests that outside her role as her father's daughter, Abida has no other reason to live.

14 Premila Paul & Padmanabhan Nair, "Varieties of Loneliness in *Fire on the Mountain*" R.K. Dhawan, (ed.) *Indian Women Novelists* Set I: Vol.III, New Delhi: Prestige Books, 1991 (p.232)

15 In a thought-provoking and insightful analysis of the mentality that produced the frenzied destruction of the Babri mosque in 1992 in Ayodhya, Agarwal points to the continuity in the rhetoric of the Hindu right which led to a communalising of identities that enabled violence. Agarwal cautions that we should not miss "the continuity that exists between a Savarkar, a Chinmayanand, a Vinay Katyar and a rapist on the street." The links between rightist ideologue, religious leaders and individual activists are on the same continuum, and have to be seen as parts that form the larger

whole. Purshottam Agarwal, "Savarkar, Surat and Draupadi," Sarkar & Butalia, (eds.) *Women and the Hindu Right*, New Delhi: Kali for Women, 1995 (p.33)

16 The name Parvati is significant. It recalls the goddess Parvati associated with domesticity.

17 A recurrent issue, which requires a deeper study beyond the scope of this work, is that of religion and class in the formation of the cultural fabric of these domestic spaces.

18 Forster. E.M., *A Passage to India*. (1924). Harmondsworth: Penguin Books, 1977.

19 Lal, Malashri. *The Law of the Threshold : Women Writers in Indian English* Indian Institute of Advanced Study: Shimla, 2000.

20 The illness could also be seen as self-punishment. Dr. Cecilia Chan of Hong Kong University suggests that psychologically, lupus is often seen as a self-inflicted punishment because of guilt feelings. (personal conversation)

21 In David Malouf's *12 Edmonstone Street*, for instance, there is certainly a strong element of the rejection of the house being seen in terms of a betrayal.

22 Susie Tharu, "The Impossible Subject: Caste and Desire in the Scene of the Family," *Thamyris* Vol.4 No.1, (Special Issue "Gender in the Making: Indian Contexts" Guest Editor Rajeswari Sunder Rajan) Amsterdam: Najade Press, Spring 1997 (p.167)

23 For a wonderful discussion of the kinds of problems faced by women writers and the 'gendered' nature of this censorship among women writers see *Storylines* and *Just Between Us: Women Speak About Their Writing*. Ammu Joseph, Vasanth Kannabiran, Ritu Menon, Gouri Salvi, Volga (eds.) Women's WORLD (India), and Asmita Resource Centre for Women: 2003 & 2004. (p.4)

24 Sudhir Kakar. *The Inner World: A Pscho-analytic Study of Childhood and Society in India*. Delhi: Oxford University Press. (1978, 1981) (p.135-136)

25 In their magisterial work *The Madwoman in the Attic*, Gilbert and Gubar suggest that the pen could be read as a phallic symbol. I do not intend to insist here that the trunk is a symbol of female sexuality and female writing, but in the light of Gilbert and Gubar's work such a linkage cannot be totally ignored either.

26 For a fuller discussion of women and autobiographies see Chanda, Geetanjali Singh "Writing Home: Indian Women's Autobiographies", *Fiction and Drama*. Volume 11, 1999.

27 The following writers, most significantly, have all written about diaries being a genre particularly favoured by women. Shari Benstock, "The Female Self Engendered: Autobiographical Writing and Theories of Selfhood," *Women's Studies*, Vol.20, 1991. Elizabeth Abel, *Writing and Sexual Difference*, London: The Harvester Press, 1980, Malavika Karlekar, *Voices from Within: Early Personal Narratives of Bengali Women*, Delhi: Oxford University Press, 1991/1993, Karuna Chanana, (ed.) *Socialisation, Education and Women Explorations in Gender Identity*, Delhi: Orient Longman, 1988.

28 Ammu Joseph, Vasanth Kannabiran, Ritu Menon, Gouri Salvi, Volga. (eds.) *Storylines* and *Just Between Us: Women Speak About Their Writing*. Women's WORLD (India), and Asmita Resource Centre for Women: 2003 & 2004.

29 Mirabai's birth is estimated to be around 1498 A.D. and death around 1546. Three factors about Mira and the Bhakti tradition provide a deeper understanding of this novel. Linguistically, these poet-saints often expressed themselves in the vernacular and common language of the people rather than only in the high tradition of Sanskrit. Thus they did away with the need of a priest or a mediator. Secondly, there was a disregard for social conventions, including family life. An individual's personal connection with the divine was highlighted. Thirdly, as a social protest, Bhakti did not deny the underlying assumptions of society. It was a protest that did not call for a revolution but could be accommodated within the existing social ideology because it emphasized the transcendence of existing social bonds.

If one were to push the parallel between the two Miras, Mira's encounter with Venu in this novel neatly echoes the poet-saint Mira's confrontation with the Krishnaite theologian Jiv Gosvami who also tried to dismiss her because she was a woman. For a full account of the incident and for a general study of other Bhakti Saints, see John Stratton Hawley & Mark Juergensmeyer, *Songs of the Saints of India*, New York, Oxford: Oxford University Press, 1988.

30 A popular story tells of the Rana's efforts to destroy Mira by sending her a cup of poison. Mira laughingly drinks it, but even that does not succeed in killing her.

31 In her autobiography, *My Story*, Kamala Das notes a generational change between herself and her Nair ancestress' in that she will not allow her poems to gather dust, closeted away in some secret drawer. I have elaborated upon this theme in a paper, "Writing Home: Indian Women's Autobiographies," delivered at the Asian Women Writers Conference entitled "Re-cognizing language, culture and identity," (University of Malaya, January 1997).

32 Abraham, Ayisha & Meena Alexander on "Writing and Contemporary Issues," *The Toronto South Asian Review*, winter 1993. (p.25)

33 Walker. Alice, *In Search of Our Mothers' Gardens*, San Diego, New York: Harvester-Harcourt Brace Jovanovich, 1984.

34 Brownmiller. Susan. *Against Our Will: Men, Women and Rape.* New York: Simon & Schuster, 1975. (p.14)

35 Libert. Florence, "Discrepancy Between the Inner Being and the Outside World," Robert L. Ross, (ed.) *International Literature in English: Essays on the Major Writers*, New York: Garland Publishing, 1991 (p.576)

36 Agarwal. Purshottam, "Savarkar, Surat and Draupadi: Legitimising Rape as a Political Weapon," Tanika Sarkar & Urvashi Butalia, (eds.) *Women and the Hindu Right*, Delhi: Kali for Women, 1995.

37 The name of the goddess Lakshmi can also be spelt as Laxmi. I have used the former spelling, except where the text indicates the other spelling.

38 Kishwar & Vanita, *In Search of Answers*, 1984. (p.13)

39 For an historical account of sati and bride-burning issues, see Kumar, *The History of Doing*, 1993. For a complex discussion on sati see Lata Mani, "Contentious Traditions: The Debate on Sati in Colonial India," Sangari & Vaid, (eds.) *Recasting Women*, New Delhi: Kali for Women 1989. pp.88-126

40 Lata Mani, "A Sense of Detail and a Sense of Order: Anita Desai Interviewed by Lalita Pandit," Patrick Colm Hogan and Lalita Pandit, (eds.) *Literary India: Comparative Studies in Aesthetics, Colonialism and Culture*, Albany: State University of New York Press, 1995 (p.157)

41 Mani, "A Sense of Detail," Hogan & Pandit, eds. *Literary India*, 1995. (p.157)

42 In the same interview Desai insists: "The fire is a real fire, but it's also a symbolic fire of course. It's the little girl who has grown more and more impatient through the summer with Nanda Kaul's fantasies and fabrications. She senses that they are all lies and illusions, where she herself is only interested in the truth of things — stones, pine-cones, solid objects — and finally she sets fire to that whole illusory world, from the ashes of which some kind of truth should show through." "A Sense of Detail and Sense of Order" Hogan & Pandit, (eds.) *Literary India*, 1995. (pp.166-167)

43 Brownmiller explains that this is one of the standard justifications for shifting the blame. See Brownmiller, *Against Our Will*, 1975/ 1986. (pp.343-370)

44 As early as 1884 Engels linked the "world historic defeat of the female sex" to the congruence of the rise of private property, the isolation of women, a coercive state that reinforced the domination of the rich over the poor, and the entrenchment of the patriarchal family that controlled and subjugated women. The resultant change in sexual mores, especially for women, destabilized the power balance that confined them within the patriarchal family and domesticity. See. Engels, Fredrick. *The Origin of the Family, Private Property, and the State*. (1884). Introduction by Evelyn Reed. New York: Pathfinder Press, 1972.

45 For a discussion of "Woman" as a subject of discourse see Judith Butler, *Gender Trouble: Feminism and the Subversion of Identity*, New York: Routledge, 1990. Carol Smart, (ed.) *Regulating Womanhood: Historical Essays on Marriage, Motherhood and Sexuality*, London: Routledge, 1992.

46 See especially Barbara Smith, (ed.) *Home Girls: A Black Feminist Anthology*, New York: Kitchen Table: Women of Color Press, 1983. Judith Butler, *Gender Trouble: Feminism and the Subversion of Identity*, New York: Routledge, 1990. Radha Kumar, *The History of Doing: An Illustrated Account of Movements for Women's Rights and Feminism in India, 1800-1990*, New Delhi: Kali for Women, 1993.

47 Overuse has diminished the powerful potential of the term "sisterhood." But as Radha Kumar notes, it has been a formative concept in feminism, one that has even affected names chosen by women's organisations. Saheli (Friend), the name of a Delhi based group for instance, suggests the centrality of friendship between women.

6

India As Home

Prime Minister Jawaharlal Nehru's first speech, "at the stroke of the midnight hour" announcing the birth of independent India on 15 August 1947 evoked an image of India as a house. He ended the famous 'tryst with destiny' speech: "We have to build the noble mansion of free India where all her children may dwell".[1] The image of the nation as a house or a dwelling was permanently etched on the national imagination. Nationhood and the idea of home are not new in any literature. But in postcolonial Indian English literature particularly, we are asked to imagine a Janus faced home that looks both backwards at its past and forward to its future. This house is in constant conversation with memory and aspiration, "Indias of the mind" as Salman Rushdie terms it or what Sunil Khilnani calls "the idea of India".[2] The house of India is an inherited house where "all her children" have to live by negotiating the rules and strictures of an anchoring past. They cannot forsake or shed the past without destroying the house too. Continuity is premised upon the inheritance or the legacy of Indian history. Both the memory of, and aspiration for, the state of India (the pun is deliberate) stems from the interaction of the individual author or their protagonists with history. In *Culture and Imperialism* Edward Said succinctly articulates the links between the novel genre and imperialism showing how the novel was almost a vehicle for inculcating a specific colonial value system. He, among many others, has reiterated the symbiotic relationship between nation and narration. The novel, particularly, as Said, Homi Bhaba, Gauri Viswanathan and other postcolonial critics demonstrate, has played a crucial role in the project of nation building. In India, the novel as a genre came in with colonialism and novels in English as well as in regional languages or *bhashas* originate in a political awakening of nationhood. But novels can also be the voice of resistance or alternative histories, "stories .... [b]ecome the method colonized people use to assert their own identity and the existence of their own history."[3] Post-colonial fiction writers particularly, as the literary critic Jon Mee notes, have modified our linear conceptions of history. Authors like, "Rushdie, Kesavan, Arundhati Roy and others have tended to thematize the idea of history as a sea of stories". [4] In the novels, the partial and fragmented versions of particular moments in history shape the relationships of the characters to India and their place in it.

India figures as a political background, and as emblematic of certain cultural values. The national past evoked is firmly located in specific political moments where the country, the government, and the citizens are called to book to judge the renovations made in their house. Two such particular moments are the partition of India at independence in 1947 which called into question the idea of India as a secular, pluralistic, democratic state, and the other is the Emergency of 1975 imposed by the then Prime Minister Mrs. Indira Gandhi, daughter of Jawaharlal Nehru. Although the anti–Sikh riots in Delhi (1984), the destruction of the Babri mosque in Ayodhya (1992), and the Gujarat massacre (2002) have yet to be addressed by Indian English literature, these moments have already penetrated and framed popular and cinematic discourse.

It may be rather simplistic to dismiss these moments as merely the kinds of "pan-India themes" that anchor an otherwise rootless literature and they do of course fall into the category of themes that Meenakshi Mukherjee delineates as being common to Indo-English writers.[5] But, aside from being markers of time and place that link authors and readers across regions, these moments are not mere backdrop but a serious questioning and critique of whether the postcolonial nation state has lived up to its promise. It is possible to read these novels as following in the genre of novels like Achebe's *Things Fall Apart* [6] which are outright indictments of the postcolonial nation state. Nayantara Sahgal, Jawaharlal Nehru's niece and a leading novelist, reflecting back on the body of her work, notes that although it was not part of any deliberate plan, her novels do "form a kind of chronological sequence from the high idealism of freedom to ... well, disillusionment and decay and the way it affected the country".[7]

Indian English literature has come a long way from the early, mainly linguistic, angst about the tensions of expressing in the English language an essentially Indian sensibility. At a literary level, a notion of Indianness rooted in its history, politics and social mores has been central in the development of this literature. K.R. Srinivasa Iyengar, an early literary critic and pioneer who popularised the term "Indo-Anglian" literature, asserts:

> What makes Indo-Anglian literature an *Indian* literature, and not just a ramshackle outhouse of English literature, is the quality of its "Indianness." (*Emphasis in the original*)[8] (8)

Nayantara Sahgal's *Rich Like Us* (1983), Meena Alexander's *Nampally Road* (1991), and Arundhati Roy's *The God of Small Things* (1997) are a self-conscious and self-reflective exploration of the quality of this Indianness. Other novels considered so far, like *Sunlight on a Broken Column* or *Tara Lane*, are also located in a specifically Indian socio-political context but these novels take those articulations of India and carry forward the discussion. A specific political moment in the larger history of India provides a lens through which to view and take stock of the nation. Each of the novels disrupts the national narratives of power and privilege to assert an alternative vision and voice. Sahgal and Alexander look at the Emergency as a moment of India's political betrayal and Roy's novel provides a searing indictment of a pre-colonial and the specifically Indian issue of continuing caste oppression. All three novels specifically engage and question the idea of history as a force of enrichment and identification as well as of destruction, violence and exclusion by the state.

The Indianness of India

Rushdie's off hand claim that "Literature has little or nothing to do with a writer's home address," is deeply problematic.[9] A politics of location has become a critical factor in other, often more dangerous realms of existence, like the communalisation of India. In recent years fundamentalist or right-wing groups and factions have gained monetary strength and a voice in the international media because of the support of overseas Indians. Rajeswari Sunder Rajan's elaboration of the implications of such a location is evident in life as in literature. She notes:

> Location, however, is not simply an address. One's affiliations are multiple, contingent and frequently contradictory . . . . Location is fixed not (only) in the relative terms of centre and periphery, but in the positive (positivist?) terms of an actual historical and geographical contingency.[10]

Location is important not merely as a geographic place but it is crucial in the inclusion and evocation of the history of that place. The shadows of the past impose their lessons on the present. An understanding and experience of history account for how authors conceive of their plots and characters. In each of the novels considered here, history is variously viewed as a decrepit, forgotten Sultan's tomb in *Rich Like Us,* a neglected graveyard in *Nampally Road,* and an abandoned, haunted house as in *The God of Small Things.*

In an interview about her novel *The God of Small Things* Arundhati Roy rather disingenuously claims, "I have to say that my book is not about history but biology and transgression" [11] and yet it is impossible to separate either biology or transgression from the borders and boundaries of the specific home address of India and of casteism at a particular moment in Indian history. The story is set in the small-town of Ayemenem, in communist governed Kerela during the late 1960s. It is told from the perspective of Rahel and Estha, a set of fraternal twins who are 7 years old at the beginning of the story. The family home consists of their grandmother, uncle, and grand-aunt Baby. The catalyst for the unfolding of the plot is the accidental death-by-drowning of their visiting English cousin, Sophie. Investigation into the death reveals Ammu, the twins' divorced, high-caste mother's affair with an untouchable, Velutha. The two events cause a ripple effect of other catastrophic consequences—Velutha is beaten to death, Estha stops speaking and is returned to his father; Ammu banished from home, dies ill and alone; Rahel is expelled from school, drifts into marriage with an American and moves to America, only to leave him later and return to the now semi-deserted Ayemnem home and to Estha.

In fact, in *The God of Small Things* the children who don't even understand history yet are witnesses to the final, terrible denouement between the forces of good and evil that have been shaped by the history of caste relations. The 'history house' with its persistent links to racial and sexual transgressions from colonial times is a richly layered, quiet archive. But in the present, the house is the stage of continuing sexual and caste transgressions that have to be mercilessly punished. The conflict between the police as representatives of a brutal state (albeit in the democratically elected communist and supposedly egalitarian regime in Kerela) and Velutha, the untouchable, powerless victim who dares to disobey the laws of history, unfolds at the 'history house'. It is important to note that Velutha's marginalization is systemic and not that of just an individual. It is the legacy of a past where caste divisions were integral to the structural hierarchy of a society. The text clearly states, "they were not arresting a man, they were exorcizing fear" (309). Over the years the divisions have blurred somewhat but the novel suggests that neither political ideology nor individual effort has erased the traces of that legacy.

Worse, it seems to suggest that there is no political will in independent India to erase those boundaries. Velutha's murder by the police is explained as "merely inoculating a community against an outbreak"(309) and the outbreak referred to is of course that of the transgression of boundaries, and, in this case, caste boundaries in particular.

In *The God of Small Things*, the history house is one of three central and deeply symbolic locations, the others being the Ayemnem family home and the Pickle factory. History in *The God of Small Things* is pictured "like an old house at night. With all the lamps lit. And ancestors whispering inside" (52) In the children's literal imagination, Kari Saipu's (the Black Sahib's) house is the history house. Narratorially too, this particular house is overtly linked to Conrad's *Heart of Darkness*—evocative for breaking the rules of class, gender and race. The deliberate and specific inter-textual reference sets up a dual dynamic linking Kurtz of Conrad's work and 'The Black Sahib'—colonials or sahibs who 'go native' and Velutha who also transgresses but in the other direction. Velutha's father, who discovers the liaison, betrays his son because his conditioning and fear of caste transgression benumbs his love for his son. Velutha may not "know his place" as an untouchable but history blinds even his imagination. It is only when he sheds "history's blinkers" that he is able to see, want and attain "things that had been out of bounds so far" (176). But even that little transgression is severely and inexorably punished. The punishment is meted out by no other than "history's fiends" who reclaim Ammu and Velutha—the ones who break the rules, "to rewrap them in its old, scarred pelt and drag them back to where they really lived. Where the Love Laws lay down who should be loved. And how. And how much"(177). But even caste laws are gendered and apply differently to women and men. Whereas Ammu and Velutha are punished for their love, Mamachi ensures that a back door is specially built for Ammu's brother Chako's secret assignations; men after all have their needs she avers. Chako's liaisons with lower caste women are dealt with efficiently by paying them off thereby sloughing off the responsibility and morality of the unequal situation. Even historically ritual caste pollution is of less consequence when it comes to high caste men using low caste women.

The text demonstrates quite unambiguously that being "trapped outside their own history" (52) is no excuse, and, people who do not know their history will be condemned to relive it. And so, "while other children of their age learned other things, Estha and Rahel learned how history negotiates its terms and collects its dues from those who break its laws"(55). In Roy's view, history is a hard and unforgiving taskmaster. The brutal killing of Velutha is neither random nor an individual aberrational act of passion. The objective lesson of history is explicitly stated, "This was an era imprinting itself on those who lived in it. History in live performance" (309). At the end, not only have Velutha, the twins and their mother paid their dues to history but history has also rejected or "turned its back on Ayemenem"(125). The house and pickle factory have been mostly abandoned while the history house has been turned into a commoditized and commercialized tourist complex where history is dumbed down and served in bite size pieces to crass tourists who have only the most superficial interest in sampling the "regional flavour".

Sahgal and Alexander on the other hand have a much more benign view of history than does Roy. They both see history as enabling knowledge. It adds completion and depth to the characters and anchors them so that they can negotiate the future with confidence. In *Nampally Road*, the England returned protagonist Mira suggests that for a younger generation that feels distanced from India's past, a conscious participation in contemporary political events can create an active sense of community and provide another entry point into India. She, as representative of that generation, bemoans her alienation from Indian history as one of the reasons for her general alienation and inability to find her own voice. As a fledgling writer, her inability to write, for instance, stems from her guilt at her privileged position and her dislocation from the Indian historic, cultural, and religious past. Her evocative description of being blindfolded and trapped in this grave-yard of a national past is poignant:

> [A]s for the Indian past, what was it to me? Sometimes I felt it was a motley collection of events that rose in my mind, rather like those bleached stones in the abandoned graveyard the boy picked his way through. I had no clear picture of what unified it all, what our history might mean. We were in it, all together, that's all I knew. And there was no way out (28).

Marooned in the graveyard, she has no sense of commu-nity with others who share the space with her; nor can she separate herself enough to write her own story. The continu-ity and connection of past and present is what makes India home for this foreign-returned Indian. Even without the out-right engagement with history that we see in *The God of Small Things*, in both *Rich Like Us* and *Nampally Road* the pickling factory and 'history house', a thirteenth century sultan's tomb and a Muslim graveyard are iconic reminders of the central-ity of the past. These recurrent images are silent sentinels whose very presence insists on both a specific location and the necessity of integrating the past.

The Legacy

The historic legacy in both *Rich Like Us* and *Nampally Road* is seen as more positive and almost even positivist than in *The God of Small Things*. The Emergency is a phase in India's politi-cal history and there is hope that it is just that—a phase—a temporary bump in the longer road of Indian democracy. Prime Minister Indira Gandhi was reeling from a High Court ver-dict that found her guilty of charges of election malpractice in her 1971 election campaign. Among widespread popular calls for her resignation based on accusations of political corrup-tion, on 26th June 1975 Mrs. Gandhi scrapped the civil govern-ment and declared a state of Emergency. Under the Mainte-nance of Internal Security Act (MISA), hundreds of her politi-cal opponents were jailed without trial, opposition parties were banned and press censorship imposed. Basic civil liberties were suspended and forced sterilization and slum clearance schemes under the leadership of her son and heir apparent Sanjay Gandhi, marked the next two years. Swollen with hubris and confident of victory, surprisingly, Mrs. Gandhi called for national elections in 1977 and was roundly defeated.

Sahgal and Alexander's personal histories frame their view of India and Indian history and the Emergency in particular. Both novels, to an extent, mirror the authors', personal situations and ideologies. Poet and novelist Meena Alexander's *Nampally Road* foregrounds a concern with the specific postcolonial identity crisis rooted in the idea of displacement—of what is aptly described as post colonial theory's "concern with the development or recovery of an effective identifying relationship between self and place".[12] The approach is undoubtedly coloured by her own zig-zag trajectory traced in her memoir *Fault Lines*, from Sudan to England to India and then to a resident and a professor in America. Alexander specifically attributes her awareness of India to her idealist grandfather. She says, she was "thrown ferociously into a new India .... My grandfather was a great idealist who really believed that there was a new India waiting, a new world based on issues like land reform and equality for all people.... [Through him] I had this extraordinary world available to me".[13] The particular familial link to India and Indian politics in both Alexander and Sahgal looks back, often nostalgically, to the euphoria and hope of an emergent Indian nation.

The novel, *Nampally Road*, maps the protagonist Mira's return home to India at the end of her academic sojourn in England. Mira's new appointment—teaching English at the university in Hyderabad—brings her back to India after four years of studying abroad. The India she returns to is that of Indira Gandhi's autocratic Emergency period of the mid-1970s. *Nampally Road* takes Mira out to the turbulent city where she is caught up in the violence and the state-sponsored "goonda raj" of the Chief Minister Limca Gowda. The gang-rape of a poor woman, Rameeza Be, while in police custody—an incident that actually took place in Hyderabad in 1978[14]—forces Mira to recognize that her pursuit of wholeness would be relevant only within the context of an active community life. Ramu, her friend, lover, comrade, and guide urges her on to the path of activism. Nampally Road, however, also brings Mira to Durgabai or Little Mother, who is "obstetrician, gynecologist, and pediatrician all rolled into one" (16). Mira stays in Little Mother's house as a paying guest but she is treated like a daughter. Although Ramu is her guide in the male world of action and public protest, women are clearly implicated in this world both as victims—embodied by Rameeza Be—and as builders of a healthier community symbolized by Little Mother.

Nayantara Sahgal was born into India's first family. Her uncle Jawaharlal Nehru was India's first Prime Minister and her mother Vijay Laxmi Pandit was India's first ambassador to the UN. Sahgal graduated from Wellesley College (USA) the year India became independent. Her political commentaries and essays as well as the majority of her dozen or so novels, including Rich Like Us, are informed by both a personal and a familial involvement in Indian politics. The Emergency imposed by Mrs. Gandhi, the then Prime Minister of India who is Sahgal's aunt, frames this narrative. The author in fact, resigned her membership of the Sahitya Akademi's Advisory Board for English in protest against the Emergency. In 2002 her alma mater, Wellesley College awarded her the Alumna Achievement Award, "for bravely confronting authority in defence of the world's largest democracy".[15] Rich Like Us could be read as a meditation on the distance travelled by India from independence in 1947 to the Emergency of 1975. This is a span of history that Sahgal herself had participated in and observed. The political direction of the country is at stake. Indian politics and the centrality of a certain core concept of India as a secular democracy is the issue.

Rich Like Us spans a long period from 1932 to the mid 1970s weaving in various critical moments in Indian history that Sahgal herself had been intimately involved with: the Freedom struggle, the Independence and Partition of India, and finally the Emergency called by Indira Gandhi from 1975 to 1977. The story begins in 1932 when a cockney shop-girl, Rose, falls in love with an Indian businessman, Ram. They marry and she returns to India with him to be the second wife in his polygamous household. During partition, the family moves from Lahore to Delhi. At the onset of the Emergency Ram, has a stroke and is paralysed, unaware of what is going on in the business now run by his son, Dev. Realizing that Rose is suspicious of his underhand dealings, Dev has Rose murdered. A parallel story is that of Rose's friend Sonali, an Oxford graduate whose father was also a nationalist civil servant. The idealistic Indian Administrative Service officer, Sonali, is transferred from her Delhi posting because she challenges the corruption of the government during the Emergency period.

The protagonists in both *Nampally Road* and *Rich Like Us* are women who are trying to make India home. Although one is British and the other Indian, both have to negotiate their place in India. Rose had managed to find a place and make her peace and home in an unusual joint-family situation as a co-wife and was even responsible for "Indianising" her very Western husband. But the Emergency crystallizes for both women—older and younger, English and Indian—how profoundly un-at-home they are in this aberration of the India that was. The novels resolve the question of their ends in very different ways. Rose, who managed to create a life for herself through all the other crises in India, finally lies murdered in another man's tomb, whereas the foreign returned Indian, Mira, comes to terms with the moral and political horror of the Emergency by an individual and womanly empathy and connection with Rameeza— a victim of the Emergency. Both *Nampally Road* and *Rich Like Us* are political novels in the traditionally accepted definition of being novels where political events and ideas dominate or are a backdrop against which individual lives are played out. In Sahgal's fiction generally, and in *Rich Like Us* particularly, politics and personal stories are thematically linked. The moral corruption of an individual like Dev mirrors the corruption of the Indian political system. Sahgal claims,

I have developed this [the technique of having a specific political situation as a backdrop] as a genre, as a whole style of
political novel, which uses political background but tells a
story of human life against that.[16]

In both novels individual and community life is deeply
intertwined with the specific political moment of the Emergency of 1975.

In both *Nampally Road* and *Rich Like Us* the Emergency marks
what the Indian nation has allowed itself to become since independence. The hooligan or 'goonda Raj' of the Youth Congress
is a threatening presence in civil society that also wreaks havoc
in personal relations. However, some justify it as,

...just what we needed. The troublemakers are in jail. An opposition is something we never needed. The way the country's
being run now, with one person giving the orders and no one
being allowed to make a fuss about it in the Cabinet or in
Parliament, means things can go full steam ahead without
delays and weighing pros and cons for ever. Strikes are
banned. It's going to be very good for business.(10)

This kind of pragmatic justification is provided in the text
and it was certainly the view of a section of the population
during the Emergency who claimed that too much freedom
had led the country towards chaos. In *Rich like Us*, a helpless
beggar with no arms, stumps for legs—broken by police (state)
brutality, who is more insect than human, is the symbol of this
time. The acme of helplessness is that being armless, he cannot
even wipe his own tears. The image recalls Nehru's first Independence Day speech where, referring to Gandhi, he said, "The
ambition of the greatest man of our generation has been to
wipe every tear from every eye."[17]   The message is quite clear
that in the goonda raj of the Emergency there is no place for
the innocent. And in fact, Sahgal all but suggests that blindness
and silence are what paved the way for a smooth dynastic suc-
cession from Indira Gandhi to her son Sanjay Gandhi.[18] Sonali,
the protagonist in *Rich Like Us*, questions her own role in this
as an administrator and an integral part of the government
machinery: "Where had the tradition we were trying to build

gone wrong?" (28) And she lays the blame squarely on the administration and the citizens, "We were all taking part in a thinly disguised masquerade, preparing the stage for family rule. And we were involved in a conspiracy of silence"(29). In both novels, the Emergency is clearly seen as a betrayal of Indian civil society and of the legacy of Nehru and Gandhi's India. The somewhat romantic and nostalgic legacy of that hopeful India is explicitly connected and contrasted with the disease and political corruption of the present India of 1975.

In *Rich like Us*, Dev's corruption is seen in terms of an illness and attributed to a lack of historical understanding which is almost the cause of his greed and corruption. Those who are locked out of the history house, be it the twins Estha and Rahel in *The God of Small Things* or Dev in this novel, they cannot but re-live it till they understand. Trapped in the bubble of the present, Dev has no connection with past or future, "... a more piteous malady in Dev. He had nothing in his head except the present. ...Locked up in the present like in a cell, he's a lunatic of another kind, cut off from continuity before or behind" (157). Illness and violence are projected as natural outcomes of individuals or societies that do not know their history. A nation ignorant of its historical legacy is portrayed as a nation that has lost its way.

In British literature, Gilbert and Gubar's study amply demonstrates that the metaphor of illness signals a larger sickness of society.[19] We see in *Sunlight on a Broken Column*, Baba Jan's old age and prolonged illness parallel the end of feudalism and the partition of India. Similarly the period of the Emergency, embodied by the figure of Ram lying paralysed in bed, is also shrouded in an atmosphere of disease. It is described as a malady that strikes both individuals and the country. In *Nampally Road*, Little Mother's fever and delirium reflect the chaos that grips Hyderabad. Her body reflects and internalizes the pain of the city/country, "It was as if the unrest that was creeping through the city has entered her feverish soul" (61). And Mira notes, "in her [Little Mother's] sickness I found an image of our lives. The fever that rose, swelling her hands and feet and face, was part of the same fever that was tearing apart the city" (62). Similarly in *Rich Like Us*, as a victim of the Emergency, Sonali is felled by her demotion and hepatitis on the same day. The text explicitly links the two noting that news of her transfer felt like a physical assault (32), and Kachru (her replacement) and hepatitis "struck" the same day (33). The doctor, in fact, grumbles that "hepatitis this year was as common as colds and coughs" (33). The malaise is of course meant to be read as a sign of corrupt times. The Emergency and its fallout are an attack on the body politic just as illness is on the human body. The naïve assumption that because of democratic institutions like the Parliament, independent India would automatically run well masks the creeping rot that has entered the soul of the nation. Sonali notes, "yet an epoch had come to an end in ways we did not recognize." (35) And Rameeza Be's rape while in police custody signals the agency and involvement of the state in brutalizing the nation, especially the poor and the disenfranchised.

For Sahgal particularly, the political legacy she harks back to is the secular democratic aspirations of the Nehruvian era. As Paranjape notes,

> ...in Sahgal's world, politics is an area in which we Indians have our own positive tradition because of the national struggle for independence. This tradition, chiefly, is the combined legacy of Mahatma Gandhi and Jawaharlal Nehru. There is in it the Gandhian emphasis on truth, nonviolence, Satyagraha, social justice, prayer, poverty, simplicity, and so on, and the Nehruvian emphasis on socialism, democracy, and progress.[20]

Gandhi and Nehru are also poignantly recalled by Alexander. In *Nampally Road* Gandhi's statue stands neglected in the middle of the square and the photographs of "two visitors from our history" (57)—Nehru and Gandhi—dominate the police station. But even in that particular space they are helpless witnesses to state corruption in the merciless beating and rape of the innocent Rameeza Be. And in the end neither the photos nor even their metal frames remain. The police in both *Nampally Road* and *The God of Small Things*, as noted earlier, are instruments of state brutality.

Rich Like Us particularly presents an idealistic bureaucratic view point and focuses on the administrative legacy of India. The Indian Civil Service (ICS) was the precursor to the Indian Administrative Service (IAS), the "steel frame" (28) with which the British ruled India. Sonali is a young officer of the IAS, like her father before her who was a member of the colonial ICS. In spite of the fact that her father often felt a sense of disjointedness being a nationalist and yet serving the colonial administration (more of that later) but when she passes the exam and enters the service, he feels as though he has passed on "a precious responsibility" (28) to her. Her inheritance is the "machinery" of administration as well as the ideology of nationhood. Father and daughter are both equally aware of the significance of the moment, "...this passage from British-trained to Indian-trained machine" (28). Their views about the role of the government are steeped in an idealistic nationalist ethos of earlier times. Sonali is deeply aware that her view of her work is in no small measure colored by her father: "Papa's work had been his life. His memories of it had been my inheritance" (28). The inheritance that Keshav hands down to his daughter is a joint share in the "mystique" of the new nation: "we had a new tradition to create, our own independent worth to prove" and, he tells her proudly, "'Sonali, people like you, especially women like you, are going to Indianize India'"(28). It is worth noting that the traditions of political India are handed over specifically to the women just as the traditions of the home were also specifically handed over along a womanly line of inheritance. It is this Indian political and administrative legacy that most interests Sahgal. In an interview, she claims, "What I am writing is the story of India. I am not writing about ethnic stuff. I am interested in what politics does to human beings."[21] And the novel is a testimony to how politics affects individual lives and reactions in very specific ways. The quality or specific sensibility of Indianness that Sahgal refers to is not what she dismissively terms "the ethnic stuff" but concrete political structures and values espoused by Gandhi and Nehru during the struggle for independence.

On her last day in her office, Sonali muses,

> I sat looking at the decrepit office furniture, the beige-brown unevenly hung curtains, the air conditioner thrumming anciently. This shabby sixteen by twenty foot area I had never bothered to refurnish, so the grant had lapsed, was more to me than home. It was my share of what we were trying to build.(32)

Again, it is not so much the physical room and the status that it gives her, but, the nationalism and idealism inherent in what it symbolizes. The room is not a mere work-space; it is larger than both her work and her home. It is imbued with an almost mystic quality of nationalism. Sonali clings to the mantel of political structures that she has inherited and vowed to safeguard. A large part of her nationalism includes the idea of ownership. This is a country and a system in which Sonali has a stake, what she calls her "share" or input into nation-building. Her office, like the country, may be shabby but it does not need refurbishing because the ideas seemed age-old and solid. As Sonali looks out of her window at "Lutyens' orderly mathematical New Delhi" (32) and the Parliament house just beyond, they are solid visual and institutional ethical reminders, if not icons of the democracy and independence that India had fought for and won.

As the inheritor of this legacy of nationhood, Sonali questions how the Emergency is indicative of her failure as a citizen and an administrator. Sahgal unambiguously places the blame not only on opportunist administrators like Kachru or businessmen like Dev but also on those who kept silent and saw, yet did not see—citizens and administrators alike. Sonali muses,

> What must an administrator do who sees a citizen kicked and cuffed and arrested for standing on the pavement talking? And if I had never before seen power and authority so nakedly displayed on the pavement, wasn't something very wrong the day it was? (35)

The naked display of power and authority lead Ramu and Mira to activism but for Sonali, since she is a participant in what the state has become, her only option is to resign from the IAS. Sahgal makes it abundantly clear, as Paranjape notes, "that there is no place for the honest and law-abiding officer in the new regime."[22] In fact, Sahgal's view is even more pessimistic than Alexander's because not only does Sonali have to resign, but Rose is murdered, Ram continues to be in a coma, and Dev's father-in-law is jailed for no apparent reason. Clearly there is no place for the honest or the innocent in this India. The only ray of hope is in the fact that Kachru, Sonali's sycophantic colleague who had defended the misdeeds of the regime, finally risks his career and speaks out. The political idealism that viewed administrative officers and politicians as "servants of the people" is badly frayed but not completely discarded yet.

The Inherited House of India

There is a dangerous imbalance in the transition from India's feudal, patriarchal past to a threatening modernity. National political corruption touches and corrodes everything from social institutions to even the most insignificant of its citizens. The careful location of the house in Meena Alexander's *Nampally Road* though offers an optimistic way of integrating a gentler past and the fraught present of the Emergency. In *Sunlight on a Broken Column,* aunt Abida's house which cannot change with the times becomes in the end her mausoleum; and Laila too has to leave the house to be able to ultimately reclaim it. Similarly in *Inside the Haveli,* Geeta chooses to accept the rules of the house because for her, at least, the old system and class privilege ensures a secure future for her children. In *The God of Small Things* the hopelessness of the decaying old house surrounded by the History House and the Pickle Factory do not bode well for the remaining inhabitants. *Rich Like Us* forces us to consider the past as both a threat and a refuge. It presents an interesting juxtaposition between Ram's glitzy new house with the enormous cellar to stash away illegal cash and materials and a 13th century tomb. Rose stumbles upon the old tomb during the construction of the new house, specifically referred to as "Ram's new house". The house and the tomb are paralleled because ultimately the new house becomes Ram's tomb. Even though he is alive and breathing, he is in a coma, and powerless to influence or stop his corrupt son. And the actual tomb, Rose's sanctuary away from the house, becomes her tomb too as she is murdered there. Time triumphs over both Rose's and the 13th century Sultan's unsung passages through India. But even the rather frivolous Nishi, Rose's step-daughter-in-law, feels an atavistic attraction to the tomb that compels her away from the house. The looming past is clearly important and cannot be ignored. But the authors negotiate this past in very different ways.

Time and space are poignantly linked in *Nampally Road* as Siddhartha, a fellow exile, plots Mira's road home on an old calendar from five thousand miles away in the Midlands in England. His directions to Durgabai — his mother's house — nostalgically recall every turn and bend in the road. The huge peepal tree, which provides shade and protection to all is a crucial landmark on the road recalling a "natural" rural and agrarian past. Unlike the banyan tree of *Inside the Haveli*, though, Alexander does not privilege the past or the rural connection over the more urban markers of city life like the cinema "Sagar Talkies," and the optical and the bicycle repair shops. The road is foregrounded as a marker of assimilation where disparate symbols co-exist. Although Mira looks out onto the graveyard from her window, she is keenly aware of the road that links and makes both her and the house a part of a flowing continuum of time.

In an interview, Meena Alexander notes that her poem "The Storm" is, "a journey poem" which she says "was a prototype in some ways for the autobiography" — *Fault Lines*.[23] That journeys are central to Alexander's writings is again foregrounded, even by the title, of her first novel *Nampally Road*. For Mira, the aspiring writer and protagonist, Nampally Road is at the centre of her "stitching together" of various aspects of herself. The road is an insistent reminder of mobility and a link to the larger community outside the self.

Durgabai or Little Mother's house is an inherited patriarchal space like many of the houses under discussion. But its location in the middle of a busy thoroughfare is unique. Little Mother herself seems to blur the boundaries of class and gender as she does of time: "For Little Mother there was no gap between Krishna's world and ours . . . . And time was all of a piece" (18). Time and natural decay are accepted as part of the life cycle and no attempt is made to preserve, pickle or emphasize the ancient lineage or past glory of the house:

> In the upstairs quarters the velvet-backed chairs and brocade-lined screens stood huge and mute under their dusty sheets. Tiles were cracked in the courtyard. Paint had chipped off the shutters or ran in little streaks down the walls after a series of rough monsoons. The city had grown up around the house, and Nampally Road which was once fairly quiet, had turned into a noisy thoroughfare (16).

Although "now the grand days of the house were over" (16), this house, unlike Ashiana (*Sunlight on a Broken Column*) or History House (*The God of Small Things*), will not be allowed to disintegrate into an empty shell awaiting destruction and/or kitsch, commercial redevelopment. The rooms may be empty and shuttered but that is seen as a temporary, almost cyclical phase. The old house, empty of the younger generation studying or working abroad, recalls the fears of India losing its young to the West. But they are expected to return as Mira does, even claiming Siddhartha's mother as her surrogate parent. The description of the house is woven into Little Mother's personal history and her profession and both are located in India. The very specific location of the workplace, the clinic "...in one of the poorest parts of town" (17) that is accessible to the poor is indicative of an awareness of class and of a specific professional and political choice. Similarly the location of the house on a busy thoroughfare is not coincidental. The street intrudes and disrupts the isolation of this house involving it in the changes outside. Little Mother's house, like Nampally Road, does not resist change. The descriptions of the house and the street insist on blurring the boundaries of inside-outside, or public and private existence. Little Mother is herself an agent of change. Reversing the normal inheritance pattern from father to son, it is her name — "Durgabai Gokhale" — her professional medical qualifications — "MD, Gyni-Obstetric" — and the address that announce her ownership on the name-board outside the house proudly facing Nampally Road and welcoming all. She inherited the house from her father, a court physician who served the Nizam. She, in turn, is a physician of the people and serves the community. People like Little Mother and Rose (*Rich Like Us*) are witnesses to history. They are not passive witnesses but active participants in the process of change. Rose actively Indianizes Ram to adjust to the post colonial situation and speaks out when others are silent during the Emergency. Little Mother, Mira's surrogate mother is proactive and deliberate in nurturing the younger generation. Mira notes, "I might have been a young intern, preparing for a bout in the villages. She wanted to show me life" (25). Durgabai sees her job as physician in much the same way as Keshav and Sonali see their jobs in the administrative machinery as "service" or "nation's work" rather than a mere job. She reprimands a patient for following some arcane custom saying, "This is modern India. Did we fight the British for this? Did we gain Swaraj so your child could catch an infection?" (24)

The younger generation—Sonali, Siddhartha and Mira— are all implicated in India's continuity. The Emergency as a specific moment of stock-taking will force them to choose sides. In all three narratives the analogy between the house and country is foregrounded. In *Nampally Road*, Little Mother's house like the empty house of India, is bereft of its young by the westward "brain-drain" but both house and country await their return to reclaim their legacy. It is possible to see Siddhartha and Mira's choice between staying on abroad or coming home as a political choice. Neither Mira nor Siddhartha can, however, return to their respective mothers' houses of stifling tradition. But some of these traditions have been shed at least in Nampally Road. The problem though is the inchoate sense of duty that is the particularly Indian baggage of even those youngsters who have left home. (This will be discussed in detail in the next "Diaspora Homes" chapter). The links between mother-country and biological mothers are obvious. Mira can adopt Little Mother as her surrogate mother, but her status in the house is still that of a guest. In the early stages, this could be read as a lack of commitment on Mira's part but that changes as the narrative progresses. The question is how does this younger generation return or fit-in in a home that often seems distant from their realities? History, in its broadest sense is proposed as one key way of engaging with the house of India.

The Post-colonial Female Subject

Rich Like Us is dedicated "To The Indo-British Experience and what its sharers have learned from each other". Nostalgia definitely colours this novel as it does many others including *Sunlight on a Broken Column* and *Inside the Haveli*. But nostalgia apart, there is no denying the impact of the British in India at various levels of everyday life, especially for the urban, educated elite. In 1915, Sonali's grandfather wrote,

> Wars change worlds. But can even war cause greater upheavals than those a new language and its legacies have brought to our shores in the past hundred years and which will become part of what future Indians will call heritage? I write in English and that is a sign of it, but changes go deeper than language. (131)

Meenakshi Mukherjee points to the disjunct in Indo-English writing in reconciling "two sets of values."[24] The Indianness of the home address that Rao, Iyengar, Rushdie and Sunder Rajan among many others, talk about is not merely locational. Indian English literature's dual parentage, as we have seen (in the "Introduction"), affects not only language, form and content but also affects the literature's sense of its place in the tradition of Indian Literatures. In these narrations of nation, the characters have to similarly either find their place in India or find ways of making India home despite the disjunct that may be caused by their sense of belonging to both the Indian and English traditions.

The colonial experience, for instance, marked Sonali's father, Keshav (an Indian officer of the Colonial civil service) directly. He was conflicted by the sense of rupture it created in him—a nationalist working for an imperial power meant he would have to enforce their rules on fellow colonial subjects. He articulates his confusion, "as two people, at home and in exile, ecstatic and wretched, Indian and British, saved and doomed" (67). But Sahgal, in an inspired reversal, provides a parallel in a British woman, Rose, whose experience of India is curiously similar to Keshav's. For her the "twoness" is on a domestic front as her home is not quite her home as a co-wife, and India is home and not-home for her. Keshav acknowledges that it is the colonial Rose, whose commonsense and positive acceptance of her situation shows him the path. (We will return to Rose's search for home later.) But one can stretch the colonial interpretation too far and Sahgal, like Alexander, offers a more human and simple, if not almost simplistic, idea of love or individual human connections, as something that make a place a home. Rose's ability to empathize is a simple, human understanding that transcends borders of nationality just as Mira is able to transcend barriers of class. However, Roy strongly rejects such a simple solution. In her India, neither Velutha and Ammu's love for each other, nor the twins love for their mother and Velutha, is able to save them. They are deeply scarred and marked by the boundaries that history does not allow them to ignore.

Textually, in *Rich Like Us* there is a too easy resolution of two-ness in the postcolonial subject, Keshav. Sonali notes, "[f]or Papa the seesaw stopped at Independence. He worked harder than ever but with the energy of a whole, not a divided man. Things fell together for him though it was a fallen-apart world we became free in" (165). Pre and post independence India join together almost seamlessly and in this past and present

coming together all the earlier accoutrements of coloniality become part of the mix, as they become 'Indianized', "[t]he civil
service was part of the join. So were English, Parliament, Commonwealth and the Word of Lord Jesus Christ. And Byculla
Souffle and Tipsy Trifle" (163). In this view, post-colonial is a
mere temporal marker that ends colonialism on 15 August 1947.
It does not take into account the lingering process of the emotional impact of colonialism that has been so sharply theorized
by Franz Fanon, Ashis Nandy, Homi Bhabha and many others.

A part of the questioning in these novels is how a
non-resident Indian or even a postcolonial subject can make
India home. Sonali, though she lives in India, faces a similar
dilemma as Mira but her problem is not of colonial or western
influence as much as the fact that she has been brought up on a
diet of Nehruvian idealism and not taken note of the political
changes that run contrary to her idea of what India should be.
Alexander's *Nampally Road* explores the sense of "two-ness" in
a younger generation. Mira is a 25 year old, English educated,
"tangled up inside" postcolonial subject. On the one hand, aware
that she can't go "home" to her mother and be married off nor
can she continue with her life in England, away from what she
sees as her community. To this is also added Mira's acute sense
of the very different ways in which she as a woman perceives
her place in the world and the way her lover, Ramu does. The
gender dynamic is important because the legacy that the
women in at least *Rich Like Us* and *Nampally Road* claim seems
to be one that is passed on by a woman to woman connection.

As a modern Indian woman writer, Mira's homecoming
project is a gentle piecing together:

> a few poems, or a few prose pieces, I could start to stitch it all
> together: my birth in India a few years after independence,
> my colonial education, my rebellion against the arranged
> marriage my mother had in mind for me, my years of research
> in England (30).

During her "English sojourn" (29), Mira's other experiments at "remaking" herself by eating with the "polluted left-

hand" (29) had fallen flat. No one in the Midlands knew or understood the extent of the rebellion involved in that single gesture. Her "homecoming" to a familiar cultural background frames the quest to "make up a self that had some continuity with what I was" (30). The English as well as the Indian experiences are both important parts of who she is that Mira needs acknowledged and integrated for her to feel at home. The two-ness does not necessarily need to merge but both sides need to be accepted wherever she is for it to be home.

Mira's concern about the relevance of her kind of writing and of finding a voice is central to her "homecoming." These are paralleled by Alexander's similar concerns articulated in her other writings. The authorial and autobiographical voice seems often to slip into the narratorial voice of Mira. Wordsworth and the Romantic poets are Alexander's area of specialization as they are Mira's and Mira teaches at Hyderabad University where Alexander herself taught. Mira voices the anxiety of Indian English writers generally when she questions what it means to be writing in English in India. As elsewhere, Alexander has written that:

> ...this process of tearing away, of stripping the language of its canonical burden, of its colonial consolations - by which I mean the curious elegiac mask that the Wordsworthian moment sets up against any powerful resistance to hegemony —is hard indeed.[25]

In what words can such a writer, Wordsworth, Alexander, Mira, whose privileged background and linguistic association with colonialism describe the hurly-burly and messiness of an Indian reality? Alexander's articulation recalls Aijaz Ahmad's trenchant suggestion that instead of dwelling on whether or not English is an Indian language we should really be questioning how English has been assimilated in India. Both Ahmad and critic Sujit Mukherjee call for a systemic way of studying the question. A way that does not privilege English but considers it at par with, and, in the context of, the plurality of Indian languages and literatures. The language issue is not limited to writing alone; Mira's job — teaching English literature — also poses the same dilemma: "why study Wordsworth in our new India?" (54). The irony of the question is underlined by the fact that the college where Mira teaches canonical English texts used to be the house of the nationalist and poet, Sarojini Naidu, whom Gandhi referred to as "India's nightingale." The joint reference to Naidu and Wordsworth complicates the question of relevance: are they both equally irrelevant because they are anachronistic Romantic poets whose idyllic pastorals are drowned in the roar of the cruelly violent "Eveready" motorcade of Hyderabad's mini dictator Limca Gowda in the India of the Emergency? Or is it the job of the post-colonial subject to reconcile the dichotomies and make them both relevant?

In an interview, Alexander explains the dichotomy embodied by Sarojini Naidu. She notes that Naidu, "a powerful nationalist figure," was very different from Naidu the poet, whose "women were pale, imprisoned creatures, modeled on the female images of the Decadents."[26] Alexander elaborates that Naidu's political activism even led to a changed writing style. Her poetry tends to be extremely lyrical, almost orientalist, but her political speeches in English demanding freedom for India are very different. And Mira's awakening follows a similar trajectory. Her deep involvement with Rameeza Be is both a personal and a political connection that firmly links her as a writer and as a woman to the life of the Hyderabadi and larger Indian community:

> Our streets were too crowded, there was too much poverty and misery. The British had subdued us for too long and now that they had left, the unrest in rock and root, in the soul of men and women, was too visible, too turbulent already to permit the kinds of writing I had once learned to value (32).

Mira's use of the possessive pronoun "our", used for the first time in the passage quoted above, completes her homecoming and firmly establishes her as part of the Indian community. Her writing ultimately emerges as self-discovery and protest, blurring the boundaries between private and public.

Commenting on Mira, Alexander notes that, "She [Mira] realises that Wordsworth's `solitary spirit' has nothing to do with the turbulent experiences of these men and women in India."[27] Wordsworth ultimately cannot be a useful model, Mira concludes, because "the lines between inner and outer he valued so deeply were torn apart in our lives" (31). Mira's writing, like Nampally Road, has to function as both a literal and a metaphorical link that reiterates a woman's access to both the home and the world.

In fact, Mira does not seek an isolated story. She seeks herself as an integrated member of the community and society to which she has returned. Her return home is premised upon the desire to establish a sense of community which she feels is denied her by living abroad. She confesses, "I could not figure out a line or a theme for myself, "the life that made sense was all around me" (28). Fragments of her personal past are mapped onto a cultural past. Her attempt is to make sense of the totality of who she is by weaving them together and linking them to the present through a lived and active participation in the everyday life of the community.

Creating Home

Home and community are linked positively in *Nampally Road* and in *Rich Like Us* but in *The God of Small Things* the links are fractured and tenuous. In Roy, both home and community are ultimately destructive. However, in the former two novels, community is created by association with a select group of people who share the same values. Individual connections become a way of both accepting the legacy of the past and carving a niche for oneself in the Indian present. The insistence on that connection is palpable in *Nampally Road* where Mira equates not being connected to a past to being homeless and incomplete. Wholeness, for her, is inextricable from the past and a sense of community.

> [I]t wove the world together. It made a past. Listening to her [Little Mother], I lost the bitter sense I often had of being evicted, of being thrust out of a place in which lives had meanings and stories accreted and grew. The present was flat and sharp and broken into pieces. (69)

If ethnicity, history and culture are key elements to this wholeness then a Mira can come home, blend in with the local population in Hyderabad, and claim her share of the legacy. But can a foreigner ever claim a different place as home? In *Rich Like Us*, Sahgal reverses the paradigms through the character Rose. Rose is as English as her name suggests. She is conceived of as a "powerful" and "whole" character because she comes from a "whole culture." "Rose," Sahgal explains, "comes out of that East End Cockney culture of London and is firmly rooted in its values."[28] Her English-ness is just a part of who she is, like "the flow of Cockney, unleavened by forty-odd years of being a memsahib in India" (33). No apologies are offered for either; they are just two among the many ways of situating her. Our first view of her — "a woman in a sleeveless print dress, her hair dyed a peremptory scarlet" (11) — marks her as "other." Her ethnicity is the primary marker of her difference. Neuman, her step-son's business associate, imagines her in the 1930s, "the electric effect of her unquenchable hair and whiteness, all red, white and blue of her — a veritable Union Jack — at the till of the shop in Lahore" (13). Rose as a "veritable Union Jack" in colonial India plays a complicated role of maintaining her own English identity yet Indianizing both herself and her westernized husband enough to fit into a feudal familial structure. Rose can almost be seen as a cipher for Englishness though not for colonialism.

Neuman's simplistic categorization, however, is one that Rose herself firmly refuses. Her involvement with Indians, through her husband Ram and his friends, puts her in an in-between state, defined by negatives: "not the mistress of the house" (11) and "neither wife nor widow" (79). She shares this see-saw position with other westernized Indians like Keshav and Zafar and instinctively understands their dilemma "in her bones." The shared "two-ness" constantly disturbs and problematises notions of home and identity based on exclusion of gender, ethnicity, language, and religion or too-easy alignments among them. Inter-textually, an interesting parallel could be drawn between Rose and Laila (*Sunlight on a Broken Column*), both of whom share this sense of two-ness and yet are "whole" characters. At the end even her father-in-law Lalaji, and the community accept her as the 'angrezi bahu' the foreign daughter-in-law and very much a part of the household. (In much the same way as Sonia Gandhi, Indira Gandhi's widowed Italian daughter-in-law, has been accepted by the Indian nation.) Rose is not alone, she follows in the line of other foreigners, women and men in India, like CF Andrews, Annie Besant, and Mira Ben who were considered Indians at heart because they identified with and participated in the struggles of the Indian people against colonialism.

Cythera as Home

Rose's desired home does not have a fixed location or a permanent address. Maybe the only way she, as a foreigner, at that moment in time can create a home is through Benedict Anderson's idea of an imagined community of horizontal friendships, but one that is not circumscribed by either history or geography. The idea of Cythera encapsulates how she makes India home.

The narrative shifts between Rose-as-guest, even after forty-three years in India, and Rose as the foreign wife who is responsible for "Indianising" her husband. It is not coincidental that the home Rose is looking for is Cythera. The text explains that Cythera is essentially a dreamlike, mythical place, "Cythera is where you embarked for when you left your native shores'" (73). Rose's dictionary search reveals that it is linked to Venus and Aphrodite. A real island, she discovers, but "an island for believers in love" (74) In the explanation under Watteau's print of 'L'embarquement pour L'ile de Cythere' Rose finds an elaboration – "The voyage was a quest, it said, and Cythera a paradise, an impossible dream, towards which pilgrims journey but never arrive" (203). The kind of home that Rose aspires to is a Cythera – beyond physical boundaries and where the quest is more important than the arrival.

Cythera is not Rose's quest alone. The text suggests various possibilities of Pakistan as Cythera, India as Cythera, but in the end, rejects them all. Pakistan/Cythera — a "homeland" for the believers — is not only a geographic location but conceptualized as a religio-mythical space in the 1930s when Rose first arrives in India. Cythera also recalls the awakening of India "at the stroke of the midnight hour" to the reality of independence. Partition and Emergency are the dark side of Cythera. India as a possible home/Cythera is the story of political and personal betrayals. Rose is framed by, and a participant in this historical narrative of India from the 1930s to the 1970s. Rose and Sonali, though separated by age and nationality, are both implicated in India's history, and linked by their resistance to forces that undermine a universal humanism. Sahgal, however, does not encourage us to see Cythera as India. *Rich Like Us* maps the betrayal of Cythera — a dream turned nightmare located in an India that is both home and not-home for both the young, Indian woman Sonali as well as for the older English woman Rose.

Although geographically at home in England where Ram courts her, Rose even there is "out in strange territory and had lost her way home". She is lost not only emotionally but also linguistically and historically. Some of the normally accepted aspects of home—language, religion, ethnicity, culture that often make one feel at home are missing for Rose even in England. Ram 'teaches' her her own language often correcting her pronunciation and grammar. He is well versed in both Indian and British history. He talks of Anne Boleyn and Henry VIII "as though it was his country's history and not hers"(42). Her 'knowledge' is of a lived and felt reality. Experience grounds her more securely in herself and among people than does Ram's more 'bookish' learning. But Ram's talk bridges cultural and class boundaries. It creates a world where she is an insider—till the door shuts her in. She does not have the vocabulary or grammar to resist his word/world creation. For Rose, the idea of home itself is Janus-faced from its very inception, and not only because the home is going to be in India. In Ram's wooing of the young chocolate shop girl in London, the idea of imprisonment is almost palpable in his "talk erecting a world around her, drawing her deep into it, the door shutting, Rose inside" (42). This initial seduction through words creates a placeless home for Rose so that the physical reality of India is not registered by the text. Ram is the home rather than India.

The physical descriptions of Rose's place in the house especially in the Delhi house raises more questions than they answer. Rose is aware that the house, "was his [Ram's] world, from roof terrace to alcove, and she an idle guest, housed, feasted and invited to enjoy herself" (63) It would be too easy to read into this an analogy with the British presence in India. But even in the new house they build after partition, we see Rose's room described as "an island off the mainland of the house" (39). Sonali notes, "[E]verything she [Rose] owned was in it [her room]. To concentrate her whole being there, with not a stray cushion or an ashtray of hers anywhere else in the house, showed what a desert the rest of the house must have seemed to her" (253). It is no surprise then that Rose's idea of home is a mythical Cythera. Sonali claims, "but Rose had transcended those things, blood, race, distance" (259). But could she really have found home in India or elsewhere without transcending ethnicity, history and geography? Again *The God of Small Things* is very different in that there is no sense of home or community formation. In fact, the community is ignored if not rejected outright. The twins, Rahel and Estha, finally can turn only to each other – they are each other's home. They assuage and complete each other when the world at large seems to have rejected them. They are rooted in a very definite home and community that destroys them and does not allow any easy escape.

Sahgal, like Rushdie, suggests that it is possible for somebody like Rose to dwell in an India of the mind that can be a placeless reality. But the idea of community is still essential to being at home in a place. And both Alexander and Sahgal suggest that women like Rose, Sonali, Little Mother and Mira create home through a strong bond with other women. These emphatic bonds allow them all to make connections across history and class. Sonali sees a female continuum in Rose, Mona, and Sita (*Ramayana*) as all defenseless against a willful male will. She acerbically attributes this to "an exercise of sheer male prerogative" (215). The linking is subtle and the idea is not to perpetuate the bonding of women as victims, used by men and "murdered by society" (75) but rather revelatory of how each woman becomes for other women, a role model of individual resistance that will not passively accept injustice.

Women's Homes

Rich Like Us and *Nampally Road* suggest a woman to woman connection as a primary linking factor that makes India home for women even if they are marginalized or second class citizens. The idea of womenspace physically delineated in haveli dwellings and extended in women-only homes is recreated in *Rich Like Us* and *Nampally Road* though in a different way. Although the basic idea of community formation around and through women is similar, both *Nampally Road* and *Rich Like Us* enables women in the house of India to reach beyond family and household. Women reach out to women transcending bonds of nationality, race, age and class to establish womanly bonds that sustain. These bonds reiterate Gomathy and Fernandez' observation that, "Almost all women in our society have experienced women-only spaces for confidence-sharing, healing, mutual comfort and support."[29] The woman to woman connection, in both Sahgal and Alexander is sometimes overly romanticized but is based on a conscious idea of community formation deemed possible through an empathy and an instinctive understanding that is often wordless.

In a continuation of a female pattern, Mira, the surrogate daughter, rather than the distant son who has left mother and motherland, is chosen to inherit the legacy of Little Mother as home-maker and community-healer. Durgabai, though firmly rooted in India's past, is aware of her role in the present. The traditions of healing associated with women are reinforced by Durgabai's medical degrees which are a sign of both her modernity and a public assertion of professionalism that allow her legitimate access and entry into the public sphere. Her occupation as a qualified medical doctor places her firmly in the scientific age of modern India. The text carefully maintains the balance between Durgabai the physician who heals bodies through scientific medication and Durgabai the holistic healer of spirits (16). Her art of assimilating male and female spheres and yet linking with other women is passed on to Mira imperceptibly in the daily rituals of sharing a home, much like they were passed on in *Inside the Haveli* to Geeta the new daughter-in-law. Although, of course, what is passed on is very different. In the havelis it is the patriarchal, feudal haveli ethos that is handed on to the new daughter-in-law to safeguard whereas in both *Nampally Road* and *Rich Like Us* a secular, humanist and democratic idea of nationhood is the legacy. Durgabai takes Mira to her clinic so she can also participate in the public aspect of her life. Mira recognizes that for her the newcomer, the clinic, the street, the house and the college are all on the same continuum of places of learning. Conscious of Little Mother as her teacher, she remarks, "I might have been a young intern, preparing for a bout in the villages. She wanted to show me life" (24). As a surrogate mother, Durgabai is her guide and friend, and her house offers Mira an alternative to her biological mother's home. Mira the returnee daughter, in this richly layered text, reciprocates in kind. It is possible to read a parallel in Mira the surrogate daughter, nursing Little Mother—her mother-country—back to health.

If Durgabai weaves Mira into the cocoon of an affective past, Rameeza Be flings her headlong into the violence of India in the present. Rameeza, the young Muslim village woman, gang-raped by the police, becomes the embodiment of the brutal and unequal struggle Mira witnesses on the streets. It is not coincidental that both Rameeza and Velutha in *God of Small Things* are of lower status and voiceless. But Alexander and Roy treat these marginalized characters in starkly different ways. In Roy's narrative the stranglehold of history necessitates Velutha's violent death. Rameeza, though, is given a chance at not only survival but also of finally finding her voice as her wounded mouth heals and she is able to speak. Mira's moment of epiphany occurs as she sees "a small fire blazing in the water" (40). The vision evokes the chilling presence of Rameeza Be, "The eyes of the unknown Rameeza, black as the deepest pools in our river, filling me, sucking me down into a world from which there was no escape" (40) It becomes clear that the line from Nagarjuna that prefaces the novel, "If fire is lit in water, who can extinguish it?" is the key question posed by the text. If the way of renunciation is proposed as the traditional Indian spiritual way, then Mira vehemently proposes an alternate way through passionate involvement. Mira's entry into India and to finding her place in it is through an instinctive, individual empathy. Rameeza, at this moment, is only a felt presence and a name, but Mira is already involved in her story because she relates to her as a woman.

In the second instance, when Mira sees Rameeza physically, she remains nameless and is alluded to indirectly. For the whole length of the paragraph, the pronouns "she" and "her" (57) designate Rameeza's tangible and battered presence. There is an element of voyeurism in Mira's gaze as she first focuses on Rameeza's sari "stiff with blood"(57), which changes to complete identification as she tentatively leans forward through the cell bars to touch "her damp forehead" (57). The gesture betrays a tender wonderment, almost as if Mira could not distinguish between herself and Rameeza. The mutual absorption of the two women is completed when Rameeza draws Mira's dream:

> She was drawing the great pyramid with stones of flesh that I had seen in my dreams. The stones with water rushing under them, where I had hung. The stones with voices. I was so close to her now that I felt I was writing with her hand, that her hand was my hand writing (81-82).

The lyricism of the passage makes it hard to tell where Rameeza ends and Mira begins. The class barrier is transcended, at least for this moment, even though Rameeza remains voiceless and we see this scene entirely from Mira's perspective. A similar moment of absorption occurs in *Rich Like Us* when the two co-wives Rose and Mona are visualized as mirror images. The authorial intention seems to insist upon an instinctive empathy between the women despite differences of race and status, "Rose and Mona seeing each other's face in mirrors, bound by never-to-be-broken sacraments, Rose in India, in Cythera, her exile, her home"(74) It is unclear if Rose and Mona see each other in mirrors or if they are mirror images. Both views are suggested by the text. And home is definitely exile and home for them both.

The completion of Mona/Rose is in "the thin sobbing sound of pure grief no one was meant to hear, [which] froze Mona's tears in Rose's eyes" (105). The co-wives turn to each other even in their final moments but Ram is not excluded either, and the "family" comes full circle when at Mona's death, it is Rose who "burst into helpless weeping, shedding the tears he [Ram] couldn't" (105). From being the outsider, Rose becomes the one who holds the family together. The physical restrictions of a space that is written over are transcended as Mona's complete volte face and triumphant cry of "we are sisters" (155) overtly acknowledges that barriers of class, race and even shared wifehood are not insurmountable.

Similarly, Mira's recognition of herself in Rameeza opens the space for a wider community formation, and the community is one that primarily celebrates women's friendships. Mira, Rameeza and Durgabai intuitively recognize and extend each others thoughts. They are self-consciously cognizant of their instinctive empathy for each other as women and the connections that cross generation and class barriers to form a common human, womanly history. Rameeza and Mira's mutual recognition is extended by Mira when she reiterates the sense of oneness she feels with the activists in the truck protesting Limca Gowda's autocratic rule as well as with the anonymous woman whom she does not recognize. She insists on gender as the primary linking factor. She explains to her lover Ramu,

There's nowhere people like us can be whole. The best I can do is leapfrog over the cracks in the earth, over the black fissures. From one woman's body into another. From this Mira that you know into Little Mother, into Rameeza, into Rosamma, into that woman in the truck on the way to the Public Gardens (92-93).

Alexander and Sahgal's descriptions of these moments of instinctive empathy amongst women are romantic. The texts' positioning of Mira, Rose or Sonali distracts the reader's attention. We are swept along in Mira's epiphany quite forgetting the erasure and silence of Rameeza Be as a subject and the fact that the charity of crutches for the beggar in *Rich Like Us* is a placebo to appease our conscience. Mira and even Sonali are allowed an escape that is firmly denied to Ammu and the twins in *God of Small Things*. And although Rose is murdered and Rameeza and Sonali's futures are uncertain, we the readers are comforted by Mira and Sonali's resolution of their place in society.

The naïve romanticism of these solutions is a problem but, as Spivak counsels, "that is a danger one must face, because the other side of romanticizing is censorship."[30] The romanticism should also not detract from the important recognition of, to use Rajeswari Sunder Rajan's term, "women's collective identity."[31] In Sahgal and Alexander, as in other women novelists, the consciousness of a collective identity may not yet have translated into collective action but there is hope in Mira's finding her voice, her own specific writing style, and a sense of home despite the shadows that sometimes loom over the house of India.

References

1   Nehru, Jawaharlal. "Tryst with Destiny" 14 August 1947. *The Vintage Book of Indian Writing 1947-1997.* (eds.) Salman Rushdie and Elizabeth West. (p.2)

2   Khilnani, Sunil. *The Idea of India.* London: Hamish Hamilton, 1997

3   Said, Edward W. *Culture and Imperialism.* London: Vintage, 1993. (xiii)

4   Mee, Jon. "Not At Home in English? India's Foreign-Returned Fictions". *The Round Table.* (2001) 362. (p.717)

5   Mukherjee, Meenakshi. *The Twice Born Fiction Themes and Techniques of the Indian Novel in English.* New Delhi, Heinemann (Educational Books) 1971.

6   Achebe, Chinua. *Things Fall Apart.* London: Heinemann, 1958.

7   Ammu Joseph et al. (eds.) *Storylines: Conversations with Women*

Writers. New Delhi: Women Unlimited, Womens World, and Asmita Resource Centre for Women 2003 (p.44)

8   Iyengar, K.R. Srinivasa. "Indian Writing in English: Prospect and Retrospect," Ramesh Mohan, (ed.) *Indian Writing in English*, Mumbai: Orient Longman, 1978 (p.8)

9   Rushdie, Salman. "Damme, This is the Oriental Scene For You!" *New Yorker*, 1997 (p.56)

10 Sunder Rajan, Rajeswari. *Real and Imagined Women: Gender, Culture and Postcolonialism*. London, New York: Routledge 1993. (p.8)

11 Arundhati Roy. Interview http://website.lineone.net/ ~jon.simmons/roy/tgost6.htm

12 Ashcroft, Bill et al, (eds.) *The Empire Writes Back: Theory and Practice in Post-Colonial Literatures*. London, New York: Routledge 1989. (p.9)

13 Nelson, Emmanuel S. (ed.) *Writers of the Indian Diaspora: A Bio-Bibliographical Critical Sourcebook*. West Port, Conn.: Greenwood Press 1993 (p.1)

14 See Kumar, Radha. *The History of Doing: An Illustrated Account of Movements for Women's Rights and Feminism in India, 1800-1990*. London, New York: Verso, New Delhi: Kali for Women 1993 (pp.128-129)

See also Meena Alexander's prose piece "Mosquitoes in the Main Room," *House of a Thousand Doors: Poems and Prose Pieces*, Washington D.C.: Three Continents Press, 1988. (pp.51-52)

15 Ammu Joseph et al. (eds.) *Storylines: Conversations with Women Writers*. New Delhi: Women Unlimited, Womens World, and Asmita Resource Centre for Women 2003. (p.42)

16 Kohli, Devindra. *Indian Writers At Work*. New World Literature Series: 43, New Delhi: D.K. Publishers, B.R. Publishing Corporation, 1991. (p.115)

17 Jawaharlal Nehru : Speech on the Granting of Indian Independence, August 14, 1947. http://www.indhistory.com/partition-independence.html

18 Indeed that may have happened but for Sanjay Gandhi's death in a flying accident when the mantel was passed on to his elder brother, the supposedly reluctant politician, Rajiv Gandhi. Rajiv Gandhi was later assassinated by a terrorist bomb. His wife, Sonia Gandhi, was in line to take over but her Italian origins became a contentious issue and she declined the Prime Ministership and instead took over as the head of the Congress party.

19 Gilbert, Sandra and Susan Gubar. *The Mad Woman in the Attic: The Woman Writer in the Nineteenth Century Literary Imagination*. New

Haven: Yale University Press, 1979.

20 Paranjape, Makarand. "The Crisis of Contemporary India and Nayantara Sahgal's Fiction". *World Literature Today*, Spring 94, Vol. 68, Issue 2.

21 Rao, Parsa Venkateshwar, Interview: "Presenting the Past," *Indian Express Sunday Magazine*, 18 July 1993.

22 Paranjape, Makarand. "The Crisis of Contemporary India and Nayantara Sahgal's Fiction". *World Literature Today*, Spring 94, Vol. 68, Issue 2.

23 Abraham, Ayisha & Meena Alexander on "Writing and Contemporary Issues," *The Toronto South Asian Review*, 1993 (p.23-26)

24 Mukherjee, Meenakshi. *Realism and Reality: The Novel and Society in India*. Delhi, New York: Oxford University Press, 1985. (p.7) 1985./1994. (p.7)

25 Alexander, Meena. "Piecemeal Shelter: Writing, Ethnicity, Violence," *Public Culture 5*. 1993. (pp.621-625)

26 Ayisha Abraham & Meena Alexander on "Writing and Contemporary Issues", *The Toronto South Asian Review*. 1993. (pp.23-26)

27 Silva, Paul. "Indian Writers on Tour: Meena Alexander Talks to Paul Silva." *Cascando*. 1993 (p.73)

28 S. Varalakshmi, "An Interview with Nayantara Sahgal" R.K. Dhawan, (ed.) *Indian Women Novelists*. New Delhi: Prestige,1993.

29 Gomathy N.B. and Bina Fernandez. "Fire, Sparks and Smouldering Ashes" in Narrain and Bhan (eds.) *Because I Have a Voice*. New Delhi: Yoda Press, 2005 (p.201)

30 Spivak, "Transnationality and Multiculturalist Ideology," Bahri & Vasudeva, (eds.) *Between The Lines: South Asians and Post-coloniality*. Philadelphia, P.A.: Temple University Press, 1996. (p.86)

31 Sunder Rajan, Rajeswari, "The Feminist Plot and the Nationalist Allegory: Home and The World in Two Indian Women's Novels in English," *Modern Fiction Studies*. 1993.

7

Diaspora Homes

Diaspora Indians are thrice alienated—from the India they left behind, from their new host country and from their children. Homes in South Asian Diaspora fiction are in constant conversation with the meta-home that is India. The Indian home is an orienting device, like some airplane's in-flight maps that point towards Mecca while flying at 30, 000 feet above the earth in a borderless world. The hazily glowing green arrow on the map in the womb-like darkness of the plane reassuringly provides a directional compass for prayer.[1] Similarly the Indian home left behind is both an orienting device as well as an exemplar home.

But why do we need the reassurance of the glowing arrow orienting us to Mecca, or to the meta-Indian home? The orienting arrow is a reminder and a guide towards an idea of an original home of acceptance and belonging. Displacement accentuates the nostalgia of original homes, homes left behind. It colours the loss and longing for not merely the home country or a parental home, but for that feeling of entitlement and belonging often associated with childhood homes. In "Imaginary Homelands," Salman Rushdie articulates how recreations of "Indias of the mind" are inflected by loss and retrieval.[2] Rushdie describes his journey from a photograph of his ancestral home to the concrete structure of that home in Bombay.

The photograph reminds him that "it's my present that is foreign, and that the past is home, albeit a lost home in a lost city in the mists of lost time."[3] Rushdie suggests that home is retrieved and changed by describing it: "redescribing a world is the necessary first step towards changing it."[4] The desire to reclaim lost homes he suggests often results in the creation of a different version of home rather than recalling a particular lost home. For expatriate writers like himself, he says:

> our physical alienation from India almost inevitably means that we will not be capable of reclaiming precisely the thing that was lost; that we will, in short, create fictions, not actual cities or villages, but invisible ones, imaginary homelands, Indias of the mind.[5]

Nostalgia, loss, betrayal and duty are the foundations of new homes as diasporic Indian protagonists adjust to new countries. In adjusting to new homes abroad issues of acculturation and/or assimilation become the focal point as immigrants and first or second generation Indians negotiate the un-balance of their hyphenated identities. Who is classified as Indian, by whom and for what purpose is an integral part of diaspora women's novels in English.[6] Ravinder Randhawa's *A Wicked Old Woman* (1987), Bharati Mukherjee's *Jasmine* (1989), Anita Rau Badami's *Tamarind Woman* (*Tamarind Mem*) (2002) and Jhumpa Lahiri's *The Namesake* (2003), explore the construction of Indianness, and trace the patterns of nest and prison woven into Indian homes abroad. Some Indians cling to food and clothes as the most overt markers of Indianness that sets them apart and reinforces their difference. The insistence on this difference is often a deliberate statement of belonging to another place. Whereas others, and especially second generation Indians, erase and reject those very markers in an effort to pass in the dominant culture. Particular textures of Indianness— a familiarity with material culture, values, rituals and familial bonds that create a home-space, albeit, imaginary, help anchor some whereas for others often that very Indianness is envisioned as the albatross that prevents assimilation in the new or dominant culture.

The interplay of nostalgia, duty and desire in these novels are reflective of migration patterns, class experiences and age as they inflect the shape of new homes. The homes under consideration are located in the United States, England and Canada. Each of these locales imbues the homes with their own specificity that influences the particular manner in which new homes are conceived. However, the ways in which these diaspora Indian homes are marked as American, English or Canadian and therefore different from each other are beyond the scope of this work. The authors deliberately invoke community and conversation in the interface of the new homes with Indian homes as a way of creating a balance between the two sides of the hyphen of Indian-Americans (or British or Canadian). The interactive link with India and Indianness, a characteristic that distinguishes this second phase of diaspora from that of the earlier indentured labour phase, shapes these diaspora characters living abroad, be they immigrants or first and subsequent generation ethnic Indians.

India in Diaspora

The India's invoked in Bharati Mukherjee's *Jasmine* and Jhumpa Lahiri's *The Namesake* could not be more different from each other. *Jasmine* opens in rural Punjab of the 1980s against the larger backdrop of the threatening rumblings of an emerging fundamentalist violence of the Lions of Punjab or Babbar Khalsa movement. A sinister astrologer's dramatic prophecy of widowhood and exile for the then seven year old protagonist Jyoti Vijh haunts her. A couple of year later, it seems that there is no escaping destiny, when her engineer husband, preparing to leave for higher education in America is killed by a terrorist bomb. Jyoti has two choices, either she can quietly submit to her fate or she can find another way. Jyoti, renamed Jasmine by her husband, chooses the other way. She packs her bags, acquires a false passport and leaves for America. Her perilous passage and journey through America transform her from a shy, village girl into an intrepid woman "greedy with wants and reckless from hope." (241) She arrives in New York, settles in, initially as a home-help, with Taylor and his daughter Wylie. One day she spots the terrorist who killed her husband and flees to Iowa. In Iowa she marries a banker, Bud and they adopt a Vietnamese boy. Bud is semi paralyzed by a shooting incident. In the end, a heavily pregnant Jasmine leaves Bud to head west with Taylor; she acknowledges, "I am not choosing between men. I am caught between the promise of America and old-world dutifulness." (240) The promise of America is self-evident in the literary pioneering trope invoked of heading West.

The "old-world dutifulness" Jyoti flees is an exoticised India embodied in the astrologer and in escaping him, Jyoti escapes him, her destiny and India itself. This fleeing is but the first of her many attempts to run away from her past. The star shaped wound, acquired when she fell after the astrologer's prediction marks her with all the overtones of the mark of Cain and the scarlet letter but it is re-configured in another exotic trope of the third eye of the god Shiva. This third eye gives Jyoti insight, wisdom and the courage to escape her destiny. In her construction of India, it is a site of violence and terrorism, of both fundamentalists and the state. Escape and rejection can be read as both inevitable and almost necessary. That would be an astute condemnation and commentary on the narration of nation at a particular political and historical moment. But the political backdrop remains just that, a backdrop. It does not assume the complex dense reading seen in Sahgal's *Rich Like Us*, Roy's *The God of Small Things* or Alexander's *Nampally Road*. The moment is glossed over as India takes on the familiar contours of a Western orientalist imaginary in the style of Katherine Mayo's 1920's controversial book *Mother India*. There are no redeeming features to the India Jyoti leaves behind and her desperate desire to assimilate and buy into the American advertisement slogans of 'be what you want to be' and 'just do it' are not merely condescending but dismissive and judgmental of other immigrant realities such as those of the Wadehra family that initially give her refuge in New York. But Jyoti, and to an extent Mukherjee herself, does not see this. Mukherjee's *New York Times* essay

"Two Ways to Belong in America" portrays her own assimilation as a choice but does not see her sister's desire not to assimilate, in fact her insistence to retain her "resident alien" status as an equally valid choice.[7]

The Namesake, unlike *Jasmine*, opens less dramatically and more poignantly with a pregnant Ashima hungrily recreating and literally consuming India in her concoction of *"jhaal moori"*. But her cravings remains unappeased as she cannot find the right ingredient, there is always something missing, a certain lack in her approximation of the common-place, popular Indian snack. Homesick for the foods, smells and companionship of home and family her American existence reflects the same nostalgia, lack and approximation as did her attempts to replicate *"jhaal moori"* with rice crispies. They are valiant substitutes but initially just that—substitutes, until the taste buds have been re-trained to forget the original tastes and smells. India is the reference point for Ashima's home in America. The original home is evoked not only because of the loss caused by dislocation but the loss is further exacerbated because she is expecting a baby. The baby heralds the beginning of a new life—but it is a life that will begin in a 'foreign' land. It also marks a new beginning for Ashima the new bride now about to embark on motherhood without the support of family and community. As noted earlier, in *Imaginary Homelands* Rushdie emphasizes that the past itself becomes a sort of lost home.[8] For Ashima, memory and recreating the new home furnished with memories of the old home and even in the mould of the old becomes a way of recovering the lost past and its attendant sense of kin and community. The geographic, chronologic, spatial and material dislocation here is articulated in the everyday longings for the tastes, smells and sounds of the home left behind. The story begins with the newly wed Ashoke and Ashima Ganguli's departure from Calcutta to Boston. Professionally, Ashoke climbs the American professorial ladder to tenureship. However, socially their lives revolve around other immigrant Bengali families in the area. Their two children Gogol and Sonia are born and brought up in an affluent, immigrant American existence. Gogol in many ways typifies the ABCD (American Born Confused Desi) as he struggles between his pet name Gogol and his real name Nikhil. He, the first born, Ivy-leaguer son, has all but been assimilated into his girl friend Maxine's lifestyle when his father dies of a heart attack. Gogol is drawn back into his natal home and marries another Non Resident Indian (NRI). But the marriage does not last. Indian origins and similar pasts are not strong enough to keep them together. His mother Ashima, now a widow, decides to sell their home and divide her time between India and America. At that moment, confronted by the loss of his father, his home and life as he knew it, Gogol realizes the full significance of his name and the meaning of home, family and identity.

Jhumpa Lahiri won the Pulitzer Prize for fiction in 2000 for her collection of short stories *The Interpreter of Maladies*. One reviewer calls Lahiri, "the interpreter of immigrant dreams especially for Bengali immigrants".[9] At an autobiographical level Lahiri has much in common with Gogol, the protagonist of *The Namesake*. Like him and many other Indians, not just Bengalis, she has two names, Nilanjana and Jhumpa. And like Gogol she too is a second generation Indian-American which according to her is more problematic because, "that's much harder to write about, it's much closer to me."[10] But her response to a question about whether there were significant differences of experience between immigrants and their American born and brought-up children provides a rare insight into Gogol. She says,

> The question of identity is always a difficult one, but especially so for those who are culturally displaced, as immigrants are, or those who grow up in two worlds simultaneously, as is the case for their children. The older I get, the more aware am I that I have somehow inherited a sense of exile from my parents.[11]

This inheritance of loss is the sense of exile that Gogol, like other second generation Asian Americans, struggles with. The not always articulated or acknowledged sense of 'something missing' does not allow him to be at home in a completely white America nor is he at ease in the community of immigrant Bengalis that were the mainstay in an alien land for his parents. To return to the food metaphor, Ashima at least had a memory of the *"jhaal moori"* she was trying to replicate. Gogol only has her version of the real thing and no evocative context of associations with that particular food. His associations of India are seen through his parents' lens of nostalgia and his own reluctant and infrequent visits when he feels 'not Indian enough' and is treated as 'too American' to fit in comfortably.

Rejection, escape and nostalgia are not the only possible reactions to past homes. Recreating or reliving the past sometimes becomes a way of finding direction when displacement erases familiar identity markers. In the London based *A Wicked Old Woman*, Ravinder Randhawa suggests that for second generation Indians, being twice removed from the original home and home-country loosens the framework of life. She compares the situation of British Indians to that of (the fairy tale characters) Hansel and Gretel who do not have the stone markers to guide them back to where they came from. She likens the situation to being in a jungle and not recognizing a single animal. Diaspora Indians try and balance their homes and existence between overly-strict and ossified parental homes and the homes in the dominant culture which promise freedom and hostile racism in equal measures. First generation parents, Randhawa suggests, try to recreate the life patterns in homes left behind, but are stranded without any points of reference. She comments,

> They attempt to replicate the frames that informed their lives, but they can't hold on because the frames they make here are constructed of material foreign to them and like anti-climbing paint it repels their grip (Randhawa.104)

The desire to replicate the frames that provided stability and held families together are the frames of the meta-Indian home that continue to contextualize these new homes. Old homes become the blueprint for home in an alien land. The lack of a guiding arrow or an orienting device of memory can render one homeless—both literally and emotionally.

Kulwant is the eccentric middle-aged narrator of *A Wicked Old Woman*. She recalls and evaluates her past and forms a new network of contacts to try and make sense of her life. As the daughter of first generation immigrant parents and a schoolgirl in London, she tried to fit in by conforming to British mainstream norms like acquiring a boyfriend. However, in reaction to a racist society she swings the other way—the way of the Indian, especially immigrant mainstream, and opts for an arranged marriage which ends in divorce. She wanders around like an anonymous, homeless, bag-lady but that does not afford her whatever she is looking for either. Distanced from her sons and daughters-in-law who are wary of her, she builds a network of connections through chance encounters with others. Her reminisces are interwoven with the parallel stories of other immigrant Indians like Rani/Rosalind struggling with similar issues. Colour and class are squarely confronted around the hospital bed of Rani/Rosalind who hangs between life and death. Rani's story is a cautionary tale. She ran away from home at sixteen, killed a house-mate in self defense and now has to figure out how and if she can reclaim her life. Randhawa charts a path between the confining rules of the old community desperately trying to resist change and that inevitably alienates the younger generation who have to fend for themselves in an alien and often racist environment; and the freedom and anonymity offered by the new community that comes at a price. And the price is change and conformity to a different set of cultural rules.

In Anita Rau Badami's *Tamarind Mem,* or *Tamarind Woman* as it was renamed in its American edition, provides the duality of a past inflected less by culture than generation and distance. In the two part structure of the novel — the voices of 'Kamini' and 'Saroja' echo the distance between Canada and India, daughter and mother. This is one of the first in the genre of mother-daughter novels in Indo-English writing. The novel immediately locates Kamini alone and cold in her silent, Canadian basement apartment looking out at a snow covered land-scape, her yearning conjuring up memories of a sun-filled, spacious and peopled Indian home. But she is unable to tell her mother "how I yearned to get away from this freezing cold city where even the traffic sounds were muffled by the snow." (2) Kamini's Calgary is reduced to this basement apartment. Her only communications are with her mother and sister, on the telephone or through letters. We know that she works at a chemical engineering research centre but there is no sign of a life outside the basement. Here she sits sorting out and recalling memories of her Indian homes and her childhood, the basement location in itself signals her inability to emerge from the past. A part of her need to uncover the past is rooted in Kamini's ambivalent relationship with her mother. "I was never sure about Ma's feelings for me. Her love, I felt sometimes, was like the waves in the sea, the ebb and flow left me reaching out hungrily." (14) This hunger necessitates Kamini's painstaking uncovering the past to come to terms with her absent present. In their different versions of the past, Kamini's daughterly version maps the daily minutiae of her childhood viewed from far-away Canada and through the rose tinted lens of nostalgia. For her the present is definitely "a foreign country" as she re-plays her past endlessly. Although she escapes to Canada physically, she never really leaves India. Canada remains an absence. For her the memories of homes in India and her past are virtual prisons that do not allow her to leave her basement apartment even in Calgary. The basement location in itself signals her in-ability to emerge from the past. She blames her mother for the constant unhappiness that permeates their house.

The mother, Saroja, recalls the past quite differently. Following familial convention, she was forced to give up her ambition to have a career, possibly as a doctor and is married to an older railway engineer. Their peripatetic existence as railway families and her husband's emotional and physical absences, as well as her own thwarted ambition turn Saroja into the acid-tongued, tamarind woman of the title. She has an affair with an Anglo-Indian mechanic, Paul da Costa, and bears his daughter but refuses to run away with him because he seems to offer just another kind of dependence. After her husband's death, she chooses to live on her own rather than moving in with one of the daughters. In the end, on a train trip across India, unmoored from the walled confines of home, she tells her stories to the group of random younger women who share her compartment.[12] As in Anita Nair's *Ladies Coupe*, the train compartment signals both community formation as well as a journey of self-discovery. In the telling of their stories Saroja sees how much India has changed from the time when she was a young wife and mother while Kamini gains some understanding of the social constrictions women like her mother faced. Saroja and Kamini's narration of their various homes and the relationships within point to a generational rather than a cultural conflict. Cultural conflict is absent in Saroja's mother's and grandmother's homes because the houses are in India. Kamini too does not attribute her own inability to settle in Canada to problems of acculturation.

Indianness as a quality, however, is not perceived as an unmitigated blessing in this literature. Meenakshi Mukherjee notes that, "[w]eighed down by the heavy burden of Indianness, they [Indo-English writers] wrote as if India has a homogenous culture."[13] The homogenisation is, of course, one problem in the evocation and portrayal of India. But, from the viewpoint of the protagonists, another problem is the sense of confinement imposed by an amorphous sense of Indianness. Home and country often merge and bleed in and out of each other in these evocations.

India as a meta-home is different for immigrants and first or second generation settlers. The differences, at one level, replicate the two phases of diaspora immigration, as delineated by many scholars such as Vijay Mishra, Makarand Paranjape and Jasbir Jain among others. The stories of the first wave of indentured labourers remains largely absent in this fictional terrain. The second wave of professionals dealt with in these novels, came voluntarily mainly to the West, to better their prospects. Vinay Lal aptly classifies the distinction between the 'old' and the 'new' Indian diasporas as marked, respectively, by "labour and longing."[14] Nostalgia and longing for the homes left behind are the foundations of new Indian diaspora homes in the West. But even in this second phase of the diaspora there is a marked difference between the parental generations that move abroad, and their children who are often born abroad. Gogol remarks on the numerical demographic difference even between the time of his birth and growing up years on Pemberton Road when there were relatively few Indians, and twenty years later when they are ready to sell the house there is a huge community of Indians in and around their area.

As a new immigrant, Ashima Ganguli feels compelled to recreate at least a semblance of an Indian home with pieces of embroidery and pictures that visually reiterate the Indianness of the home. Paranjape notes that the reproduction or replication of Indianness by these visual signs was far stronger in first generation and poorer immigrants whose ties with the homeland were virtually severed once they left India.[15] However, in the twenty–first century, spatial and emotional distances have been reduced by the popularity and availability of Bollywood cinema, music, cheaper telephone communications and availability of Indian foods. Vijay Mishra's "Hindu toolbox" of an assortment of icons, pictures and outfits that might help familiarize and Indianize homes in an alien land are less of a necessity today.[16] Yet Ashima's visual reminders of the Indianness of her home are not merely a nostalgia-driven recreation of her past but a way of assuaging her loneliness in alien surroundings and of anchoring herself with familiar objects. When her first child, Gogol, is born there is an urgent necessity to perpetuate the continuity of an Indian home. Ashima knows that it is only at home where he can be acculturated as an Indian and be taught the "Indian family values". This home will assure and anchor him in a different and older cultural past that will link the child to the parent. But it is also this home that separates him and alienates him from the everyday reality of his life in America.

Makarand Paranjape says that the diaspora "...must involve a cross-cultural or cross-civilizational passage."[17] My disagreement is with Paranjape's claim that, "the crossing must be forced, not voluntary; otherwise, the passage will only amount to an enactment of desire-fulfillment" (6). I would contend that the cross-cultural passage could be metaphoric. Second-generation Indians may have never literally crossed the *kala pani* as it were, to get to England or America, as Gogol and others have, but their daily lives involve a struggle or to use Paranjape's words "a significant tension between the source and target cultures." (6) I don't wish to trivialize the suffering, loss and displacement of immigrants but it may be equally unfair to minimize the inchoate sense of loss and un-belonging faced by subsequent generations who are born in one country but tied to another by bonds of familiar affection as well as hostility. Their claims of identity are not affirmed or validated either by other Indians or by the host country. Gogol, for instance, is born in America but to an Indian family that tries to keep the Indianness alive in language, clothing, food and values. And although he may aspire for Maxine's un-hyphenated American identity, he is never allowed that luxury. He is constantly reminded of his otherness by sharp, pin-pricks like at his birthday party when Maxine's family friend insists that being Indian he must not suffer the heat, dust and sickness from visits to India. Not only is this stereotypical image of India prevalent in the imaginary of even well educated and well heeled Boston Brahmins, but more telling is Gogol's acceptance and defensive reaction. He insists that like any good American family, "we get sick all the time. We have to get shots before we go. My parents devote the better part of a suitcase to medicine." (157)

Gogol's relationship with Maxine ends after his father's death because that relationship was enclosed in a bubble of her world. The distance between Gogol's sense of "inherited exile" and Maxine's very American sense of entitlement dooms their relationship especially at the moment of his father's death when his sense of personal and cultural loss is magnified. She has no interest in his past and it is not possible for him to separate his individual past, however much he may want to, from his parents, and, his experience of not just being Indian but also and more importantly of being seen as Indian. Maxine's complete lack of interest in issues that have shaped him such as his name change or his parents struggles to adjust to life in America make him turn to another NRI, Moushumi. Although that relationship does not work out either, their recognition that, at some level, the specificity of their experience as hyphenated Indian-Americans is important to them is worth noting. Characters like Gogol are dislocated by the neither / nor syndrome. They see themselves as neither quite Indian nor quite American. Others—Indians and Westerners, too, reinforce this non-belonging by casting them as other.

Indian House of Duty versus Western House of Freedom

Generationally and culturally, the Indian home in diaspora novels is figured primarily as a house of duty. Allegiance to a familial and a larger Indian community, and adherence to the idea of duty are the primary markers of Indianness. A character in Ravinder Randhawa's novel, A Wicked Old Woman ironically asserts, "Respect. Obedience. Hard Work. The three penances for being born Indian you know!" (187) [18] But this sense of duty afflicts older and younger generations alike. As the narrator in A Wicked Old Woman remarks, "Children were a pleasure that was taxed by duty, the duty to bring them up Right according to the rules, of whatever pond you swam in." (7) Particularly in a non-Indian location, duty and Indianness become synonymous and are wrapped together in notions of loyalty to home and home-country. The performance of ethnicity begins (and is reinforced) at home, in the domestic sphere, especially in gendered behaviour patterns, food and clothing. As the host country and the children born in it pull in one direction, the nostalgia for the original home pulls in the other. Indian homes abroad caught between the two become fraught sites of negotiations.

Indianness as duty is acidly articulated by Saroja, living in

India. Her mother's home is the archetype Indian house of duty that haunts diaspora Indian protagonists in all these novels. It is worth reiterating that the resistance to the idea of a rigid duty is couched in generational rather than cultural terms in *Tamarind Woman* whereas in other novels it is projected as a conflict between the traditional home culture and a more individualistic Western ethos. Saroja describes her mother's patriarchal house as "long, narrow...plain, ugly" and insists that, "A house needs a name to suit its character, the people who live inside it. The only name that suits our stern house is "Dharma" – duty, the word by which we live" (156). She continues:

> My father goes to work every morning because it is his duty as the man of the house to earn money for his family; my mother cooks and cleans and has children because she is his wife; and it is our duty as children to obey them, respect their every word. Even the neem tree in the front yard, with none of the knots, gnarls or hollows that give a tree character, obligingly blooms in March to provide the buds and flowers needed to make bitter-sweet *bevu-bella* for the Yugadhi feast (156)

A rather narrow sense of 'dharma' translated as duty, hierarchy and separation of gender roles become the relational markers of the house. Even nature seems to bow to the rules of the house with the sleek Neem flowering at the appropriate time. This house of duty is aptly located on Mahatma Gandhi Street next to the Krishna temple. Gandhi and Krishna (at least the Krishna of the *Mahabharata*) are evoked as specifically Hindu paragons of duty. Saroja escapes her mother's hidebound, rigidly Hindu, patriarchal home but it is not much of an escape. Her husband, she says, "fulfils his obligation to society by acquiring a wife. I am merely a symbol of that duty completed." (228) He conforms to the spirit of duty and gender roles that were part of her parental home, even if he does not necessarily accept the rigid Hinduism of that home.

The dutiful relationship is subverted when Saroja moves into an open house that can be entered through twelve different doors. In this house, transgressing class and caste hierarchies, she has an affair with a non-Hindu, an Anglo-Indian car mechanic and handyman — breaking the rules not only of caste and class but also violating the norms of wifely fidelity. In the airy, twelve-door railway home, at least for a brief sojourn, Saroja is able to defy the rules. But for her children, and especially for Kamini, that home is so permeated with secrets, hidden ghosts and sadness that even though physically on another continent she is unable to sort out or escape from the shadow of her mother's home. Kamini remembers, "my mother's constant unhappiness, which ran like a dark thread right through our lives." (16)

In diaspora Indian homes allegiance to a familial and/or a larger Indian community and adherence to the idea of duty have to be read more densely as the primary markers of Indianness. In non-Indian locations, specifically, duty and Indianness become synonymous. The acceptance of and adjustment to new homes is premised upon the evaluation of India and what they see as their duty to it—in terms of parents and notions of conformity to Indianness. Kamini's inability to leave her Canadian basement is because she is still entrapped in the prison of her past and of her memory—of her mother and of India.

India itself, though, is evoked differently in each of the novels. In *Jasmine* the grandmother sees India as, "A houseful of widows, that's what my son's house has become!" she wailed. "House of Sorrows! House of Ill Fortune!" (98) India is formulated as a geographic and historic reality at a particular moment in time. The specific history is of the rise of Sikh fundamentalism with the collusion of then Prime Minister Indira Gandhi due to intra party rivalries. Unfortunately this powerful idea of the state of India—the independent, post-colonial nation state remains a mere back-drop, enabling rejection and ultimately escape. The India invoked is embodied in the trope of the fortune-teller and the mark of destiny. Jasmine rejects and needs to flee this India—"the house of ill fortune". This construction of India validates the immigrant Jasmine's departure. It enables her to assuage the immigrant guilt of abandonment—of both mother and mother-country and in-deed even turns the tables to blame the country for the neces-sity to escape rather than to posit it as a choice. Her unques-tioning acceptance of America is in fact, premised upon her rejection of India. In contrast to the often grim but always concrete reality of India, Mukherjee invokes America as an idea, if not a utopian ideal, a foil to her India: "America that is an idea, not political, social, or ethical, but rather a stage for transformation."[19]

The protagonist, Jasmine, has to escape both her home and India the home-country for survival. Orientalist mark-ers of Indianness invoked by stereotypes of fortune tellers, destiny and the status of women frame her leaving as not a mere justification but almost a necessity. A reviewer notes that *Jasmine* is,

> A story of a young widow who uproots herself from her life in India and re-roots herself in search of a new life and the im-age of America. It is a story of dislocation and relocation as the title character continually sheds lives to move into other roles, moving further westward while constantly fleeing pieces of her past. In it, Mukherjee *rejoices in the idea of assimilation and makes it clear that Jasmine needs to travel to America to make something significant of her life*, because in the third world she faced only despair and loss. What Mukherjee hoped that people would read in the story is not only Jasmine's story and change, but also the story of a changing America. [*My emphasis*][20]

In this reading, not only India but the whole of the "third world" is visualised as a site of "despair and loss". Jasmine's survival is premised on a rejection of India and only assimila-tion into America will enable her to render her life meaning-ful. Mukherjee's India is a specific geographic locale burdened by history and stereotypes; her America on the other hand is an abstract idea full of promise. The realities of America and especially of the diversity of immigrant experiences are glossed over. In other novels, however, the negotiations are less Manichean. Indianness and Westernness are not necessarily pitted in a battle for the soul of the diasporic Indian. The efforts to strike a balance between the two homes are tinged with the colours of loss, betrayal, and, a defensive assimilation rather than an outright rejection.

Name Changes: Escape, Rejection and Categorization

In three of the four novels, Randhawa's *A Wicked Old Woman*, Mukherjee's *Jasmine* and Lahiri's *The Namesake*, name changes are a trope for identity change. In *A Wicked Old Woman* Kulwant even experiments with a visual change, as she dons cast-off clothes from the local charity and pretends to be a homeless local. But the problem is as much within as it is without. Changing appearances or names are suggested as a possible path of escape from Indianness. Rani and Jasmine reject their names as markers of Indianness and in doing so they also reject India or at least their versions of it. As Kulwant's son Arvind/Arnold says he chose a British wife Shirley, "not because he wanted to be English but because he hated to be Indian, especially the kind of Indian his family approved of." (91-92) Both Rani and Jasmine articulate that taking on new names, Rosalind and Jane, are symbolic of taking on new cultural identities. By the name change they think they have moved closer to the dominant, white mainstream of England and America. But neither Rani/ Rosalind nor Jasmine escape gender and race as the defining characteristics of their Indian identities. However, each one uses their new names and personas in different ways to re-adapt into the new culture. For Rani/Rosalind who is found and nursed back to health by the South Asian community, a compromise and reconciliation is suggested. But for Jasmine the name changes are a part of the American ideology of "transformation" and remaking oneself. But it appears to be a transformation towards a different conformity and adapting or fitting in better in mainstream society.

Jasmine's name changes are problematic as both an Indian and as a woman. Rani's deliberate name change is of her own volition and marks her specific desire to not belong to a confining Indian community nor to a mainstream Britain. Jyoti's name changes, however, cannot be read as conscious acts of agency.

She avers, "My grandmother may have named me Jyoti, Light, but in surviving I was already Jane, a fighter and adapter." (40) Each of Jyoti's name changes are instigated by the various men in her life. She is the first to acknowledge, "I have had a husband for each of the women I have been. Prakash for Jasmine, Taylor for Jase, Bud for Jane. Half-Face for Kali" (197). Each new name signals a particular man's vision of what he wants her to be. Can this woman, who so courageously takes her destiny in her own hands and flees India, so obediently accept the new names bestowed upon her by different men? Is her name change any more significant than that of say a Mira/Nirmala in *The Binding Vine*? (See chapter on "Women's Homes") Mira in her writing vehemently resists the traditionally required name change. Even though she outwardly acquiesces to the custom of her in-laws family where even the first name of the bride is changed to erase their individual past and initiate them into the new family culture as a tabula rasa. Jyoti's marriage to Prakash is not arranged nor does he have a family who force their will upon her, yet she lovingly recounts her transformation from Jyoti to Jasmine:

He [Prakash] wanted to break down the Jyoti I'd been in Hasanpur and make me a new kind of city woman. To break off the past, he gave me a new name: Jasmine. He said, "You are small and sweet and heady, my Jasmine. You'll quicken the whole world with your perfume (77).

She sees the breaking down of Jyoti as more benign than Mira does. For Mukherjee, despite the violence inherent in a word like "break down", the name change is seen as transformatory. In Prakash's desire to remould Jyoti from a rural to an urban woman, there is an unquestioned rejection and dismissal of rural values as backward and superstitious that hold women down. The educated, urban, English-speaking, ambitious, male who is going for higher education to America will rescue and transform the Indian village girl and make her a worthy companion for him. The myth of the urban Indian male rescuer seamlessly replaces the myth of the white knight in shining armour of colonial times.[21]

In Iowa, as banker Bud's 'Jane', Jasmine defiantly asserts that "plain Jane" is all she wants to be because "Plain Jane is a role, like any other." But she recognizes that the real reason for playing this particular role is that her foreignness frightens him. The foreignness is a double edged sword that can both frighten and intrigue. She acknowledges that, "Bud courts me because I am alien. I am darkness, mystery, inscrutability. The East plugs me into instant vitality and wisdom." (200) Jasmine/Jane manipulates the Orientalist mystique to work for her in a way that Rani/Rosalind cannot, will not or does not. Yet, what does "foreign" mean here? The reader is left wondering if Jasmine has become foreign not only to Bud but also to herself. Is the foreignness a threat even to her because she does not recognize her new self or is it because of her location in a context that marks her as so other?

In diaspora novels, both women and men see duty and Indianness as synonymous but, for women especially, Indianness is inseparably intertwined with notions of sexuality and independence. New homes and countries seem to promise freedom. But unmoored from old homes and ideas of duty however, often seems to cast them adrift on a sea of empty loneliness. The contradictory impulses of flight and anchor complicate diaspora homes. In A *Wicked Old Woman*, Shanti angrily questions her daughter Rani's running away and her so-called search for independence. She sees her escape as merely a desire for sexual freedom and questions the price of that freedom: "For what? A bed-sitter? A strange man's bed? Social security? Freedom? How happy are they with their freedom? How happy are you?" And the answer – "Perhaps happier than if I had stayed at home", (40) does little to appease her for either her daughter's pain or for her own. For Rani, whatever other sense of freedom and escape she may have had in mind, it is translated as sexual freedom. Similarly in rural Punjab, Jyoti too would not have had the opportunity to travel or have the kinds of relationships with Taylor and Bud that she, as Jasmine, does in New York and Iowa. But here too, there is little sense of agency; to the contrary, as she accepts the names chosen for her she also moulds herself to suit those names and images.

Gogol's name change is quite different from both Rani and Jasmine. For males, like him, sexuality is not an issue. His various relationships do not evoke parental or societal wrath. He chooses between two names—his pet name and his official name —both of which were chosen for him. In a sense it is not much of a rebellion and yet it consumes him. The reasons for his wanting to change his name are not so much to mask his Indian identity as is the case with Rosalind/ Rani and Jane/Jasmine, but to be more firmly at least part of an ethnic group that he looks like. The purpose seems to be to make categorization easier. He is an Indian-American saddled with a Russian name. That is the confusion that bothers him. His gesture of changing his official name back to Nikhil is a bid to ease his own confusion and firmly belong to at least one side of his hyphenated Indian-American identity rather than answer to a third, a Russian name. But, merely changing names or adopting different lifestyles do not make Gogol, Rani or Jasmine un-Indian or even less Indian.

Diaspora Aspirations

Rani, Gogol and Jasmine reject some aspects of India and Indianness also because they aspire to a certain kind of admittance to the dominant society in England and America. Rani's quest for independence from her parents is simpler than what moves Gogol and Jasmine. Jasmine understands that, "There are no harmless, compassionate ways to remake oneself. We *murder* who we are so we can rebirth ourselves in the images of dreams." (29) [*my emphasis*] Violence is inherent both in Jasmine's departure from India and her arrival in America and so she cannot conceive of a remaking of the self without the murder of the old Jyoti/Jasmine. Gogol's desire to belong and be accepted in America, on the other hand, is predicated on certain unarticulated and probably subconscious aspirations to class and to a more carefree way of life. Jasmine and Gogol each fall in love not so much with particular individuals—Taylor and Maxine—but for the Americanness they represent. Jasmine says, "The love I felt for Taylor that first day had nothing to do with sex. I fell in love with his world, its ease, its careless confidence and graceful self-absorption" (171).

Gogol's similar desires are embodied by his Boston Brahmin girlfriend Maxine's parental home. It is no surprise that he, the son of immigrants, is seduced initially by the un-hyphenated solidity of their house. For him it represents not only a particular lifestyle but an easy sense of entitlement and belonging to American culture and society of a particular class. A society where his own belonging is suspect because of his ethnicity and colour. He gazes longingly at the house almost as if it were an objet d'art. As an architect his professional and aspirational gazes merge as he notes its pedigreed architectural lineage — Greek revival; Gogol notes with breathless awe the "pedimented window lintels, the Doric pilasters, the bracketed entablature, the black cruciform paneled door" (130). The casual, understated tastefulness is echoed in the detailed and loving description of the meal and conversations about the "cosmopolitic's" urban New York life comprised of museums, shops, shows and restaurants.[22] The food, the hospitality, and the conversation, in fact everything, seems to show up his parents and their home as sadly lacking. Even as he settles down to a family meal with Maxine and her parents, Gogol feels "... a sudden gratitude for the day and where it has brought him" (133). When he moves in with Maxine "He feels free of expectation, of responsibility, in willing exile from his own life" (142). Clearly class—wealth and status—can ease the transformation of identity and homelessness into Rushdie's celebrated idea of hybridity and plurality. Sangeeta Ray calls this affluent set "cosmopolitics" rather than cosmopolitans because she feels that the politics of centre and margin are rehearsed in their choices.[23] The homes of 'cosmopolitics' like Jasmine and Gogol are located in metropolitan urban centers.[24] The narrator of The Namesake notes that "Quickly, simultaneously, he [Gogol] falls in love with Maxine, the house, and Gerald and Lydia's [her parents] manner of living..." (137)

A part of Jasmine and Gogol's attraction to Taylor and Maxine is, indubitably, the desire to assimilate into upper middle-class white America, but, part of it is also the desire to be that image of Jasmine and Gogol that is reflected back at them in the eyes of Bud and Maxine. Jasmine says, "I wanted to become the person they thought they saw: humorous, intelligent, refined, and affectionate. Not illegal, not murderer not widowed, raped, destitute, fearful." (171) In Gogol's case it is a white-washed image of him, all traces of Indianness covered, if not erased. Maxine and her liberal family call him Nick and accept him as American, almost as one of them, because he was born in America. He is grateful to Maxine for loving him in spite of his Indianness.

Integration: Assimilation and Acculturation

K.S. Maniam, a Malaysian author and critic, notes that in fact diaspora Indians are often seen as 'inauthentic' by both cultures and thereby equally silenced by both. He suggests two possible ways of living in multicultural societies—the way of the tiger or the way of the chameleon. The former is embraced by stability seeking "cultural patriots" who tend to live apart from the mainstream; the latter is embraced by the new diaspora who "live within an ever-widening sense of the world."[25] But even within this ever widening sense of the world the need for the idea of the meta-Indian home remains undiminished.

The integration of immigrants and their children or subsequent generations settling into their new domiciles depends, among other factors, on the reaction of the hosts to their 'guests'. The politics of assimilation in each of the countries (England, Canada and USA) and the often unspoken pressures on diaspora citizens influence the degree to which they need the kind of luminous direction of the green arrow on the map to point them home. The idea of a home where one belongs and that is one's birthright acts as a talisman against an alien if not outright hostile community and country. In this uneasy space, even the rigid rules of home appear to be structures of stability and order—nomos building institutions. The clear rules are especially longed for in an alien land where all the conventions are different and anomie threatens at every step. The vague fear of chaos is accentuated by the real racism of the society. Even in an otherwise celebratory and assimilationist novel like *Jasmine*, the narrator notes, "This country has so many ways of humiliating, of disappointing." (29) But this is clearer for her to see in the case of her adopted Vietnamese son Du than in the case of a fellow-Indian, the pathetic professorji who lives in a Punjabi dominated apartment block in Flushing, New York, but that is another story.

Racism is curiously not an issue in *The Namesake*. Lahiri's America is surprisingly a-racist. The novel is set in 1968 and ends in about 2000, it was published in 2003, two years after the September 11 attacks on New York's World Trade Centre and the Pentagon. In spite of both historical markers—the tumult of the 1960s and 70s marked by the anti-war, student and women's movements and the racial hate crimes in the aftermath of September 11, 2001—the novel is colour blind. Race awareness and discrimination are not new in America and yet in Gogol's Boston and New York it is possible for him to be completely unaware of his surroundings. Blinkered, he conforms to the model minority stereotype of the studious and hardworking Asian who is only interested in assimilating into the white mainstream. In all the novels race, ethnicity and culture are suggested as almost interchangeable categories where one often stands in for the other.

In Jasmine's bleak picture, India is not only a house of duty but a confining cultural prison. Destiny, women's oppression and India are so intertwined that they have to be accepted or rejected together as one thing. The narrator notes,

> If we could just get away from India, then all fates would be cancelled. We'd start with new fates, new stars. We could say or be anything we wanted. We'd be on the other side of the earth, out of God's sight (85).

Gayatri Spivak and Uma Narayan, among others, have written eloquently of the orientalist argument about how Indian (and other coloured) women, particularly, are perceived as in need of being saved from their own men, and, sometimes their own, so-called, backward cultures. This (essentially colonialist) argument is often deployed to justify the 'saving' of oriental women by Western men and Western enlighten-ment ideals.[26] In Mukherjee's vision, even the liberal and entre-preneurial post-colonial Indian male, Prakash, does not mea-sure up. He cannot save himself from the dark forces of des-tiny let alone rescue or change Jasmine's fate. For that she has to escape to far-off America and be saved by a real, white American male. The attitude is explicitly stated in *A Wicked Old Woman*, where Shanti recalls her experience of seeking help from the British police in locating her missing daughter Rani:

> And they said do you know how many runaway Asian girls there are? But you know they say it with delight, as if she has done a wonderful thing. The papers also. If they could, they would encourage every Asian girl to leave home(40)

The response underlines a racist viewpoint prevalent even today, where women become the site of machismo battles of cultural superiority. Narayan notes how even feminist critics unthinkingly use culture as an explanation, if not an excuse, to justify and ignore violence against third-world women in their own communities. At one level, the cultural relativity argu-ment lets other women and men off the hook from condemn-ing obvious violence against women. And on the other hand it can also provide a justification for interference or for colo-nial rule, as was the agenda in Katherine Mayo's *Mother India*. In either case the end result is the perpetuation of an East-West dichotomy.[27] The 'culture card' or what Narayan calls "death by culture" can and is often used by a hostile host society as a weapon of domination if not destruction. Diaspora Indian communities may want to inculcate and preserve pat-terns of Indian homes in their new homes abroad, but those patterns may, and often do, accentuate and enlarge the dis-tance between children and their parents.

In both *The Namesake* and *A Wicked Old Woman* assimila-tion even if desired is tinged with shades of betrayal as if in accepting even aspects of the new culture automatically means a betrayal of the old. This guilt of betrayal haunts diaspora characters. As Kulwant recounts,

Having snatched a fraction of freedom she'd smile and laugh
with others and seem to agree as they applauded her courage
in defying her backward and traditional society, in trying to
escape her primitive background; the smile sticking to her
lips like painted plastic while her insides folded in around
an agitation that said this is treachery. (7)

Feelings of betrayal and treachery hark back to "the original sin" which is the lot of most immigrants—of having left
the home country. However, the diaspora sense of
homelessness also stems from what Paranjape articulates as
the "tension between the source and target cultures" (6).[28]
This could be read as the tension between racism and a blind
insistence on the melting pot ideology of assimilation against
the desire to preserve some semblances of a home culture
perpetuated through family and community memories and
rituals. Sociologist Patricia Uberoi notes, "Indian 'family values' are proposed as the crucial markers of Indianness" and
these values are transmitted mainly in the home.[29] So the
home becomes a site of initiation into Indianness, and by extension the home country, India, becomes an almost sacred
concept. Denying or deviating from the accepted notion of
Indianness is coloured in terms of treachery and betrayal.

Indian Homes and Intermediary Spaces Abroad

The hospital, in Randhawa's *A Wicked Old Woman*, is an apt
site of generational and cultural negotiations. It signals the
crisis ailing the Indian community in Britain. The many immigrants each have their individual stories of struggling families,
runaway daughters and betrayed wives that are not openly
talked about and therefore cannot be dealt with. The hospital
in this novel becomes the key site for recovery of not only Rani
but also of Kulwant, Maya and the community as a whole.

The novel opens in the hospital with Kulwant wanting to
be treated for a mysterious ailment but the nurse cannot even
begin to understand the problem. And, in the hospital, again
Rani's parallel story becomes the focus of attention. An Indian girl, Rani, runs away from home at age sixteen, changes
her name to Rosalind, and deliberately rejects all things Indian. She lives on the margins of society with other dropouts,

finding odd jobs and managing to eke out subsistence. Her father dies of a heart attack and her mother, Gandhari-like, blindfolds herself, with the single-minded quest of finding her daughter. Rani/Rosalind accused of murder finally lies in the hospital hovering between life and death, refusing to speak.

The hospital is literally a space of illness and recovery. Can a person wounded by both the home and the local community survive? In this specific location, the British and Indian communities are drawn together and have to work together to renegotiate their relationships with each other to enable Rani/Rosalind to recover. It is a more neutral place than either the home that Rani had escaped (read India) or the communal house (read Britain) where she committed murder to avoid being raped and killed. Cure and death are both possible in this liminal space that is neither Western nor Indian. Initially Rani is willfully uncooperative in her own recovery and refuses to close her eyes or to talk. The community, especially the women, gathers around and keeps a twenty-four hour vigil by her bedside; tempt her with food and their presence. It is perhaps unsurprising that the very Indianness that she had so vehemently rejected tempts her back to life. The sensory aromas of Indian food, the tactile touch of many hands caressing and nursing her, the visual colours of the bright salwar-kameez offered her, the aural conversations in lilting, Indian inflected English and, most importantly, the concern of the women and men around her bed finally awaken her. The community literally wills her back to life.

The hospital is also the site of an adult re-birth. When Rani is released on bail and her mother will not take her back from hospital. When asked why she will not let Rani come home Shanti replies, "A child can ask for unconditional love and protection; an adult has to earn it" (203). Having forsaken her home once, Rani too has to recognize the pain she [it] has caused. She, like Gogol and Kamini, cannot claim the safety of her mother's home as an entitlement. Shanti insists that in this re-birth or second lease of life, Rani has to consciously chart her own path. Mother-daughter duos like Shanti-Rani (*A Wicked*

Old Woman) or Saroja-Kamini (*Tamarind Woman*) resist the stereotypes of the mother-daughter relationships, especially Asian
mothers and daughters. This is the less talked about "tough
love" between mothers and daughters.

Both *A Wicked Old Woman* and *Tamarind Woman* see community formation as central to an individual's well being. In
Tamarind Woman (like in the earlier *Ladies Coupe*) even though
the interaction with the women in the train is short-lived, its
intensity and sense of sisterhood provides the women with the
sustenance to carry on. In *A Wicked Old Woman* the community
discusses their problems as a community around Rani's bed
and in nursing her back to health they also heal themselves. In
fact the idea for the creation of an Asian women's shelter
emerges from the discussions around Rani's bedside about the
need of a space where women can be safe away from both
home and the street to sort themselves out. *A Wicked Old Woman*
offers two specific locales—Greenham Common and the Asian
Centre as literal and metaphoric spaces of political and cultural
intermingling and community formation. Kulwant the protagonist and sometimes narrator sees the Asian Centre as,

> ...simulation Sub-Continent. Misbegotten child of a guilty
> conscience, Frankenstein patched together with the flotsam
> of travel posters, batik work ... It was supposed to be inviting,
> user friendly: a home away from home for the Asian woman
> trapped in the isolation of her house; a helping hand for the
> Asian man shell-shocked from dealing with the revolving
> door racism and vagaries of white bureaucracy (30-31).

But despite the ironic tone and the ambivalence towards
the centre, it does eventually become a real place of discussions and interactions largely within the Asian community
rather than a neglected space for individual drop-ins. The invocation of Greenham Common, on the other hand, transcends
ethnic community barriers for solidarity on the basis of
gender and politics. It·invokes a particular historical moment
in the 1980s when Greenham Common became the sine qua
non of peaceful women's protests against militarization and
their resistance to nuclear weapons. By organizing to take

food to the women's camp, Randhawa suggests solidarity among women beyond community and class lines. The food is jointly prepared to assuage Ammi's nightmares but in fact, it links Asian women together to join in a worldwide protest against violence at both a personal and a political level. Both sites are interesting authorial solutions of community formation along political, gender and racial lines to transform potentially hostile sites into safe havens.

Dialogue between Old and New Homes

Perhaps, rather than the orienting arrow on the in-flight map, Edward Said's musical metaphor of contrapuntality might be a more apt analogy for this conversation between two homes, because the dialogue is not unidirectional. It is often the new home reacting *against* as well as *to* the old home. Said notes,

> For an exile, habits of life, expression or activity in the new environment inevitably occur against the memory of these things in another environment. Thus both the new and the old environments are vivid, actual, occurring together contrapuntally (172).

The new fictional homes of Diaspora literature are located in the West, but, because they are homes of exiles, immigrants, and diaspora citizens, their unique perspective provides, what Said would call, a "... plurality of vision [which] gives rise to an awareness of simultaneous dimensions" (172).[30] The plurality is often more confusing than the simple two-way traffic or Indian homes versus Western homes. The 'confused' sobriquet of ABCD stems from the instability of this positioning between two or more cultures.

The continuity of Indianness is pitted against the dominant mainstream Americanness of the new culture in all four novels. The schism between an Indian home embedded in the larger American context is initially accentuated by the duality or rather clear demarcation of a Western exterior and an Indian interior. The home and the world spatialization of the private and the public or women's and men's spaces recalls

Partha Chatterjee's historical conceptualization of the construction of Indianness as a private space that resists colonial Western exterior that was harder to challenge in the colonial period. A specifically Indian home space served as a bulwark against the larger whole of a colonized India. The home is seen as a mystical, real and unassailably Indian space normally presided over by women who were responsible for maintaining its cultural purity, whereas the exterior is Western, commercial and, to an extent, superficial. In diaspora literature too, there is a similar sense of resistance to colonization by the dominant culture in the way homes are configured. From the outside, Gogol's parental home, the "small patch of America to which they lay claim" (51) looks like the other all-American homes in the mainly all white Pemberton Road neighbourhood. The meticulous counting, categorization and listing of – four modest bedrooms, one and one-half bathrooms, seven foot ceilings, one car garage, and household appliances like refrigerator, TV, blenders etc, are a testimony of what this immigrant family has achieved—their attainment of the American dream. But the interior is balanced with Indian memorabilia, "A watercolor by Ashima's father, of a caravan of camels in a desert in Rajasthan" (52) and other such artifacts that anchor and remind them of their Indianness. Socially too Ashima's three address books full of names of other Indian families are a testimony to their belonging to this specific immigrant community. The divisions between home and the world are not watertight. It is unsurprising that Gogol's own home as a single adult in New York is tiny, noisy and obviously not-home. "On the stove sits a teakettle he has never filled with water, and on the countertop a toaster he's never plugged in" (126). This home has the feel of a waiting room or a transitional space; where street noises so invade the apartment that the inside feels like the outside.

The Indianness in the homes built abroad can be read as assertions of identity and difference but they also offer a kind of resistance to the dominant culture. The older generation sees their children slipping away from them as they become assimilated or "fluent" as Lahiri says, in the new culture.[31] The home serves as a primary site of grounding children in the ways of the parents—a way of maintaining links between generations. Equally it is not possible to ignore the guilt trip that parents lay on the children reminding them that these new houses, liberties and opportunities have been made possible by the sacrifice (even if a willing and voluntary sacrifice) by the parental generation. They want the children to validate them and their suffering by acknowledging it. And one way of acknowledgement becomes acceptance of the 'Indian' way— whatever that may mean to the particular family. Moving away from these notions of Indianness is often seen as disloyalty and betrayal.

The continuity of Indianness is thus pitted against the dominance of mainstream Americanness. In this 21st century diaspora, unlike earlier diasporas, spatial and emotional distances have been reduced by the easy access to things Indian, be they Bollywood cinema, music, cheaper telephone communications and availability of Indian foods. Vijay Mishra's "Hindu toolbox" of portable Indiana is less of a necessity today.[32] Yet Ashima's visual reminders of the Indianness of her home are not merely nostalgia-driven recreations that assuage her loneliness in alien surroundings. The familiar objects anchor her to a sense of self. When her first child Gogol is born, there is an urgent necessity to ensure that the over-arching dominant culture does not subsume that past and alienate her child from her. The perpetuation of Indianness in the home ensures intragenerational links and continuity. Knowledge and acknowledgement of that parental past and a larger ethnic, cultural past provide the necessary glue for continuity and community building.

Indubitably, class, economic and educational privileges do allow immigrants like Gogol to ease into a new culture and a new way of life with minimum trauma. Technology has played a key role in bridging the distance between India and abroad. The relative abroad is now only a phone call away. As Gillespie, among others, has pointed out, the VCR and Bombay cinema have dramatically helped bridge the cultural and generational distance between India and the world and among Indians.[33] However, even NRIs who can slip in and out of the "source and target cultures" still hark back, albeit very differently, to the meta-home of India. It is critical to note the gendered nature of the tension between old and new homes. For sons, like Gogol, Indianness is coded as respect for parents and elders, general conformity and social mobility. Parents want to be able to prove to themselves and to the community that, despite feelings of guilt and betrayal at having left home and country, they have managed to inculcate home values even on alien soil. The cherished values — an ability to speak a home language, manners, respect for hierarchy etc.,— in their children are seen as manifestations of their continuing links and even allegiance to India.

Gogol, the stereotypical ABCD is intent on distancing himself from his parents who have become the embodiment and the site of his unease. A simple and normal generational embarrassment about parents is enlarged to include and specifically manifest itself as a cultural cringe. Gogol all but holds his parents responsible for almost willfully not fitting in. Their difference is located in their colour, their middle class aspirations, their accented English, their clothes and their food. External differences aside, the Indianness that Gogol shies away from is what he sees as the twin hallmarks of his home — duty and obligation. Both Gogol and Saroja (*Tamarind Woman*) seek to escape from their "house of duty". But Gogol's escape is not merely generational: it is complicated by ethnicity and culture. His desire to escape is painted in shades of his aspiration to whiteness, with all the privileges that it entails—but also coloured by the initial "betrayal"— his word, of ethnicity seen in his ignorance, if not rejection, of his own name, duty and obligation to country, culture, parents and ultimately himself.

The notion of duty that Jasmine, Rani and Gogol seek to cast off is that of an ethnic and gendered conformity and propriety. Born-in-America children clamour for more of the freedom associated with Western lifestyles. But often, at least in their parent's eyes, they fail to even acknowledge the suffering and deprivation of the earlier generation that has made their lives easier. Rani cannot slip back into a natal home as a birthright once she has broken the rules of the house. As her mother heartbreakingly says, "It is like entering a different world, when you find that your child is a stranger. A door shuts on the past." (40) The relationship with the house and with her mother (and mother country) has to be renegotiated. This was exactly Ashima's fear at Gogol's birth that without the extended family and the Indian context he would be a stranger to her past and hence to her. Gogol's appreciation and understanding of the hardships his parents suffered for the 'success' they achieved for themselves and the opportunities created for the children is what may allow him a new beginning. His final moment in his Pemberton Road home is not quite a moment of epiphany but at least there is hope that Gogol will emerge out of his boringly blinkered and self-centered existence.

Kamini's alienation in Canada, unlike Gogol's in the United States, stems not so much from an ethnic displacement in a foreign country but from her awareness of the murky waters churning beneath the placid surface of her own childhood in India. Canada merely provides her with the necessary distance – literal and metaphoric from her mother. Because Kamini is struggling with her past and her relationship to her mother, she has not yet had time to realize that she is in Canada and to come to terms with the cultural implications of living in a different place. In *Tamarind Woman*, *The Namesake* and *A Wicked Old Woman*, cultural and generational negotiations within various communities are crucial to building a new kind of home.

Conclusion

Racial and cultural otherness in the majority community combined with a generational and (to some extent) cultural alienation from one's own ethnic community leaves hyphenated Indians trapped in the space of the hyphen between two cultures. Gogol's many visits to India and his very Bengali Boston home are the markers of the meta-Indian home from which he seeks to escape. But only Randhawa's *A Wicked Old Woman* attempts to unpack the issue of how these new, out-of-India homes need to be reconfigured through compromise and negotiation, not only intra-generationally (within the Indian community) but also between British and Indian cultures. Destruction or death mark the end of a particular phase that forces the younger protagonists to take stock. The looming threat of Rani's death and the sale of Gogol's natal, parental home become the catalysts for rethinking Indian homes abroad that can stifle and imprison the younger generation as well as provide them with a certain anchor. Despite the ironic tone of *A Wicked Old Woman,* the authorial solution to Indian homes abroad is posited unambiguously as community formation along political, gender and racial lines to transform potentially hostile sites into safe havens.

India and Indian homes – homes of duty and desire, love and hate, anchor and flight — remain the icons of Indian homes abroad be they first or second generation homes. New homes are constructed on emotional mindscapes and mapped onto the sites of these original homes. Diaspora Indians cannot be at home unless they acknowledge the Indianness of past homes, whether in terms of origins, cultural affiliations or even duty. The acknowledgement can manifest as rejection or acceptance, but the conversation between homes remains dynamic and a necessary pre-requisite of settling. The Indian community plays a crucial role in this home-formation either as implacable guardians of the old culture who punish any transgression or as a comfort base and support network that nurtures and teaches by example. All the novels except Mukherjee's *Jasmine* point to the crucial importance of a cross-cultural and cross-generational conversation. The hyphenated status of Indians who live abroad often causes them to feel homeless because they are not fully accepted—neither by their ethnic communities nor by their adopted communities. The hybridity of the diaspora has a brooding underside of discontented disconnect. In all these novels, the significance of the past in terms of home patterns, Indian values, family and community are reiterated. The new does not arise, phoenix like, from the ashes of the old, but rather, the old is the guiding green arrow that allows one to renegotiate and yet not lose ones bearings.

References

1 Many airlines, especially Middle Eastern carriers, have a floating luminous green arrow pointing towards Mecca on their ever-changing in-flight maps showing the progress of the plane. The directional arrow enables Muslim passengers to face Mecca as required while they pray.

2 Rushdie, Salman 'Imaginary Homelands,' *Imaginary Homelands: Essays and Criticisms* 1981-1991, London: Granta Books, 1991.

3 Rushdie, Salman. *Imaginary Homelands*, 1991 London: Granta Books, (p.9)

4 Rushdie, Salman. *Imaginary Homelands*, 1991 London: Granta Books, (p.14)

5 Rushdie, Salman. *Imaginary Homelands*, 1991 London: Granta Books, (p.10)

6 Lal notes two primary ways of classifying Indianness based on origins or cultural affiliations and to this list one could also add language and religion among other categories. Vinay Lal, "Labour and Longing" *Seminar* (June 2004) http://www.india-seminar.com/semsearch.htm

7 Mukherjee, Bharati. "Two Ways to Belong in America" September 22, 1996: *New York Times*. [http://personalwebs.oakland.edu/~kitchens/150c/mukherjee/]

8 Rushdie, Salman. "Imaginary Homelands" *Imaginary Homelands: Essays and Criticism 1981- 1991*. London: Granta Books, 1991 (p.9)

9 Roy, Sandip. "Still Bengali at heart" October 19, 2003. *Mid Day*.

10 Roy, Sandip. "Still Bengali at heart" October 19, 2003. *Mid Day*.

11 A Conversation with Jhumpa Lahiri. http://www.houghtonmifflinbooks.com/readers guides/interpreter maladies.shtml#conversation

12 The road-trip genre is a train-trip genre in Indian English literature. Anita Nair's *Ladies Coupe'* (2001) was probably one of the first Indo-English women's novels in this genre.

13 Mukherjee, Meenakshi. "Towards Liberation: Four Recent Novels

from India," *Westerly* 28.4, December 1983.(pp.66-72)

14 Lal, Vinay. "Labour and Longing" *Seminar* (June 2004) http://www.india-seminar.com/semsearch.htm

15 Paranjape, Makarand. "Displaced Relations: Diasporas, Empires, Homelands" *In-Diaspora: Theories, Histories, Texts* Delhi: Indialog Publications, 2001 (p.9)

16 Mishra, Vijay. "New Lamps for Old: Diasporas Migrancy Border" *Interrogating Post-Colonialism: Theory, Text and Context.* (ed.) Harish Trivedi and Meenakshi Mukherjee Shimla: Indian Institute of Advanced Study. 1996 (pp.67-68)

17 Paranjape, Makarand. "Displaced Relations: Diasporas, Empires, Homelands" *In-Diaspora: Theories, Histories, Texts.* Delhi: Indialog Publications, 2001 (p.6)

18 Randhawa, Ravinder. *A Wicked Old Woman.* London: The Women's Press, 1987 (p.187)

19 Dirks, Emilie. "Bharati Mukherjee and the Heart of Light" http://www.suite101.com/article.cfm/literature_of_women/22580

20 *Voices from the Gaps: Women Writers of Color.* University of Minnesota. http://voices.cla.umn.edu/vg/

21 In Bollywood films like—there is an interesting inversion where it is the Indian woman, often a village belle who brings the erring urban often NRI male back to essential India, often seen as rural and to Indian values of family and community.

22 Ray, Sangeeta. "Through The Looking Glass" *Seminar* (June 2004) http://www.india-seminar.com/semsearch.htm

23 Ray, Sangeeta. "Through The Looking Glass" *Seminar* (June 2004) http://www.india-seminar.com/semsearch.htm

24 This has most recently been restated in Suketu Mehta's *Maximum City: Bombay Lost and Found.* New York: Alfred A. Knopf, 2004

25 Maniam, K.S. "The New Diaspora" *International Literature.* 1996 http://www.ucalgary.ca/UofC/eduweb/engl392/492/maniam-dias.html

26 An argument that was used to great effect by Katherine Mayo in *Mother India* (1927). A highly polemic and controversial book which many have seen as a propaganda tract to justify British colonial rule in India.

27 Narayan, Uma. "Death by Culture" *Dis-locating cultures: Identities, Traditions, and Third-World Feminism* New York: Routledge, 1997. The argument is of course not new. We see it as early as in Katherine Mayo's thinly veiled justification of colonialism in *Mother India*, and

Margaret Daley's support of the text as primarily a critique of patriarchy. This idea of the 'white knight' rescuing the oriental woman is also prevalent in films. See Gina Marcetti (1993) and Ford & Chanda (1999).

28 Paranjape, Makarand. "Displaced Relations: Diasporas, Empires, Homelands" *In-Diaspora: Theories, Histories, Texts.* Delhi: Indialog Publications, 2001.

29 Uberoi, Patricia. "The Diaspora Comes Home: Disciplining Desire in DDLJ", *Tradition, Pluralism and Identity.* New Delhi: Sage Publications, 1999 (p.167)

30 Said, Edward W. "Reflections on Exile" *Granta* 13. 1984 (pp.159-172)

31 Lahiri, Jhumpa. "My Two Lives". March 6, 2006. http:// www.msnbc.msn.com/id/11569225/site/newsweek/

32 Mishra, Vijay. "New Lamps for Old: Diasporas Migrancy Border", *Interrogating Post-Colonialism: Theory, Text and Context.* Trivedi and Mukherjee (eds.) Shimla: Indian Institute of Advanced Study. 1996 (pp.67-68)

33 Gillespie, Marie. "Technology and Tradition: Audio-Visual Culture Among South Asian Families in West London" *Cultural Studies* 3, (1989):226-239 shows how Bombay cinema especially via the growing video industry creates a space for inter-generational communication within the home for diaspora families.

8
Conclusion

The yearning for 'home' with all the emotional weight invoked by that word is central in Indo-English women's fiction. Homes are described in intimate physical and emotional detail both as a way of recalling the past but also as a means of changing and rebuilding from that past. Along with recollections of actual homes, sometimes, there are tantalising pictures of alternate homes—family homes or summer homes—that serve as blueprints for the houses of desire. Physical location is a part of what the home-space is all about but the key criteria of these new homes are the links to the past, relationships and personal spaces they provide. The space to be oneself in a safe and supportive environment. Integration within a larger community and access to a community of women are seen as essential components of these dwellings.

Focusing on women as the subject, this book has attempted to explore the implications of Indianness, domesticity, gender and nation through Indo-English women's fiction. Reading the subtext and examining how the issues of women and home are framed and what they are being opposed to brings them into a sharper and sometimes different focus. Because of the close interrelationship between author, text and context, this conclusion steps out of the world of fiction into the 'real' world to draw upon the arguments of Madhu Kishwar, political activist and founder editor of the feminist journal *Manushi*, and author and psychologist Sudhir Kakar.

Indian and Woman

Kishwar pits Indianness against Westernness in a feminist context whereas Kakar posits Indianness as primarily a male community of which Woman is a part but Other. These two scholars in particular have been chosen because both are well-known in India and globally, and both claim to speak for or explain the Indian point of view. There are many instances where their viewpoints either mirror or contradict arguments suggested by the novels. But in exploring Kishwar and Kakar's notions of Indianness through the novelistic lens we see a more nuanced exploration of these issues. From the novelistic or literary perspective both Indianness and womanhood are often seen as confining categories. The intent here is not to repeat these arguments but to show how a pointedly anti-Western stance and/or a specifically male perspective often become the hallmark of what is generally accepted as 'Indian'.

Kishwar blames a Western imported feminism for serious problems in countries like India. Her main argument is that Western feminism's insistence on judicial rights is unacceptable in the Indian context because it alienates and isolates Indian women from their families, which are their mainstay. Unlike other mainstream views, hers, however, does not see women's assertiveness as particularly Western. In fact, she is unnecessarily defensive in claiming:

> We Indians have a much longer history of individual women's assertiveness than the West, and a well-established tradition of making space for women whose aspirations draw them beyond stereotypical paths.[1]

However, she condemns the assertion of individual rights and in particular women's rights at the cost of community and family integration. She asserts that, "many of us believe life is a poor thing if our own dear ones don't honour and celebrate our rights, if our freedom cuts us off from others."[2] In Kishwar's view, a protest or assertion of individuality that might alienate one from family and community is un-Indian, a Western import. She asserts that this viewpoint is not "slavery to social opinion" but rather a way of social and communal integration. She rightly questions handing social reform over to authoritarian state institutions like the police or the judiciary which have a dubious track record.

The problem with arguments like Kishwar's is that the suggested alternative of the good community, figured as "our own dear ones," is no less suspect. Individual men can be and are held responsible for particular actions. But the problem is systemic and inherent in the culture of the community. Often, "the good community" even if it does not actively support patriarchy, remains deafeningly silent to patriarchal injustices against women. Newspaper reports about village Panchayats punishing a woman by gangraping her illustrate the problem of the so called "good community" in daily life.[3] Historically too, both classic and contemporary literature reveals a pattern of community betrayal—Draupadi in the *Mahabharata*, Sita in the Ramayana, Ila in *Fire on the Mountain*, Kalpana in *The Binding Vine* amongst many others. The reliance on the "good community," is equally problematic in both life and literature.

Kishwar's politics are part of a current trend in "contemporary studies of third world women" where, as Julie Stephens points out, "erasing 'the West' has come to be a pre-requisite for subjecthood and hence liberation."[4] This assertion of Indianness by an opposition to or negation of Westernness doubly disenfranchises Indo-English women writers. Linguistically, writing in English, as already noted, suggests their inauthenticity as Indian; and as women who speak out and sometimes stand apart from their community, they are once again re-framed as un-Indian. Kishwar appears to silence plurality by her insistence that only conformist and mainstream voices are authentically Indian.

In contrast to Kakar and Kishwar's views, the novels reveal an authorial awareness and anxiety about this negative equation of non-western as Indian. The protagonists are self-reflective and articulate about their sense of alienation because of supposed Western attributes like education, privacy, and individuality. And class is of course a key though not always stated factor in these notions of Indian and Western. The challenge to feminism, often also seen as a Western import, is equally visible in the field of literature as Kishwar says it is in real life. The word "feminist" has come under attack at home and abroad, both from some feminists who now refuse the label, and literary critics like Malashri Lal who claim that Indian women for the most part are wary of the term. Lal's two-fold argument premised on guilt and erasure claims that first, "A female guilt about the likely overturning of the status quo through 'feminist' action is widespread in India even today."[5] The argument goes on to detail how women blame themselves even when they are victims of attack. The second part of her argument explains that although women now are more visible in public spheres, they are asked to erase themselves as much as possible. She suggests that individual women and women's groups should strategically accommodate this message by refusing the term feminist, and adopt instead the more acceptable terminology of "women's cause" or "gender." However, Lal admits that the matter is one of nomenclature rather than belief. In the West too, some feminists, especially feminists of colour, reject the term because of its associations with white, middle-class values. But, like Kishwar, Lal's opposition is language based. She claims that "'Feminism' is an imported word for which there is no equivalent in the Indian language."[6] Lal's self-styled "Indocentric" methodology therefore excludes the term feminist although she acknowledges the influence of feminist literary theory. The language argument is fallacious as there are many foreign words for which there are no Indian equivalents and yet they have been easily accepted and assimilated into Indian languages. A rejection on the grounds of its non-Indianness is extremely subjective and plays into the parochial politics of "Asian values."

Kakar, like Kishwar, emphasises the centrality of community in Identity formation. He defines identity as, the process of synthesis between inner life and outer social reality as well as the feeling of personal continuity and consistency within oneself. It refers to the sense of having a stake in oneself, and at the same time in some kind of confirming community.[7]

Again this faith in a "confirming community" like Kishwar's "our own dear ones", ignores the fact that community and even family are often not affirming. In fact, to the contrary, community and family tend to be the first to punish non-conformity and reject those individuals who challenge the prevailing norms. In the novels we see that for women particularly, community and family are as much a source of annihilation as they are of sustenance. And while the novels explore what happens if the community does not confirm the individual, neither Kakar nor Kishwar raise that question. Nor do they note how the unequal power balance between women and men, in both the family and the community, marginalise women.

Kakar's innate conviction of, or perhaps his desire for, equality between women and men presumes that, as in his notion of the family noted earlier, all the members are in fact equal.[8] Elsewhere in his work, Kakar remarks on the existence of a specifically female community which he suggests is a bulwark for the girl child in a society that values males. But this insight is not factored into his argument regarding the formation of women's identities. Kakar's conception of a female community is in many respects similar to the notion of womenspace that has been elaborated here. However, there are problems in both his elaboration of a female community and its relationship to the general community which, by contrast, and by his distinction, has to be seen as a male community. Before remarking on the divergence between Kakar's viewpoint and the one indicated by the novels, it would be worthwhile to first briefly examine Kakar's delineation of a female community.

Kakar notes that "in traditional India, every female is born into a well-defined community of women within her particular family."[9] He characterises the "femininity and domesticity"

of this sphere by three prominent aspects: one, it has "a special kind of inviolate feminine privacy," two, it is "independent of the patriarchal values of the outside world," and three,
women are "allies against the discriminations and inequities"
of the outside world. Kakar's elaboration of these three aspects of the female community differs in some fundamental
respects from the one elaborated in the novels. Indo-English
women's novels emphasise the translation of female friendships from the home to the community at large, whereas Kakar
firmly delimits women's place in the home. He insists that,

> the existence of this exclusive sphere of femininity and domes-
> ticity gives women a tangible opportunity to be productive
> and lively, to experience autonomy and to exercise power.[10]

His notion of "feminine privacy" reiterates the strictly
domestic role of a woman where through apprenticeship she
learns "the mandatory skills of householding" which enable
her to establish "her place in this primary world".[11] A skill
seductively passed on from mother-in-law to daughter-in-law
in, *Inside the Haveli*.   Other novels like *Thousand Faces of Night*
or *The God of Small Things are* not so sanguine in their acceptance of this tradition of "householding" passed on from woman
to woman. They seek to blur the distinction between the outside and the domestic worlds. Even when housekeeping models are passed on, women protagonists are keenly aware of
the politics of power inherent in domestic relations.

The most troubling of Kakar's notions is the complete
segregation and separation between female and male spheres.
His writing reinscribes the idea of separate spheres in ways
that are more concrete and rigid than the ones portrayed by
the novels and ideologically even recreate the segregated
world of havelis. Kakar completely elides the connection between the two worlds, failing to note that the female sphere
is secondary and exists, even by his own description, for the
maintenance of the male sphere. In his version, these isolated
spheres seem to have no spaces of overlap. From his viewpoint, it would appear that all women inside the homes are
allies who resist patriarchal domination. Kakar ignores what

the novels clearly show, that patriarchal values can and are internalised by women who, for a variety of reasons, become transmitters of these values even if the values perpetuate, as Anita Desai suggests, the oppression of women by other women.[12] Kakar envisions this female space as transparent and not written over by the dominant patriarchal values of mainstream society. Having noted elsewhere, that often women gain power in the household, and even within the female community, because of their relationship or access to men who are in positions of seniority, Kakar fails to take this into account in his portrayal of a female community.

Kakar's explanation conflates women and domesticity, firmly closing the door so that women remain inside the walls of the home turned prison. The only site of resistance offered to women is that of "the 'underground' of female culture" as reflected in folk-songs, ballads, and jokes where women band together as "allies" in an unfair world. Kakar's argument trivialises the kinds of oppression women suffer and in suggesting that ballads and jokes are an adequate, if not the only response, negates the possibility of political and social activism in pursuit of change. Significantly, this is so in spite of the visibility and wide coverage of street protests in Delhi as well as other metropolitan and some rural areas organised by a very active women's movements in the 1970s. Kakar does not even consider women's political community formation and direct action outside the home. The notion of community invoked in both Kakar and Kishwar is defined by negation—non-woman and non-Western. The experiential and lived reality of a plural India is papered over by the binary and oppositional categorization of India as non-West. Also, maintaining the patriarchal status quo is seen as being community-centered, whereas a more equitable balance of power and woman-centeredness is seen as threatening and therefore unacceptable.

Indo-English women's fiction registers the tensions illustrated above, between notions of Indianness and notions of womanhood. Literary critics like Lal, as noted earlier, and often even the novelists themselves are wary of the term "feminist" even when they clearly invoke feminist ideologies. In *The Binding Vine,* Shashi Deshpande's negative characterization of Preeti, the avowed feminist reflects a stereo typical mainstream view while in an interview Nair vehemently asserts, "No, this is not a feminist book at all. I have no problems with men."[13] Aside from Nair's automatic and knee-jerk reaction that feminists "have problems with men" both assertions signal a deep unease if not outright rejection of the term. But unlike Nair, Deshpande's delineation of Urmila, who is never called a feminist but in true feminist spirit seeks to give women a voice, signals authorial awareness and willingness to consider if not espouse, issues raised by feminists in the literary and extra-literary spheres. In India, as in other countries, a part of the rejection of the term feminism is due to the negative image projected in popular culture. But in India specifically another part of the rejection, is due to the perception of feminism's association with Western values. However, feminist critical inquiry has opened doors to thinking about women and has provided methodologies of critical analysis that have enabled a fresh look at language and literature. The first chapter sketched the development of Indo-English women's writing, here, the conclusion raises issues about women as subjects and of women's place that would not have been possible but for feminists having blazed the trail in all spheres of life and literature.

Sexuality and Domesticity

The final issue reconsidered here is the link between women and home. Domestic novels as a genre have been seen as women's forte in international literatures like English, American, and Latin American, to name but a few. Antoinette Burton, in her study of the house in a family memoir, notes how in novels particularly, the house is a central locus:

> The frequency with which women writers of different "nations" have made use of home to stage their dramas of remembrance is a sign of how influential the cult of domesticity has been for inhabitants of structurally gendered locations like the patriarchal household.[14]

The link between home and nation is not a new one. But the role of women as both central characters and as iconic manifestations of the hearth and the nation frame this discussion of women and domesticity. Mark Wigley has eloquently demonstrated how the house is a mechanism of the control of female sexuality.[15] In linking house and nation, this book explores how home and nations serve as mechanisms of control. Notions of Indian womanhood are constructed and shaped by what it means to be both Indian and woman. Kakar and Kishwar provide one such lens through which we see the subject Indian woman. In a rigid ideological context where Indianness is seen as non Western and femaleness is negatively defined by a gendered frame of non-male then border crossings and the blurring of boundaries become problematic and women's individuality and ability to speak out is severely restricted. Mahatma Gandhi's call to women to participate in the nationalist struggle, as Ketu Katrak notes, brought women out of the home but it did not question the ideology of separate spheres or of patriarchy.[16]

Houses are contradictorily gendered as female when in fact they celebrate patriarchy and patrilineality. The association of women and domesticity has often foregrounded the house as a site of women's actions and location, whereas, as Mark Wigley persuasively argues, it is much more a mechanism for controlling women:

> As the mechanism of, rather than simply the scene for, this control, the house is involved in the production of the gender division it appears to merely secure.[17]

Wigley claims that the house underpins institutions of motherhood and wifehood by domesticating what is believed to be women's uncontrolled sexuality. Houses offer shelter from the outside and the elements but they also protect women from other men, as aptly demonstrated by the contrast between Nanda and Ila in *Fire on the Mountain*. Wigley concludes that "its [the house's] primary role is to protect the father's genealogical claims by isolating women from other men."[18]

Women, as is seen in Geeta's gradual assimilation into the haveli *(Inside the Haveli)*, develop a stake in this patriarchal house because it offers them and their children security and protection. Rather than an ally of other women even in a segregated women's sphere as Kakar would have us believe, Geeta's absolute internalization of patriarchal and feudal values is what allows her to assimilate and become a part of the haveli and all that it stands for. The wife at the center of the house, which is a physical manifestation of Berger's nomos-building structure, becomes its guardian. However, Wigley sees the wife's role in more Foucauldian terms. He notes that "The wife assumes this burden of internal surveillance as the `overseeing eye' monitoring the house."[19] In this vision, she is transformed from guardian to jailer. She may be a benign jailer as were the elite and dignified women of Sangram Singh's haveli in *Inside the Haveli* or they could be servants—guardians turned jailers—like Paro in *Daughters of the House*.

While keeping Wigley's general framework of the house in mind, this book has sought to focus more specifically on the implications of his argument for Indian women at home, in the nation, and in the homes of fathers and husbands. The Gandhian concept of service brings women and servants together, as they jointly tend the home. However, and more importantly, presenting their roles as practically interchangeable suggests their joint dependency. In his essay on Indian nationalism and female sexuality, Ketu Katrak traces how women were mobilised in the anti-colonial struggle but reincorporated into the new patriarchy of nationalists.[20] The houses women had stepped out of, in answer to Gandhi's nationalist call, might have been repainted, but they were substantially unchanged from the ones they had left and were expected to return to after serving the nation. Even so, in an article provocatively entitled "What Women Learned When Men Gave Them Advice", Judith Walsh posits a definite choice for women between "two patriarchal alternatives": the older orthodoxy inscribed in Sanscritic texts and the "new patriarchy, inscribed in the nationalist discourse."[21]

In the new patriarchies, as in the old, women as guardians of the home were expected to defend the very structures that they sought to transform. Katrak astutely remarks, "Home and hearth assumed an overdetermined reality that women needed both to protect and to be protected in."[22] They were the protectors as well as the embodiments of an essentialised Indian interiority threatened by a Western colonising power but equally they had to be protected from the changes that this power represented. Katrak notes, "The belief that women even more than men were the *guardians of tradition*, particularly against a foreign enemy, was used to reinforce the most regressive aspects of tradition."(Emphasis in the original).[23] Seen from this perspective, it is clear why Kishwar's rejection of feminism as an imported or Western phenomenon becomes problematic. The Indainness and community that Kishwar promotes can and often is the suffocating home/prison that confines women. The gendered configurations of home and community affects women's place both in the home and in the world.

Regulating female sexuality was of course the most direct way of ensuring the purity of home and nation. The threat of female sexuality was not viewed merely in terms of the home and the world but was inherent in the man-woman relationship: "Female sexuality, understood as female power, must be controlled and bounded through social custom, primarily within marriage."[24] Indian mythology provides endless exemplars of dutiful wives and heroic, suffering mothers to reinforce the message of conformity and suffering. In particular the message of female suffering as inevitable and purifying is the bedrock of both classical and popular Indian culture, and one that has been internalised by women themselves. Gandhi's emphasis on these specific self-sacrificing aspects of Indian femininity which inherently qualified them to be the guardians of home and nation followed a traditional mythological model that contemporary Indo-English women's literature is only just beginning to interrogate and reinterpret.

The specific threat posed by the outside is that of a sexuality that cannot be controlled. Homes are seen to protect women from themselves. Wigley notes,

A woman's interest let alone active role in the outside calls into question her virtue. The woman on the outside is implicitly sexually mobile. Her sexuality is no longer controlled by the house.[25]

In the *Ramayana*, Sita's abduction as she steps out of the protective Lakshmana rekha reveals her sexual vulnerability. In Desai's *Fire on the Mountain*, Ila Das, despite her age, is equally vulnerable because she is alone outside in what is seen as a male space, and she has no affiliations to a patriarchal house. In her case though, she is a threat not merely because of her presence in the male sphere but also because her work, stopping child marriage, challenges the existing patriarchy and its customs. The father of the child-bride to be is incensed that Ila—a woman—dares to question his authority. She is 'taught a lesson' for stepping out and for challenging a male in his role as father in the family and a patriarch in the society. In each of the novels, we see that the separate spheres ideology is premised upon ideas of male ownership of women. The male space, which used to be any public space, is dangerous territory for women because they are vulnerable, especially sexually, and, other men pose that threat. But, for women, sexual freedom is also one of the attractions of the outside, as we see in Lakshmi's choice of leaving the haveli (*Inside the Haveli*). But Tara's (*Tara Lane*) cocooning descriptions of the house and her married state similarly reveal her fear of a sexuality that is not "sanctioned." Nothing in her education or her upbringing, despite her reading of D.H. Lawrence's *Lady Chatterley's Lover*, prepares her to step out of the stifling protection provided by the house. The ideology of separate spheres is particularly problematic for Indian women in fiction and in life because the rewards and punishments of the choices made are stark and intransigent.

Alternate Homes

In the exploration of havelis, bungalows and apartments the novels also propose alternate homes and changed relationships within them. The alternate homes are often located on 'free spaces' like hill-stations or by the sea which signal a carefree, holiday spirit. Others are located in natal villages that signal homes of happy childhood or security. These particular homes provide insights into the patterns of existence that women might desire. The 'desired home' as a microcosm also refocuses the vision of India as home. The novels emphasise a geographic, political and cultural delimitation of the home space that is in constant dialogue with notions of Indianness and womanhood. Authors, expatriate and Indian, are involved in the construction of fictions of both India and home. The book maps the idea of home in Indo-English women's novels by tracing the delineation of specific homes be they an ashram, a shop or an apartment, etched within this broader concept of India. The aspects of loss, retrieval, and recreation, invoked by Rushdie in "Imaginary Homelands," are central to the way these new homes are imagined.[26] The recreation of "Indias of the mind" is the starting point of a journey that reminds us, as it did Rushdie that "it's my present that is foreign, and that the past is home, albeit a lost home in a lost city in the mists of lost time."[27] Rushdie suggests that home is retrieved and changed by describing it: "redescribing a world is the necessary first step towards changing it."[28] Similarly these novels not only redescribe the homes of the various phases of the protagonists lives—childhood, marital and older, often single women's homes—but they also present ideas of alternate homes that they would like to inhabit. The desire to reclaim lost homes, Rushdie suggests, often results in the creation of a different version of home rather than recalling a particular lost home. For expatriate writers like himself, he says:

> our physical alienation from India almost inevitably means that we will not be capable of reclaiming precisely the thing that was lost; that we will, in short, create fictions, not actual cities or villages, but invisible ones, imaginary homelands, Indias of the mind.[29]

His particular vision authorizes, even expatriates like himself, to speak for and about India. An authorization that similarly bestows legitimacy on Indian English writing as simply

Indian writing, without the anxieties that might burden the writing.

In Indo-English women's novels, India figures as a political background, and as emblematic of certain cultural values. Political and historical events anchor the texts in a specific time period. Events like the 1947 Partition or the Emergency in 1975 imposed by Prime Minister Indira Gandhi are the kinds of "pan-India" themes that Meenakshi Mukherjee describes as being common to Indo-English writers.[30] But, aside from being markers of time and place that link authors across class and across a non-region based readership, these events are also indicative of the mood or social atmosphere of that period. The larger malaise that afflicts society provides both a significant backdrop against which the particular novels are set and also mirror the issues and trials of specific characters. In Attia Hossain's *Sunlight on a Broken Column* the partition and breakup of a nation are paralleled in the dissolution of a lifestyle and a home and the quest for identity of both the new nation and the young protagonist Laila. A kinship with history is at the core of both Arundhati Roy's *The God of Small Things* and Meena Alexander's *Nampally Road* but in markedly different ways. In Roy the empty and haunted "history house" is a sinister reminder of the cliché that those who do not know their history are condemned to relive it. Alexander's is a more romantic vision. In *Nampally Road*, the protagonist Mira suggests that political events and social activism create a sense of community and provide an entry point into India especially for returning Indians like herself, and perhaps this is a crucial way in for a younger generation who feel distanced from India's past. Mira, as representative of that generation, bemoans her alienation from Indian history and sees that as a cause for her outsider status and consequent inability to find her own voice. She, a writer, cannot write because of her guilt at her privileged position and her dislocation from the Indian historic, cultural, and religious past. In her evocative description, she is blindfolded, trapped and marooned in the abandoned graveyard of Indian history. She has no sense of community with others who share the space with her; nor can she separate herself enough to write her own story. In fact, she does not seek an isolated story. She seeks herself as an integrated member of the community and society to which she has returned. Her return home is premised upon the desire to establish a sense of community which she feels is denied her by living abroad. She confesses, "I could not figure out a line or a theme for myself. The life that made sense was all around me . . ." (28). A lived national event—the Emergency - actively shared with others is what makes India 'home' for this returnee. Mira's India is constructed through an individual woman-to-woman connection. In her narration India does not take shape through a description of its physical landscape of rivers and mountains a la Jawaharlal Nehru's *Discovery of India*. She focuses instead on people, and an event becomes the catalyst for Mira to create a sense of community between the reader, the writer, and the text.

Community: Author, Text and Culture

The relationship between the author, text and a cultural community is multi-layered and sometimes problematic. I am not suggesting that these novels can or should be read in Jamesonian fashion as "masked autobiographies". However, it is important to note that often the lines between the authorial, the narratorial and even the critical voice can blur. Malashri Lal's critique of Rama Mehta's *Inside the Haveli*, mentioned earlier, exemplifies the difficulty of keeping the voices separate.[31] Autobiographical knowledge can, of course, provide an additional perspective and insight to the novel. Again, *Inside the Haveli*, poised at a time when the financial viability of princely houses was being threatened by the abolition of privy purses, wishes to arrest time, and posits feudal values as quintessentially Indian and as framing values of the desired Indian home. Rama Mehta's own haveli experience and training as a sociologist can be read as informing the novel. The confusion and deep sense of dislocation evoked in Hosain's Partition narrative *Sunlight on a Broken Column*, similarly reflects a personal experience. In an interview, Hossain states: "We belong to a generation that has lived with our hearts in pieces."[32]   In fact, as Aamer Hussein notes, Attia Hosain's limited output—a novel and a collection of short stories—harks back to the Partition experience:[33] "Reticence and unresolved pain, she told me, stopped her [Hosain] from writing more."[34] Similarly Nayantara Sahgal's *Rich Like Us* maps the journey from pre-Partition India to the Emergency in which she has been a participant and a spectator. Kamala Markandaya's *Nectar in a Sieve* is the only novel amongst these that nostalgically evokes a rural Indian past which is projected as an ideal Indian home. The antagonistic relationship between urban and rural lifestyles is in fact a recurrent feature in her other novels. Markandaya's sentimental and romantic portrayal of an idealised village life is perhaps better understood in the context of her own location in a distant England.

The other aspect of 'India as home' that the authors portray is cultural. In a majority of the novels, local and diaspora, Indian tradition is generally seen as restrictive. Culture weighs heavily on Kulwant in England (*A Wicked Old Woman*) as it does on Gogol in America (*The Namesake*); Ancestry is a heavy burden for Geeta (*Inside the Haveli*) and Laila (*Sunlight on a Broken Column*). Laila feels suffocated by tradition, even in her natal home. The shadows of her ancestors whose "ghosts had stood sentries over all action, speech and thought" (39) loom large over her. But ancestry and cultural traditions also provide a sense of security and rootedness as has been noted earlier in Geeta's case in *Inside the Haveli*. This recognition or acknowledgement of a past and belonging to a community accords an individual her or his place in that community and signals a reassuring continuity. In Santha Rama Rau's *Remember the House*, the protagonist Baba's flirtation in the "contact zone" via the young American couple ultimately reveals that the distance between them could only be attributed to something as amorphous and indefineable, and yet, rock solid as Indianness. In these novels, the sense of belonging to a nation, community and family is an essential part of the individual's identity. The link between past and future, and recognition of the individual's place in the history of the community is what makes

Saleem *(Sunlight on a Broken Column)* feel at home in India even though he has chosen to live in Pakistan. It is the same sense of belonging that stymies Tara *(Tara Lane)* and makes her so utterly fearful of stepping out in any way. In Indo-English Women's novels, the narration slips easily between nation, house, and body. The three are integrally linked, but also the one is a synecdoche for the others. An invocation of the house, for example, automatically encompasses the nation and the body. In Hariharan's *The Thousand Faces of Night*, and Alexander's *Nampally Road*, the India that both young protagonists reject is their mother's house of arranged marriages. Cultural conformity and acceptance of tradition in the form of arranged marriages is a part of Indianness that is rejected even if it means a rejection of mother's house or motherland. And both novels find innovative ways of linking back to India circumventing these suffocating traditions. In *Nampally Road*, Mira does not even return to her biological mother's house. She finds a surrogate in Little Mother, and her house becomes home for Mira. In *The Thousand Faces of Night*, the author does not permit the simpler solution of side-stepping or rejecting the mother's house. Devi has no alternative but to come to terms with her mother's house. Ultimately, the author proposes a transformation of the house to enable a freer existence for both the mother and the daughter.

Although not discussed here, it is interesting to note that Sahgal's novel *The Day in Shadow*, written twenty years before *Nampally Road* and *The Thousand Faces of Night*, does not suggest that customs like arranged marriages are an insurmountable obstacle of a particularly Indian tradition. The protagonist, Simrit, marries against her parents' wishes and her divorce does not make her an outcaste. Again, it is possible to invoke autobiographical information to account for Sahgal's very different version of India but that does not necessarily enrich a reading of the text. In Rich Like Us Sahgal shows that bigamy and an unmarried, single status are, like divorce, viable options even in a supposedly traditional Indian society.

Female and Male Spheres

The issue of separate feminine and masculine spheres as invoked by Kakar also recurs in a majority of these novels. This separation marks the female sphere as home and as India in all the novels. Framed at either extreme by Mehta's *Inside the Haveli* and Gyaltsen's *Daughters of the House*, the other novels propose a negotiation and a narrowing of the gap between women's and men's worlds. The segregation which can be traced back to the haveli has proved to be a mixed blessing. The novels show that the haveli dwelling pattern contributed to a lack of communication between women and men which continued beyond the haveli into bungalow lifestyles as in *Ladies Coupe, The Binding Vine and Tara Lane*. However, an un-looked for advantage of this segregated space is its potential transformation into a womenspace. This allowed women to build friendships in the domestic sphere, and when a segregated domestic sphere was no longer available, to extend the friendship among women beyond the domestic into the community. The friendships among women in train compartments or hospitals cut across class, caste and age barriers providing a concrete and tangible sense of a women's community that was not limited to the domestic as Kakar would have us believe but extended out of the domestic, personal and familial spaces into the public as instinctive gender empathy and as political and social coalitions, however temporary they may be.

The question of community is what makes India home, both politically and culturally. Chapter One suggested that individual texts rather than authors provide a possible alternative method of deciding to which community Indo-English literature belongs, and who can be categorised as an Indian writer. The variety and diverse versions of India that these novels claim suggest that all writers, whether or not they are resident Indians, create their own particular fictions of India as home. Realism in a literal sense or authenticity based on what passports authors hold or where they live, tend to be arbitrary as criteria for categorising what or who can be considered Indian. The integrity of the plurality of India, even in this limited selection of novels, suggests that neither India nor home are static or fixed concepts.

Embedded in the larger canvas of imaginary homelands are pictures of alternative homes that the protagonists of these novels would like to inhabit. None of the novels suggest a utopia or an ideal space but the protagonists draw upon elements from houses that are familiar to suggest a different kind of dwelling. The elements that go into imagining these alternative homes may be rooted in the nostalgia and memory of past homes but they extend beyond that into uncharted futures.

This alternative space is often timeless and placeless—an idea of home and of India. The main characteristic of this imagined home is the blurring of boundaries between inside and outside and between male and female spaces. The configuration of home as past and the poignant sense of loss, evoked by Rushdie, are central in Indo-English women's novels. Novels like Hosain's *Sunlight on a Broken Column*, Gyaltsen's *Daughters of the House*, and Anita Rau Badami's *Tamarind Mem*, are stories of memory and retrieval. They are journeys back in space and time in search of a home. From the vantage point of motherhood and maturity, the narrators look back, often nostalgically, at homes that had provided them with a sense of wholeness, belonging and stability. Laila, in *Sunlight on a Broken Column* and Chchanda in *Daughters of the House*, return home to narrate themselves into existence linking past, present and future in seamless time. Their search is not only to make sense of a present that seems foreign but also to structure a future based on a formative past.

Gyaltsen's *Daughters of the House* and Anita Desai's *Fire on the Mountain* are fascinating mirror images of what a house of women can look like. Gyaltsen explores the creation of a womenspace in a house owned and recognised by its patriarchal lineage whereas Desai's house has a strictly female lineage. Unlike other, sometimes abstract, notions of a womenspace, Gyaltsen locates the house of women physically in a hill station, in the midst of a little forest, demarcated by a stream. Desai's Cariagnano is also located in a hill station and is marked by its deliberately sought isolation. In Gyaltsen,

Panditji's house is a little oasis isolated from the town and the world of men but constantly threatened by their presence. The image of Chchanda standing at the river with her daughter in her arms recollecting how they have averted the threat of men in the form of Pratap and preserved the sanctity of the house of women is deeply troubling. In this novel, the price of keeping men at bay seems to be to imprison women. Both, Chchanda's mother and aunt pay the price of escape with their life. Ultimately only the servant Paro, and Chchanda, are the guardians and inhabitants of this house. Madhumita's birth signals a continuity of sorts but this house of women is no less confining and restrictive than the tyrannical patriarchal houses it rejects. *Daughters of the House* suggests that a physical place for women apart from men is only possible as a kind of prison, whereas living with men is envisioned as being "nagged by tyrants with penises"(11). The two equally unacceptable alternatives offered to daughters in this house are the same as those offered in patriarchal houses—to live as willing prisoners within or to die by breaking the rules of the house.

Marital homes are unambiguously rejected in Desai's *Fire on the Mountain* but the patterns of those homes continue to shape future homes. The promise of safe-haven, foregrounded in locating these houses in hill-stations like Kasauli are belied in their revelation as exiles rather than refuges. Some of these homes, especially of older women, pretend to be much sought retreats nested in beautiful hill stations. But they are no more than a flawed paradise, a place of self-exile. In distancing herself from her husband's home where she had dutifully performed to perfection her role as mother and wife, she does not really escape her past. The hill-house is a mere facade maintained by a dutiful if bitter wife who has nowhere else to go. Even when they are able to leave their husbands' homes, for wives like Nanda and Sita *(Thousand Faces of Night)* the other houses that they retreat to cannot become the havens they seek. Nanda carries the imprint of the marital home in her. That home, with its unending demands and constant traffic of people, has so numbed her sensitivity that she finds it impossible to reach out or connect to people even in this other house. Nanda views her great granddaughter, Raka, and her childhood friend, Ila, as continuations of an old pattern of demands that she is now unable or unwilling to empathise with. The isolation and distance that these older women protagonists seek in order to find themselves are seen as exile rather than retreat. These novels suggest that if a haveli-type joint-family existence can isolate and destroy, then detachment and physical escape from people equally can render a home into a cell for solitary confinement. They suggest destroying the system of house-prisons but do not propose any alternatives. In fact, in novels like *Fire on the Mountain* often the protagonist herself is annihilated.

Hosain and Futehally too, do not propose an ideal house but they do indicate what the necessary elements for such a house would be. In *Sunlight on a Broken Column*, Laila returns to the village home to seek refuge, and in *Tara Lane*, Tara views Munra, their vacation, family-home by the sea as a haven. The physical location of these houses, in the ancestral village and by the sea, significantly highlights what is most important in each novel. For Laila *(Sunlight on a Broken Column)*, the return to the village home in Hasanpur after Baba Jan's death, is a return to her roots for a reaffirmation of who she is and where she belongs at a moment of change. A similar introspective moment is staged in Laila's return to Ashiana, at the end of the novel. She revisits the old home to gather herself before she is willing to let go of her memories of Ameer and start a new life probably with her cousin Asad. In both *Sunlight on a Broken Column* and *A Matter of Time* houses, and specially natal homes are visualised as both the embodiment and the container of the past. These are memories of "a space that does not seek to become extended, but would like above all still to be possessed."[35] In Sumi's return to the "big house" the past is seen as "destiny". She has to confront the secret of the house and her parent's marriage and almost retread the same path before she can be free to find a new home. Similarly, even in choosing Asad and returning to confront Ashiana, Laila reiterates the importance of family and a shared past. The village house in Hasanpur and Ashiana are equally familiar to Asad and Laila, and though neither of them wants to return to that lifestyle, they realise that these houses have shaped them. The recognition and assimilation of the past guide both Sumi and Laila's future choices. The houses of their childhood are an essential component of any future house that, Laila especially, can envisage. Laila exemplifies psychologist Kakar's claim that, "the feminine role in India also crystallizes a woman's connections to others, her embeddedness in a multitude of familial relationships".[36] Laila's sense of self, her identity is embedded in the family and she sees the house as a symbol of the collective memory or what Antoinette Burton sees as an historical archive. Reclaiming and foregrounding history and roots are essential for Laila as they are for Sumi. In the final scene in *A Matter of Time* after Sumi's death, our final vision is of Aru and her grandmother together at the window. They are the guardians of the house and ensure its continuity. But both texts insist as Deshpande's novel clearly notes, that the way forward is possible only via the past.[37]

In Tara's ecstatic escape to Munra, in *Tara Lane*, Futehally suggests a house that is a family home of ancestry and continuity but its location by the sea is a very different setting from Laila's return to a feudal and rural past. The assumption and recognition of class and wealth are marked in both novels. The orchards that surround the house by the sea indicate a financial security crucial to Tara, just as the ancestral lands surrounding the Hasanpur home assure Laila and the family of their status and wealth. Tara perceptively comments that upon arrival at Munra, her mother always glances at the orchards first. This glance will later be fearfully replicated by Tara because as she grows older, she too, is made more aware of the source of her privilege, and fears its loss.

The unresolved dichotomy between the factory and the house on *Tara Lane* is carried forward even to this house which Tara sees as an escape from the lane. But Munra also offers Tara an openness and freedom beyond the confines of the house. Whereas the village house cocoons Laila ensuring her of her place within, Munra offers Tara a limitless vista denied her in her city home. Tara joyfully describes Munra in terms of unlimited space and light, exulting at the lack of obstacles to where and how far she is allowed to go. Tara's journey to wifehood and beyond is dogged by her fear of overstepping the limits of propriety and going too far:

> And it was only on this stretch of sand, of all places in my life, that I felt you could go on and on. You could gaze at the sky, taking in more and more till you were filled up and light; you could watch the waves roll in without end, one after the other after the other after the other; you could walk on and on and on; you could never go too far. Here, you were *meant* to go far, and allowed to go on. It was very different from being at home, where you were constantly reminded that you must halt somewhere. (42-43) (*Emphasis in the original*).

The incantary, mantra-like repetition reiterates Munra's promise of unlimited freedom. The permission, as well as the expectation, of "going too far", offers Tara possibilities that her education and her domestic existence as daughter, wife and mother have curtailed. Significantly, this is not a place she shares with her husband.

Three houses stand out as alternative houses of the future: Meena Alexander's *Nampally Road*, Gita Hariharan's *The Thousand Faces of Night* and Shashi Deshpande's *The Binding Vine*. The first two are husbandless homes although the possibility of admitting men is not eliminated, and the last is definitely a heterosexual home that emphasises the importance of dialogue or conversation between wives and husbands. The fourth and larger perspective of home and community is seen in Randhawa's *A Wicked Old Woman*, where the Indian community in England, gathers around the hospital bed to finally try and revive and recreate a mutually caring community through conversation rather than through punishment and tired notions of duty and allegiance to a home and way of life left behind in the old country. *Nampally Road* and *The Thousand Faces of Night* have already been discussed earlier, here; I would like to highlight the promise of these houses as blueprints for future homes.

In *Nampally Road*, Mira is offered two ways of integrating with the community. Little Mother, by her own example, suggests social-work and healing the poor as one way, while Mira's companion, Ramu, offers her the path of political activism. For Mira, writing is the only way she knows of creating a home. In Little Mother's home, Mira is given the space to write but it is through Ramu's political involvement that she initially establishes links with society.

Ramu's impatience with her writing as something which stymies action—"It doesn't let you turn right or left. And what do you do with it, after all?"(28)—reveals his basic lack of understanding and compels Mira to hide her writing from him. She feels that Ramu senses "a lack in me he could hardly heal" (93). In a Freudian moment, maybe to fulfill that "lack", she takes off her sari "for him". The strategic positioning of where they make love is revelatory:

> We lay down on the cool stone floor in my room, between the metal bed with its mosquito netting all tied back with ribbons and the small desk where my pen and paper still lay. (34)

The desk is a reminder of a crucial aspect of Mira's self discovery. It is a symbol of her recognition of a lack, but for her it is a different kind of lack. She writes to make herself whole, to "make up a self that had some continuity with what I was" (30). Ramu's rejection of her writing is tantamount to a rejection of her. Mira's example suggests that the kind of home she envisages will include a sisterhood with other women like Little Mother and Rameeza Be which bridges barriers of generation and class. She would like it to include a Ramu-type companion, but one who will encourage and accept all aspects of her personality. However, in the novel, fathers, husbands, and sons are yearned for but remembered by their absence.

The Thousand Faces of Night is less optimistic about men. In this novel, men as husbands are less than adequate but as fathers they are accorded a daughterly sympathy and understanding. The servant Mayamma's husband is the only one who physically abuses her but the other wives—Parvati, Devi, and Sita—are either obliged to transform themselves or leave in order to survive marital homes. Sita's transformed house by the sea is a viable alternative home where mothers and daughters can live. Its location by the sea recalls Munra in *Tara Lane*, and the same promise of space and wildness. But in this house, the unkempt garden is a clear statement rejecting housekeeping. The wild, overgrown garden signals Sita's lack of concern for her public image, and her abandoning the role of perfect wife and mother according to society's standards. Nanda and Raka's *(Fire on the Mountain)*, attraction to the arid and unkempt Kasauli landscape is a similar rejection of house-keeping associated with the marital state. Nanda explicitly invokes the piece on "When a Woman lives Alone" in *The Pillow Book* of Sei Shonagon to justify how sparseness and aus-terity are almost the dues of women who lived alone. The untended garden marks Nanda's change from the busy, orderly housewife who is constantly looking after other peoples' needs to a woman who does not need to do so. Sita and Devi's house by the sea emphasises the rejection of house-keeping, and offers a space where women can follow their own creative instincts, audible in the resurrected sounds of Sita's veena. This house is primarily a women's dwelling but it does not replicate the prison-like atmosphere of *Daughters of the House*.

Shashi Deshpande's *The Binding Vine*, unlike the previous two novels, quite firmly suggests a heterosexual home. This bungalow dwelling recalls a joint-family haveli type arrange-ment. The protagonist Urmila's wider involvement with other people like Shakutai and Bhaskar reveals to her the growing aridness of her relationship with her husband, Kishore. Bhaskar her new doctor friend, not only asks her about herself but, more importantly listens intently, which makes Urmila realise that she does not talk in the same way to Kishore. Urmila assumes some of the responsibility for the failed communica-tion and wonders "Have I never let Kishore become part of my real world?"(175). She resolves to correct the balance in their relationship by ensuring that dialogue, in its real sense as a two person communication, becomes an integral part of their lives. However, her friend Mira's idyllic moment is a female centered one and the house she recalls is her grandmother's home where she grew up. The moment she remembers is the time of her first pregnancy, and most importantly she recalls being part of a female world; being with women who had experienced pregnancy and birth and who were intensely involved with and empathetic to what she was feeling made this time the most meaningful and idyllic in her life. Conversations with husbands or other males do not and will not preclude or replace the female friendships that are a central part of a woman's life. Urmila looks to create a home that will allow the space for all these relationships but most importantly she is committed to ensuring that women's voices, Mira's, Kalpana's and her own, are not silenced. She does not deny the centrality of familial relations but notes that often because of these relationships and their ties of affection and duty, women choose silence over speaking out.

A study of these novels as a body of work indicates certain patterns although there is not necessarily a chronological development or progression. A significant feature of Indo-English women's novels is the desire to project the past, or at least some elements of it, into the future. They propose alteration rather than a radical transformation of homes that they have known. In the more recent novels, for example, although the haveli is not the locus of action, the haveli ethos continues to shape relationships even in bungalow dwellings. Female friendships constitute one positive extension of a segregated space which is then carried out of the domestic sphere into the wider community. The novels recommend reviewing and even changing those aspects of traditional family life that silence women but acknowledge the overall importance of both family and tradition. The houses of fiction alter and extend the realistic models they invoke, suggesting a strategy of change from within.

References

1   Kishwar, Madhu. "The Feminist Missionary," *Far Eastern Economic Review*, 16 May 1996, (p.30)

2   Kishwar, "The Feminist Missionary," *Far Eastern Economic Review*, 1996, (p.30)

3   See D.S. Kunwar, "Panchayat sentences Woman to Gang-rape," *Times of India*, Delhi: 26 July 1996 p.1. and *Pioneer*, Delhi: 26 July 1996
    My thanks to Surbhi Mallik of the Women's Feature Service for tracing these articles for me.
    The "good community" is also the underlying premise in some judicial discourse. See B.B. Pande, "Creating A Right to Die - An Exercise in Futility," *Islamic and Comparative Law Quarterly*. Vol.VII:2. June 1987. (pp.112-120) and "Right To Life Or Death?: For Bharat Both Cannot Be Right". *Supreme Court Cases* (1994) 4 SCC (J) (pp.19-29).

4   Julie Stephens, "Feminist Fictions: A Critique of the Category `Non Western Woman' in Feminist Writings on India," Ranajit Guha, (ed.) *Subaltern Studies. VI*. Delhi: Oxford University Press, 1989/1992, (p.101).

5   Lal, *The Law of the Threshold*, 1995, (p.26.)

6   Lal, *The Law of the Threshold*, 1995, (p.27.)

7   Kakar, *The Inner World*, 1989, (p.2.)

8   See Chapter Four, "Of Wives."

9   Kakar, *The Inner World*, 1989, (p.61.)

10 Kakar, *The Inner World*, 1989, (p.61.)

11 Kakar, *The Inner World*, 1989, (p.61.)

12 See Chapter Three, "Of Mothers and Daughters."

13 Kakar, *The Inner World*, 1989, (pp.61-62.)

14 http://www.chennaibest.com/cityresources/Books and Hobbies/anithanair.asp

15 Burton, Antoinette. "House/ Daughter/ Nation: Interiority, Architecture, and Historical Imagination in Janaki Majumdar's `Family History". in *The Journal of Asian Studies*. 56, no.4, November 1997, (p.922.)
    My thanks to Dr Norman Owen for bringing this to my attention.

16 Wigley, Mark. "Untitled: The Housing of Gender," Beatriz Colomina, (ed.) *Sexuality and Space*, Princeton: Princeton Architectural Press, 1992.

17 Katrak, Ketu H. "Indian Nationalism, Gandhian 'Satyagraha,' and Representations of female Sexuality", A. Parker et al., eds. *Nationalisms and Sexualities*, New York and London: Routledge, 1992.

18 Wigley, "Untitled," Colomina, (ed.) *Sexuality and Space*, 1992, (p.336)

19 Wigley, "Untitled," Colomina, (ed.) *Sexuality and Space*, 1992, (p.336)

20 Wigley, "Untitled," Colomina, (ed.) *Sexuality and Space*, 1992, (p.340)

21 Katrak, "Indian Nationalism," A. Parker et al., (eds.) *Nationalisms and Sexualities*, New York and London: Routledge 1992.

22 Judith Walsh, "What Women Learned When Men Gave Them Advice," *The Journal of Asian Studies*, Volume 56, Number 3, August 1997, (p.646)
    My thanks to Dr Norman Owen for bringing this to my attention.

23 Katrak, "Indian Nationalism", *Nationalisms and Sexualities*, 1992, (p.400.)

24 Katrak, "Indian Nationalism," *Nationalisms and Sexualities*, 1992, (p.398.)

25 Katrak, "Indian Nationalism", *Nationalisms and Sexualities*, 1992, (p.398.)

26 Wigley, "Untitled," *Sexuality and Space*, 1992, (p.335.)

27 Rushdie, Salman. 'Imaginary Homelands,' *Imaginary Homelands: Essays and Criticisms 1981-1991*, London: Granta Books, 1991.

28 Rushdie, *Imaginary Homelands*, 1991, (p.9.)

29 Rushdie, *Imaginary Homelands*, 1991, (p.14.)

30 Rushdie, *Imaginary Homelands*, 1991, (p.10.)

31 Mukherjee, *The Twice Born Fiction*, 1971. See Chapter One, "Introduction."

32 See Chapter One, "Introduction," Section I.

33 Hussain, Aamer. "Obituary" Attia Hosain, *The Guardian*, 31 January 1998. My thanks to Susanna Hoe for bringing this obituary to my attention.

34 Hosain, Attia. *Phoenix Fled And Other Stories*. (1953) London: Virago Press, 1988.

35 Hussain, Aamer. in Attia Hosain's obituary. *The Guardian*, 31 January 1998.

36 Bachelard, *The Poetics of Space*, 1958/1964, (p.10.)

37 Kakar, Sudhir. *The Inner World: A Psycho-analytic Study of Childhood and Society in India*, Delhi: Oxford University Press, 1978/1989 (p.62.)

38 Hussein notes that this was true of Hosain herself, who, "[d]espite her cosmopolitanism, ... was passionate about her roots." Hussein, *The Guardian*, 31 January 1998.

Select Bibliography

I Indo - English Women's Novels

Aikath-Gyaltsen, Indrani. *Cranes' Morning.*, New Delhi: Penguin, 1993.

—. *Daughters of the House.* New Delhi: Penguin, 1991.

Alexandar, Meena, *Manhattan Music,* San Francisco: Mercury House, 1997.

—. *Nampally Road.* San Francisco: Mercury House, 1991.

Appachana, Anjana. *Incantations.* London: Virago, 1991.

—. *Listening Now.* New York: Random House, 1997.

Badami, Anita Rau. *Tamarind Mem.* Canada: Penguin, 1996.

Balse, Mayah. *Indiscreet.* New Delhi: Orient Paperbacks-Vision Books, 1977.

—. *The Stranger.* New Delhi: Bell-Vikas Publishing, 1977.

Chand, Meira. *The Bonsai Tree.* London: John Murray, 1983.

—. *Last Quadrant.* London: John Murray, 1981.

Dalal, Nergis. *The Sisters.* Delhi: Hind Pocket Books, 1973.

Das, Kamala. *Alphabet of Lust.* (1976). New Delhi: Orient Paperbacks-Vision Books, 1980.

——. *A Doll for the Child Prostitute*. New Delhi: Himalya Pocket Book-India   Paperbacks, 1977.

David, Esther. *The Walled City*. Madras: Manas-East West Books, 1997.

De, Shobha. *Second Thoughts*. New Delhi: Penguin, 1996.

——. *Shooting From the Hip*. Delhi: UBS, 1994.

——. *Sisters*. New Delhi: Penguin, 1992.

——. *Socialite Evenings*. New Delhi: Penguin, 1989.

——. *Sultry Days*. New Delhi: Penguin, 1994.

Desai, Anita. *Baumgartner's Bombay*. New York: Horizon-Alfred A. Knopf, 1989.

——. *Bye-Bye Blackbird*. Delhi: Hind Pocket Books, 1971.

——. *Clear Light of Day*. Harmondsworth: Penguin, 1980.

——. *Cry, the Peacock*. London: Peter Owen, 1963.

——. *Fire on the Mountain*. (1977). Harmondsworth: King Penguin, 1981.

——. *In Custody*. London: Heinemann, 1984.

——. *Journey to Ithaca*. London: William Heinemann, 1995.

——. *The Village by the Sea: An Indian Family Story*. (1982). New Delhi: Allied   Publishers, 1983.

——. *Voices in the City*. Delhi: Orient Paperbacks, 1965.

——. *Where Shall We Go This Summer*. (1982). New Delhi: Orient Paperbacks-Vision   Books, 1994.

Desai. Kiran. *Hullaballoo in the Guava Orchard*. New Delhi: Viking-Penguin, 1998.

Deshpande, Shashi. *The Binding Vine*. Delhi: Penguin, 1993.

——. *Come Up and be Dead*. New Delhi: Vikas, 1983.

——. *The Dark Holds no Terrors*. New Delhi: Vikas, 1980.

——. *A Matter of Time*. New Delhi: Penguin, 1996.

——. *Roots and Shadows*. New Delhi: Sangam-Orient Longman, 1983.

——. *That Long Silence*. New Delhi: Penguin, 1988.

Devi, Shakuntala. *Perfect Murder*. New Delhi: Orient Paperbacks, 1976.

Divakaruni, Chitra. *The Mistress of Spices*. New York:

Bantam-Doubleday, 1997.

Dharker, Rani. *The Virgin Syndrome*. New Delhi: Penguin, 1997.

Futehally, Shama. *Tara Lane*. Delhi: Ravi Dayal, 1993.

Ganesan, Indira. *Inheritance*. New York: Knopf, 1998.

—. *The Journey*. New York: Knopf, 1990.

Gokhale, Namita. *Gods, Graves and Grandmothers*. New Delhi: Rupa, 1994.

—. *Paro: Dreams of Passion*. London: Hogarth Press, 1984.

Gupta, Sunetra. *The Glassblower's Breath*. New Delhi: Penguin, 1993.

—. *Memories of Rain*. New Delhi: Penguin, 1992.

—. *Moonlight into Marzipan*. New Delhi: Penguin, 1995.

Gupta, Shakti M. *Women on Men*. New Delhi: Sterling Publishers, 1976.

Hariharan, Githa. *The Ghosts of Vasu Master*. New Delhi: Viking-Penguin, 1994.

—. *The Thousand Faces of Night*. Delhi: Viking-Penguin, 1992.

Hosain, Attia. *Sunlight on a Broken Column*. (1961). Delhi: Arnold-Heinemann, 1980.

Kalhan, Promilla. *Forbidden Bride*. New Delhi: Sterling Publishers, 1975.

Kumar, Anita. *The Night of the Seven Dawns: a War Novel*. New Delhi: Bell-Vikas Publishing, 1979.

Lannoy, Violet Dias. *Pears from the Willow Tree*. Washington D.C.: Three Continents Press, 1989.

Mahindra, Indira. *The Club*. New Delhi: Rupa & Co., 1993.

—. *The End Play*. New Delhi: Rupa & Co., 1994.

Markandaya, Kamala. *The Golden Honeycomb*. London: B.I. Publications in association with Chatto & Windus, 1977.

—. *A Handful of Rice*. New Delhi: Orient Paperbacks-Vision Books, 1966.

—. *Nectar in a Sieve*. (1954). Bombay: Jaico Publishing, 1973.

—. *The Nowhere Man*. (1974). Delhi: Sangam Books-Orient Longman, 1975.

—. *Pleasure City*. London: Chatto & Windus, 1982. Reprinted as *Shalimar*. New York: A Cornelia & Michael Bessie Book-Harper & Row, 1982.

—. *Possession*. (1963). Bombay: Jaico Publishing, 1978.

—. *A Silence of Desire*. London: Putnam, 1960.

—. *Some Inner Fury*. London: Putnam, 1955.

—. *Two Virgins*. New Delhi: Bell-Vikas Publications, 1973.

Mathai, Manorama. *Mulligatawny Soup*. New Delhi: Penguin, 1993.

Mehta, Dina. *And Some Take a Lover*. Calcutta: Rupa & Co. 1992.

Mehta, Gita. *A River Sutra*. New Delhi: Viking-Penguin, 1993.

Mehta, Rama. *Inside the Haveli*. Delhi: Arnold-Heinemann, 1977.

Moorthy, Nirmala. *Maya*. New Delhi: Penguin, 1997.

Mukherjee, Bharati. *Wife*. New Delhi: Sterling Publishers, 1976.

—. *Jasmine*. New York: Viking, 1990.

—. *The Holder of the World*. New Delhi: Viking-Penguin, 1993.

Nagpal, Veena. *Compulsion*. New Delhi: Sterling Publishers, 1975.

Narasimhan, Raji. *The Heart of Standing is You Cannot Fly*. Calcutta: Writers Workshop, 1972.

—. *Forever Free*. Delhi: Hind Pocket Books, 1979.

Narayan, Kirin. *Love, Stars and All That*. New Delhi: Penguin, 1994.

Nimbkar, Jai. *Come Rain*. Bombay: Disha Books, Orient Longman Limited, 1993.

—. *Temporary Answers*. New Delhi: Orient Longman, 1974.

Paintal, Veena. *An Autumn Leaf*. Delhi: Hind Pocket Books, 1976.

Paintal, Veena. *Serenity in Storm*. Bombay: Allied Publishers, 1966.

Parmeswaran, Tara. *Once Bitten Twice Married*. New Delhi: Mayfair Paperbacks- Arnold Heinemann, 1976.

Raina, Vimala. *Ambapali*. Bombay: Asia Publishing House, 1962.

Rama Rau, Santha. *The Adventuress*. (1971). Delhi: Hind Pocket Books, 1973.

Rama Rau, Santha. *Remember the House*. London: Victor Gollancz, 1956.

Rao, Shanta Rameshwar. *Children of God*. Delhi: Sangam Books- Orient Longman, 1976.

Roy, Arundhati. *The God of Small Things*. New Delhi: IndiaInk, 1997.

Roy, Anuradha Marwah. *The Higher Education of Geetika Mehendiratta*. New Delhi: Disha Books-Orient Longman, 1993.

Sahgal, Nayantara. *The Day in Shadow*. New Delhi: Bell-Vikas Publications, 1971.

—. *From Fear Set Free*. Delhi: Hind Pocket Books, 1962.

—. *Mistaken Identity*. London: Heinemann, 1988.

—. *Rich Like Us*. (1983). Kent: Sceptre-Hodder and Stoughton, 1987.

—. *Storm in Chandigarh*. London: Chatto & Windus, 1969.

—. *This Time of Morning*. London: Victor Gollancz, 1965.

—. *A Time to be Happy*. (1952). New Delhi: Sterling Publishers, 1975.

Sarabhai, Mrinalini. *This Alone is True*. (1952). Delhi: Hind Pocket Books, 1977.

Shah, Deepa. *The Solitude of Surabhi*. New Delhi: Penguin, 1997.

Shrinagesh, Shakuntala. *The Little Black Box*. London: Secker & Warburg, 1955.

Sibal, Nina. *Yatra (The Journey)*. London: The Women's Press, 1987.

Singh. Mina. *A Partial Woman*. New Delhi. Kali for Women, 1997.

Srivastava, Atima. *Transmission*. New Delhi: Penguin, 1992.

Syal, Meera. *Anita and Me*. New Delhi: Indus, 1996.

Thakore, Dolly. *The Eccentricity Factor*. New Delhi: Vikas Publishing, 1980.

Vasudev, Uma. *The Song of Anasuya*. New Delhi: Bell-Vikas, 1978.

—. *Shreya of Sonagarh*. New Delhi: UBSPD, 1993.

II General Readings

Abel, Elizabeth, ed. *Writing and Sexual Difference*. Great Britain: The Harvester Press, 1982.

Abraham, Ayisha & Meena Alexander. "On Writing and Contemporary Issues." *The Toronto South Asian Review*, Winter 1993 (23-26).

Abu-Lughad, Lila. "A Community of Secrets: The Separate World of Bedouin Women." *Feminism and Community*. Penny A. Weiss & Marilyn Friedman (eds.). Philadelphia: Temple University Press, 1995.

Adigal, Prince Ilango. *Shilappadikaram (The Ankle Bracelet)*. Translated by Alain Danielou. New York: New Directions Books, 1965.

Afzal-Khan, Fawzia. *Cultural Imperialism And The Indo-English Novel*. Pennsylvania: The Pennsylvania State University Press, 1993.

Agarwal, Purshottam. "Savarkar, Surat and Draupadi Legitimising Rape as a Political Weapon." *Women And The Hindu Right*. Tanika Sarkar & Urvashi Butalia (eds.). Delhi: Kali for Women, 1995.

Agarwal, Bina. "Positioning The Western Feminist Agenda: A Comment." *Indian Journal of Gender Studies* New Delhi: Sage Publications 1.2, 1994.

Ahmad, Aijaz. *In Theory: Classes, Nations, Literatures*. Bombay: Oxford University Press, 1992.

Alexander, Meena. *Fault Lines*. New York: The Feminist Press, 1993.

—. "Mosquitoes in the Main Room". *House of a Thousand Doors*. Washington, D.C.: Three Continents Press, 1988. (51-52)

—. "Piecemeal Shelter: Writing, Ethnicity", *Public Culture* [The University of Chicago Press] 5 1993: (621-625).

Alston, A.J. *The Devotional Poems of Mirabai*. Delhi: Motilal Banarsidass, 1980.

Altekar, A. S. *The Position of Women in Hindu Civilization*. (1938). Delhi: Motilal Banarsidass, 1978.

Anand, Mulk Raj. "The Changeling". *Indian Writing in English*. Mohan Ramesh (eds.). Bombay: Orient Longman, 1978.

—. "Attia Hosain: A Profile". *Sunlight On a Broken Column*. Hosain, Attia. Delhi: Arnold-Heinemann, 1980.

Anderson, Benedict. *Imagined Communities: Reflections on the Origin and Spread of Nationalism*. London: Verso Editions and NLB, 1983.

Apte, Mahadeo L. "Reflections of Urban Life in Marathi Literature." *Urban India: Society, Space and Image*. Richard G. Fox (eds.). Duke University, Program in Comparative Studies on Southern Asia. Monograph and occasional Papers Series. Monograph Number Ten: 1970.

Ardener, Shirley, (ed.) *Women and Space: Ground Rules and Social Maps*. London: Croom Helm Ltd, 1981.

Asaf Ali, Aruna. *The Resurgence of Indian Women*. New Delhi: Radiant Publishers, 1991.

Ashcroft, Bill, Gareth Griffiths, Helen Tiffin., (eds.) *The Empire Writes Back Theory and Practice in Post-Colonial Literatures*. London, New York: Routledge, 1989.

Asnani, Shyam. "New Morality in the Modern Indo-English Novel: A Study of Mulk Raj Anand. Anita Desai and Nayantara Sahgal", R.K. Dhawan, (ed.) *Indian Women Novelists* Set 1: Vol.I (New Delhi: Prestige Books, 1991) p.109.

Asthana, R. K. "Tradition and Modernity in Inside the Haveli". *Indian Women Novelists*. Set I: Vol.IV. R.K.

Dhawan (ed.). New Delhi: Prestige Books, 1991.

Bachelard, Gaston. *The Poetics of Space*. Translated by Maria Jolas. Boston: Beacon Press, 1964 (French edition 1958).

Bahri, Deepika and Mary Vasudeva, eds. *Between The Lines: South Asians and Postcoloniality*. Philadelphia: Temple University Press, 1996.

Barker, Diana Leonard, and Sheila Allen. *Dependence and Exploitation in Marriage*. London: Longman Group Limited, 1976.

Basu, Tapan Kumar. "Class in the Classroom: Pedagogical Encounters with Nectar in a Sieve." *The Lie of the Land: English Literary Studies in India*. Ed. Rajeswari Sunder Rajan. Delhi: Oxford University Press, 1993.

Beauvoir, Simone de. *The Second Sex*. (1949) New York: Alfred A. Knopf, 1993.

Beerbohm, Max. "Servants." *And Even Now*. London: William Heinemann, 1920.

Belsey, Catherine. *Critical Practice*. London & New York: Methuen, 1980.

Benstock, Shari. "The Female Self Engendered: Autobiographical Writing and Theories of Selfhood." *Women's Studies* 20. 1991.

—, ed. *The Private Self Theory and Practice of Women's Autobiographical Writings*. London: Routledge, 1988.

Berger, Peter & Hansfried Kellner. "Marriage and the Construction of Reality: An Exercise in the Microsociology of Knowledge." *The Psychosocial Interior of the Family* (fourth edition). Gerald Handel & Gail C. Whitchurchn (eds.). New York: Aldine de Gruyter, 1994.

Berger, Peter L. *The Social Reality of Religion* (or *The Sacred Canopy*) London: Faber and Faber, 1969.

Beverley, John. "The Margin at the Center: On Testimonio" (Testimonial Narrative). *Modern Fiction Studies*. 35.1. [Spring 1989].

Bhabha, Homi K., (ed.) *Nation and Narration*. London &

New York: Routledge, 1990.

Bhatia, Gautam. *Punjabi Baroque And Other Memories of Architecture*. New Delhi: Penguin Books India, 1994.

—. *Silent Spaces And Other Stories of Architecture*. New Delhi: Penguin Books India, 1994.

Bhattacharji, Sukumari. "Motherhood in Ancient India". *Economic and Political Weekly*, 20-27 October 1990 (50-57).

Bird, Jon, et al., (eds.) *Mapping The Futures Local Cultures, Global Change*. London: Routledge, 1993.

Bloch, Ruth H. "American Feminine Ideals in Transition: The Rise of the Moral Mother, 1785- 1815". *Feminist Studies*, "Special Issue: Towards a Feminist Theory of Motherhood", Volume 4, Number 2, June 1978.

Blunt, Alison and Gillian Rose, (eds.) *Writing Women and Space: Colonial and Postcolonial Geographies*. New York, London: The Guildford Press, 1994.

Boehmer, Elleke. "Motherlands, Mothers and Nationalist Sons: Representations of Nationalism and Women in African Literature". *From Commonwealth to Post-Colonial*. (ed.) Anna Rutherford. Sydney: Dungaroo Press, 1992.

Bourdieu, Pierre. "Social Space And Symbolic Power". *Sociological Theory*. 7.1. Spring 1989 (14-25).

Brownmiller, Susan. *Against Our Will: Men, Women, and Rape*. Toronto, New York: Bantam Books, 1975/1986.

Brownstein, Rachel M. *Becoming a Heroine reading about Women in Novels*. UK: Penguin, 1982.

Brydon, Diana & Helen Tiffin. *Decolonising Fictions*. Sydney: Dangaroo Press, 1993.

Bull, J.A. *The Framework of Fiction Socio-cultural Approaches to the Novel*. London: Macmillan Education Ltd., 1988.

Burton, Antoinette. "House/Daughter/Nation: Interiority, Architecture, and Historical Imagination in Janaki Majumdar's `Family History'". *The Journal of Asian Studies*. 56, no.4, November 1997.

Butalia, Urvashi. "Blood". *Granta*. 57. Spring 1997. (13-22).

Butler, Judith. *Gender Trouble: Feminism and the Subversion of Identity.* New York: Routledge, 1990.

Cameron, Deborah. *Feminism and Linguistic Theory.* London: Macmillan Press Ltd., 1985.

—, (ed.) *The Feminist Critique of Language: A Reader.* London: Routledge, 1990.

Campbell, Joseph with Bill Moyers. *The Power of the Myth.* New York: Double Day, 1988.

Certeau, Michel de. *The Practice of Every Day Life.* (1984) Trans. Steven Rendall. Berkeley: University of California Press, 1988.

Chakravarty, Uma. "Whatever Happened to the Vedic Dasi? Orientalism, Nationalism and a Script for the Past". *Recasting Women: Essays in Colonial History.* Kumkum Sangari & Sudesh Vaid(eds.). New Delhi: Kali for Women, 1989.

Chanana, Karuna, (ed.) *Socialisation, Education and Women Explorations in Gender Identity.* Delhi: Orient Longman, 1988.

Chatterjee, Bankimchandra. *Rajmohan's Wife: A Novel.* With a Foreword, Notes and an Afterword by Meenakshi Mukherjee. Delhi: Ravi Dayal Publisher, 1996.

Chatterji, Lola, (ed.) *Woman Image Text: Feminist Readings of Literary Texts.* New Delhi: Trianka Publications, 1986.

Chatterjee, Partha. *The Nation and its Fragments.* Delhi: Oxford University Press, 1994.

Chavan, Sunanda P. "Inside the Haveli: Inadequate as A Work of Art". *Indian Women Novelists.* Set I: Vol.IV. R.K. Dhawan (ed.). New Delhi: Prestige Books, 1991.

Chodorow, Nancy. *The Reproduction of Mothering: Psychoanalysis and the Sociology of Gender.* Berkeley: University of California Press, 1978.

Clifford, James. *The Predicament of Culture: Twentieth-Century Ethnography, Literature, and Art.* Cambridge(Mass): Harvard University Press, 1988.

Colomina, Beatriz, ed. *Sexuality and Space.* New York: Princeton Architectural Press, 1992.

Combellick, Katherine Ann. *Feminine Forms of Closure:*

‌‌‌‌‌, *Deming and H.D.* Michigan: University Microfilms International, 1993, Ph.D. 1984. State University of New York at Binghamton.

Cornillon, Susan Koppelman, (ed.) *Images of Women in Fiction: Feminist Perspectives.* Ohio: Bowling Green University Popular Press, 1972.

Copland, Ian. *The Burden of Empire, Perspectives on Imperialism and Colonialism.* Oxford: Oxford University Press, 1990.

Costello, Jeanne. "Taking the 'Woman' Out of Women's Autobiography: The Perils and Potentials of Theorizing Female Subjectivities". *Diacritics.* [Summer/Fall 1991].

Cowasjee, Saros. *So Many Freedoms: A Study of the Major Fiction of Mulk Raj Anand.* Delhi: Oxford University Press, 1977.

Craig, David, ed. *Marxists On Literature: An Anthology.* Middlesex, UK: Penguin Books, 1975/1977.

Crane, Ralph J. *Inventing India (A History of India in English-Language Fiction).* London: Macmillan, 1992.

Cronin, Richard. *Imagining India.* London: Macmillan Press, 1989.

Culler, Jonathan. *Barthes.* Great Britain: Fontana Paperbacks, 1983.

Daly, Mary. *Gyn/Ecology.* Boston: Beacon Press, 1979.

—. "Sin Big". *The New Yorker.* (Special Women's Issue) February 26 & March 4, 1996 (76-84).

Das, Kamala. *My Story.* Delhi: Sterling Publishers, 1976.

Desai, Anita. "A Secret Connivance." *Times Literary Supplement,* 14-20 September 1990.

—. "Introduction". *Sunlight on a Broken Column.* Hosain, Attia. London: Virago Modern Classics, 1988.

Desai, Neera & Maithreyi Krishnaraj. *Women and Society in India.* Delhi: Ajanta Publications, 1987.

Devi, Jyotirmoyee. *The River Churning: A Partition Novel (Epar Ganga Opar Ganga).* Trans.(from Bengali) Enakshi Chatterjee. New Delhi: Kali for Women, 1995.

Devi, Mahasveta. "Untapped Resources." *Seminar.* 359.

July 1989 (15-19).

Dhawan, R.K., (ed.) *Indian Women Novelists.* Set.1: Vol.I. New Delhi: Prestige Books, 1991.

—, (ed.) *Indian Women Novelists.* Set I: Vol.II. New Delhi: Prestige Books, 1991.

—, (ed.) *Indian Women Novelists.* Set I: Vol.III. New Delhi: Prestige Books, 1991.

—, (ed.) *Indian Women Novelists.* Set I: Vol.IV. New Delhi: Prestige Books, 1991.

—, (ed.) *Indian Women Novelists.* Set II: Vol.1. New Delhi: Prestige Books, 1993.

—, (ed.) *Indian Women Novelists.* Set II: Vol.IV. New Delhi: New Prestige Books: 1993.

—, (ed.) *Indian Women Novelists.* Set II: Vol.V. New Delhi: New Prestige Books: 1993.

Donaldson, Laura E. *Decolonizing Feminisms Race, Gender and Empire-Building.* Chapel Hill and London: The University of North Carolina Press, 1992.

Dutta, Sangeeta. "Relinquishing the Halo: Portrayal of Motherhood in Indian Writing in English." *Economic and Political Weekly*, 20-29 October 1990.

Eagleton, Mary, (ed.) *Feminist Literary Theory: A Reader.* Oxford: Basil Blackwell Ltd., 1986.

Eck, Diana L, and Devaki Jain. *Speaking of Faith: Cross Cultural Perspectives on Women, Religion and Social Change.* Delhi: Kali for Women, 1986.

Erikson, Erik H. *Gandhi's Truth: On The Origins of Militant Nonviolence.* New York: W.W. Norton, 1969.

Flax, Jane. "The Conflict Between Nurturance and Autonomy in Mother-Daughter Relationships and Within Feminism". *Feminist Studies*, "Special Issue: Towards A Feminist Theory of Motherhood", Volume 4, Number 2, June 1978.

Forster, E. M. *A Passage to India.* (1924) Harmondsworth: Penguin Books, 1977.

Fox, Richard G., (ed.) *Urban India: Society, Space and Image.* Duke University, Program in Comparative Studies on Southern Asia. Monograph and occasional Papers Series. Monograph Number Ten: 1970.

Fox-Genovese, Elizabeth. *Within The Plantation Household: Black and White Women of the Old South.* Chapel Hill & London: The University of North Carolina Press, 1988.

Futehally, Shama. "Portrait of a Childhood". *In Other Words: New Writing by Indian Women.* Urvashi Butalia, & Ritu Menon (eds.). Delhi: Kali for Women, 1992.

Gajjala, Radhika. "Representation and Identity: The Not-Subaltern Indian/South Asian Woman's Dilemma", http://pitt.edu/~gajjala.

Ganesh, Kamala. "Mother Who Is Not A Mother: In Search of the Great Indian Goddess." *Economic and Political Weekly.* 20-27 October 1990 (58-64).

Gelley, Alexander. *Narrative Crossings Theory and Pragmatics of Prose Fiction.* Baltimore & London: The Johns Hopkins University Press, 1987.

Gemill, Janet P. "The City in the Indo-English Novel." *India: Cultural Patterns and Processes.* Eds. Allen G. Noble & Ashok K. Dutt. Boulder, Colorado: Westview Press, 1982.

Genette, Gerard. *Narrative Discourse Revisited.* Trans. Jane E. Lewin. Ithaca: Cornell University Press, 1988. (Nouveau discours du recit, by Gerard Genette was published in French, Editions du Seuil, November 1983.)

—. *Narrative Discourse An Essay in Method.* Trans. Jane E. Lewin. (1st pub. Seuil, 1972) Ithaca: Cornell University Press, 1980.

Geyh, Paula E. "Burning Down the House? Domestic Space and Feminine Subjectivity in Marilynne Robinson's Housekeeping". *Contemporary Literature.* 34.1.(University of Wisconsin Press) Spring 1993.

Gilbert, Sandra and Susan Gubar. *The Mad Woman in the Attic: The Woman Writer in the Nineteenth Century Literary Imagination.* New Haven: Yale University Press, 1979.

Gilman, Charlotte Perkins. *The Yellow Wallpaper.* (1892) London: Virago Press Ltd., 1981.

Gilmore, Leigh. *Autobiographics: A Feminist Theory of*

Women's Self Representation. Ithaca & London: Cornell University Press, 1994.

Glenn, Evelyn Nakano, Grace Chang, and Linda Rennie Forcey, (eds.) *Mothering Ideology, Experience, and Agency.* New York: Routledge, 1994.

Godden, Rumer. "Faith and Love in A Village in India." *New York Herald Tribune Book Review*, 15 May 1955, (p.3) rpt *Contemporary Literary Criticism*, Vol. 38 (p.320).

Goodwin, K.L., (ed.) *National Identity.* London: Heinemann Educational Books, 1970.

Greene, Gayle & Coppelia Kahn., (eds.) *Making A Difference: Feminist Literary Criticism.* Gen Ed. Terence Hawkes. London: Methuen, 1985.

Guha, Ranajit, (ed.) *Subaltern Studies VI.* Delhi: Oxford University Press, 1992.

Habermas, Jurgen. *The Structural Transformation of the Public Sphere, An Inquiry into a Category of Bourgeois Society.* Trans. Thomas Burger with the assistance of Frederick Lawrence. England: Polity Press, 1989.

Hall, Stuart, David Held and Tony McGrew, (eds.) *Modernity and its Futures.* Cambridge: Polity Press, 1992.

Harasym, Sarah, (ed.) *The Post-Colonial Critic, Interviews, Strategies, Dialogues, Gayatri Chakravorty Spivak.* New York & London: Routledge, 1990.

Hawley, John Stratton and Mark Juergensmeyer. *Songs of the Saints of India.* New York, Oxford: Oxford University Press, 1988.

Hays, Michael. *Critical Conditions Regarding The Historical Moment.* Minneapolis: University of Minnesota Press, 1992.

Heilbrun, Carolyn G. *Writing A Woman's Life.* New York: Ballantine Books, 1988.

Hitchcock, Peter. *Dialogics of the Oppressed.* Minneapolis and London: University of Minnesota Press, 1993.

Hobsbawm, Eric and Terence Ranger, (eds.) *The Invention of Tradition.* Cambridge: Cambridge University Press, 1983.

Hochschild, Arlie Russell. *The Managed Heart Commercialization of Human Feeling.* Berkeley: University of California Press, 1983.

Hogan, Patrick Colm and Lalita Pandit, (eds.) *Literary India: Comparative Studies in Aesthetics, Colonialism and Culture.* Albany: State University of New York Press, 1995.

hooks, bell. *Yearning: Race, Gender, and Cultural Politics.* Boston: South End Press, 1990.

Horner, Avril and Sue Zlosnik. *Landscapes of Desire: Metaphors in Modern Women's Fiction.* New York: Harvester Wheatsheaf, 1990.

Hosain, Attia. *Phoenix Fled and Other Stories.* (1953) London: Virago Press, 1988.

Hossain, Rokeya Sakhawat. "Sultana's Dream." (1905). *Women Writing in India.* Susie Tharu & K. Lalita (eds.). New York: The Feminist Press, 1991 (342-352).

Humm, Maggie. *Border Traffic: Strategies of Contemporary Women Writers.* Manchester: Manchester University Press, 1991.

Hussain, Aamer. "Obituary" Attia Hosain. *The Guardian*, 31 January 1998.

Iyengar, K. R. Srinivasa. "Indians Writing in English: Prospect and Retrospect." *Indian Writing in English.* Mohan Ramesh (ed.). Bombay: Orient Longman, 1978.

—. *Indo-Anglian Literature*, Bombay: International Book House, 1943.

Jain, Pratibha and Rajan Mahan, (eds.) *Women Images.* Jaipur, New Delhi: Rawat Publications, 1996.

Jameson, Fredrick. "Third World Literature in the Era of Multinational Capitalism." *Social Text* V15, 1986: (65-88)

Jaworski, Adam. *The Power of Silence: Social and Pragmatic Perspectives.* California: Sage Publications, 1993.

Jayakar, Pupul. *The Children of Barren Women: Essays, Investigations, Stories.* New Delhi: Penguin Books, 1994.

Jayawardena, Kumari. *The White Woman's Other Burden: Western Women and South Asia During British Rule.* New York: Routledge, 1995.

Joshi, Svati, (ed.) *Rethinking English: Essays in Literature, Language, History.* New Delhi:Trianka, 1991.

Josselson, Ruthellen & Amia Lieblich, (eds.) *The Narrative Study of Lives.* London, New Delhi: Sage Publications, Newbury Park, 1993.

Jung, Annes. *Breaking The Silence: Voices of Women from around the World.* Delhi: Penguin Books/ UNESCO Publishing, 1997.

Jussawalla, Feroza and Reed Way Dasenbrock, (eds.) *Interviews with Writers of the Post-Colonial World.* Jackson & London: University Press of Mississippi, 1992.

Kachru, B. "Indian English." *Seminar.* 359. July 1989 (30-35).

Kakar, Sudhir. *The Inner World: A Psycho-analytic Study of Childhood and Society in India.* (1978) Delhi: Oxford University Press, 1981.

—. *Intimate Relations: Exploring Indian Sexuality.* New Delhi: Viking-Penguin Books, 1989/1990.

Kapur, Ratna. (ed.) *Feminist Terrains in Legal Domains: Interdisciplinary Essays on Women and Law in India.* New Delhi: Kali for Women, 1996.

Karlekar, Malavika. *Voices from within Early Personal Narratives of Bengali Women.* Delhi: Oxford University Press, 1991/1993.

Katrak, Ketu H., "Decolonizing Culture: Toward a Theory For Postcolonial Women's Texts." *Modern Fiction Studies.* 35.1. Spring 1989.

—. "Indian Nationalism, Gandhian 'Satyagraha' and Representations of Female Sexuality". *Nationalisms and Sexualities.* A. Parker et al (eds.). New York and London: Routledge, 1992.

Kaur, Iqubal. (ed.) *Gender and Literature.* New World Series - 60. Delhi: B.R. Publishing Corp. DK Publishers, 1992.

Khan, Naseem. "Private Space to Public Places: Contemporary Asian Women Writers". *Daskhat: Journal of South*

Asian Literature. 1. Autumn/Winter 1992.

King, Adele. "Shashi Deshpande: Portraits of an Indian Woman." *The New Indian Novel in English, A Study of the 1980s.* Viney Kirpal (ed.). Delhi: Allied Publishers, 1990.

King, Bruce. *The New English Literatures — Cultural Nationalism in A Changing World.* London: Macmillan (New Literature handbooks), 1980.

King, Anthony D. *The Bungalow: The Production of a Global Culture.* London: Routledge & Kegan Paul, 1984.

Kingston, Maxine Hong. *The Woman Warrior: Memoirs of A Girlhood among Ghosts.* England: Penguin, 1976/1977.

Kinsley, David. *Hindu Goddesses: Visions of the Divine Feminine in the Hindu Religious Tradition.* Delhi: Motilal Banarsidass, 1986.

Kirpal, Viney. *The New Indian Novel in English: A Study of the 1980's.* Delhi: Allied Publishers, 1990.

—. "How Traditional can a Modern Indian be: An Analysis of Inside the Haveli." *Indian Women Novelists.* Set I: Vol.IV. R.K. Dhawan (ed.). New Delhi: Prestige Books, 1991.

—, (ed.) *The Girl Child in 20th Century Indian Literature.* New Delhi: Sterling Publishers, 1992.

Kishwar, Madhu. "The Feminist Missionary." *Far Eastern Economic Review.* Hong Kong: 16 May 1996 (30).

—. "Introduction". *Manushi* (Tenth Anniversary Issue, Women Bhakta Poets). 50,51,52. New Delhi: 1989 (3-8).

—. "Yes to Sita, No to Ram!: The Continuing Popularity of Sita in India". *Manushi.* 98. January-February 1997. (http://www.arbornet.org/~radhika/manushi/issue98/sita.)

Kishwar, Madhu & Ruth Vanita, (eds.) *In Search of Answers: Indian Women's Voices from Manushi.* London: Zed Books, 1984.

Kohli, Devindra. *Indian Writers At Work.* New World Literature Series:43, Delhi: D.K Publishers, B.R. Publishing Corporation, 1991.

Krishna Rao, A.V. "The Other Harmony : Nayantara

Sahgal's Non-Fiction". *Indian Women Novelists*. Set II: Vol.IV. Ed. R.K. Dhawan. New Delhi: Prestige Books, 1993.

Krishnamurty, J., (ed.) *Women in Colonial India: Essays on Survival, Work and the State*. (Indian Economic and Social History Review), Delhi: Oxford University Press, 1989.

Krishnaswamy, Shantha. *The Woman in Indian Fiction in English*. New Delhi: Ashish Publishing House, 1984.

Krupat, Arnold. *Ethnocriticism Ethnography History Literature*. Berkeley: University of California Press, 1992.

Kumar, Radha. *The History of Doing: An Illustrated Account of Movements for Women's Rights and Feminism in India, 1800-1990*. New Delhi: Kali for Women, 1993.

Kundera, Milan. *The Art of the Novel*. Trans. Linda. Delhi: Rupa & Co. 1988/1992.

Kunwar, D.S. "Panchayat Sentences Woman to Gang-rape." *Times of India*. Delhi: 26 July 1996.

Lacapra, Dominick, (ed.) *The Bounds of Race, Perspectives on Hegemony and Resistance*. Ithaca and London: Cornell University Press, 1991.

Laing, Stuart. *Representations of Working-Class Life 1957-1964*. London: Macmillan Publishers, 1986.

Lal, Malashri. "Anita Desai: Fire On The Mountain." *Major Indian Novels, An Evaluation*. (ed.) N.S. Pradhan. New Jersey: Humanities Press, 1986.

—. *The Law of the Threshold: Women Writers in Indian English*. Shimla: IndianInstitute of Advanced Study. 1995.

Lefebvre, Henri. *The Production of Space*. Trans. Donald Nicholson-Smith. Oxford: Basil Blackwell Ltd., 1974/1991.

Leitch, Vincent B. *Cultural Criticism, Literary Theory, Poststructuralism*. New York: Columbia University Press, 1992.

Levi-Strauss, Claude. *Tristes Tropiques*. (1955) Trans. John and Doreen Weightman. Harmmondsworth: Penguin Books, 1978.

Libert, Florence. "Discrepancy Between The Inner Being and the Outside World." Robert L. Ross, (ed.) *International Literature in English: Essays on the Major Writers*. New

York: Garland Publishing, 1991.

Liddle, Joanna and Rama Joshi. *Daughters of Independence: Gender, Caste and Class in India.* London: Zed Books, 1986.

Lim, Shirley Geok-lin. *Writing S.E./ Asia in English: Against the Grain, Focus on Asian English-language Literature.* London: Skoob Books Publishing, 1994.

Lionnet, Francoise. *Autobiographical Voices Race, Gender, Self-Portraiture.* Ithaca:Cornell University Press, 1989.

Loveridge, Patricia. "Approaches to Change: The All India Democratic Women's Association and a Marxist Approach to the Woman Question in India". *Indian Journal of Gender Studies.* 1.2. New Delhi: Sage Publications 1994.

Malouf, David. *12 Edmonstone Street.* Australia: Penguin Books, 1985/1989.

Mani, Lata. "Contentious Traditions: The Debate on Sati in Colonial India". *Recasting Women: Essays in Colonial History.* Kumkum Sangari & Sudesh Vaid (eds). New Delhi: Kali for Women, 1989.

Manu. *The Laws of Manu.* Translated by Wendy Doniger and Brian K. Smith. London: Penguin, 1991.

Massey, Doreen. *Space, Place and Gender.* Cambridge: Polity Press, 1994.

McHale, Brian. *Constructing Postmodernism.* London: Routledge, 1992.

Mehta, Ved. *A Family Affair: India Under Three Prime Ministers.* New York: Oxford University Press, 1982.

Menon, Ritu and Kamala Bhasin. *Borders & Boundaries: Women in India's Partition.* New Delhi: Kali for Women, 1998.

Merewether, Charles. "Zones of Marked Instability: Woman and the Space of Emergence." *Rethinking Borders.* John C. Welchman (ed.) Minneapolis: University of Minnesota Press, 1996.

Merton, Robert K. *The Sociology of Science: Theoretical and Empirical Investigations.* ed and intro. Norman W. Storer. Chicago & London: The University of Chicago Press, 1973.

Mies, Maria, Veronika Bennholdt Thomsen, Claudia von

Welhof. (eds.) *Women The Last Colony*. Delhi: Kali for Women, 1988.

Miller, Nancy K. *Subject to Change: Reading Feminist Writing*. New York: Columbia University Press, 1988.

—, (ed.) *The Poetics of Gender*. New York: Columbia University Press, 1986.

Minogue, Sally, (ed.) *Problems for Feminist Criticism*. Routledge: London, 1990.

Modjeska, Drusilla, (ed.) *Inner Cities: Australian Women's Memory of Place*. Sydney: Penguin Books, 1989.

Moers, Ellen. *Literary Women: The Great Writers*, London: The Women's Press, 1977.

Mohanty, Chandra Talpade, Ann Russo, Lourdes Torres, (eds.) *Third World Women and the Politics of Feminism*. Bloomington and Indianapolis: Indiana University Press, 1991.

Moi, Toril. *Sexual Textual Politics: Feminist Literary Theory*. General Editor Terence Hawkes, New Accents. London and New York: Routledge, 1985/1995.

Moore Jr., Barrington. *Privacy Studies in Social And Cultural History*. Armonk, New York, London: M.E. Sharpe Inc., 1984.

Mukherjee, Meenakshi. "The Language of the Indo-Anglian Novelist". *Indian Writing in English*. Ramesh Mohan (eds). Bombay: Orient Longman, 1978.

—. "The Problem". *Seminar*. 359. July 1989 (12-14).

—. *Realism and Reality: The Novel and Society in India*. (1985) Bombay: Oxford India paperbacks, Oxford University Press, 1994.

—. "Towards Liberation: Four Recent Novels from India". *Westerly*. 28.4. December 1983 (66-72).

—. *The Twice Born Fiction: Themes and Techniques of the Indian Novel in English*.Delhi: Arnold Heinemann, 1971.

Mukherjee, Sujit. *Towards A Literary History of India*. Simla: Indian Institute of Advanced Study, 1975.

Mukherjee, Prabhati. *Hindu Women: Normative Models*. Orient Longman Limited, Delhi: 1978.

Nabar, Vrinda. *Caste as Woman*. New Delhi: Penguin Books, 1995.

Naik, M. K. *A History of Indian English Literature*. Delhi: Sahitya Akademi, 1982.

Nair, Hema N. "Bold Type: The Poetry of Multiple Migrations". *Ms*. January/February 1994 (71).

Nandy, Ashis. *The Intimate Enemy: Loss and Recovery of Self Under Colonialism*. Delhi: Oxford University Press, 1983.

Narasimhan, Raji. *Sensibility Under Stress: Aspects of Indo-English Fiction*. New Delhi: Ashajanak Publications, (no publication date given).

Nehru, Jawaharlal. *The Discovery of India*. (1946) Delhi: Oxford University Press, 1946/1985.

Newton, Judith L., Mary P. Ryan & Judith R. Walkowitz., (eds.) *Sex and Class in Women's History*. London, Boston: Routledge & Kegan Paul, 1983.

Olney, James, (ed.) *Autobiography Essays Theoretical and Critical*. New Jersey: Princeton University Press, 1980.

Palmer, Phyllis. *Domesticity and Dirt: Housewives and Domestic Servants in the United States, 1920-1945*. Philadelphia: Temple University Press, 1989.

Pande, B.B. "Creating A Right to Die - An Exercise in Futility". *Islamic and Comparative Law Quarterly*. Vol.VII:2. June 1987 (112-120).

—. "Right To Life Or Death?: For Bharat Both Cannot Be `Right'." *Supreme Court Cases* (India) (1994) 4 SCC (J) (19-29).

—. "Creating A Right to Die - An Exercise in Futility." *Islamic and Comparative Law Quarterly*. Vol.VII:2. June 1987 (112-120).

Pande, Mrinal. *Daughter's Daughter*. New Delhi: Penguin Books, 1993.

—. Devi. Delhi: Penguin, 1996.

Pandit, Lalita. "A Sense of Detail and a Sense of Order: Anita Desai Interviewed by Lalita Pandit". *Literary India: Comparative Studies in Aesthetics, Colonialism and Culture*. Patrick Colm Hogan and Lalita Pandit (eds.) Albany: State

University of New York Press, 1995.

Parmar, Pratibha. Interviews Trinh T. Minh-ha. Woman, Native, Other *Feminist Review*. 36 (London), Autumn 1990.

Pateman, Carole. *The Disorder of Women: Democracy, Feminism and Political Theory*. Cambridge: Polity Press, 1989.

Paul, Premila & R. Padmanabhan Nair. "Varieties of Loneliness in Fire on the Mountain", *Indian Women Novelists* Set I: Vol. III. (ed.) R.K. Dhawan. New Delhi: Prestige Books, 1991.

Pradhan, N.S., (ed.) *Major Indian Novels: An Evaluation*. New Jersey: Humanities Press, 1986.

Prakash, Gyan. "Subaltern Studies as Postcolonial Criticism". *The American Historical Review*. 99.5. December 1994.

Pramar, V. S. *Haveli: Wooden Houses And Ma sions Of Gujarat*. Ahmedabad: Mapin Publishing, 1989.

Prasad, Sunand. "The Havelis of North India The Urban Courtyard House". Vol.I. Diss., The Royal College of Art, Visual Islamic Arts Unit, Faculty of Fine Art, London, June 1988.

Punja, Shobita. *Daughters of the Ocean: Discovering the Goddess Within*. Delhi: Viking-Penguin India, 1996.

Rao, Parsa Venkateshwar. Interview, "Presenting the Past." *Indian Express Sunday Magazine*. 18 July 1993.

Rao, Vimala. "Submission And Revolt: The Dialectic of Girlhood in Markandaya's *Two Virgins* and Desai's *Fire on the Mountain*". *The Girl Child in 20th Century Indian Literature*. Viney Kirpal (ed.). New Delhi: Sterling Publishers, 1992.

Reagon, Bernice Johnson. "Coalition Politics: Turning the Century". *Home Girls: A Black Feminist Anthology*. Ed. Barbara Smith. New York: Kitchen Table: Women of Color Press, 1983.

Rich, Adrienne. *Blood, Bread and Poetry: Selected Prose 1979-1985*. London: Virago Press, 1987.

—. "Compulsory Heterosexuality and Lesbian Existence." *Powers of Desire: The Politics of Sexuality*. Eds. Ann Snitow, Christine Stansell & Sharon Thompson. New York:

Monthly Review Press, 1983.

——. *Of Woman Born: Motherhood as Experience and Institu-tion*. New York: Bantam- W.W. Norton & Company, 1976/1977.

——. *On Lies, Secrets, and Silence Selected Prose 1966-1978*. New York, London: W.W. Norton & Company, 1979.

Richardson, Laurel / Verta Taylor. *Feminist Frontiers II: Rethinking Sex, Gender, and Society*. New York: Random House, 1986.

Robbins, Bruce. *The Servant's Hand: English Fiction from Below*. New York: Columbia University Press, 1986.

Rodriguez, Ileana. *House, Garden, Nation: Space, Gender, and Ethnicity in Postcolonial Latin American Literatures by Women*. trans. Robert Carr and Ileana Rodriguez. Durham NC, London: Duke University Press, 1994.

Roland, Alan. *In Search of Self in India and Japan: Towards A Cross-Cultural Psychology*. Princeton: Princeton University Press, 1988.

Romines, Ann. *The Home Plot: Women Writing and Domestic Ritual*. Amherst: The University of Massachusetts Press, 1992.

Rose, Gillian. *Feminism and Geography: The Limits of Geographical Knowledge.* Cambridge: Polity Press, 1993.

Roy, Modhumita. "'Englishing' India: Reinstituting Class and Social Privilege". *Social Text*. 39. Summer 1994 (82-109).

Roy, Anjali & Manasi Sinha. "Growing up In a Zenana Sunlight on a Broken Column". *The Girl Child in 20th Century Indian Literature*. Viney Kirpal (ed.). New Delhi: Sterling Publishers, 1992.

Roy, Kumkum. "'Where Women are Worshipped, there the Gods Rejoice': The Mirage of the Ancestress of the Hindu Woman". *Women and The Hindu Right: A Collection of Essays*. Tanika Sarkar and Urvashi Butalia (eds.). New Delhi: Kali for Women, 1995.

Rudolph, Lloyd I. & Susanne Hoeber Rudolph. *The Modernity of Tradition: Political Development in India*. Chicago

& London: The University of Chicago Press, 1967/1984 Midway Reprint.

Rushdie, Salman. "Damme, This is the Oriental Scene for You!" *The New Yorker*. 23 & 30 June 1997 (50-61).

—. *Imaginary Homelands: Essays and Criticism 1981 -1991*. London: Granta Books, 1991.

Ruthven, K.K. *Feminist Literary Studies: An Introduction*. London: Cambridge University Press, 1984.

Rybczynski, Witold. *Home: A Short History of an Idea*. New York: Penguin Books, 1986/1987.

—. *Looking Around: A Journey through Architecture*. New York: Penguin Books, 1992.

S. Varalakshmi. "An Interview with Nayantara Sahgal." *Indian Women Novelists*. Set II: Vol.IV. Ed. R.K. Dhawan. New Delhi: Prestige Books, 1993.

Sage, Lorna. *Women in the House of Fiction: Post-War Women Novelists*. New York: Routledge, 1992.

Sahgal, Nayantara. *Indira Gandhi's Emergence and Style*. New Delhi: Vikas Publishing House, 1978.

—. "The Schizophrenic Imagination". *From Commonwealth to Post-Colonial*. (ed.) Anna Rutherford. Sydney: Dungaroo Press, 1992.

Sahgal, Nayantara and E. N. Mangat Rai. *Relationship: Extracts from a Correspondence*. New Delhi: Kali for Women, 1994.

Said, Edward W. *Culture and Imperialism*. London: Vintage, 1993/1994.

—. *Orientalism*. (1978) London: Peregrine-Penguin Books, 1985.

Sangari, Kumkum & Sudesh Vaid, (eds.) *Recasting Women: Essays in Colonial History*. Delhi: Kali for Women, 1989.

Sarkar, Tanika & Urvashi Butalia, eds. *Women and the Hindu Right*. New Delhi: Kali for Women, 1995.

Scott, Joan W. & Louise A. Tilly. "Women's Work and the Family in Nineteenth-Century Europe". *Comparative Studies in Society and History*. 17. 1975 (36-64).

Shirwadkar, Meena. *Image of Woman in the Indo-Anglian*

Novel. New Delhi: Sterling Publishers, 1979.

Showalter, Elaine. *A Literature of their Own: British Women Novelists from Bronte to Lessing,* New Jersey: Princeton University Press, 1977.

—, (ed.) *The New Feminist Criticism: Essays on Women, Literature and Theory.* New York: Pantheon Books, 1985.

Silva, Paul. "Indian Writers on Tour: Meena Alexander Talks to Paul Silva". *Cascando.* (UK) 1993.

Singh, Bhupal. *A Survey of Anglo-Indian Fiction.* London: Oxford University Press, 1934.

Singh, Amita Tyagi and Patricia Uberoi. "Learning to `Adjust': Conjugal Relations in Indian Popular Fiction". *Indian Journal of Gender Studies,* Volume 1, Number 1, New Delhi: Sage Publications, 1994.

Singh, Khushwant and Keki N. Daruwala. Interview *Zee News.* 31 December 1997.

Sinha, Mrinalini. "Introduction". *Selections from Mother India* by Katherine Mayo. New Delhi: Kali for Women. 1998

Smart, Ninian & Richard D. Hecht, (eds.) *Sacred Texts of the World: A Universal Anthology.* New York: The Crossroad Publishing Company, 1989.

Smart, Carol, (ed.) *Regulating Womanhood: Historical Essays on Marriage, Motherhood and Sexuality.* London: Routledge, 1992.

Smith, Barbara, (ed.) *Home Girls: A Black Feminist Anthology.* New York : Kitchen Table: Women of Color Press, 1983.

Snitow, Ann, Christine Stansell & Sharon Thompson, (eds.) *Powers of Desire: The Politics of Sexuality.* New York: Monthly Review Press, 1983.

Soja, Edward J. *Postmodern Geographies: The Reassertion of Space in Critical Social Theory.* London: Verso, 1989.

Spivak, Gayatri Chakravorty. "A Literary Representation of the Subaltern: Mahasweta Devi's "Standayini"' & Spivak's translation of the story (Appendix). *Subaltern Studies V: Writings on South Asian History and Society.* Ranajit Guha. (ed.) Delhi: Oxford University Press, 1987/1992.

—. "The Political Economy of Women as seen by a

Literary Critic." *Coming to Terms: Feminism, Theory, Politics.* Elizabeth Weed (ed.) New York: Routledge, 1989.

—. Interview with Rashmi Bhatnagar, Lola Chatterjee, and Rajeswari Sunder Rajan, "The Post Colonial Critic." *The Post-Colonial Critic: Interviews, Strategies, Dialogues.* Sarah Harasym (ed.). New York: Routledge, 1990.

—. Interview with Deepika Bahri and Mary Vasudeva, "Transnationality and Multiculturalist Ideology". *Between the Lines: South Asians and Postcoloniality.* Deepika Bahri & Mary Vasudeva (eds.). Philadelphia: Temple University Press, 1996.

Sprinker, Michael, ed. *Edward Said: A Critical Reader.* Oxford (UK) & Cambridge (USA): Blackwell, 1992.

Stephens, Julie. "Feminist Fictions: A Critique of the Category `Non Western Woman' in Feminist Writings on India". *Subaltern Studies.* VI. (ed.) Ranajit Guha. Delhi: Oxford University Press, 1989/1992.

Stubbs, Patricia. *Women and Fiction: Feminism and the Novel 1880 -1920.* New York: Harper and Row Publishers, 1979.

Sunder Rajan, Rajeswari, guest editor. *Thamyris: Mythmaking from Past to Present.* (Special Issue, Gender in the Making: Indian Contexts) 4,1. [Najade Press Amsterdam], Spring 1997.

Sunder Rajan, Rajeswari. "The Feminist Plot and the Nationalist Allegory: Home and The World in Two Indian Women's Novels in English". *Modern Fiction Studies.* Spring 1993.

—. *Real And Imagined Women: Gender, Culture and Postcolonialism.* Routledge: London and New York, 1993.

—, (ed.) *The Lie of the Land: English Literary Studies in India.* Delhi: Oxford University Press, 1993.

Tambling, Jeremy. *Narrative and Ideology.* Open Guide to Literature series. Philadelphia: Open University Press, Milton Keynes, 1991.

Tannen, Deborah. *You Just Don't Understand: Women and Men in Conversation.* New York: Ballentine Books, 1990.

Taylor, Charles. *Multiculturalism and "The Politics of*

Recognition" (an essay) Commentaries by Amy Gutmann,(ed) Steven C. Rockfeller, Michael Walzer, Susan Wolf. Princeton: Princeton University Press, 1992.

——. *Sources of the Self: the Making of the Modern Identity.* Cambridge: Cambridge University Press, 1989.

Tharu, Susie and K. Lalita, (eds.) *Women Writing in India: 600 B.C. To The Present.* Volume I. New York: The Feminist Press, 1991.

——. , (eds.) *Women Writing in India: The Twentieth Century.* Volume II. New York: The Feminist Press, 1993.

Tharu, Susie. "The Impossible Subject: Caste and Desire in the Scene of the Family". *Thamyris,* Vol.4 No.1, [Najade Press, Amsterdam] Spring 1997 (Special Issue 'Gender in the Making: Indian Contexts', Guest Editor Rajeswari Sunder Rajan).

——. "Tracing Savitri's Pedigree: Victorian Racism and the Image of Women in Indo-Anglian Literature". *Recasting Women: Essays in Colonial History.* Kumkum Sangari & Sudesh Vaid (eds.). New Delhi: Kali for Women, 1989.

Thorne, Barrie with Marilyn Yalom, (eds.) *Rethinking the Family: Some Feminist Questions.* New York & London: Longman, 1982.

Tilly, Louise A., Joan W. Scott & Miriam Cohen. "Women's Work and European Fertility Patterns". *The Journal of Interdisciplinary History.* 6. 1975-76 (447-476).

Todd, Janet. *Feminist Literary History.* Routledge: New York, 1988.

Trevor, James. *English Literature from the Third World.* Harlow: Longman York Press, 1986.

Trivedi, Harish and Meenakshi Mukherjee, (eds.) *Interrogating Post-Colonialism Theory: Text and Context.* Shimla: Indian Institute of Advanced Study, 1996.

Tryambakayajvan, *The Perfect Wife (Stridharmapaddhati).* Selected from the Sanskrit with an introduction by I. Julia Leslie. New Delhi: Penguin India, 1989.

Uberoi, Patricia. "Hindu Marriage Law and the Judicial Construction of Sexuality". *Feminist Terrains in Legal Domains:*

Interdisciplinary Essays on Women and Law In India. Ed. Ratna Kapur. New Delhi: Kali for Women, 1997.

UNI report *Pioneer.* "Gangraped Woman Struggling for Life." Delhi, 26 July 1996, p.1.

Viswesawaran, Kamala. *Fictions of Feminist Ethnography.* Minneapolis, London: University of Minnesota Press, 1994.

Wacziarg, Francis & Aman Nath. *Rajasthan: The Painted Walls of Shekhavati.* London: Croom Helm Ltd, 1982.

Walker, Alice. *In Search of our Mothers' Gardens.* San Diego, New York: Harvester- Harcourt Brace Jovanovich, 1984.

Walsh, Judith. "What Women Learned When Men Gave Them Advice." *The Journal of Asian Studies.* Volume 56, Number 3, August 1997.

Weed, Elizabeth, (ed.) *Coming to Terms: Feminism, Theory, Politics.* New York, London: Routledge, 1989.

Weiner, Myron. *The Child and the State in India.* Delhi: Oxford University Press, 1991.

Welchman, John C., (ed.) *Rethinking Borders.* Minneapolis: University of Minnesota Press, 1996.

Wigley, Mark. "Untitled: The Housing of Gender." *Sexuality and Space.* Beatriz Colomina (ed.). Princeton: Princeton Architectural Press, 1992.

Wiley, Norbert W. "Marriage and the Construction of Reality: Then and Now". *The Psychosocial Interior of the Family.* (fourth edition). (eds.) Gerald Handel & Gail C. Whitchurch. New York: Aldine de Gruyter, 1994.

Williams, Patrick and Laura Chrisman, (eds.) *Colonial Discourse and Post-Colonial Theory: A Reader.* New York: Harvester Wheatsheaf, 1994.

Willis, Ellen. "Abortion: Is a Woman a Person?" *Powers of Desire The Politics of Sexuality.* Ann Snitow, Christine Stansell & Sharon Thompson, (eds.) New York: Monthly Review Press, 1983.

Winternitz, Maurice. *History of Indian Literature.* Vol.I. (1981) Delhi: Motilal Banarasidass, 1987.

Zelliot, Eleanor. "Literary Images of the Modern Indian City." *Urban India: Society, Space and Image.* Ed. Richard G.

Fox. Duke University, Program in Comparative Studies on Southern Asia. Monograph and occasional Papers Series. Monograph Number Ten: 1970.